Korean Religions in Relation

SUNY SERIES IN KOREAN STUDIES
————————
Hongkyung Kim, editor

Korean Religions in Relation
Buddhism, Confucianism, Christianity

Edited by

Anselm K. Min

Cover image: iStockphoto.com / sunset over Gyeongbokgung Palace in Seoul, South Korea

Published by State University of New York Press, Albany

© 2016 State University of New York

All rights reserved

Printed in the United States of America

No part of this book may be used or reproduced in any manner whatsoever without written permission. No part of this book may be stored in a retrieval system or transmitted in any form or by any means including electronic, electrostatic, magnetic tape, mechanical, photocopying, recording, or otherwise without the prior permission in writing of the publisher.

For information, contact State University of New York Press, Albany, NY
www.sunypress.edu

Production, Diane Ganeles
Marketing, Fran Keneston

Library of Congress Cataloging-in-Publication Data

Names: Min, Anselm Kyongsuk, editor. | Kang, Wi Jo, honouree.
Title: Korean religions in relation : Buddhism, Confucianism, Christianity / Edited by Anselm K. Min.
Description: Albany : State University of New York Press, 2016. | Series: SUNY series in Korean studies | Includes bibliographical references and index.
Identifiers: LCCN 2016007298 (print) | LCCN 2016008296 (ebook) | ISBN 9781438462752 (hardcover : alk. paper) | ISBN 97811438462769 (pbk. : alk. paper) | ISBN 9781438462776 (e-book)
Subjects: LCSH: Korea—Religion. | Buddhism—Relations. | Confucianism—Relations. | Christianity and other religions—Korea.
Classification: LCC BL2234 .K67 2016 (print) | LCC BL2234 (ebook) | DDC 201/.509519—dc23
LC record available at http://lccn.loc.gov/2016007298

10 9 8 7 6 5 4 3 2 1

*These Essays Are Dedicated
to the Honor of Professor Wi Jo Kang,
Mentor, Colleague, Friend*

Contents

Professor Wi Jo Kang: A Tribute   ix
Preface   xi
Acknowledgments   xiii
A Note on Romanization   xv

1. A Relational Approach to the Study of Korean Religions: An Overview   1
   Anselm K. Min

Part I
Buddhism and Confucianism: Accommodation and Conflict

2. Interactions between Buddhism and Confucianism in Medieval Korea   19
   Jongmyung Kim

3. Philosophical Aspects of the Goryeo-Joseon Confucian-Buddhist Confrontation: Focusing on the Works of Jeong Dojeon (Sambong) and Hamheo Deuktong (Gihwa)   53
   A. Charles Muller

Part II
Confucianism and Catholicism: Conflict and Assimilation

4. Catholic God and Confucian Morality: A Look at the Theology and Ethics of Korea's First Catholics   89
   Don Baker

5. On the Family Resemblance of Philosophical Paradigm:
   Between Dasan's Thought and Matteo Ricci's *Tianzhu Shiyi*   119
   Young-bae Song

Part III
Protestantism and Korean Religions: Exclusion and Assimilation

6. A Genealogy of Protestant Theologies of Religions in Korea,
   1876–1910: Protestantism as a Religion of Civilization
   and Fulfillment   155
   Sung-Deuk Oak

7. What Can Christianity Learn from Korean Religions?
   The Case of Ryu Yongmo   189
   Young-Ho Chun

Part IV
Confucianism, Christianity, and the Challenges of the Modern World

8. Resurgence of Asian Values: Confucian Comeback and
   Its Embodiment in Christianity   215
   Namsoon Kang

9. Korean Confucianism and Women's Subjectivity in the
   Twenty-First Century   241
   Un-sunn Lee

10. Confucianism at a Crossroads: Confucianism and
    Democracy in Korea   263
    Young-chan Ro

11. Between Tradition and Globalization: Korean Christianity
    at a Crossroads   285
    Anselm K. Min

Contributors   311
Index   315

Professor Wi Jo Kang
A Tribute

The essays of this volume are offered in honor of Professor Wi Jo Kang, a pioneer in the study of Korean religions.

Dr, Kang received the PhD in history from the University of Chicago in 1967, and taught at Columbia University, Valparaiso University, Concordia Seminary, and for twenty years (1980–1999) at Wartburg Theological Seminary where he served as Wilhelm Loehe Professor of Mission. He also served as visiting professor at Yonsei University, Seoul National University, Japan Lutheran College and Seminary, Tokyo, and the University of California–Los Angeles, where he taught as Henry Luce Distinguished Visiting Professor (2001–2002) during the last year of a long, illustrious teaching career. He has also been a very prolific writer on a wide range of subjects from various Korean religions to Korean Protestant missions to religion and politics in Korea, new religions, world Christian mission, and peace and reunification on the Korean peninsula. In addition to countless articles in journals and anthologies, he authored, among others, *Religion and Politics in Korea under the Japanese Rule* (Edwin Mellen, 1987), *Word and World: Theology for Christian Ministry*, co-edited with Steven Charleston and Peter J. Paris (Luther/Northwestern Theological Seminaries, 1992), and *Christ and Caesar in Modern Korea* (SUNY Press, 1997). A Korean War veteran, he had started his career as an aspiring teacher of Korean and Korean literature, whose literary and poetic talent later saw the light of day in a novel, *Lullaby* (2009), on the life of a young Korean soldier attached to the U.S. Army during the Korean War; a play, *A Korean Nurse Who Went to Germany* (2009); and a book of poems, *Longing for Home: Dreaming of the Unification of the Korean Peninsula* (2014). As editor of the present volume I am proud to add the personal note that he is the one who first introduced me to

Asian religions when I took his summer course, Religions of East Asia, at Columbia University in 1965.

We are honored to pay tribute to Professor Kang for his pioneering scholarship in Korean religions, his collegial leadership in the community of Korean-American scholars, and his always inspiring and encouraging friendship with the younger ones in that community.

Preface

The publication process is a debt-incurring process. I would like to thank the contributors to this volume, who so willingly responded to my invitation to join in honoring Professor Kang each with his or her own insightful essay that distinguishes the present volume. It was a great pleasure to work with them in the often laborious process called publication. My professional thanks also go to the two anonymous reviewers, whose criticisms and suggestions helped improve the quality of this volume in both content and form.

As always, I owe a great debt of gratitude to my indispensable research assistant, Shane Akerman, a doctoral candidate in philosophy of religion and theology at Claremont Graduate University, whose diligent and meticulous editorial work in the various stages of this volume significantly contributed to the professional appearance of the chapters.

Acknowledgments

Two chapters of this volume have previously appeared in different venues. Chapter 8, "Resurgence of Asian Values: Confucian Comeback and Its Embodiment in Christianity" by Namsoon Kang, appeared as chapter 10 of her own book, *Diasporic Feminist Theology: Asia and Theopolitical Imagination* (Minneapolis: Fortress Press, 2014), 292–321. Chapter 9, "Korean Confucianism and Women's Subjectivity in the Twenty-First Century," by Un-sunn Lee, was published as "Confucianism and Development of Korean Women's Subjectivity in the Twenty-First Century," in *Madang: An International Journal of Contextual Theology in Asia* 18 (2012), 73–94. I would like to thank both publishers for permission to reprint their respective material in this volume.

A Note on Romanization

Today there exist two main methods for Romanizing Korean, the McCune-Reischauer method (MR) and the Revised Romanization method (RR). The MR method has been used since 1937 and is the preferred method used by the international community of scholars in North America, Europe, and by many Korean scholars in and outside Korea. The Library of Congress and many U.S. university libraries (Harvard, Chicago, Columbia, among others) use this method. The RR method was officially adopted by the Korean Ministry of Culture and Tourism in 2000 based on the recommendation of the Academy of the Korean Language and is required of all government documents, road and street signs, and government-funded research in Korea. Younger Korean scholars are using this system more and more, as are increasingly many international scholars.

However, scholarly debate still continues on the relative merit of each method, as is evident in the divided opinion among the contributors to this volume. Given the division of scholarly opinion I have decided to allow both methods in this volume as long as the same method is followed throughout the chapter. The MR method is followed in chapters 2, 4, 6, and 10, and the RR method is followed in Chapters 3, 5, 7, 8, 9, and 11. Chapter 1, which introduces the content of each chapter, uses the method followed in the chapter it is introducing in order to avoid confusion.

1

A Relational Approach to the Study of Korean Religions

An Overview

Anselm K. Min

There are many ways of studying religions, Korean or non-Korean. We can study each of the religions in itself, its history, its theology, its politics, its art and music. Most studies of religions, one can say, belong to this category. There exist all kinds of histories of Buddhism, Christianity, Hinduism, Islam, and other religions, each taken in itself, which then can be subdivided into ancient, medieval, and modern, depending on the particular period the author decides to concentrate on. There also exist philosophical, theological, or doctrinal studies of each religion, as there are sociological, political, and cultural studies of each. There are many studies of each of the major Korean religions from these and other perspectives. There are also comparative studies of Korean religions that compare different religions with one another at the doctrinal level, pointing out their conflicts, their similarities, their possible convergences.

There exist, however, relatively few studies of Korean religions *in their mutual relations*. How have Korean religions, mainly Buddhism, Confucianism, Catholicism, and Protestantism behaved and related to one another and with what consequences? It is well known how Buddhism prospered as the dominant religion during the Goryeo dynasty, but not many are aware of the fact that Confucianism was the political ideology of the state. How, then, did the two treat each other? It is well known that Catholics were martyred by the Confucian state throughout the nineteenth century, but it is not known in any significant detail how some Confucian scholars tried to integrate Catholic teachings on morality into the reigning Neo-Confucian philosophy of human nature. How was this kind of Confucian assimilation of Christianity possible? Was there also a Catholic assimilation of Confucianism? It is well known that Korean Protestantism has been intolerant and exclusivist toward traditional Korean religions, but it is little known that many of the early Protestant missionaries wrestled with what we today would call an "inclusivist" approach to other religions. What, then, was the relation between Protestantism and other religions in the early twentieth century? Sheer conflict, practical accommodation, or even assimilation, or a combination of these? Confucianism is patriarchal and hierarchical and has a history of oppressing women and obstructing democracy, but is it not conceivable that Confucianism may also have insights and doctrines that can contribute precisely to the causes of women and democracy in the contemporary world, and how would Confucianism and Christianity compare in this regard?

It is this relational approach to the study of Korean religions that I am introducing in this collection of essays. This is neither a general survey of Korean religions nor a study of a particular religion in isolation. It is a historical study of how the three Korean religions, Buddhism, Confucianism, and Christianity, thought of and treated one another in terms of three categories—conflict/exclusion, practical accommodation, and assimilation/dialogue—taking these categories in a very broad, flexible sense. The relation is approached historically, politically, sociologically, philosophically, and even theologically, depending on the nature of the relation under discussion. The need for a relational approach of this sort to the study of Korean religions should go without saying today when relations among religions are so critical to peace in society and the world. As far as I know, we do not have a comprehensive in-depth study of the relations among the three religions in Korean history.

Nor do I claim that this volume is such a comprehensive, exhaustive study of those relations. I am only too keenly aware of so much more yet to be done on the subject. I am confident, however, that this is the first major study of those relations from a variety of perspectives by a team of experts, each with a distinguished record of scholarship in his or her field, and do hope that more comprehensive studies will follow that will also include Tonghak and other religions of Korean origin. Many readers will note the absence of any formal discussion of animism and shamanism, which it is widely recognized are pervasive of Korean religions and culture. Many recognize the presence of shamanism in Buddhism and Christianity in particular, often with a decisive impact on the character of Korean Buddhism and Korean Christianity, both Catholic and Protestant. Certainly, a more comprehensive treatment of Korean religions in relation should have included an adequate discussion of animism and shamanism. I regret that time and space did not permit inclusion of these religions in this volume.

Let me now introduce the basic concerns and arguments of each of the ten essays that follow. We begin in part I with the story of the encounter of Buddhism and Confucianism during the Goryeo period. One of the conventional assumptions accepted by both scholars and laypersons in Korea is that the Goryeo dynasty was a Buddhist state and that Buddhism dominated all areas of life during the period. The period is still remembered as the period in which Buddhism pervaded the whole of Korean culture with its spirit, as a gloriously Buddhist age, in much the same way that the European Middle Ages are sometimes looked at, rightly or wrongly, as a gloriously Catholic period. In chapter 2, "Interactions between Buddhism and Confucianism in Medieval Korea," Professor Jongmyung Kim of the Academy of Korean Studies in Seoul develops a novel and provocative thesis that demolishes this conventional view. The Goryeo dynasty (918–1392 CE) was a Confucian state, not the Buddhist state it is often described to be, although Buddhism was the most dominant religious influence; and the Buddhism that was so influential was a Buddhism transformed and degraded into the political tool of a Confucian state, a deviation from its original purity in the teachings of the Buddha.

In order to develop this claim Kim mobilizes not only historical sources from this period and existing scholarship on the subject but also his vast knowledge of the history of the relation between Confucianism and Buddhism in China, which had an impact on Korean politics as an exemplar of Confucian statecraft. The state during this period was a thoroughly Confucian state for which the Confucian classics set the paradigm of kingly rule; and while kings favored Buddhism in so many ways, such privileging was all political, that is, to use Buddhism, its beliefs, its spirituality, and its rituals to ensure the prosperity of the royal families, invoke blessings on the nation in times of foreign invasions and natural disasters, and strengthen the Confucian ideals of kingship. Buddhism was not a state religion in the sense in which Confucianism was one during the Joseon dynasty (1392–1910), and coexisted with other religions such as Daoism, Confucianism, shamanism, geomancy, and astrology, in a multireligious society. In the process, Buddhism lost the political influence it used to enjoy during the preceding Silla period, and became Confucianized, reinterpreted in the Confucian terms of humanity or *jen*, filial piety, loyalty to the king, yin and yang, and the theory of heavenly warning, and using its doctrines to support the political aims of the state and its rulers with little regard for the Four Noble Truths and the paths of spiritual liberation they demand. This essay has significantly altered my conventional view of the relationship between the two religions during this period, highlighting the central political role of Confucianism, of which I was not fully aware, and relativizing the role of Buddhism, which I thought was the all-dominant influence on Korean culture at the time. One could say that according to Kim, the relation *between the two religions was one of practical accommodation accompanied by a Buddhist* assimilation of major Confucian virtues, with no major conflicts.

Different religions in Korea coexisted in relative peace and practical mutual accommodation both during the Three Kingdom period and during the Goryeo dynasty. With the explicit foundation of the Joseon dynasty on the ideology of Confucianism or Neo-Confucianism, however, the relation between Confucianism and Buddhism seems to change from practical accommodation to explicit confrontation. In chapter 3, "Philosophical Aspects of the Goryeo-Joseon Confucian-Buddhist Confrontation: Focusing on the Works of Jeong Dojeon (Sambong) and Hamheo Deuktong (Gihwa)," Professor A. Charles Muller of the University of Tokyo tells the fascinating story of this confrontation in some detail from historical, comparative-religious, and doctrinal perspectives. As Prof. Kim illuminated the history of accommodation between Confucianism and Buddhism in Korea with the prehistory of that relation in China, so Prof. Muller sheds light on the conflict between the two toward the end of the Goryeo dynasty and the beginning of the Joseon dynasty with the Chinese antecedents of that confrontation. As the Chinese monk, Zongmi (780–841), responded to the critique of Buddhism by Han Yu (768–824) during the Tang period, so the monk Gihwa (1376–1433) responded to the Neo-Confucian critique of Buddhism by Jeong Dojeon (1342–1398). The notable thing here is the astonishing degree to which the Korean Neo-

Confucian critique of Buddhism and the Buddhist reply to that critique repeat their Chinese antecedents.

According to Muller, there are two sides to the Korean confrontation between Buddhism and Confucianism, the sociopolitical and the philosophical. The sociopolitical side refers to the tense political situation toward the end of the Goryeo dynasty when the Confucian intellectuals and activists were increasingly alienated from the Buddhist establishment because of its pervasive religious, political, and economic corruption and ended with a call for the overthrow of Buddhism from the center of national life and the founding of a new dynasty on the explicit foundation of Neo-Confucianism. Buddhism completely lost its credibility, incurring the outrage of the political elite, a situation that explains the polemical vehemence of the Neo-Confucian critique of Buddhism even to the point of being exclusivistic. The philosophical side refers to the Confucian critique of Buddhist doctrines. Here Korean Neo-Confucians largely repeat the Chinese Neo-Confucian critique of the Song period that Buddhism is antinomian, escapist, antisocial, and nihilistic in its doctrine of emptiness, and that it neglects the duty of cultivating one's humanity by practicing the social virtues and participating in the life of this world.

After this prehistory and introduction Muller devotes the main part of his essay to the discussion of the exchange between Jeong Dojeon, the chief architect of the new dynasty who also provided the most substantial philosophical critique yet of Buddhism, and Gihwa, who was himself a disciple of Jeong Dojeon at one time and who converted to Buddhism in his later life and wrote the most thoughtful response to Jeong's and generally Neo-Confucian critique of Buddhism. Basically, Jeong's criticism, which covers every major doctrine of Buddhism, especially Seon Buddhism, is not only that Neo-Confucianism is superior to Buddhism but also that Buddhism is dangerous to society and only fit for extinction because of its antisocial, escapist, and nihilistic tendencies. In an equally thorough response Gihwa provides a point-by-point rebuttal for every criticism Jeong makes, but his central point is that that Confucian practice, which allows the killing of animals, is not consistent with its theory of humaneness and the interdependent unity of all things, which Confucianism shares with Buddhism and Daoism. What is most distinctive of Gihwa's response is his inclusivist view that Buddhism, Confucianism, and Daoism are three different ways to the same truth, the interconnected unity of all things. Muller also goes on to reflect on the conditions for interreligious dialogue, especially the sharing of a certain worldview without which no dialogue can proceed, something useful to keep in mind today. He singles out the conceptual pair of essence and function as such a shared worldview in the debate between Jeong and Gihwa.

As we leave the religious world of the Goryeo dynasty marked first by practical accommodation and then by conflict between Buddhism and Confucianism, and enter the world of the Joseon dynasty (1392–1910), we observe different forms of relation between Christianity and Korean religions, the Confucian-Catholic relation as seen through the eyes of Catholic converts and a sympathetic Neo-Confucian intellectual in part II, and in part III the relation between Protestantism and Korean religions as seen from two Protestant perspectives, that of Protestant theologies of non-Christian religions and that of a Protestant theologian who tried to appropriate essential insights of various Korean religions into an indigenized Christian theology. We see here the rejection and exclusion of Catholicism by official Confucianism, a Confucian attempt to appropriate something of the Catholic tradition into its own philosophy of human nature, a Protestant attempt to include Korean religions in its perspective against its own exclusivist tendencies, and a creative Protestant appropriation of the substance of Korean religions. It is no longer practical mutual accommodation as during the Goryeo period but serious mutual encounter in various forms such as rejection and exclusion, tolerance and inclusion, and substantive appropriation of the other.

In chapter 4, "Catholic God and Confucian Morality: A Look at the Theology and Ethics of Korea's First Catholics," Professor Don Baker of the University of British Columbia provides a provocative analysis of the encounter between Neo-Confucianism and Catholicism in eighteenth-century Korea that challenges much received interpretation with original insights and enlightening backgrounds. In a three-part narrative he shows the radical nature of the break Catholic converts risked with their religious culture, describes the backgrounds that might have motivated some Neo-Confucians to embrace Catholicism, and ends with a description and analysis of three paradigmatic examples taken from among the first Korean converts with regard to what they were expecting to receive from the Catholic faith. His narrative is based on documents left behind by the martyrs and records of government interrogation.

For Baker, conversion to Catholicism meant a radical break with existing Korean religious culture. Catholicism was monotheism, and there had been no monotheism in Korean history prior to the introduction of the Catholic faith. Most Koreans, including most Buddhists, had been polytheistic, and Neo-Confucianism, although not atheistic, did not consider God as relevant. There had been no clear concept of the human soul or life after death except some nebulous idea of the continued existence of the dead. The emphasis of the culture had been on behavior and ethics, not on beliefs and theology, and the result had been the nonexistence of any concept of religion as an organized community of faith with its own distinctive set of beliefs that would separate it from other communities. It is no wonder that there had been no urgent call for the separation of church and state in traditional Korean culture. We today do not fully appreciate the radical challenge posed by Catholicism with its clear monotheistic faith. Baker wonders, therefore, why, of all groups, some Neo-Confucians, for whom the question of God was irrelevant, found Catholicism attractive.

Baker surmises that there were two crises facing eighteenth-century Korean society that might have motivated some Neo-Confucians to turn to Catholicism. The first is the demographic crisis, the sharp decline of the population through a whole series of natural disasters, drought, famine, epidemics, and flood that caused mounting deaths and sicknesses to the entire population, which naturally turned many to religion. Coupled with this was the sense of guilt and responsibility on the part of some Confucian elite for the eruption of natural disasters: lack of virtue on the part of the rulers, according to the Confucian tradition, was the cause of natural disasters besetting a nation. The demographic crisis led to the moral crisis, the failure of the Confucian ruling elite to live up to the ideals of Confucian virtue. Is there any religion that can help with a better theory of human imperfection and a greater hope of rescue from that moral crisis? Baker insists that it is this moral crisis, not the modern political ideal of equality nor interest in Western science and technology, as some history books claim, that motivated some Neo-Confucians at this time to convert to the Catholic faith. It was a moral and religious motive, not a political or scientific one.

In order to demonstrate his thesis Baker examines three examples from the first Catholic community. In the case of Paul Yun, the first Catholic convert to be executed for not performing the Confucian ancestor veneration rite on his mother's death, it is clear from the records of government interrogation that his motive for accepting the Catholic faith, even to the point of martyrdom, was his conviction that it is more imperative to obey his divine Father in heaven and his commandments than to obey parents and rulers on earth. It was filial piety, the main Confucian virtue, but transferred to God the Father, not his belief in the Trinity, the Incarnation, the death and resurrection of Jesus, and/or the specifically Catholic doctrines, of which no mention is made, that proved decisive. In the case of Tasan Chong Yagyong (1762–1836) (more of him in the next chapter), it was his conviction that morality needed a foundation in a personal God or Sangje, not an impersonal principle like *li* as taught by Neo-Confucianism, something he found in Matteo Ricci's *The True Meaning of the Lord of Heaven*, not the specifically Catholic doctrines, that moved him to the Catholic faith, but which was also decisive in his renouncing that faith once he learned that Catholics were not allowed to perform ancestor veneration rites so central to Confucian morality. He accepted Catholicism as a means to Confucian morality and could easily renounce it when it was found to contradict that morality. In the case of his own brother, Chong Yakchong, however, it was the total Catholic faith from the Trinity and Incarnation to the death and resurrection of Jesus and the eternal life it promised that he accepted and accepted to the point of renouncing his own life through martyrdom. His faith was a truly religious faith, not merely a means to morality as in the case of his brother.

Tasan Chong Yagyong, perhaps the most important Korean thinker of the nineteenth century, is the best exemplification of the dialogue of Neo-Confucianism and Catholicism at the philosophical level. Baker already indicated something of this. In chapter 5, "On the Family Resemblance of Philosophical Paradigm between Tasan's Thought and Matteo Ricci's *Tianzhu shiyi* [*The True Meaning of the Lord of Heaven*]," Professor Young-bae Song of Seoul National University provides a full philosophical discussion of this dialogue. He first presents some of the essentials of Ricci's critique of Neo-Confucianism, and then shows how Tasan uses that critique to modify and transform the existing Neo-Confucianism of his time, providing a significant synthesis of East and West, of Confucianism and Catholicism, without, however, accepting Catholicism in its totality, a paradigmatic example of a Confucian assimilation of some aspects of Catholicism.

On the basis of an Aristotelian-Thomistic metaphysics, Matteo Ricci (1552–1610), the Jesuit missionary, provided a critique of contemporary Neo-Confucianism on the issues of human nature, moral life, and the nature of ultimate reality. Human beings are endowed with an intellect and a free will, which distinguishes human beings from animals who only follow their pre-given instincts; and it is the possession of the free will that makes moral life, responsibility, the imputation of good and evil, possible for human beings. Human goodness or moral perfection is not a matter of an inherited *qi* but one of moral practice in which one struggles to cultivate virtue by means of consistent free choices against the animal tendencies of human nature. The Neo-Confucian ultimate, *Taiji* or *Li*, cannot be truly ultimate because they are at best accidents and formal causes, not individual substances that alone can act and cause other things. More ultimate is the personal, intelligent, and spiritual being, *Sangje* or Lord of Heaven, who alone can be the efficient and final cause of the universe.

Tasan accepts this critique of Neo-Confucianism by Ricci. He too rejects Zhu Xi's attribution of the same original nature or *li* to all beings, human and nonhuman, with *qi* as the only differentiating principle. It is not true that all beings possess the same nature, an idea Tasan attributes to a Buddhist influence, and one of the fundamental differences is between nonintellectual and intellectual beings. Human beings as intellectual beings have the capacity to reason and choose between good and evil, even against animal desires, which nonintellectual creatures do not. Thus, moral life belongs only to human beings, not to all beings as Neo-Confucianism claims. The source of moral evil is not the body but the mind and its free choice. Tasan clearly rejects the Neo-Confucian determinism of *qi*. Furthermore, moral perfection is not the result of theoretical meditation on *li* or *tao* but that of moral practice strenuously and consistently carried out throughout one's life. Likewise, for the same reasons as given by Ricci, Tasan argues that *taiji* or *li*, both accidents and impersonal, cannot be the ultimate efficient and final cause of the universe, its movement, its moral order, its teleology; only an intelligent, personal being, who "watches over us like the sun," from whom we cannot hide anything and who rewards the good and punishes the evil, can be such a cause.

Korean Protestantism has long been fundamentalist and exclusivist toward other religions, but it has not always been so, argues Professor Sung-Deuk Oak of the University of California–Los Angeles, who, in chapter 6, "A Genealogy of Protestant Theologies of Religions in Korea, 1876–1910: Protestantism as a Religion of Civilization and Fulfillment," traces the early history of Protestant attitudes toward Korean religions and advocates retrieving some of these early discussions today to counteract the rather dogmatic exclusion of Korean religions from the possibility of salvation still prevailing in much of Korean Protestantism. These discussions between 1880 and 1910 reveal an open-minded evangelicalism that is both "inclusive" of other religions as stages toward Christianity as their "fulfillment" and eager to see points of contact with and even to learn from them. In a theologically fascinating and historically informative documentary survey Oak presents the internal discussions of four different groups, each with an impact on the attitudes of Korean Protestants toward Korean religions. They are the theologies of religions produced by the late nineteenth-century North American scholars that formed the theological background of the early American missionaries on Korean religions, the theological discussions by Western Protestant missionaries in China during the nineteenth century whose Chinese texts were available to educated Korean Christians, the works by North American missionaries themselves based on their experience of Korean religions, and finally the works produced by Korean Protestant intellectuals under the impact of all of these.

The North American contribution to the theology of religion is represented by five authors, James Freeman Clarke, William E. Griffis, Frank Field Ellinwood, George M. Grant, and Samuel H. Kellogg, authors of books on comparative religion reflecting the tension between the progressive view of non-Christian religions as not false but incomplete to be fulfilled by Christianity ("fulfillment theory") and the conservative view that regards them as false religions, as degradations from primitive monotheism in need of salvation through Christianity ("degradation theory"). The Chinese contribution is presented on the basis of works by John L. Nevius, William A. P. Martin, and the two Shanghai missionary conferences of 1877 and 1890, again reflecting the tension of the open-minded accommodation of Confucianism and ancestor veneration on the model of Matteo Ricci (minority) and the conservative condemnation of ancestor veneration and other elements of Asian religions as idolatry (majority). The Korean missionary contribution focuses on the works of missionaries themselves such as G. Heber Jones, George O Engel, and Horace G. Underwood, and the conversion of some missionaries to the theory that healing miracles and demon-possession did not stop with early Christianity but still continued, as testify the experience of Korean Christians. These Korean missionaries likewise show a tension between the theory of degradation and that of fulfillment. Finally, the story of how these three influences were integrated by the early Korean Protestant leaders is told through an analysis of the works by Choe Pyeongheon, Hong Chonghu, and Kil Seonju. These were highly educated intellectuals who were steeped in the classics of Confucianism and up-to-date on the theologies of religions promoted by the missionaries in China, and argued that Christians and Confucians worship the same God although Confucianism still needs fulfillment by Christianity. As a theologian with a special interest in the contemporary discussion of various theologies of religions, I have found this chapter especially theologically fascinating and informative with regard to the early history of Korean Protestantism, a history crying out to be told again today.

Ryu Yongmo (1890–1981), perhaps the most original thinker of Korean Protestantism and the greatest synthesizer of Confucianism, Buddhism, and shamanism on the basis of Christianity, grew up in the period when Korean Protestantism was still open to the voices of greater openness and theological accommodation of Korean religions. In chapter 7, "What Can Christianity Learn from Korean Religions? The Case of Ryu Yongmo," Professor Young-Ho Chun of Saint Paul School of Theology tells the fascinating story of how at least one Korean Protestant theologian grappled with the challenges of traditional religions and tried to push the fulfillment theory as far as it could go by integrating many of the essential elements of traditional religiosity into a reconstruction of the Christian faith.

Committed to the idea of affirming and learning from whatever is good and true in other religions, Ryu provides a thoroughgoing reconstruction of the Christian faith by reformulating and integrating its traditional content into the terms and perspectives of Confucianism, Buddhism, and shamanism. According to Chun, his conversion to Christianity did not entail the rejection of other religions; it was but part of the journey of "awakening" to the most ultimate and comprehensive truth to which other religions also had an important contribution to make in a process of mutual learning and mutual transformation. Ryu's theology is the result of this process of learning and transformation, as Chun illustrates it in terms of certain basic concepts taken from Confucianism, Buddhism, and shamanism, such as *eol* (얼, indigenous Korean term, of shamanistic origin), *seong* (性, "nature" in Neo-Confucianism), *bulseong* (佛性, Buddha nature), and filial piety (chief Confucian virtue), which Ryu employs as the chief hermeneutic categories of his theological reconstruction. Ryu identifies God with *seong*; *eol* or spirit is the presence of God in nature and human life, the invisible but real core of living things; and *bulseong* is the divine nature immanent in all things to be awakened by all *eols* in their spiritual journey to maturity. With no use for the traditional incarnational Christology of the hypostatic union, Ryu considers

Jesus as the being who was thoroughly and only human in whom the *eol* of God was fully realized, especially through his self-sacrifice on the cross to the will of the Father, achieving sagehood and becoming a *gunja* [君子] in Confucian terms, a paradigmatic example of filial piety for all to follow. Chun concludes with theological reflections on the tension between the orthodox Christian faith and Ryu's reconstruction.

Part IV, the last section, brings Confucianism and Christianity (Catholicism and Protestantism) together in their encounter with the challenges of the modern world, especially, feminism, democracy, and globalization. In chapter 8, "Resurgence of *Asian Values*: Confucian Comeback and Its Embodiment in Christianity," Professor Namsoon Kang of Texas Christian University conducts a comparative analysis and critical evaluation of the concept of the family, regarded as the core of Asian values, in Confucianism and Christianity from the feminist perspective, and examines the historical impact of misguided Confucian familism on Korean society as a whole and on Christianity in particular.

For Kang, so much of the talk about "Asian values" is merely a reversion of Said's "Orientalism" now only used to put in a positive light exactly those Asian values that used to be dismissed as retrogressive with all the problems of Orientalism. The discourse on Asian values is dangerous for several reasons: it overlooks both the vices of the so-called Asian communitarianism with its hierarchy and patriarchy and the virtues of Western ethical individualism, masks the root cause of women's oppression by idealizing the patriarchal family structure, and justifies and perpetuates the hierarchical and gender inequalities of inherited social status. She goes on to describe the classical ideal of the family according to Confucian classics as centered on filial piety and its patriarchal, patrilineal, and patrilocal emphasis, and contrasts it with a variety of Christian views on the family, advocating what she calls "critical familism" as constructed by contemporary Christian feminists centered on doing the will of God, justice, and mutual care. The Confucian view reduces human beings to their role in the family and subjects women to men in so many oppressive ways, while the Christian view relativizes the family in light of God's will and justifies ethically responsible individualism, legitimizing the possibility of human rights, which Confucianism has trouble accepting. Kang goes on to show how Confucian familism has also contaminated the Korean Christian view of the family and the institutional life of the churches with endemic patriarchy, producing a "Confucianized" Christianity with all the problems of Confucian familism.

While Kang's perspective on Confucian familism is clearly negative and critical, in chapter 9, "Korean Confucianism and Women's Subjectivity in the Twenty-First Century," Professor Un-sunn Lee of Sejong University, Seoul, presents an opposite, positive view of the Confucian view of the family and the role of women in the contemporary world where the family and civic life in general seem to be collapsing, and does so by retrieving certain—often neglected—aspects of classical Confucianism and Neo-Confucianism. I want to note here that Professor Kang and Professor Lee were not explicitly responding to each other's essay, yet they do have a history of arguing and dialoguing with each other in Korean journals as representatives of two very contrasting perspectives on the relation between Confucianism and feminism. These essays were published elsewhere as remarked on in the Acknowledgments, and are being reprinted here, with some revisions, with their consent to my invitation. I am delighted to include both essays next to each other because Lee also seeks, as does Kang, to address the same issue, the Confucian potential for feminism, although from an opposite point of view. If Kang's ultimate concern is the protection of justice and human rights, Lee's concern is the restoration of the family and proper human relationships in the public realm when both are radically challenged today. Lee is fully aware of the fact that Confucianism did contribute to the repression of women but quite hopeful that there are still Confucian resources that can help us in promoting women's subjectivity and community life. It is precisely the purpose of her essay to explore and retrieve them.

Lee argues that it has been central to Confucianism to promote the public realm in which we live together and the common good and condemn individualism, the seeking of private, personal interests, an important aspect to be revived in the contemporary world where self-interest and individualistically conceived subjectivity have been the ruling ideology to the collapse of authentic public life or life with others and its reduction to the Hobbesian "war of all against all." In this context it is one-sided to regard Korean Confucian women's lives, especially during the Joseon dynasty, as passive, lowly, and miserable, a misunderstanding derived from the failure to appreciate the religious aspect of Confucianism, which is to sanctify all lives without distinction between private and public, through the virtue of sagehood, the way to authentic humanity or *jen*, which is to "become one with all things in the universe" through compassion and care. The traditional dedication of women to their role of giving birth to and taking care of lives must be understood precisely as a

Confucian way of sanctifying all lives by ritualizing and civilizing them. There is also plenty of evidence that Korean women took this religious aspect seriously and positively with the full realization of their equality with men in the pursuit of sagehood and authentic humanity, which lies in the cultivation of self through the service of others, not in the pursuit of self-interested subjectivity. Korean women's dedication to their role as mother, daughter, and wife was not the source of their oppression as is often argued but the transcendent, religious source that empowered them to cope with the difficulties of life with faith and hope, seeing the ultimate not in heaven (as does Christianity) or in the inward self (as does Buddhism) but in the concrete *other* before them, their children, ancestors, husbands, guests, and neighbors in need of care. Lee illustrates this aspect of Confucianism and Korean Confucian women's experience with examples from classical Confucianism, Korean Neo-Confucianism, and Korean women's lives, both from the Joseon and contemporary periods, and Hannah Arendt.

We now move on to another contemporary topic, democracy. How have Confucianism and Christianity been doing with regard to democracy in Korea? Have they been progressive or retrogressive forces? In chapter 10, "Confucianism at a Crossroads: Confucianism and Democracy in Korea," Professor Young-chan Ro of George Mason University reviews the Confucian tradition in light of the democratic challenges facing Korea, especially its failure to promote democratic institutions, and tries to retrieve its classical humanism, especially its concern for the well-being of the people as the primary norm of all politics, as moral resources for the integrity of democracy now under great tension and strain.

Ro readily admits that Confucianism did not make a positive contribution to the democratization of Korea even though it may have contributed to the economic prosperity of the nation as it did in Singapore, Taiwan, and China with its emphasis on hard work, discipline, loyalty to the nation, and the promotion of family values. He attributes the introduction of democracy to Korea to Western culture and Christianity, the two sources responsible for the modernization of Korea from the end of the Joseon dynasty. This does not mean that Confucianism did not have some of the democratic values. Confucianism was anthropocentric or humanistic, believed in the equality of all human beings in their potential to become sages, and regarded the mind of the people as the mind of heaven. Why, then, wonders Ro, did Confucianism not develop democracy while Western culture did?

According to Ro, Confucianism had the democratic "ideology" that regards the people as the "foundation" of all government (*minbonjuŭi/ minbenzhuyi*, 民本主義), but it could not develop the necessary democratic "institution" in the sense of the government that is at once "of" the people, "by" the people, and "for" the people because of its optimistic view of human nature. It considered every human being capable of being a sage, requiring only proper "learning" and "cultivation," not political institutionalization. It also regarded the government "for" the people as the best form of government to be secured by the properly educated and cultivated kings; its ideal was sage-cracy, not demo-cracy. Lacking a doctrine of "original sin," Confucianism trusted the system of education and cultivation, especially for rulers, which it did extensively develop, to make up for any failures of the ruling class. Even dictatorship was acceptable as long as it was by a virtuous and enlightened ruler. Believing in human perfectibility, it failed to develop institutions of checks and balances that would prevent human beings from falling into evil and corruption. Ro attributes this failure to the predominance of the Mencian line in the tradition to the neglect of the realistic insights of Xunzi (298–238 BCE). It is time today, for Ro, that serious Confucian scholars should study ways of retrieving and institutionalizing Xunzi's idea of "propriety" (*ye/ li*, 禮) and contribute to the creation of a uniquely Korean form of the democratic system.

While Professor Ro discusses Korean Confucianism at a crossroads in the face of the institutional challenges of democracy, Professor Anselm Kyongsuk Min of Claremont Graduate University discusses Korean Christianity, both Catholicism and Protestantism, now facing a crossroads of its own, in the last chapter, chapter 11, "Between Tradition and Globalization: Korean Christianity at a Crossroads." Contemporary Korean Christianity confronts the daunting task of renewing and defining itself in the double contexts of tradition and globalization. It has to somehow come to terms with the Korean religious and cultural tradition, a problem that usually goes by the name of indigenization, so as to consider itself authentically Korean, and it has to respond, as do all other Korean religions, to the impossibly complicated challenges of globalization now engulfing the whole of Korean society with the force of a hurricane in order to fulfill its mission in contemporary Korea.

Min first presents the relation of tension between Christianity and other religions in Korea in its historical context while also calling attention to a universally neglected phenomenon: Korean Christians already embodying much of Korean religions in their mentality and behavior and this de facto indigenization of Christianity already operative in them, which requires theological reflection prior to all the talk about interreligious dialogue and mutual appropriation among religions at the explicit conceptual and practical level. Min goes on to describe the essential challenges of globalization, which he considers to be *the* context of all contexts for *all* major human endeavors. He ends with a critical analysis of a debilitating problem facing Korean Protestantism and Korean Catholicism, individualist fragmentation and clerical authoritarianism, respectively, and with a suggestion for a three-step methodology of indigenizing Christianity precisely in the contemporary context of the globalizing world. He argues that the indigenizing retrieval of ancient sources, whether Buddhist, Confucian, shamanist, or Christian, requires a hermeneutic of suspicion in terms of an ideology critique, a social-scientific analysis of the contemporary context, and a political theory that mediates between the ancient world and the contemporary context. Without these steps, retrieval runs the danger of becoming irrelevant antiquarianism, a repressive ideology, or a confusing mix of the two. He concludes with former president Kim Dae Jung's approach to updating the Confucian ideas of loyalty to the king and filial piety as a good illustration of this method.

Part I

Buddhism and Confucianism
Accommodation and Conflict

2

Interactions between Buddhism and Confucianism in Medieval Korea

Jongmyung Kim

Introduction

Buddhism and Confucianism have been in close relationship since the Three Kingdoms period of Korea (first century BCE–668).[1] However, the relationship between the two was different by period. They were in dialogue from the fourth to the thirteenth century, but they came into conflict from the thirteenth to the fourteenth century. Confucianism became the dominant of the two from the fifteenth to the early twentieth, and they still coexist in contemporary Korea. The purpose of this article is to examine the interactions between Buddhism and Confucianism in medieval Korea, which corresponds to the Koryŏ Dynasty (918–1392).

There exist only some fragmentary materials for understanding the Koryŏ people's views of Buddhism and Confucianism (Pak 2004, 91), and as a result, scholarly discussions of the relationship between the two traditions are few both in Korea and overseas.[2] In addition, active contacts between Buddhism and Confucianism did not occur until after the late thirteenth century, i.e., toward the end of the Koryŏ Dynasty, when Neo-Confucianism (Sŏngni hak) was introduced to Korea (Ch'oe 2001, 7–28; Pak 2004, 91–105; Pyŏn 2005, 43–81) and produced some works on the relationship between Buddhism and Confucianism (Pyŏn 2005, 43–81).[3]

Therefore, this study is crucial for a better understanding of the nature of Korean religious traditions and, by extension, of the relationship between politics and religion in East Asia. The Koryŏ period is also important in that it connects ancient Korea to modern Korea, but it has attracted less attention among scholars than other periods.

Following a tradition set in the Silla period,[4] Buddhism and Confucianism coexisted during the Koryŏ Dynasty, but their influence on Koryŏ society was different by period.[5] This article will primarily focus on the role of the ruler[6] in the development of the religious traditions from the reign of King T'aejo (918–43), when the dynasty was founded, to that of King Hyŏnjong (1009–31), when Confucian bureaucracy was firmly established.[7] In particular, the reign of King T'aejo will be the focus of analysis because the vicissitudes of state customs depended on the ruler in pre-modern Korea (Kim 2013b, 6–7). As founder of the Koryŏ kingdom, the king was the final arbiter who determined the nature of Buddhism and Confucianism in medieval Korea, enabling the two religious traditions to coexist as major ideologies (Yun et al. 2002, 31). His Buddhist activities developed in close relation to his Confucian statecraft, which had become the time-honored tradition until the demise of the Koryŏ kingdom.[8]

One of the prevailing views of medieval Korea among both scholars and non-scholars is that Buddhism was the state religion with a predominant role in determining every aspect of Korean culture and society at the time. In articulating the interaction between Buddhism and Confucianism it is also my hope to correct this view and provide a more balanced perspective on the relative importance of the two religions. There is no denying the dominance of Buddhism as a religion, but it should be balanced by the fact that Confucianism was the dominant political ideology which often exploited the potential of Buddhism to serve the preservation and prosperity of the ruling dynasty, Confucianizing Buddhism in many important respects in the process.

This study consists of three sections. It will first examine the political position of Buddhism and Confucianism; second, describe the role of Buddhism in Confucian statecraft; and finally, analyze the relationship between Buddhism and Confucianism. It will do this by employing the textual criticism of extant sources, largely focusing on the *Koryŏ sa* (*History of the Koryŏ Dynasty*, hereafter, *KRS*).[9] It will be argued that as far as extant materials are concerned, Confucianism was the ruling ideology of Koryŏ while Buddhism was the dominant religious spirit that also reinforced Confucian virtues such as humanity (Kor.* *in*; Ch. *jen*) and filial piety (Kor. *hyo*; Ch. *xiao*).¹⁰

The Political Position of Buddhism and Confucianism

Koryŏ society was a multireligious society in which a variety of religious traditions coexisted. From its initial period the Koryŏ kingdom accepted diverse religious and philosophical traditions, which included Buddhism, Confucianism, Taoism, shamanism, astrology, and geomancy (Kim 1994, 3), forming a pluralist society (Breuker 2010, 48–84) characterized by unity within variety and openness (Park 2013, 1–1). No state religion as such existed in Koryŏ (Yun, et al. 2002, 50). In this respect, Koryŏ was quite different from the Christian and Islamic kingdoms of the same period (Yun et al. 2002, 24) as well as from the Chosŏn Dynasty that would follow (1392–1910). King T'aejo's religious policy was that of religious pluralism in the modern sense, which other Koryŏ kings also faithfully followed (Yi 2011, 242). Buddhism and Confucianism were the most important ones among these religions, but they were not state religions.

Prior to medieval Korea, Buddhism had been regarded as more important than Confucianism in governing the state. However, the political position of the two was reversed during Koryŏ, where Confucianism was considered more important than Buddhism. In Koryŏ Buddhism was the dominant religious force, but Confucianism was the official ideology of the state. While eminent monks until the eleventh century viewed Buddhism as superior to Confucianism, Confucian scholar-officials in general were critical of Buddhism.

Buddhism as a Dominant Religious Force

Buddhism in Koryŏ was the dominant religious force (Yun et al. 2002, 24).¹¹ Koryŏ kings engaged in Buddhist events in various ways, receiving Buddhist precepts, constructing temples, instituting monastic offices, and performing Buddhist rituals.

As a lay Buddhist follower, King T'aejo emulated Emperor Wu (502–49) of Liang China (*NYK* 1996, 1: 268) and respected Buddhism and monks

---

*Abbreviations: Ch.: Chinese; Jp.: Japanese; Kor.: Korean; Skt.: Sanskrit

(*NYK* 1996, 1: 192–5).[12] In particular, through his Injunctions[13] King T'aejo said that Buddhism was the foundation of his kingdom, noting:

> The success of every great undertaking of our state depends upon the favor and protection of the Buddha. Therefore, the temples of both the Meditation and Doctrinal schools should be built, and monks should be sent out to those temples to minister to the Buddha. (*KRS* 2, 15a1–3)[14]

In particular, one of the most intriguing aspects of Buddhism during the Koryŏ period was the abundance and variety of Buddhist rituals (Vermeersch 2008, 313). More Buddhist rituals were held by kings during the period than at any other time in Korean history, a frequency also unprecedented in China or Japan (Kim 1994, xiii; Kim 2001, 8–9).[15] In this regard, King T'aejo admonished his successors to value the Assembly of Eight Prohibitions (*P'algwanhoe*) and the Lantern Festival (*Yŏndŭnghoe*) (*KRS* 2, 16a1–5), the two most significant Buddhist rituals in medieval Korea.[16] The engraving of the Korean Buddhist canons[17] was another achievement of this period. Buddhist canons were engraved only twice during the entire history of Korea, and both happened during the Koryŏ Dynasty: The *Ch'ojo Koryŏ taejanggyŏng* (*First Korean Buddhist Canon*) engraved in the eleventh century but with most of it burned due to the Mongol invasions in the mid-thirteenth century, and the *Chaejo Koryŏ taejangyŏng* (*Second Korean Buddhist Canon*), a product of the thirteenth century still preserved in Haein Monastery as part of the UNESCO World Heritage.[18]

It is also quite notable that Buddhism was interpreted in the context of Confucianism, which included the concepts of loyalty, filial piety, yin (negative cosmic energy) and yang (positive cosmic energy), and the theory of heavenly warning (Kor. chŏn'gyŏn chaei sŏl or chŏnin kamŭng sŏl; Ch. tianqian zaiyi shuo), a traditional Confucian system of thought systematized by the Chinese ideologue Dong Zhongshu (ca. 179–104 BCE) during the Han Dynasty according to which natural disasters are warning signs of misgovernment sent by Heaven.[19]

Confucianism as the State Ideology

From the very beginning of the Koryŏ Dynasty, Confucianism served as the state ideology (Yi 1984, 1; Yun et al. 2002, 27)[20] upon which state administration and social order were in principle based (Yi 2011, 225). In addition, the royal ancestor worship ritual had been one of the most significant state events throughout the history of the dynasty from beginning to end. Texts considered essential for kings and princes to gain necessary knowledge of state governance were all Confucian texts, with priority accorded to the *Shu jing* (Book of History) and the *Li ji* (Book of Rites). In particular, the *Book of History* had been used throughout the dynasty as a book of political ideology, which was based on the idea of the unity between heaven and man and emphasized the ruler's morality (Kim 2001, 277). Most of Koryŏ kings were also buried after their death in accord with Confucian customs (Kim 2010, 276–82).

King T'aejo played a most significant role in accepting the Chinese system and culture. He not only adopted Confucianism as the political ideology of the state, which was to remain so throughout the dynasty (Pak 2011, 171–220), but also personally composed works with emphasis on Confucian leadership such as "*Chŏnggye*" (Political Admonitions) and "*Kye Paengnyo sŏ*" (Admonitions for All Officials) to promote the Confucian ideas of loyalty and filial piety (Pyŏn 2005, 49). In his Injunction, King T'aejo admonished his successors to be well informed of the chapter of "*Wui*" ("Against Luxurious East") in the *Book of History* (*KRS* 2, 7a6–9).[21] The king also founded the National Academy (*Kukhak*) and the Royal Ancestral Shrine (*Chongmyo*) (Cho 2006, 16). For King T'aejo, politics meant reforming public morals and bringing peace to the people (Chŏng 1992, 115) according to the ideals of Confucian statecraft.[22]

King Kwangjong (949–75) was the first king to adopt the Confucian civil service examination from Song (960–1279) China in Korean history. King Sŏngjong (981–97) was so eager to accept Chinese culture as to incur criticism for excesses (*KRS* 94, 3b5–6). It was during his reign that Confucianism was fully accepted as the governing ideology of the state (Yi 1984, 39–50). As Ch'oe Sŭngno (927–89), an influential scholar-official, pointed out, "Behavior based on Confucianism is the foundation of governing the state ... Governing the state is what we have to do today" (*KRS* 93, 114–15), which indicates something of the consensus among the ruling elite regarding Confucianism as the principle of their politics (Yi 2009, 321; Pak 2011, 198–99). It was during the reign of King Sŏngjong that the National Confucian Academy (*Kukchagam*), a possible reorganization of the National Academy, was established (Yi 1984, 1).

In the tradition of Confucian politics (Yi 2011, 226), King Hyŏnjong promoted the art of kingship or kingcraft. (Kim 2008, 246). His reign saw the completion of Confucian bureaucracy. In particular, he developed reform politics aimed at the fulfillment of Confucian ideals, i.e., the strengthening of kingship, increasing the wealth of the nation, and the building of a strong army with the support of the Confucian scholar-officials (Kim 2008, 132–54), who were selected through the Confucian civil service examination system and constituted the core of political leadership of the time. Ch'ae Ch'ungsun (?–1036), an important leader of reform politics under King Hyŏnjong, argued that Confucianism served as the orthodoxy of his time,

> Your Majesty's subject [Ch'ae Ch'ungsun] is told that the ultimate mirror of a sage is hidden in the Confucian texts. Therefore, if one cultivates the texts diligently with a firm will, the orthodox teaching will take root. (*HKC*, 1984, 447: 12–13)

In addition, King Hyŏnjong published thirty-nine royal edicts, of which many were Confucian in content, a good indication of the direction of national politics of the time. (Yi 2011, 228).

In short, Confucianism had remained the political ideology of the state until the demise of the dynasty in the late fourteenth century.

Intellectuals' Understanding of Buddhism and Confucianism

Buddhism was the dominant religious force in medieval Korea. However, it should be noted that the religion also lost its position as an autonomous entity at the same time, existing only to support Confucian morals, but not vice versa. Koryŏ kings took the carrot-and-stick approach toward Buddhist circles.[23] While, until the eleventh century, eminent monks including Ŭichŏn (1055–1101), had either viewed Buddhism as superior to Confucianism or expressed no interest in Confucianism,[24] Confucian scholar-officials viewed Buddhism as a strategic partner in governing the state or criticized it.

For Koryŏ's royal families, the transfer of royal lineage for generations had been regarded as the most important benefit received from their ancestors (Kim 1994, 33; Kim 2001, 72). Religious traditions, therefore, including Buddhism, were also requested to fulfill this goal (Yun et al. 2002, 49–50). To that end and following the idea of Ch'oe Ch'iwŏn of Silla Korea, Confucian scholar-officials in early Koryŏ held that both Buddhism and Confucianism were important in the execution of royal governing. Regarding this, Ch'oe Sŭngno said,

The Three Teachings [Buddhism, Confucianism, and Taoism] all have their own special qualities, and those who follow them should not be confused but keep them separate. Practitioners of Buddhism take spiritual cultivation as the basic principle. Practitioners of Confucianism take governing the nation as the basic principle. Spiritual cultivation is valuable for the afterlife, but governing the country is the task of the present. The present is here and the afterlife is extremely distant. How could it not be wrong to sacrifice the present for the distant? (*KRS* 93, 19a3–6)[25]

According to this entry, Ch'oe Sŭngno thought that Buddhism was a religion for spiritual cultivation for the afterlife, whereas Confucianism was the political ideology for governing the state in this life, thus giving primacy to Confucianism. King Hyŏnjong also agreed with Ch'oe Sŭngno and said, "Buddhism is for inner cultivation and Confucianism is for outer governing" (*HKC*, 1984, 448: 7). Ch'ae Ch'ungsun also maintained,

Your Majesty's servant [Ch'ae Ch'ungsun] is told that a sage is an extremely exemplary man. . . . Buddhism is none other than a teaching about the mind. If we cultivate it ourselves with utmost sincerity, a blessing will naturally ensue. The so-called Three Religions [Buddhism, Confucianism, and Taoism] look disparate, but their origin is the same. . . . They all teach benevolence and filial piety. Therefore, the previous king said, 'Filial piety is the root of virtue and all teachings are derived from it. Accordingly, my kingly predecessors regarded it as the principle of governing the state. . . . As a result, the world was peaceful and calamities did not occur. There is a Buddhist text titled *Pumo ŭnjung kyŏng* (Ch. *Fumu enzhong jing*, Book of Parental Gratitude) and its core emphasizes filial piety. Therefore, both Confucianism and Buddhism regard the concept of filial piety as their essence. (*HKC* 1984, 447: 12–448: 2)

This quote makes evident the belief that both Buddhism and Confucianism are necessary in governing the state. In particular, King Hyŏnjong valued the *Book of Parental Gratitude*, which focused on filial piety in content. In his "Kaesŏng Hyŏnhwa-sa pi" (Epitaph of Hyŏnhwa Monastery in Kaesŏng), Ch'ae Ch'ungsun also said, "We follow Buddhism internally and educate people with Confucianism outwardly. The unity of the ins and outs is well communicated both in the past and in the present "(*HKC*, 1984, 448).

We can say, therefore, that in Koryŏ Confucianism served as a political ideology for this life while Buddhism did as a means to spiritual cultivation (*susin chi to*) for the afterlife or as a religion for blessings.

The Role of Buddhism in Confucian Statecraft

The Political Position of Buddhism

As far as extant sources are concerned, the political position of Buddhism and Confucianism in medieval Korea was not equal: Confucianism was dominant over Buddhism.

Koryŏ kings considered themselves to be *bodhisattvas*. The idea of the identity of the ruler with the Buddha or a *bodhisattva* first emerged in Northern Wei (386–534). Empress Zetian (625–705) claimed that she was an incarnation of the Maitreya Buddha. It was during the period of Tang (618–907) China that the regulation that monks should bow to the ruler was established (Zhang 2014, 74–75). Shizu (1260–94) of Yuan was also identified with a Buddha. During the Northern Song period (960–1126) Confucian scholars insisted that the emperor should be identified with the Buddha and should not bow in front of a Buddhist image. In particular, the idea that the emperor was a *bodhisattva* developed in Liusong (420–79) China, and rulers received the bodhisattva precepts. This tradition was popular during the Sui (581–618) and Tang dynasties.

In Korean history, Kungye (?–918), the founder of Later Koguryŏ (901–18), was the only ruler who identified himself with the Buddha. He composed Buddhist texts in person and lectured on them himself, which was rare in China and Korea (Nam 2005, 85–86). In Korean history kings received Buddhist precepts before the seventh century. King T'aejo of Koryŏ followed suit, and it had been tradition throughout the dynasty, which was different from pre-modern China, where the tradition was only intermittently followed (Nam 2005, 83–87).

Some eminent Korean monks were respected as *bodhisattvas* or even as Buddhas from the ninth to the tenth century. The tradition in which the ruler makes a vow to an eminent monk and takes him as a

National Master (*kuksa*) had begun in the ninth century in Korea and was firmly rooted by the tenth century, a practice unique to Korea and not found in contemporary China.²⁶ This tradition was transmitted to Koryŏ. Koryŏ adopted the system of National Master and Royal Master (*wangsa*) from the very beginning, symbolizing the privilege accorded to Buddhist monks as spiritual and ethical leaders by the state. In particular, the system of Royal Master was unique to Koryŏ, probably a product of King T'aejo's policy of embracing various Buddhist circles of his time (Nam 2005, 88–99). The monastic examination was also adopted in the tenth century, and the monastic ladders (*sŭnggye*) were firmly set up after the tenth century (Wŏn 2010, 58).

However, the actual aim of the appointment of high monks in medieval Korea was to make them devote themselves to the welfare of the state. In this regard, King T'aejo's remark is telling:

> The reason why the state regulated the grade of temples is to treat eminent monks well . . . How can I as the ruler be stingy in selecting such figures who will bring happiness to the state? (*KMC* 1, 1986, 367)

In addition, from the beginning of the dynasty, kings received *bodhisattva* precepts and were considered *bodhisattvas*. However, these facts do not mean that monastic power was superior to secular power in medieval Korea. After all, the king had the power to appoint National and Royal Masters.²⁷

Koryŏ rulers controlled the monastic circles for their political purposes and had much more effective control over the appointment of abbots than their Chinese counterparts (Vermeersch 2004, 9).²⁸ From the very beginning of Koryŏ the king claimed the right to appoint abbots. Korean monastic communities were not an autonomous entity, as was the case with the Catholic Church in medieval Europe. King T'aejo's policy regarding Buddhist offices was different from that of Silla. In Silla temples served as venues for state-supporting cults and constituted the basic units in the administrative system supervising all temples in the country. However, the system of temple-based overseers in Silla was replaced by a completely new system under King T'aejo (Vermeersch 2008, 203–19).

In short, the political position of Buddhism in medieval Korea was not independent of secular power but subject to its control.

The State and Buddhism

Buddhist circles in medieval Korea were under the direct and indirect control of the state (Wŏn 2010, 82).[29] In that context, Buddhism served as a political tool, a support of Confucian morals, and a religion for good fortune.

Koryŏ Kings' Attitude toward Buddhism

In traditional Korea, including Koryŏ, kings in general understood the Buddha as a divine figure with compassion and Buddhism as the teaching for praying for blessings with emphasis on loyalty and filial piety (Kim 2013b, 359–92). In particular, Koryŏ society in general depended on Buddhism (Ro 2002, 63) and most of Koryŏ kings were not Confucianized due to their concern with Buddhism, following the tradition from Silla.[30] However, their Buddhist policies were not the same[31] and Koryŏ kings were different from some of Silla kings in their attitude toward Buddhism. Kings Pŏphŭng (514–40) and Chinhŭng (540–76) of Silla took Buddhism as their political ideology and became Buddhist monks after dethronement. However, Koryŏ kings, including King T'aejo, were never ordained as monks. In addition, Confucian scholars in medieval Korea viewed Buddhism as a religion for spiritual cultivation for this and the next life rather than as a "life education system."[32]

Buddhism as a Political Tool

In China Buddhism came under the control of the state from around the seventh century, and such a relationship was firmly established during the Song period (960–1279) (Nam 2005, 81). Korea was not an exception in this regard. Already, from the initial period of their emergence on Korean soil in the fourth century, Buddhist circles were under the control of the state, and this tradition was transmitted to Koryŏ. However, King T'aejo prohibited his opponents from founding temples. The king said, "If villainous courtiers attain power and come to be influenced by the entreaties of bonzes, the temples of various schools will quarrel and struggle among themselves for gain. This ought to be prevented" (*KRS* 2, 15a4–5).[33] In addition, the primary motive of Koryŏ kings in supporting Buddhism was their expectation of the perpetuity of the royal family, which was an expression of filial piety. In this regard, Ch'ae Ch'ungsun said,

The great performance of Buddhist events is to prolong the achievements of our forefathers. . . . The filial piety of my lord [King Hyŏnjong] will continue down to ten thousand generations (*HKC* 1984, 447: 1–3).

In this context, King Hyŏnjong used Buddhism actively to win the hearts of the people, depending on the Buddha's miraculous power (Yi 2011, 239). Buddhist events, including the engraving of the *First Korean Buddhist Canon*, were also products to fulfill his political purposes. It is highly possible that King Hyŏnjong's special life career as a monk before his enthronement made him especially interested in Buddhist affairs. Regulations to control monks were stronger during his reign than during that of King Sŏngjong, who professed to take Confucianism as his political ideology. Prohibitions included brewing wine in monastic areas, transforming one's house into a temple, a woman's ordination as a nun, and seizure of the people's property (*KRS* 85, 8b3–10a1). King Hyŏnjong also required monks to observe Buddhist precepts through the control of the monastic community and imposed penalties when the monastic communities could not fulfill their duties or had problems with Buddhist precepts (Yi 2011, 239). Except for such regulations, King Hyŏnjong supported the Buddhist circles in various ways, and the primary reason for his support was political.[34]

Koryŏ kings also appear to have encouraged monks to participate in war. For example, King Hyŏnjong rewarded a monk who died in war with the office of Chief Abbot (*sujwa*) (Kim 2013b, 136).

Koryŏ kings admitted that Buddhism was a means to gain the hearts of the people, whom they viewed as "crass" (*NYK* 1996, 1, 34) and "childlike" (*NYK* 1996, 1, 117).[35] As an example, King T'aejo used Buddhism as part of his political strategy. He noted that Buddhist ideas were so deeply embedded in the minds of the Silla people that they believed that life or death and fortune or misfortune depended entirely on the Buddha (Nam 2003, 35). In response, King T'aejo's Counselor Ch'oe Ŭng (898–932) remonstrated against the king's dependence on Buddhism, to which the king responded by saying that Buddhism was just a useful tool in gaining the hearts of the people (*KMC* 2, 106).[36] Yi Chibaek (fl. 983–95) also emphasized the need to perform indigenous events of the Lantern Festival, the Assembly of Eight Prohibitions, and *Sŏllang* (The Way of Immortal Youth) in order to maintain national security and peace (*KRS* 94, 1b16–3b5).

Koryŏ kings were known for cultivating good relations with many Sŏn (Ch. *Chan*; Jp. *Zen*) monks in particular, but it was not because kings had a special interest in their teaching but because the Sŏn monks were connected with local strongmen. Yi Kyubo (1168–1241), a representative man of letters, also asserted that the reason why King T'aejo favored Sŏn over other Buddhist schools was because it was more effective in repelling invaders,

> The path to Sŏn is the path to victory. The efficacy of Sŏn is very fast and it is a great carrier of blessings beyond comparison. Because of this, the Great King [T'aejo], our great ancestor, sought [teaching] from a bright master in secret and respected the supreme teaching. He established 500 Sŏn temples to widely spread the teaching of the mind. After that, the army from the north retreated by itself, and there were no longer thieves in the border areas. [Therefore,] the benefit of Sŏn is excellent. (*KMC* 1, 1986, 268)

Yi Kyubo also argued that a Sŏn monk was more efficacious than property and provisions in times of war. He said, "To raise a Sŏn monk is better than to use property and parched rice as provisions for ten thousand soldiers." (*KMC* 1, 1986, 270). In addition, although Koryŏ had a closer diplomatic relation to the Liao Dynasty (907–1125), which played a significant role in the development of East Asian Buddhism, than to Sung China, Koryŏ's Buddhist policy was different from that of the Liao kingdom, where Buddhist canonical texts were used to educate the crown prince, and monks were encouraged to be faithful to their proper duties without engaging in war even in national difficulties (Wittfogel and Feng 1961, 294).

Buddhism as a Support of Confucian Morals

The ritualization of Confucian values in Koryŏ emerged as the ancestor worship ritual, and other religious or philosophical traditions such as Buddhism, Taoism, shamanism, and geomancy also served as a means of realizing Confucian values. Conventional scholarship argued that the religious traditions of the Koryŏ kingdom were worn by Buddhist integuments (Ro 2002, 63). However, I would rather argue that in traditional Korea Buddhism was influenced by Chinese philosophical or religious traditions, Confucianism in particular, to the neglect of those principles that contain the essence of the Buddha's teachings such as the Four Noble Truths.[37] Buddhism served as a support of Confucian morals but not vice versa.

Kings in pre-modern Korea used Buddhism for the promotion of the social and political virtues of their times, of which loyalty and filial piety were considered the most important. It is worth noting in this regard what Hŭmch'un, a high ranking official of seventh-century Silla, said: "Loyalty and filial piety include risking one's life in national difficulties," and "Loyalty is the primary virtue of a subject" (Kim, 1986b, 375a6-7). This also applied to monks as subjects of the king. In his "*Anmin ka*" (Song of Pacifying the People) of 765, the monk and later Royal Master Ch'ungdam (d.u.) said, "The king is a father, subjects are lovely mothers, and the people are silly children" (Iryŏn 1993, 67: 12).[38] This tradition was transmitted to Koryŏ.

Koryŏ kings thought that the primary function of Buddhism was to promote filial piety, and many eminent monks agreed. For example, in his admonitions on the death bed, Great Master Chin'gong (855–937) said, "Monks and men of manners should respect their seniors as their parents and love their juniors like their children" (*NYK* 1996, 1, 66), emphasizing filial piety and brotherly love, which were important Confucian virtues.

Buddhism as a Religion of Good Fortune

The single most important role of Buddhism from its inception in Korean history was its service as a religion of good fortune, which included protection from natural calamities, prevention of foreign invasions, enjoyment of secular blessings, and better rebirth. Koryŏ Buddhism was also characterized by this tradition.

Natural calamities were considered a warning of misgovernment in traditional Korea and important enough, therefore, to be recorded in their historical texts. Solar eclipses, droughts, floods, earthquakes, hail, and heavy snow were all duly mentioned in the *Historical Records of the Three Kingdoms*.[39] The *KRS* was not an exception in this regard. When natural calamities occurred in Koryŏ, kings reflected on their moral failures and held religious rituals, including Buddhist rituals. Yi Kyubo's (1168–1241) "Taejang kakp'an kunsin kigo mun" (Prayer by the King and Subjects for Engraving the *Second Korean Buddhist Canon*) indicates the motive for engraving the *First Korean Buddhist Canon*. According to this record, King Hyŏnjong began engraving it in the hope of repulsing foreign enemies by invoking the miraculous power of the Buddha,

> In 1011, the second year of the reign of King Hyŏnjong, the ruler of Khitan mobilized his army in large numbers and

invaded the Koryŏ kingdom. As a result, the king fled to the south. The Khitan army was stationed in Songak and did not retreat. [The king] issued the greatest appeal to his subjects for engraving the *First Korean Buddhist Canon*. Thereafter, the Khitan army withdrew from the Koryŏ kingdom of themselves. (*KMC* 1, 1986, 272–73)

Koryŏ kings, including King T'aejo, understood Buddhism as a religion for invoking blessings. For them, Buddhist scriptures were not for learning Buddhist doctrine but for accumulating merits. Ch'ae Ch'ungsun also said that the Koryŏ people of his time understood Buddhism as a religion for blessings,

> Your subject [Ch'ae Ch'ungsun] was told that . . . Buddhist teaching is mind. Therefore, sincerity in it and respect for it will bring blessings (*pongnok*). (*HKC*, 1984, 447: 12–3)

In his "Chŏn Taejanggyŏng so" (Commentary on the Reading of the *First Korean Buddhist Canon*), Chŏng Chisang (?–1135), a scholar-official and one of the twelve poets in Koryŏ, also observed that partial readings of Buddhist literature (*chŏndok*) aimed at earthly blessings (Kim 2013b, 140–41).

Koryŏ kings wished for a better rebirth based on the theory of karma.[40] For example, quoting from the *Jin guangming jing* (Scripture of Golden Glow), King Hyŏnjong said, "One's collected karma causes him to be reborn as a human" (*HKC* 1984, 448: 2–3). Ch'ae Ch'ungsun also said that Buddhist texts were printed in the hope of a better rebirth,

> Your Sacred Highness wished to pray for the heavenly well-being of your deceased parents . . . ordered his men to print 600 fascicles of the *Tae Panya kyŏng* (Great Scripture of Wisdom, Skt. *Mahāprajñāpāramitā Sūtra*), the *Hwaŏm kyŏng* (Flower Garland Scripture, Skt. *Avataṁsaka Sūtra*), the *Kŭm kwangmyŏng kyŏng* (Scripture of Golden Light), and the *Myobŏp yŏnhwa kyŏng* (Lotus Scripture, Skt. *Saddharmapuṇḍarīka Sūtra*) and to put the printing plates at this monastery [Hyŏnhwa-sa]. (*HKC*, 1984, 450: 11–16)[41]

In short, Koryŏ kings viewed the Buddha as a divine being, his teaching as a magic pearl, and the Saṃgha as a group of thaumaturgies.

Buddhism in Koryŏ served as a political tool, a support of Confucian morals, and a religion for good fortune in the context of Confucian statecraft.

An Analysis of the Relationship between Buddhism and Confucianism

In medieval Korea kings used Buddhism for their own secular purposes in the broad context of Confucian statecraft. Based on the tradition from the Sinicized form of Buddhism, their views on the Three Treasures of Buddhism—the Buddha, the Dharma, and the Saṃgha—were not in agreement with their original meaning in early Buddhism.[42] In addition, many monks tried to find favor by endorsing royal Buddhist policies developed in such a context, often violating Buddhist doctrine for their own survival.

Royal Buddhist Policies

Unlike the commonly accepted idea that the Koryŏ kingdom was a Buddhist state (Yi 2007, 453; Li 2011, 353), Buddhism was not the state ideology but a dominant religious force. State policies toward Buddhism aimed at using Buddhism as a political expedient in support of Confucian morals. To that end, the rulers employed carrot-and-stick policies: they not only protected it, but also controlled it. However, the state control of Buddhist circles was a tradition from China, not from India, home to Buddhism, where Buddhist circles enjoyed the privilege of extraterritoriality from secular powers.

Koryŏ kings allowed the coexistence of Buddhism and Confucianism, but they differed from some Chinese and Korean monarchs in that they did not take Buddhism as their political ideology. In China Emperor Da (Sun Quan, 222–52) of the Wu Dynasty and Cao Cao (155–220), an influential general of Later Han (25–219) and the father of Emperor Wen (220–26), the founder of the Wei Dynasty (220–65), attempted to establish a new ideology through Buddhism. In particular, the latter attempted a systematic approach to Buddhism in order to set it up as a ruling ideology. Emperor Wu (502–49) of the Liang Dynasty promulgated Buddhism as the ruling ideology, received *bodhisattva* precepts, and kept Buddhist precepts, prohibiting five spicy vegetables and meat (Kim 2010, 63–74). Also in Korea, King Pŏphŭng (514–40) of Silla prohibited the killing of living beings in 555 (Kim, 1986a, 81a8). King Pŏp (599–600) of Paekche

(18 BCE–660 CE) did the same and ordered the release of domestic hawks and sparrow hawks and burned fishing tools (Iryŏn 1987, 206–07). King Sejo (1455–68) of the Chosŏn Dynasty took Buddhism as the political ideology even in an era of strong anti-Buddhist sentiments (Kim 2013b, 256–85). In striking contrast, there is no record to show that Koryŏ kings did any one of these things. For them, Buddhism was little more than a political tool to support Confucianism, the orthodoxy of their time.

Koryŏ kings' understanding of the Three Treasures were also different from their meaning in early Buddhism. Buddhism was originally "a life education system"[43] and was not a religion for the invocation of blessings. In addition, the Buddha refused to perform miracles. However, the nature of Buddhism has changed in the historical process of migrating to different cultures. Buddhism was first introduced to Korea not from India but from China. Buddhism was transmitted to China around the first century CE and underwent gradual transformation in the process of accommodating indigenous Chinese philosophical systems of thought such as Confucianism and Taoism. The Buddhism that was transmitted to Korea was such Sinicized form of Buddhism. As a result, Koryŏ kings viewed Buddhism as a religion for invoking good fortune and used it as a tool to fulfill their political goals along with Confucianism, the political ideology of the time.

The Buddha was originally not regarded as a divinity. His immediate disciples viewed him as a great teacher. However, the position of the Buddha changed, and he was deified in the gradual process of transmission. Koryŏ kings' views of the Buddha followed the tradition of the divinized Buddha, considering him a deity of mercy and miraculous power. With a rather superficial understanding of Buddhism they interpreted the Buddha's teachings from the perspective of Chinese philosophy.

The essential teachings of Buddhism, best represented by the Four Noble Truths, is clear in saying that ignorance, greed, and blind desires are the sources of man's bondage and that man can be released from this bondage with the cultivation of the mind. However, for Koryŏ kings, Buddhist texts, generally regarded as records of the oral teachings of the Buddha, were not for learning Buddhist teachings. Instead, they were used as a tool to fulfill the political goals of the royalty or as an object of worship to invoke divine blessings.

Koryŏ kings often favored particular parts of Buddhist texts. For example, the kings, including King Hyŏnjong, paid particular attention to the *Fahua jing* (*Lotus Sūtra*) from the eleventh century, which then served as the basic text for understanding Buddhism (Pak 2009, 74–87).[44] The essence of the *Lotus Sūtra* is that there is no contradiction among noumena, phenomena, and the principle that unifies both (Soothill and Hodous 1990, 276). However, the reason why King Hyŏnjong paid attention to the Sūtra was not the doctrine itself but the will of his father, who was impressed by the story of the donation of a resting place for travelers in the scripture but failed at an attempt to put it into action (*HKC* 1984, 469–70).[45]

The Buddhist saṃgha in India was independent of secular powers. King T'aejo did not want to make his kingdom a Buddhist state and thus put the monastic communities under his control (Chŏng 1992, 119). By controlling the bureaucracy and clergy, the king became the only entity exercising both secular and religious power (Nam 2003, 53) and held full authority on personnel matters of the Buddhist community (Nam 2005, 101–06).

In addition, the temples in Koryŏ primarily served as places for prayer invoking blessings for the royal house and sometimes as a military ground. This military use of temples and monks constitutes another important difference of Koryŏ and Liao (907–1125) in the matter of royal policies toward the Buddhist community. Liao exerted a significant influence on the development of Koryŏ Buddhism, but unlike in Koryŏ, in Liao, it was customary for Buddhist believers to have their eldest sons ordained. Likewise, even when the state needed to mobilize all its manpower, the Liao government still admonished Buddhist monks and nuns against breaking their vows (Wittfogel and Feng 1961, 294–95). In Koryŏ, however, eldest sons were hardly ordained, and monks were even rewarded for their military feats. In light of the fact that Buddhism, like other religions, is against war and emphasizes peace, rewarding monks for their military feats seems to be another indication of the royal use of Buddhism for political, non-Buddhist purposes.

The Saṃgha's Response to Royal Buddhist Policies

Buddhist temples were originally places for spiritual cultivation and kept separate from secular powers, and Buddhist monks were those who took an oath to dedicate their lives to following what was actually taught by the Buddha.

However, in medieval Korea the monastic communities were under the control of the state that attempted to use Buddhism as a way of fulfilling its secular goals. Eminent monks played varying roles as political advisors, subjects of the ruler, thaumaturgists, entrepreneurs, and even as warriors, while power-hungry monks ingratiated themselves with the royalty by supporting royal Buddhist policies[46] as part of "practical considerations"[47] for the sake of their survival, often violating the basic teachings of the Buddha in the process.

In China monks began calling themselves subjects from the eighth century, which became a tradition in the eleventh century. The first example of a Korean monk calling himself a subject is found in 886, when Great Master Kwangja (864–945) said that he was a subject of the king and accepted royal orders (*NYK*, 1996a, 193: 4), which became a tradition in the tenth century. In particular, monks of early Koryŏ who were associated with the Buddhist schools that could not produce national masters or royal masters began calling themselves subjects of the ruler.

In addition, unlike monks of the Liao Dynasty, who were faithful to their monastic duties even in times of national difficulties, many eminent monks in medieval Korea actively collaborated with royal Buddhist policies. For example, the monk Haerin (1038–96), National Master of Chigwang, prayed for the fulfillment of royal secular wishes such as the birth of a prince to attract royal attention (Pak 2009, 88). This tradition of conforming with royal policies was continued down to later generations, including Hyesim, Wŏno (?–1286), and Wŏnŭng (1301–82), all of whom were National Masters of their time (Kim 2013a, 24).

Transformation of Buddhist Doctrine in Confucian Statecraft

Buddhist events in medieval Korea were interpreted in the Confucian context, which included the concepts of loyalty and filial piety, *yin* and *yang*, and the theory of heavenly warning. In addition, the Buddhist doctrine that attracted royal attention was not one of the essential teachings of the Buddha such as the Four Noble Truths but skillful means such as the theory of karma and the Mt. Sumeru cosmology.[48]

The concept of filial piety was not among the basic things of the Buddha. It was clearly valued in Confucianism, and its use in politics was prominent particularly in China and Korea. The Koryŏ kingdom was not an exception in this regard, and it was one of the most significant ethical teachings emphasized in the then Buddhist community correlated with the theory of karma. The theory of *Yin* and *Yang*, not a Buddhist but a Confucian theory, along with the theory of heavenly warning,[49] was applied to the founding of temples (*HKC* 1984, 443: 5–13).

In tenth-century Korea, the theory of heavenly warning had a strong element of divination, and natural calamities were attributed not to the misgovernment of the king but to the moral failures of subjects. A typical way of resolving natural calamities was the king blaming himself for his misgovernment, resolving to govern the state well, and lowering penalties on the people (Yi 1984, 9–54).

The Mt. Sumeru cosmology served as an underlying ideology behind the carving of Korean Buddhist canons. However, the Mt. Sumeru cosmology is a symbolic expression based on the mythic cosmology of pre-Buddhist Indian people, but Buddhism claims that everything is a representation of one's mind with no substantial existence of its own

The theory of karma, correlated with the concept of rebirth, had been the philosophical underpinning behind most Buddhist events in Korean history including the Koryŏ period, such as Buddhist rituals and the printing of the Korean Buddhist canons on woodblocks. However, this theory is still being debated among Buddhist scholars who ask whether it is among the essential teachings of the Buddha. In *What the Buddha Taught*, Richard F. Gombrich argues on the basis of the evidence of the Pali canon that the doctrine of karma is central to the Buddha's teachings (Gombrich 2009, 11–16). Johannes Bronkhorst is not as certain and agrees with Gombrich conditionally. In his article, "Did the Buddha Believe in Karma and Rebirth?" he argues, "In so far as the texts allow us to reach an answer, [the answer] seems to me an unambiguous 'yes'" (Bronkhorst 1998, 16).

Gombrich, however, also argues that the oldest extant Pali canon is a product of the latter period of the first century BCE (Gombrich 2009, 98), several hundred years from the lifetime of the Buddha, which makes it difficult to accept their contents as authentic. Moreover, the theory of karma is not in agreement with the Buddhist concept of no-self, the Buddhist epistemology represented by the theory of twelve abodes of sensation (the idea that there is nothing without perception), and the Buddha's silence about the fourteen unanswerable questions asked by his disciples (Skt. *caturdaśa*).[50] Scholars of Buddhism also have characterized what the Buddha actually taught to be practical, rational, scientific, and democratic in nature. Therefore, I argue that the theory of karma is not among the essential teachings of the Buddha but rather among the skillful means developed in later times to attract people of diverse spiritual faculties.

Some Koryŏ kings were interested in Buddhist canonical texts. However, what they focused on was not the major doctrinal contents in them but those parts relevant to their secular interest. Unlike Kungye of Later Koguryŏ and Prince Shōtoku (?–622) of Japan who delivered a lecture on Buddhist scriptures such as the *Lotus Sūtra*, records rarely indicate that Koryŏ kings did the same.

In sum, unlike conventional scholarship that has argued that Buddhism in Koryŏ was the state religion, I argue that it was only the most dominant religion among others and that it functioned largely to support Confucian ethics. Koryŏ kings' attitude toward Buddhism was both support and control. From the beginning of the dynasty, King T'aejo did not allow his entire kingdom to convert to Buddhism and instead carried out Buddhist policies in terms consonant with religious pluralism (Yun et al. 2002, 18). In addition, Koryŏ kings' prime concern was not with Buddhist doctrine but with Buddhist events, and their views on Buddhism, the Buddha, the Dharma, and the saṃgha were not in conformity with their original meaning. Conventional scholarship also argued that traditional religions in Koryŏ were covered with Buddhist integuments. This argument, I suggest, needs to be revised as follows: Buddhism in Koryŏ was interpreted in the context of Chinese philosophical systems of thought such as Confucianism. For Koryŏ kings, Buddhism was a tool for fulfilling their secular purposes rather than a life education system as taught by the Buddha. They made a thorough use of Buddhism as a means to accomplish their earthly goals, such as longevity of their royal houses, based on the Confucian ideology.

Conclusion

This article examined interactions between Buddhism and Confucianism in early Koryŏ. To this end, the basic position of Buddhism and Confucianism and the role of Buddhism in Confucian statecraft were examined, and the relationship between Buddhism and Confucianism was critically analyzed.

As far as extant records are concerned, it is safe to say that in medieval Korea Confucianism served as the state ideology while Buddhism was a dominant religion in support of Confucian morals such as loyalty and filial piety. In that context, Koryŏ kings understood Buddhism primarily through the lens of Confucianism. Their prime concern was not with the essential teachings of the Buddha but with the skill-in-means such as the theory of karma and Buddhist events. They put Buddhism at the service of their secular purposes including royal longevity and keeping Buddhist communities under their control. The Buddhist establishment ingratiated themselves with the royalty by promoting royal Buddhist policies in exchange for state support, a tradition that had continued down to the end of the Koryŏ Dynasty and even thereafter.

Korean scholars have generally agreed that most contents of the *Koryŏ sa* (History of the Koryŏ Dynasty) are accurate. However, the *History of the Koryŏ Dynasty* was compiled by the Confucian scholars of the Chosŏn Dynasty in the fifteenth century, who tended to disparage traditional customs including Buddhism and to speak highly of Confucian culture (Ro 2002, 63–72). In spite of the importance of Buddhism in Koryŏ society,[51] the Confucian compilers made light of recording of Buddhist music and monastic economy and underestimated the role of eminent monks and major Buddhist rituals in Koryŏ (Kim 1994, 13–16; Kim 2001, 34–38). A similar revisionism is also found in the *Historical Records of the Three Kingdoms*.[52] Records on Buddhism in the *KRS*, therefore, contain many unresolved questions, requiring further scholarly research, which will give us a more accurate and more profound understanding of the relationship between Buddhism and Confucianism in the Koryŏ period.

Glossary

"*Anmin ka*" 安民歌
Cao Cao 曹操
"Chŏn Taejanggyŏng so" 轉大藏經疏
"Chŏnggye" 政誡
Ch'ae Ch'ungsun 蔡忠順
Ch'ildae sillok 七代實錄
Ch'oe Ch'iwŏn 崔致遠
Ch'oe Sŭngno 崔承老
Ch'oe Ŭng 崔凝
Ch'ojo Koryŏ taejanggyŏng 初雕高麗大藏經
chŏn'gyŏn chaei sŏl 天譴災異說
chŏnin kamŭng sŏl 天人感應說

Chŏnch'aek 天頙
Ch'ungdam 忠談
Ch'ungji 冲止
Chaejo Koryŏ taejangyŏng 再雕高麗大藏經
Chigwang 智光
Chin'gak 眞覺
Chin'gong 眞空
Chinhŭng 眞興
Chinul 知訥
chŏndok 轉讀
Chŏng Chisang 鄭知常
Chŏngjo 正祖
Chŏnyŏng 天英
Chongmyo 宗廟
Chosŏn 朝鮮
Dong Zhongshu 董仲舒
Fahua jing 法華經
Fumu enzhung jing 父母恩重經
Haerin 海麟
Han 漢
Haein[-sa] 海印[寺]
Honwŏn 混元
Hou Han shu 後漢書
Hŭmch'un 欽春
Hwaŏm kyŏng 華嚴經
Hyegŭn 惠勤
Hyesim 慧諶
hyo 孝
Hyŏnhwa-sa 玄化寺
Hyŏnjong 顯宗
in 仁
Iryŏn 一然
Jenwang boluo jing 仁王般若經
Jin guangming jing 金光明經
"Kaesŏng Hyŏnhwa-sa pi" 開城玄化寺碑
Kanhwa Sŏn 看話禪
"Karye chaphŭi" 嘉禮雜戲
Kim Sisŭp 金時習
Koguryŏ 高句麗

Kojong 高宗
Koryŏ 高麗
Koryŏ sa 高麗史
Koryŏ taejanggyŏng 高麗大藏經
Kukchagam 國子監
Kukhak 國學
kuksa 國師
Kŭm kwangmyŏng kyŏng 金光明經
Kungye 弓裔
Kwangja 廣慈
Kwangjong 光宗
"Kye paengnyo sŏ" 誡百僚書
Kyewŏn p'ilgyŏng chip 桂苑筆耕集
Kyŏngdŏk 景德
Kyŏnghan 景閑
Kyŏnhwŏn 甄萱
Li ji 禮記
Liang 梁
Liao 遼
Lieusong 劉宋
Mugi 無寄
Munjong 文宗
Myobŏp yŏnhwa kyŏng 妙法蓮華經
osang 五常
Paekche 百濟
P'algwanhoe 八關會
Pŏphŭng 法興
pongnok 俸祿
Pou 普愚
Pumo ŭnjung kyŏng 父母恩重經
p'ungnyu 風流
Samguk sagi 三國史記
Sejo 世祖
Sesok ogye 世俗五戒
Shizu 世祖
Shōtoku 聖德
Shu jing 書經
sijung 侍中
Silla 新羅

Sŏkkur-am 石窟庵
Sŏkpul-sa 石佛寺
Sŏllang 仙郎
Sŏn 禪
Song 宋
Songak 松嶽
Sŏngjong 成宗
Sŏngnihak 性理學
Sui 隋
sujwa 首座
sŭnggye 僧階
Sun Quan 孫權
susin chi to 修身之道
T'aejo 太祖
Tae Panya kyŏng 大般若經
"Taejang kakp'an kunsin kigomun" 大藏刻板君臣祈告文
Tang 唐
tianqian zaiyi shuo 天譴災異說
Ŭichŏn 義天
wangsa 王師
Wei 魏
Wen 文
Wŏno 圓悟
Wŏnŭng 圓鷹
Wu 武
"Wui" 無逸
wuxing 五行
Wu Yue 吳越
xiao 孝
Xiao jing 孝經
yang 陽
yangban 兩班
Yi Chibaek 李知白
Yi Kyubo 李奎報
yin 陰
Yŏndŭnghoe 燃燈會
Yuan 元
Zetian 則天

Notes

1. For example, Ch'oe Ch'iwŏn (857–?), a polymath of the Silla kingdom (57 BCE–935 CE) mentioned the close relationship between Buddhism and Confucianism, arguing that the two were the same in nature (Lee 1993, 101–02). In addition, opinions on the beginning of the Three Kingdoms of ancient Korea are divided between Korean and Western scholars. While the former locate it in the first century BCE, the latter trace it to the fourth century CE, for which see Kim 2014, 3, note 3. However, there has been no substantial dialogue between the two academic camps.

2. For trends in overseas research on Korean Buddhism, see Kim 2014, 3, note 4.

3. Duncan suggests calling Yuan-era Koryŏ as a semi-colony (Duncan 2013, 1–19).

4. The monk Wŏn'gwang's (ca. 555–638) "Five Commandments for Laymen" (*Sesok ogye*) is an early example to show a combination of Buddhism and Confucianism in Korean history. For an English translation of the Five Commandments for Laymen, see Lee 1993, 117. For a discussion of the relationship between early Buddhism and the Five Commandments for Laymen, refer to Im 2014, 7–27.

5. The relationship between Buddhism and Confucianism during the Koryŏ Dynasty can be classified into four stages: 918–97; 997–1170; 1170–1270; and 1270–1392. In the first stage the Confucian system was established, the second stage saw the increase of Confucian influence, the third stage was characterized by the flourishing of Buddhism and the recession of Confucianism, and the fourth stage saw the rise of the anti-Buddhist sentiment with the introduction of Neo-Confucianism (Pyŏn 2005, 44–46).

6. On Korean kings' views of Buddhism and their Buddhist policies from the fourth to the eighteenth century, see Kim 2013b.

7. For new approaches to research on Korean Buddhist history, see Kim 2010, 45–56.

8. According to King Kojong (1213–59), belief in Buddhism had been a hereditary custom since the reign of King T'aejo. The king said, "[Koryŏ] has set up its basis totally depending on the secret protection of Buddhism since the grandfather sage [King T'aejo]" (*KRS* 26, 4b).

9. For important primary source materials for the study of the Koryŏ period, see Kim 1994, 12–16; Kim 2001, 32–33. Among these, the *KRS* proves itself to be the most important source for the study of Koryŏ history and religions and most of scholarly works on Koryŏ have depended on the *KRS*.

10. The *Xiao jing* (Book of Filial Piety) was an important text on filial piety from the Three Kingdoms period. According to the *Book of Filial Piety*, filial piety to parents was developed as loyalty to the king (Yi 1984, 3–4).

11. For the nature of Buddhism in early Koryŏ, refer to Kim 2010, 193–94.

12. For King T'aejo's politics and Buddhist activities, see Kim 2010, 194–203.

13. King Hyŏnjong compiled the *Ch'ildae sillok* (Veritable Records of Seven Generations) in order to praise the achievements of his ancestor kings. In that process King T'aejo's Injunctions in ten articles reappeared (Kim 2008, 148–49). For an extensive discussion of the Ten Injunctions, see Breuker 2008, 1–73; Breuker 2010, 351–406.

14. This English translation was quoted from Lee 1993, 263.

15. For the history, types, and role of major Buddhist rituals in medieval Korea, see Kim 1994 and Kim 2001.

16. For a discussion of these rituals, see Kim 1994, 129–267 and Kim 2001, 115–205. For detailed accounts of the relationship between Buddhism and politics during the Koryŏ period, refer to Kim 2013b, 71–204.

17. The term *Tripiṭaka Koreana* has been used as an English translation of the *Koryŏ taejanggyŏng*. However, Buswell argues that because *the Koryŏ taejanggyŏng* is much more inclusive than tradtional tripiṭaka, it should be called either the *Korean Buddhist Canon* or the *Koryŏ taejanggyŏng* (Buswell 2013, 41). For a discussion of the *Korean Buddhist Canons*, see Kim 2002a, 154–81; Kim 2013b, 129–34, 151–55, 161–65, 186–203.

18. Accuracy in content, which is attributed to the monk Sugi's (fl. thirteenth century) effort, for which see Buswell 2004, 129–84, is one of its distinctive features.

19. The theory of heavenly warning was accepted during the Three Kingdoms period and the Unified Silla period (668–935) in Korea. The amount of records on natural calamities in the *Samguk sagi* (*Historical Records of the Three Kingdoms*) is almost equal to that of records on political events, showing that natural calamities were considered serious threats to the people during the time. In fact, natural calamities were one of the factors for the appointment and dismissal of the highest ranking official, *sijung*, in the Silla kingdom. However, the pre-Koryŏ period was the transitional period in relation to the theory (Yi 1984, 9–54).

20. The date of introduction of Confucianism to Korea is unknown, but it is presumed to have been pre-Three Kingdoms period (Yi 1984, 8).

21. For an English translation of the tenth Injunction of King T'aejo, refer to Lee 1993, 265–66.

22. For research on Confucian politics during the Koryŏ period, primarily focusing on Confucian institutions, see Yi 1984, 2. In terms of Confucian politics, the ruler's ruling by virtue stood for the materialization of heavenly mandate based on the Theory of Heavenly Warning (Yi 1984, 2–3).

23. For a close relationship between religion and the state, see Kim 2013b, 5–6.

24. That tradition was continued until the early thirteenth century. Chinul (1158–1210) (Yi 2007, 455), Hyesim (1178–1234), and Chŏnch'aek (fl. late 13th century) (Pak 2004, 92–103) were such examples. However, a change was felt after the late thirteenth century. Many eminent monks such as Honwŏn (1191–1271), Chŏnyŏng (1215–86), Ch'ungji (1226–93), and Iryŏn (1206–89) had Confucian knowledge and Confucian elements were found in their Buddhist thought (Yi 2007, 455–62). Buddhist monks in the fourteenth century, including Mugi (fl. early thirteenth century), Pou (1301–82), Kyŏnghan (1299–1374), and Hyegŭn (1320–76), argued that Buddhist ethics was analogous to the Confucian or emphasized the Keyword Meditation (*Kanhwa Sŏn*) in response to the rise of Neo-Confucianism in Koryŏ society (Yi 2007, 462–72), which eventually became the mainstream ideology of the Chosŏn Dynasty (Ch'oe 2001, 8; Pak 2004, 91).

25. This English translation was quoted from Lee 1993, 292.

26. The system of National Master was not popular in China until the tenth century (Nam 2005, 93–44).

27. National Master was the highest monastic title and Royal Master was the second highest monastic title. However, there was no clear distinction between the two in status until early tenth-century Koryŏ (Nam 2005, 101).

28. The establishment of the Doctrinal Order and the Meditative Order in sixteenth-century Korea also put monks under the control of the state (Kim 2014, 11).

29. For a discussion of the control of the monastic circles during the reign of King Hyŏnjong, see Kim 2002b, 142–43.

30. Respect for tradition had been continued to later generations in Korean history. For example, Queen Munjŏng's (1501–65) logic of favoring Buddhism in anti-Buddhist Chosŏn society was also tradition (Kim 2014, 16).

31. For example, King Sŏngjong abolished the Assembly of Eight Prohibitions and the Lantern Festival in favor of Confucianism and, in contrast, King Hyŏnjong revived them.

32. Robert Thurman views the Buddha's teaching as a life education system (Thurman 1999, "The Dharma").

33. This English translation was quoted from Lee 1993, 263.

34. The role of the king during the time when the military clan was a substantial power holder in mid-Koryŏ was to hold Buddhist rituals and fulfill kingcraft in accord with Confucian ideals. For the assessment of the relationship between Buddhism and military rulers, see Shultz 2000, 131–34. And for the patronage of Buddhism by kings and the literati at the beginning of the Chosŏn Dynasty, see Duncan 2000, 224–45, 251–56.

35. This kind of view of the ordinary people has been continued to the Chosŏn period and even to modern times. According to Kim Sisŭp (1435–93), King Sejo (1417–68) said that he translated Buddhist texts in classical Chinese into the Korean language to instruct the silly people of his time. In modern

times Korean Christian leaders during the Japanese colonial period (1910–45) and political leaders who were in charge of the New Village Movement (*Saemaŭl undong*) in the 1970s regarded the masses and farmers as ignorant people (Yang 2008, 116).

36. For an English translation of Ch'oe Ŭng's remonstration to King T'aejo, see Kim 2010, 200–01.

37. For an explanation of the Four Noble Truths, see Buswell and Lopez 2014, 304–05.

38. King T'aejo of Koryŏ composed the epitaph for Royal Master Ch'ungdam and it was the only epitaph composed by the king himself (Nam 2005, 99).

39. For the English translations of the history of each of the Three Kingdoms, refer to Best 2006 for the history of Paekche, Kim Pusik 2011 for that of Koguryŏ, and Kim Pusik 2012 for that of Silla.

40. For an explanation of the theory of karma, see Buswell and Lopez 2014, 420.

41. Hyesim (1178–1234), National Master Chin'gak, also emphasized miraculous efficacy of holding the *Diamond Sūtra* (Chŏng 2009, 426). In his royal edict of 1264, King Kojong said that *Inwang panya kyŏng* (Ch. *Jenwang boluo jing*, Book for Humane Kings) was the best teaching to protect the state and pacify the people (*KRS* 26, 4b). For understanding the relationship between Buddhism and politics focusing on the *Book for Humane Kings*, see Orzech 1998.

42. The period of early Buddhism varies among scholars, but it is in general regarded as Buddhism from the life time of the Buddha to 100 years after his death.

43. In his comments on my paper, Kim 2013a, Hugh Kang suggested the comparison of Koryŏ kings' views on Buddhism with Mahāyāna Buddhism, to which Korean Buddhism has belonged, rather than the former with early Indian Buddhism. However, Mahāyāna Buddhism, assimilating diverse local cultures, has entailed elements different from early Indian Buddhism.

44. The *Lotus Sūtra* was also the most popular among Buddhist canons published in the initial period of the Chosŏn Dynasty (Kim 2014, 18).

45. King Kojong treasured the *Book for Humane Kings* on the ground that it was helpful in protecting the state. However, what the text emphasizes is the attainment of enlightenment through the purification of one's mind.

46. Many eminent monks in later generations acted in concert with royal wishes for invoking blessings, even violating the first Buddhist precept of no killing. Hyesim was a good example. In his works, he emphasized loyalty and patriotism (*HBJ* 6, 50a).

47. Martina Deuchler suggested that certain social transformations that took place during the Chosŏn period were a result of practical considerations, i.e., of a "logic of practice," rather than of "Confucinization" as an ideal force (Walraven 2012, 106).

48. Regarding this cosmology, see Buswell and Lopez 2014, 869; for its use as an underlying ideology behind the Stone Buddhist Temple (Sŏkpul-sa), which is better known as the Stone Buddhist Grotto (Sŏkkur-am) and is on the cultural heritage list by the UNESCO, refer to Kim 2008, 184–09.

49. Sŏn Buddhist circles in thirteenth-century Korea did not accept the theory of heavenly warning (Kim 1999, 13–14); yet, the theory served as the philosophical source behind the Calamities-Solving Ritual (Kim 2001, 251–52; Kim 2007, 1–32), a favorite of King Kojong, who performed the greatest number of Buddhist rituals throughout Korean history.

50. For the contents of the fourteen unanswerable questions, refer to Buswell and Lopez 2014, 1088.

51. For example, the Assembly of Eight Prohibitions and the Lantern Festival were so important Buddhist rituals in Koryŏ that three and one official holidays, respectively, were given on the days of their performance. However, the *KRS* simply classifies them as "Karye chaphŭi" (Miscellaneous Plays in Auspicious Rituals) (*KRS* 69, 1a–33b). Regarding this, Heo Hungsik, a specialist in the Buddhist history of medieval Korea, once pointed out to me that records on Buddhist rituals in the *KRS* are hardly credible.

52. Records on solar eclipses in the *Historical Records of the Three Kingdoms* were all quoted from Chinese history books or other relevant writings, including the chapter of "Wuxing" (Five Elements) in the *Hou Han shu* (*Book of Later Han*). However, records on other natural calamities except for the solar eclipses, including droughts, floods, earthquakes, hail, and heavy snow, in the *Historical Records of the Three Kingdoms* were not referred to their Chinese counterparts, giving rise to the idea that were unique to Korea (Yi 1984, 11–33).

Bibliography

Primary Sources

Ch'oe, Ch'iwŏn. *Kyewŏn p'ilgyŏng chip* 桂苑筆耕集 (*Plowing the Cassia Grove with a Brush Writing*). Translated by Yi Sanghyŏn. Seoul: Han'guk kojŏn pŏnyŏkwŏn, 2009.

HBJ: *Han'guk Pulgyo chŏnsŏ* 韓國佛教全書 (Comprehensive Collection of Korean Buddhism). 14 volumes. Seoul: Dongguk University Press, 1979–2004.

HKC: Heo, Hungsik, ed. *Han'guk kŭmsŏk chŏnmun* 韓國金石全文. 3 volumes. Seoul: Asea munhwasa, 1984.

Iryŏn. *Samguk yusa* 三國遺事 (Memorabilia of the Three Kingdoms). Yi Minsu, *yŏk*. 1983; Ŭryu munhwasa, 1987.

Kim, Pusik. *Samguk sagi* 三國史記 (Historical Records of the Three Kingdoms). 2 volumes. Yi Pyŏngdo, *yŏkchu*. 1983; Seoul: Ŭryu munhwasa. 1986.

KMC: Koryŏ myŏnghyŏn chip 高麗名賢集 (Collection of Eminent Scholars during the Koryŏ Dynasty). 1986. 5 volumes. Seoul: Sunggyunkwan University Press.
Koryŏ taejanggyŏng 高麗大藏經 (Korean Buddhist Canon). 1976. 48 volumes. Seoul: Dongguk University Press.
KRS: Koryŏ sa 高麗史 (History of the Koryŏ Dynasty). 1991. 11 volumes. P'yŏngyang: Sahoe kwahak kojŏn yŏn'gusil; 1962; Seoul: Sinsŏwŏn.
NYK: Han'guk yŏksa yŏn'guhoe, ed. 1996. *Yŏkchu Namal Yŏch'o kŭmsŏngmun* 譯註 羅末麗初金石文 (Epigraphs around Tenth-Century Korea with Annotated Translation). 2 volumes. Seoul: Hyean.

Secondary Sources

Best, Jonathan W. *A History of the Early Korean Kingdom of Paekche*. Cambridge and London: Harvard University Asia Center, 2006.
Breuker, Remco. "Forging the Truth: Creative Deception and National Identity in Medieval Korea," *East Asian History* 35 (2008): 1–73.
———. *Establishing a Pluralist Society in Medieval Korea, 918–1170: History, Ideology and Identity in the Koryŏ Dynasty*. Leiden, Boston: Brill, 2010.
Bronkhorst, Johannes. "Did the Buddha Believe in Karma and Rebirth?," *Journal of the International Association of Buddhist Studies*, 21-1 (1998): 1–19.
Buswell, Robert E., Jr. "Sugi's Collation Notes to the Koryŏ Buddhist Canon and Their Significance for Buddhist Textual Criticism," *The Journal of Korean Studies* 9-1 (2004): 129–84.
———. "Sugi's Editing of the Second Koryŏ Canon and Historical Significance in World Intellectual History," 2013 Tripitaka Koreana Festival, International Symposium, "Idea, Culture, and System of Tripitaka Koreana," Plaza Hotel, Seoul, Republic of Korea, September 3, 2013: 40–6.
Buswell, Robert E. Jr., and Donald S. Lopez Jr., ed. *The Princeton Dictionary of Buddhism*. Princeton and Oxford: Princeton University Press, 2014.
Cho, Kyŏngch'ŏl. "Tong Asia Pulgyo sik wangho pigyo" [Buddhist Royal Titles in East Asia: A Comparison]. *Han'guk kodaesa yŏn'gu* [A Study of the Ancient History of Korea] 43 (2006): 5–38.
Chŏng, Kyŏnghyŏn. "Koryŏ T'aejo ŭi wanggwŏn" [Kingship of King T'aejo of the Koryŏ Dynasty]. In *Festschrift for T'aegwa Hŏ Sŏndo*, 100–23. Seoul: Ilchogak, 1992.
Chŏng, Pyŏngsam. "Koryŏ hugi Chŏng An ŭi Pulsŏ kanhaeng kwa Pulgyo sinang" [The Publication of Buddhist Texts and Buddhist Belief of Chŏng An in the Latter Period of Koryŏ], *Pulgyohak yŏn'gu* [Journal of Buddhist Studies] 24 (2009): 403–36.
Ch'oe, Ilbŏm. "Koryŏ chunggi Yu Pul kyosŏp ŭi ch'ŏrhak chŏk kŭn'gŏ e kwanhan yŏn'gu" [Philosophical Grounds for Interactions between Confucianism

and Buddhism in the Middle Period of the Koryŏ Dynasty], *Tongyang chŏrhak yŏn'gu* [Journal of East Asian Philosophy] 25 (2001): 7–28.

Duncan, John B. *The Origins of the Chosŏn Dynasty*. Seattle and London: University of Washington Press, 2000.

———. "Late Koryŏ Literati between Empire & Kingdom: Semi-Colonial Dilemmas?" paper presented at the conference on "Kŏryo: The Dynamics of Inner and Outer," Honolulu, University of Hawai'i at Mānoa, February 14–16, 2013: 1–19.

Gombrich, Richard F. *What the Buddha Taught*. London, Oakville: Equinox Publishing, 2009.

Im, Sŭngt'aek. "Ch'ogi Pulgyo e pich'uŏ pon Sesok ogye ŭi paegyŏng kwa kŭn'gŏ" [The Background and Basis of the Five Secular Injunctions in Terms of Early Buddhism], paper presented at the 1st Academic Seminar "Hwarang Sesok ogye ŭi hyŏndae chŏk haesŏk" [Modern Interpretations of the Five Secular Precepts for the Flagrant Knights], Sponsored by Wŏn'gwang Hwarang Institute, Unmun Monastery, Chŏngdo, Korea, May 25, 2014: 7–27.

Kim, Jongmyung. "Buddhist Rituals in Medieval Korea (918–1392)," PhD Dissertation, University of California at Los Angeles, 1994.

———. *Han'guk chungse ŭi Pulgyo ŭirye: sasang chŏk paegyŏng kwa yŏksa chŏk ŭimi* [Buddhist Rituals in Medieval Korea: Ideological Background and Historical Significance]. Seoul: Munhak kwa chisŏngsa, 2001.

———. "The *Tripitaka Koreana*: Its Computerization and Significance for the Cultural Sciences in a Modern Globalized World." In *Korea and Globalization: Politics, Economy and Culture*, edited by Lewis, James and Amadu Sesay, 154–81. London: RoutledgeCurzon, 2002.

———. "The Philosophical Underpinning of the Calamities-Solving Ritual and Its Nature in Medieval Korea," paper presented at the Buddhist Conference "Esoteric Buddhist Tradition in East Asia: Text, Ritual and Image," Yale University, U.S.A. November 9–11, 2007: 1–32.

———.*Han'guk ŭi Pulgyo segye yusan: sasang kwa ŭiŭi* [Korea's Buddhist World Heritage Properties: Thoughts and Significance]. Seoul: Jipmoondang, 2008.

———."King Taejo's Buddhist View and Statecraft in Tenth-Century Korea," *The Review of Korean Studies* 13-4 (2010): 189–215.

———."Kings and Buddhism in Koryŏ," paper presented at the conference on "Kŏryo: The Dynamics of Inner and Outer," Honolulu, University of Hawai'i at Mānoa, February 14–16, 2013a.

———.*Kugwang ŭi Pulgyo kwan kwa ch'iguk ch'aek* [Korean Kings Views on Buddhism and Their Statecraft]. P'aju: Han'guk haksul chŏngbo, 2013b.

———."The State and Monks in Medieval Korea," paper presented at the Buddhism and State in the Medieval World Symposium, Fudan University, China, October 10–11, 2013c: 1–23.

———. "Queen Munjeong's (1501–1565) Statecraft and Buddhist View in Confucian Joseon," *Korea Journal* 54-2 (Summer 2014): 1–25.

Kim, Inho. "Koryŏ sidae kugwang ŭi changnye chŏlch'a wa t'ŭkching" [Royal Funeral Procedures and Their Characteristics in Medieval Korea], *Han'guk chungse sa yŏn'gu* (Journal of Korean Medieval History) 29 (2010): 265-99.

Kim Pusik. *The Koguryŏ Annals of the Samguk Sagi*. Translated by Edward J. Shultz and Hugh H. W. Kang. Seongnam: The Academy of Korean Studies, 2011.

———. *The Silla Annals of the Samguk sagi*. Translated by Edward J. Shultz, Hugh H. W. Kang, and Daniel C. Kane. Seongnam: The Academy of Korean Studies, 2012.

Kim, Tangt'aek. "Koryŏ Hyŏnjong tae kwagŏ ch'ulsin kwalli ŭi chŏngch'i chŏk chudo kwŏn changak" [Political Hegemony of Confucian Scholar Officials in Eleventh-Century Korea]. *Yŏksahak yŏn'gu* [Journal of Historical Studies] 29 (2008): 87-112.

Kim, Yŏngmi. "Koryŏ sidae Pulgyo kye ŭi t'ongje wa yullyŏng" [The Control of Buddhist Circles and Statutes in Medieval Korea], *Sahak yŏn'gu* [The Review of Korean History] 67 (2002): 1-30.

Lee, Peter H. *Sourcebook of Korean Civilization*, Volume 1: From Early Times to the Sixteenth Century. New York: Columbia University Press, 1993.

Li, Hai-tao. "Cui Chenglao de chongru yifo guan" [Ch'oe Sŭngno's Veneration of Confucianism and Repression of Buddhism], *T'oegyehak kwa Yugyo munhwa* [Studies of T'oegye and Confucian Culture] 49 (2011): 353-66.

Nam, Tongsin. "Namal Yŏch'o kugwang kwa Pulgyo ŭi kwan'gye" [The Relationship between the King and Buddhism around the Tenth Century], *Yŏksa wa Hyŏnsil* [History and Reality] 56 (2005): 81-111.

Orzech, Charles D. *Politics and Transcendent Wisdom*. University Park, PA: Pennsylvania State University Press, 1998.

Pak, Chaeu. "Koryŏ ŭi chŏngch'i chedo wa kwŏllyŏk kwan'gye" [The Political System and Power Relations in the Koryŏ Dynasty], *Han'guk chungse sa yŏn'gu* [A Study of Medieval Korean History] 31 (2011): 195-228.

Pak, Haedang. "Koryŏ sidae ŭi Yu Pul kyosŏp" [Interactions between Confucianism and Buddhism during the Koryŏ Period], *Kangwŏn munhwa yŏn'gu* [The Journal of Studies in Gangwon Community Culture] 23 (2004): 91-105.

Pak, Kwangyŏn. "Koryŏ chŏn'gi Yugaŏp ŭi *Pŏphwa kyŏng* chŏnt'ong kyesŭng kwa kŭ ŭimi" [Emphasis on the *Lotus Sūtra* in the *Yuga* [Yogācāra] School in the Early Koryŏ Dynasty and Its Significance], *Yŏksa wa hyŏnsil* [History and Reality] 71 (2009): 63-91.

Park, Jong-ki. "The Characteristics and Origins of Koryŏ's Pluralist Society," a paper presented at the conference on "Kŏryo: The Dynamics of Inner and Outer," Honolulu, University of Hawai'i at Mānoa, February 14-16, 2013: 1-31.

Pyŏn, Tongmyŏng. "Koryŏ sigi ŭi Yugyo wa Pulgyo" [Confucianism and Buddhism in Medieval Korea], *Han'guk chungse sa yŏn'gu* [A Study of Medieval Korean History] 318 (2005): 43-81.

Ro, Myŏngho. 2002. "T'ongnyŏm kwa inyŏm e kariun Koryŏ sahoe ŭi ch'eje chŏk t'ŭkching tŭl" [Systematic Characteristics in Medieval Korean Society Covered by Common Ideas and Ideologies]. In *Han'guksa yŏn'gu pangbŏm non kwa panghyang mosaek* [Methodology and Direction in the Study of Korean History], 61-77. Collection of Papers at the International Conference of Korean History, Seoul, Seoul kyoyuk munhwa hoegwan, 2002.

Shultz, Edward J. *Generals and Scholars: Military Rule in Medieval Korea.* Honolulu: University of Hawai'i Press, 2000.

Soothill, William Edward and Lewis Hodous. *A Dictionary of Chinese Buddhist Terms.* Gaoxiong: Foguang chubanshe, Minguo 79, 1990.

Thurman, Robert. A. F. *Buddhism.* 3 parts. New York: Mystic Fire Video, 1999.

Vermeersch, Sem. "Buddhism and State-Building in Song China and Goryeo Korea," *Asia Pacific: Perspectives* V-1 (2004): 4-11.

———.*The Power of the Buddha: The Politics of Buddhism during the Koryŏ Dynasty (918-1392).* Cambridge, MA: Harvard University Asia Center, 2008.

Walraven, Boudewijn. "Buddhist Accommodation and Appropriation and the Limits of Conficianization," *Journal of Korean Religions*, 3-1 (2012): 105-16.

Wittfogel, Karl and Feng Chin-sheng. *History of Chinese Society: Liao (907-1125).* 1949; Lancaster, PA: Lancaster Press, Inc., 1961.

Wŏn, Yŏngman. "Koryŏ sidae sŭnggwanje yŏn'gu" [A Study of the Monastic Administrators during the Koryŏ Period], PhD Dissertation, Dongguk University, 2010.

Yang, Hyŏnhye. "Hwangminhwa sigi Kaesin'gyo sillyŏk yangsŏng non ŭi nolli kujo" [The Logic of the Training of Capability in the Christian Circles of Korea in the Japanese Colonial Period], *Chonggyo yŏn'gu* [Journal of Religious Studies] 50 (2008): 99-128.

Yi, Hŭidŏk. *Koryŏ Yugyo chŏngch'i sasang ŭi yŏn'gu* [A Study of Confucian Political Thought during the Koryŏ Dynasty]. Seoul: Ilchogak, 1984.

Yi, Pyŏnghŭi. "Koryŏ Hyŏnjong tae sasang kwa munhwa chŏngch'aek" (Thought and Cultural Policy in Tenth-Century Korea), *Han'guk chungse sa yŏn'gu* (Journal of Medieval Korean History) 29 (2011): 213-63.

Yi, Sich'an. "Song Wŏn sigi Koryŏ ŭi sŏjŏk suip kwa kŭ yŏksa chŏk ŭimi" [The Import of Books of Koryŏ from China during the Period of the Tenth to the Fourteenth-Centuries and Its Historical Significance], *Tongbang Hanmunhak* [Classical Studies in the East] 39 (2009): 309-420.

Yi, Tŏkchin. "Sip samsa segi Koryŏ Pulsŭng tŭl ŭi Yugyo kwan e taehan il koch'al" [A Study of the Views of Monks in the Thirteenth to the Fourteenth-

Century Korea on Confucianism, *Kyopullyŏn nonjip* [Journal of the Buddhist Association of Professors] 13 (2007): 453–78.

Yun, Ihŭm, Kim Ilgwŏn, Ch'oe Chongsŏng. *Koryŏ sidae ŭi chonggyo munhwa* [Religious Culture in Medieval Korea]. Seoul: Seoul National University. 2002.

3

Philosophical Aspects of the Goryeo-Joseon Confucian-Buddhist Confrontation

Focusing on the Works of Jeong Dojeon (Sambong) and Hamheo Deuktong (Gihwa)

A. Charles Muller

Historical Perspective: Confucianism and Daoism during the Period of Buddhist Preeminence

The geographical proximity of Korea to China, along with the concomitant extensive and continuous exchange of commodities and ideas, allowed the people of the Korean peninsula to participate in the Chinese religious and philosophical world at a relatively early point in time, and even to make significant contributions to the greater East Asian philosophical discourse, as many Korean thinkers traveled to the Tang and Song centers of learning and made their own mark. Thus, Koreans learned Chinese ways of thinking well, and bringing Chinese ideas back to their homeland, made their own enhancements, and sometimes took off in their own creative directions.

During the several centuries during which Buddhism carried out its remarkable spread throughout East Asia, the Confucian tradition maintained its position as the framework for basic literary education and as the provider of the system for civil service examinations. Thus it was the case in China—and later in Korea—that the ministers, bureaucrats, teachers, and those connected in any form with the governance of the realm automatically had a Confucian education. But this Confucian tradition could not do much to compete philosophically—or as a state religion, with the dominant position that had been taken by Buddhists in terms of providing the spiritual fabric for society—a dominance that reached its peak during the early- to mid-Tang. During this period there was relatively little in the way of new developments in Confucian philosophy, as the same classics were simply learned by rote for the purpose of passing civil service examinations. Except for occasional rumblings and purges that were usually motivated by jealousy over the political and economic influence of Buddhists (and Daoists), Confucians remained largely unable to compete in the philosophical arena.

Most of the major religious and philosophical developments of this period that lay outside of Buddhism were to be seen in the area of Daoism, in the works of the Neo-Daoists, Daoist alchemists, and the Daoist-influenced literati—all of whom were stimulated by Buddhist ideas. At the same time, Daoist views influenced the evolving tendencies of East Asian Buddhism, to the extent that sometimes their texts were almost indistinguishable from each other.[1] Thus, philosophically speaking, the first several centuries of the growth of Buddhism in China can be seen as a period of philosophical stagnation for Confucianism, but Confucianism nonetheless remained ensconced in its basic position within the educational and bureaucratic system, while most creative philosophical/religious activity took place within the Buddhist-Daoist matrix. It was a period during which most major literary figures and political persons of Confucian orientation showed neither the means nor inclination of motivating any telling resistance to the Buddhist tradition.

Yet, regardless of the lack of active philosophical resistance, the indigenous traditions transformed the incoming Buddhist religion in the very course of translating it into their own vernacular, and so a Sinicized form of Buddhism became part and parcel of everyday life. There was no sustained *philosophical* confrontation—at least during the earlier centuries, when doctrinal Buddhist schools were moving toward their final formation. But from just about the time that schools such as Huayan and Tiantai reached a level of maturity, and Chan began to emerge as prominent Buddhist movement, ideological argumentation from the Confucian side began to show itself.

Beginnings of the Criticism of Buddhism

The beginnings of an overt criticism of Buddhism by Confucian leaders are usually traced to the essays of the Tang scholar Han Yu 韓愈 (768–824).[2] Han was an elite bureaucrat as well as a literary figure of considerable stature who was troubled by the steadily growing influence of Buddhism in the imperial court. He believed Buddhism was leading the rulership to a blindness that was endangering the security and well-being of the realm. He felt strongly enough about the excesses of Buddhism that he dared to vehemently memorialize the throne, knowing well that it would lead him into trouble.

Han Yu's two best-known critical essays on Buddhism are the *Origin of the Way* 原道 [3] and *Memorial on the Buddha's Bone* 諫迎佛骨.[4] In these essays he lambasted Buddhism as a foreign religion that was leading the emperor to spend an inordinate amount of time at Buddhist monasteries and which involved great expenditure of resources for activities such as the carrying of the Buddha's *śarīra* around the capital. Han's arguments were aimed at highlighting the visible excesses on the part of the members of the Buddhist clergy and the rulers involved with them. These arguments were mostly emotional in character; they did not attempt to provide a serious criticism of the philosophical shortcomings of Buddhism. But they certainly raised enough hackles to get Han sent away into exile, and they served as the point of departure for the anti-Buddhist arguments that would be presented by later scholars.[5]

However, as the Tang drew to an end and the Song began, the philosophical matrix of China, having been now long enough steeped in Buddhist and Daoist philosophy that many important concepts were taken for granted as being simply standard philosophical categories, not as specifically Buddhist or Daoist in origin, saw the birth of a new, drastically revamped form of Confucianism known as "Song learning" (Ch. *songxue* 宋學, known in the West as Neo-Confucianism). While the Chinese philosophical matrix had had sufficient chance to assimilate Daoist notions of the *dao* and alchemical transformation, and the Buddhist principles of karma and dependent origination as well as Huayan principle (Ch. *li* 理) and phenomena (Ch. *shi* 事) and Chan meditation, the gradual waning of doctrinal Buddhism in late Tang and early Song as a state institution, and the corruption and stagnation of much of the doctrinal Buddhist tradition itself, with the arrival of Chan as the predominant tradition, had left a bit of a creative intellectual vacuum. The influence of the great doctrinal systems of Chinese Yogâcāra, Tiantai, and Huayan had faded. In their place were the flowering schools of Song Chan, which were known, even then, for the worst extremes of iconoclasm, antinomianism, and escapism, both in terms of their behavior and what was contained in the popular texts of the Song Chan schools. As de Bary points out (citing Yanagida), there were numerous texts that contained passages that provided good targets for Neo-Confucian critiques of nihilism.[6] Yet it is surprising that no Buddhist scholars appeared at the time who might have been able to point out that most of the lines cited by Zhu Xi and his predecessors were skillfully selected out of the fuller context of discussions that were, taken in their entirety, not at all nihilistic.

Regardless of the honesty or accuracy of the criticisms of Chan made by the leading figures of this reenergized Confucian movement, it is no secret that there was a strong strain of anti-intellectualism in the literature of the Chan school, and regardless of whether this "stupefaction" was really a common state of affairs, there is no doubt that the overall tendency within the Chan tradition toward academic study was different from what had been seen in the doctrinal schools.[7] This attitude demonstrated by the members of the Chan schools may well have contributed to the intellectual vacuum that would be filled by the New Confucians.

Sources of Neo-Confucian Doctrine

Although the classics that were the object of study for the Neo-Confucians were essentially the same as they had been for their Confucian predecessors (the Four Books,[8] the Five Classics,[9] and so forth), they were reanalyzed under the lens of a new hermeneutic that was the result of several centuries of Buddhist and indigenous Chinese cross-fertilization: the categories of *li* 理 (principle) and *qi* 氣 (*pneuma*, material force), which were derived from the *li* (principle) and *shi* 事 (phenomena)—popular in the Huayan and Tiantai schools—both of which were a new iteration of the classic essence-function (*ti-yong* 體用) approach. The Neo-Confucians brought this new metaphysics, which also included a heavy reliance on the *Yijing* and *yin/yang* cosmology, to re-explain the relation of humans to humans and humans to the universe, along with a much more precisely articulated path of cultivation, relying heavily on the *Mencius* and the *Great Learning*.

The most important early figures in this movement were the Neo-Confucian patriarchs Zhang Cai 張載 (1020–1077) and Zhou Dunyi 周敦頤 (1017–1073),[10] whose combined works established the bases of this new metaphysics while creating schema for a new way to understand humans and their world. What is especially noteworthy about their writings, however, is the degree to which they were energized by anti-Buddhist polemic.[11] But this polemic is only started with these two, and is not especially vehement in their works. After all, Zhou was known to have been a Chan practitioner of sorts.

It is in the writings of the Cheng brothers (Cheng Hao 程顥, 1032–1085; and Cheng Yi 程頤, 1033–1107) that a distinctive Neo-Confucian philosophy really begins to take on its mature form, as the philosophical elaboration of the categories of *li* and *qi* within the framework of commentary on the classical texts takes on sophisticated form.[12] It was Cheng Hao who developed the *li-qi* cosmological view, and rereading classical passages such as *Analects* 12:1, declared that "the humane man forms a single body with the world." Even more so than the works of the earlier generations of Neo-Confucians, the criticism of Buddhism becomes an integral part—and at times perhaps the central aspect—of the Cheng brothers' discourse. Interestingly, the brother shown to have exhibited the more mystical, or "Channish" tendencies in his writings, Cheng Hao, is the one who composed the most damaging critiques of the Chan tradition. The Cheng brothers criticized Chan Buddhism for its antinomian, escapist tendencies, and its doctrine of emptiness, which they construed as pure nihilism.[13] The arguments composed by the Chengs and their mentors were digested, explicated, and systematized in the writings of Zhu Xi 朱熹 (1130–1200), who would become recognized as the grand systematizer of the Neo-Confucian tradition—as the one most singly responsible for the reinstatement of Confucianism as the predominant ideology of the Chinese imperial government until the opening of the modern era.

It is important to reiterate that when Zhu and the Chengs talk about "Buddhism," they are talking about the form of Buddhism that was in vogue during their lifetime—which was Song Dynasty Chan—the same tradition that was in the process of compiling *gong-an* collections, teaching strike-and-shout Linji methodologies, and so forth. Popular Buddhist writings at that time contained almost nothing in the way of explanation of Indian-style dependent origination, emptiness, or the two levels of truth. The popular scriptures at the time were mostly East Asian apocrypha (such as the *Sutra of Perfect Enlightenment* and the

Śūraṃgama-sūtra) and works overtly composed within the Chan tradition (such as the *Platform Sutra*), that were suddenistic in their approaches, paying little attention to intellectual study and cultivation.

While the Chan schools were drawing continuous harsh criticism from their Confucian contemporaries, we can find virtually no literature that would represent any sustained effort made on the Chan side at written self-defense. Why the lack of works aimed at defending Buddhist teachings against these critiques? One possible explanation is that knowing the general character of Chan with its self-proclaimed dissociation from discursive argumentation, such a debate was outside the purview of what a Chan teacher was supposed to be doing. It could also be that the Buddhists were sufficiently confident of the status of their religion that they believed that such diatribes were never going to have any real concrete effect in terms of government-authorized restrictions. It may have also been the case that vibrant energy of the Neo-Confucian movement, coupled with the bright young minds being attracted to it, was simply too much for the Chan leaders to contend with.

Neo-Confucianism in Korea

During the two centuries after Zhu Xi, a confrontational situation between Neo-Confucianism and Buddhism developed in the Goryeo, although in a somewhat different context than that seen in Song China. The most important difference between the two scenarios was the markedly greater degree to which the Korean Buddhist establishment was embedded into the state power structure as compared with the situation in the Song. The Buddhist *saṃgha* owned vast tracts of tax-free territory, traded in slaves and other commodities, and was influential at all levels of government. There were too many monks who were ordained for the wrong reasons, and corruption was rampant. Thus, the ideological fervor with which Neo-Confucianism rose in Korea had a special dimension, since the venom of their rhetoric was fueled not only by the earlier philosophical arguments of the Cheng brothers and Zhu Xi, but as well by the extent of the present corruption visible in the Buddhist establishment. There was a decadent, stumbling government in place, supported by, and supporting, a religious organization plagued by scandal and corruption. Thus, in Korea, the mostly philosophical arguments against Buddhism that had originated with the Cheng brothers became the ideology of a rising movement of resistance on the part of influential members of the intelligentsia who were determined to overthrow a decaying Goryeo Dynasty (918–1392)—along with the rotting Buddhist monastic system that was deeply entangled with it. Thus, the anti-Buddhist polemical dimension of the Neo-Confucianism that developed in Korea took on a focus, a vehemence, indeed an exclusivism[14] not previously seen in China.

A major portion of the Neo-Confucian polemical attack that energized these sweeping changes was sociopolitical in nature, focusing on the excesses engaged in by the Buddhist clergy. Buddhist temples had been tax-exempt, and many Buddhist leaders enjoyed wealth and power that came in the form of the possession of prize lands, slaves, and positions of privilege in the court. There was also a philosophical component to the Neo-Confucian criticism of Buddhist doctrine and practice that developed out of the writings of the above-mentioned Song Neo-Confucian architects. The main complaint expressed in these arguments was, once again, that Buddhist practices were antisocial and escapist and that the Buddhist doctrine was nihilistic. Buddhism, according to the Neo-Confucians, led people to abandon respect for the norms of society and to forget the all-important task of cultivating one's character in the midst of human relationships.

While there were anti-Buddhist memorials presented in Korea as early as 982, serious concentrated attack on Buddhism did not begin until the mid-fourteenth century. The major initial charges, presented by scholars such as I Saek 李穡 (1328–1396), were that excessive patronage was deleterious to the well-being of the state. The attacks made on Buddhism by Jo In-ok 趙仁沃 (?–1396) and Jeong Mongju 鄭夢周 (1337–1392) were also made on political and economic, rather than philosophical and religious, bases. After this period, the anti-Buddhist polemic took a turn toward the philosophical in the writings of such prominent Neo-Confucian figures as Gang Hoebaek 姜淮伯 (1357–1402) and Jeong Chong 鄭摠 (1358–1397), both of whom were active in the late fourteenth century.[15] Toward the end of the fourteenth century the political and economic problems of the Goryeo court worsened, and with the Buddhists firmly embedded in the body of a weakened political structure, Neo-Confucian activists came to the side of the rebel general I Seonggye 李成桂 (1335–1408). I, in a sudden coup d'état, toppled the Goryeo government, establishing the Joseon Dynasty in 1392, and was automatically endowed with a cabinet composed of Neo-Confucian advisers.

With the 1392 coup, the Buddhists were thrust out of their position of political power. They would, over time, become mainly relegated to an existence in the mountain monasteries, prohibited from setting foot in the cities. The final polemical push for the Buddhist purge came in the form of the essays of Jeong Dojeon 鄭道傳 (pen name: Sambong 三峰; 1342–1398), I's main political strategist, who would end up playing a major role in the development of the political structure of the new Joseon Dynasty.[16] Jeong wrote three major philosophical essays that were critical of Buddhism: (1) The *Simmun cheondap* 心問天答 (Questions from the Mind Answered by Heaven; 1375), wherein he presented a critique of the Buddhist doctrine of karma, offering instead a Neo-Confucian interpretation of the interaction of principle and material force; (2) the *Simgiri pyeon* 心氣理篇 (On the Mind, Material Force, and Principle; 1394), where he argues that the Confucian definitions and usages of the three terms of mind, material force, and principle are clear and consistent, and those of Buddhism are vague and inconsistent, and (3) the *Bulssi japbyeon*, which was his final and most sustained anti-Buddhist polemical work, in which he carried out an extensive refutation of Buddhist doctrines and practices from a Neo-Confucian perspective, including the content of the prior two essays, along with summaries of the arguments of many of his Neo-Confucian predecessors.[17]

In these anti-Buddhist tracts Jeong's intention was to show that the Buddhist doctrine was deeply and intrinsically flawed. Thus, it was necessary not only to discipline the Buddhist establishment at the present moment: it was desirable to seriously curtail, and if possible, to permanently end the activities of this dangerous belief system. His critique is thorough, covering every major aspect of the Buddhist doctrine that was being taught at the time. Given the composition of Korean Buddhism at the time in question, the primary object of his criticism was the Seon sect, which the Neo-Confucians of course perceived as having strong tendencies toward other-worldliness, denial of the importance of human relationships, denial of respect for the state, and even denial of Buddhism's own principle of cause-and-effect.

The influence of Jeong's Chinese predecessors, primarily the Cheng brothers via Zhu Xi, is omnipresent in his writings. Almost every argument, and every example made by Jeong is a citation drawn from one of the Cheng brothers, often through the commentaries of Zhu. While Jeong is often looked down up on by Korean intellectual historians as being more of an ideologue than a philosopher, none of Jeong's worthy predecessors had ever composed such a well-organized, complete, and systematic attack on Buddhism, from every angle, that can compare with the *Japbyeon*. We will return to look at some of its contents below. First, however, we need to familiarize ourselves as to what was happening in terms of the Buddhist response.

Buddhist Responses and the Influence of Zongmi

We have noted above that despite the intensity of the critiques of Chan Buddhism by the Song Neo-Confucian leaders, there was little in terms of sustained and reasoned written response from the Chan community from the time that the criticism took hold during the Song. The most significant early response to the Confucian critique occurs at the very outset of the renewed opposition in the mid-Tang from the scholar-monk Zongmi (宗密 780–841). Those with some knowledge of the history of Korean Buddhism will recognize Zongmi as one of the Chinese scholar-monks who brought the most direct influence on the later character of the Korean Seon tradition. In the history of the development of Korean Seon, issues related to the reconciliation of various approaches to practice came to play a central role, and one of the most significant of these was that of the relation between meditation practice and scriptural study. Zongmi, who would end up with the unusual distinction of being recognized as a "patriarch" of both the Chan and Huayan traditions, advocated that the approaches of meditative practice and scriptural study were mutually complementary. His statements on this and related matters, such as explanations of the notion of intrinsic enlightenment and discussions of the relationship between sudden and gradual in practice and enlightenment, were followed and repeated by the most influential of the Korean Seon formulators, including Jinul, Gihwa, and Hyujeong. And as it turns out, the set of texts that held the greatest level of interest for these later Korean Seon masters, the *Sutra of Perfect Enlightenment*, *Awakening of Mahāyāna Faith*, *Diamond Sutra*, and *Huayan jing*, were also the subject of Zongmi's most extensive commentarial efforts.

One of the works for which Zongmi is most noted in Chinese intellectual history is his *Inquiry into the Origin of Humanity* (*Yuanren lun* 原人論).[18] Composed around 830, it was a treatise written for a broad audience. It was in some sense a work typical of Chinese doctrinal scholars from the sixth to the eighth century in being a hermeneutically oriented text that classified the teachings of Buddhism into five levels. Such classifications had been carried out before Zongmi by such people as his Huayan predecessor Fazang, de facto Tiantai founder Zhiyi, and many others.

While the *Inquiry* is primarily a textbook for understanding Buddhism that utilizes the classification scheme as a pedagogical methodology, the opening passages contain a clear polemic at Confucianism, apparently in response to the attacks by Hanyu. Zongmi criticizes indigenous Chinese philosophy for those of its doctrines that show a lack of discernment of the basic laws of cause-and-effect. Thus, he debunks the Chinese classical view of spontaneous production, the lack of reasoning for the differences in individual endowments of vital force, and the unexplained unfairness seen in the operation of the "mandate of heaven" (*tianming*).

According to Zongmi, all of these paradigms are logically untenable when really thought through, and cannot match the sophistication of even the most elementary of the Buddhist teachings—that of the law of karmic retribution. There is, nonetheless, an ecumenical character to the *Inquiry*, since, although Confucianism and Daoism are seen to be inferior to Buddhism, they are nonetheless accorded a certain amount of value, with Confucius and Laozi being regarded as bona fide sages, along with Śākyamuni. As Peter Gregory notes:

> Although it should be no surprise that Tsung-mi (Zongmi) regards Buddhism as a higher level of teaching than either Confucianism or Daoism, what is especially noteworthy is that his attitude toward the two teachings is sympathetic and inclusive. Even though his designation of them as exclusively provisional places them in a category inferior to the Buddhist teachings, it also—and far more significantly—places them within the same realm of discourse. Its concrete forms of expression may differ, but the truth realized by the three sages is universal. (*Inquiry*, 81)

Given the fact that Han Yu's tracts and Zongmi's *Inquiry* were written in the early part of the ninth century, almost five centuries before the exchange between Jeong Dojeon and Gihwa, the extent to which the content from these early predecessors from both sides finds its way into the treatises of the two Korean recipients of their respective traditions is quite surprising. Jeong, for instance, will continue to invoke Han's criticism of Buddhism as a "foreign" religion. Gihwa, for his part, will open up his own treatise by borrowing the correlation made by Zongmi between the five constant virtues of Confucianism and the five basic Buddhist precepts—a correlation first made as far back as the *Diwei Boli jing* 提謂波利經.[19] While the *Inquiry* stands out as the major precedent to Gihwa's work, there are nonetheless, significant differences in content and structure, based largely upon the circumstances in which they were written. The *Inquiry* is first and foremost a *panjiao* 判 (doctrinal taxonomy) text, which takes up the critique of Confucianism only in its opening sections. Zongmi's Buddhist tradition at the time, even if suffering from the rants of the likes of Han Yu, certainly did not have its back up against the wall. The Buddhists in the early Joseon on the other hand were "on the ropes" as it were, and so Gihwa's treatise is in its entirety a defense of the Buddhist tradition, with issues of doctrinal classification long since forgotten. There are also significant personal stylistic differences, but before addressing these, we need to introduce Gihwa.

Gihwa

Gihwa 己和 (Hamheo Deuktong 涵 得通, 1376–1433) was born just sixteen years before the Goryeo/Joseon dynastic transition. The son of a diplomat, he was educated with other upper-class sons at the recently established Seonggyun-gwan 成均館 Confucian academy—where Jeong Dojeon was a member of the faculty.[20] In the course of his studies here, Gihwa is said to have attained to a remarkable level of proficiency in Chinese philosophy and literature, as his biographer goes to unusual lengths to convey the extent to which his professors esteemed him:

> Entering the academy as a youth, he was able to memorize more than a thousand phrases daily. As time passed, he deeply penetrated the universality of the single thread, clarifying the meanings of the classics and expounding their content. His reputation was unmatched. Grasping the subtlety of the transmitted teachings, he disclosed all their profundities in his explanations. He was possessed of a sonorous voice and graceful beauty, like flowers laid upon silk brocade—even such metaphor falls short of description. People said that he would become the minister truly capable of transmitting the heavenly mandate, extending upward to the ruler and bringing blessings down to the people. In his grasp of the correct principles of society he had no need to be ashamed even if he were to appear before the likes of Zhou and Shao.[21]

Acknowledging the obvious hyperbole that is invariably seen in the hagiographical sketches written by disciples of eminent Buddhist teachers, we must nevertheless pay attention to what is contained in this passage as (1) there is not, in the entire corpus of Korean Buddhist hagiographies an appraisal of scholarly (Confucian) acumen comparable in scope to this, and (2) this strong assessment of Gihwa's early abilities is corroborated in the degree to which he, later in his Buddhist career, took such a strong interest in and showed such outstanding ability in literary/philosophical/exegetical pursuits. Furthermore, a reading of his later Buddhist works shows an unusual frequency of citation from the Five Classics, Four Books, and Daoist canon.

Despite Gihwa's deep initial involvement in Confucian learning, he is said to have been greatly affected at the age of twenty-one by the tragic death of a close friend, and as a result, turned to the Buddhist path. After a short period of wandering and study, he became a disciple of the national preceptor Muhak 無學 (1327–1405), a master of the Imje Seon 臨濟禪 (C. Linji Chan) *gong-an* 公案 tradition. Gihwa spent the rest of his days immersed in meditation, travel, teaching, and an extensive literary pursuit that included commentarial work, essay writing, and poetry. Despite the diminished influence of Buddhism, toward the end of his career he served as preceptor to the royal family. After this stint, he retired once again to the mountain monasteries, where he taught and wrote until his passing in 1433. During his life, Gihwa wrote several important and influential treatises and commentaries on Buddhist works that established him as one of the leading exegetes in the Korean Buddhist tradition.[22]

Placed as he was in the position of being the leading representative of the Buddhist saṃgha at a time when it was coming under great pressure, Gihwa no doubt felt responsible to offer an answer to the Neo-Confucian charges. Respond he did, in the form of a philosophical treatise that has become a landmark in Korean intellectual history—the *Hyeonjeong non* 顯正論 ("Exposition of Orthodoxy," hereafter abbreviated as *HJN*). In the *HJN* Gihwa attempted to answer the entire accretion of criticisms made by the Neo-Confucians that had been organized and laid out in the *Bulssi japbyeon* 佛氏雜論. Therefore the relationship between the *Japbyeon* and the *HJN* is such that we might well characterize the latter work as a fairly direct rebuttal of the former, and thus, the two together can be said to constitute a debate.[23]

As mentioned above, the circumstances of Gihwa's composition of this treatise in defense of Buddhism against Confucian-based criticisms have a direct precedent in those surrounding Zongmi's *Inquiry*. Zongmi and Gihwa held much in common, both being Chan-Seon/Huayan-Hwaeom scholars of considerable classical Chinese philosophical background and both holding an honest respect for many aspects of Confucian and Daoist learning. Both men shared in their broad vision of all three masters—Confucius, Laozi, and Śākyamuni—being genuine sages, but their way of evaluating the two non-Buddhist traditions differs somewhat.

While treating similar topics from similar perspectives, the two treatises differ in their basic line of argumentation. Zongmi's work, reflecting its author's interest in doctrinal classification, is primarily an attempt to show how Confucianism and Daoism are related to Buddhism as expedient, but nonetheless heterodox 外 (K. *oegyo*) teachings. His tone toward Confucianism and Daoism is conciliatory, but he will clearly distinguish the two from Buddhism as being even less sophisticated than the teachings of "men and gods"—basic teachings of karmic retribution for moral and immoral actions. Gihwa's argument, on the other hand, relies primarily on an understanding of interpenetration that operates equally in all three teachings of Confucianism, Daoism, and Buddhism, but that he claims has been brought to different levels of actualization by the practitioners of each of the three teachings. Gihwa perceives the three teachings as varying expressions of a singular reality. Thus, despite his conversion to Buddhism, he never really rejected his earlier Confucian and Daoist learning. Accordingly, in his Buddhist apologetic writings he did not seek to disparage the fundamental Confucian doctrine; nonetheless, while the Confucian teachings were worthy of deep respect, he argued that the Confucians had often missed the deeper implications of their own texts.

The Texts: Content Analysis

Bulssi japbyeon

The chapter headings of the *Bulssi japbyeon* are as follows:

1. Critique of the Buddhist Doctrine of Transmigration 佛氏輪迴之辨
2. Critique of the Buddhist Notion of Karma 佛氏因果之辨

3. Critique of the Buddhist Theory of Mind and Nature 佛氏心性之辨

4. Critique of the Buddhists' Conflation of Function and Nature 佛氏作用是性之辨

5. Critique of the Buddhist Notion of the Mind and its Functions 佛氏心跡之辨

6. Critique of the Buddhists' Obscuration of Principles and Concrete Entities 佛氏昧於道器之辨

7. Critique of the Buddhists' Abandonment of the Basic Human Relationships 佛氏「棄人倫之辨

8. Critique of the Buddhist Notion of Compassion 佛氏慈悲之辨

9. Critique of the Buddhist Notions of the Real and the Nominal 佛氏眞假之辨

10. Critique of the Buddhist Notion of Hells 佛氏地獄之辨

11. Critique of the Buddhist Notion of Calamity and Fortune 佛氏禍福之辨

12. Critique of the Buddhists' Practice of Begging for Food 佛氏乞食之辨

13. Critique of the Buddhists' Seon Teachings 佛氏禪「之辨

14. Critique of the Samenesses and Differences between Confucianism and Buddhism 儒釋同異之辨

15. On the Entry of the Buddhadharma into China 佛法入中國

16. Serve the Buddha and Reap Misfortune 事佛得禍

17. Abandoning the Heavenly Way and Chatting about Buddhahood 舍天道而談佛果

18. Serving the Buddha Assiduously, the Length of Reign Considerably Shortens 事佛甚謹年代尤促

19. Critique to Expose Heterodox Teachings 闢異端之辨

Jeong starts off, in the first two chapters, with a critique of the Indian notions of karma and transmigration, arguing against these "foreign" Indian paradigms, based on Chinese cosmological schema such as were developed in connection with the *Yijing* and its commentaries: *yin/yang*, the five phases (Ch. *wuxing* 五行), *hun* 魂 and *po* 魄 souls, etc. These chapters do not offer much to clearly demonstrate a metaphysical high ground for Confucianism, as Jeong's proof rests on such assertions as a declaration for the non-increase or decrease for the total number of beings in the world at a given time—positions that were never really articulated as such in the foundational Confucian works. He does make a point, however, of bringing to mind the fact that when it comes to practical matters, such as the healing of disease, virtually all East Asians of the time, Buddhists included, rely on Chinese *yin/yang* cosmology in the form of traditional medicinal practices.

It is in the third through fifth chapters that he really delves into the core of his philosophical argument, as he attacks Buddhism at one of its traditional weak points: that of the contradictory character of the discourse on nature and mind as found in the tathāgatagarbha-influenced texts such as the *Awakening of Mahāyāna Faith* and *Sutra of Perfect Enlightenment*—based on an argument that he had previously fleshed out in the *Simgiri pyeon* 心氣理篇. He provides textual examples from the *Śūraṃgama-sūtra* and from the writings of Jinul that show inconsistencies between the various accounts of the relation between mind 心 (K. *sim*) and nature 性 (K. *seong*). As Jeong shows in a series of citations, in one place, nature is equivalent to the mind; in another, it is an aspect of the mind, a principle contained in the mind; and then in another place, a function of the mind. Referring to the disparities and circular reasoning that he finds in the Buddhist descriptions of nature, he says:

> The Buddhist explanations regarding nature are all done based on nebulous supposition, rather than on explicit facts. The teachings of the Buddhists have lots of word play, but lack a definitive doctrine, and through this, their actual intentions can be understood. (SBJ 1.78b)

The Confucian teachings, are, by contrast, consistent from beginning to end. They clearly distinguish between the mind and its nature, between principle and external events. They allow for clear value and evaluation, with uniformity throughout.

A similar theme carries into the fourth chapter, where Jeong criticizes Buddhists, in this case, especially Chan Buddhists, for conflating the notion of nature with that of mundane function, citing the likes of Layman Pang, who said: "Hauling water and carrying firewood are nothing but marvelous function" (SBJ 1.78d). Jeong here relies on Zhu Xi, who said: "If you take functional activity to be [the same as] the nature, then are not peoples' irresponsible actions such as taking a sword to murder someone and transgressing the Way [also] the nature?" (SBJ 1.79b). This line of argumentation is carried into chapter 6, where the focus is directly on the relationship between the mind and its external/functional manifestations. To clarify the Confucian position (which Jeong argues is rationally and metaphysically consistent), he cites the Mencian "four beginnings" (K. *sadan* 四端) that are innate to humans, along with their four directly associated manifest functions of humaneness (*in* 仁), propriety (*i* 禮), due-giving (*ui* 義), and wisdom (*ji* 智). The Buddhists, by contrast, espouse doctrines that dissociate the innate capacities of the mind from the manifestations of human activity. This chapter contains the passage that constitutes the crux of Jeong's argument. He says:

> It is like the saying "essence and function spring from the same source; the manifest and the subtle have no gap between them."[24] The Buddhist method of study addresses the mind, but does not address its manifestations. This can be seen in the Buddhist's saying things like "The bodhisattva Mañjuśrī wanders through the taverns, but these activities are not his mind." Excuses like this for sloppy behavior abound [in the Buddhist teachings]. Is this not a separation of the mind from its activities? Chengzi said: "The study of the Buddhists includes reverence to correct the internal, but does not include justice to straighten the external."[25] Therefore those who are stuck in these [incorrect views] wither away. (SBJ 1.79c–d)

Jeong's critique runs through several chapters, addressing issues such as the Buddhists' abandonment of societal obligations, perverted application of the notion of "compassion," criticism of the idea of two levels of reality, the practice of begging, and most of all, the perceived escapist and nihilistic views of Chan. But all can be summarized with Jeong's understanding of the components of the Buddhist doctrine to be disconnected from each other, of being contradictory, conveniently used for excusing responsibility, of not providing a viable system of values. Confucianism, by contrast, is completely aligned through essence and function, is unitary, without contradictions, and teaches a concrete system of values, articulating a clear relationship between inner and outer.

Hyeonjeong non

The section titles for the *Hyeonjeong non* are as follows:[26]

1. Prologue
2. Distinctions in Levels of Teaching
3. The Constant and the Expedient
4. Śākyamuni's Attainment of Freedom from Attachment
5. Societal Obligations
6. Harming Life
7. The Meaning of Humaneness
8. Drinking Alcohol
9. Making Offerings
10. Defense of the Doctrine of Karma and Rebirth
11. Defense of the Buddhist Practice of Cremation
12. Refutation of the Complaint against Buddhism as a Foreign Religion
13. Refutation of the Accusation of Buddhism as a Harbinger of Calamity
14. Refutation of the Accusation of Monks being Parasites
15. Refutation of the Charge of Decadence in the Saṃgha
16. Refutation of the Charges of Nihilism and Antinomianism
17. The Unity of the Three Teachings

To set the tone for his argument, Gihwa goes to some lengths to clarify the Buddhist position on the nature of the mind and the relevance and gradations of methods of practices—basically summarizing the view of mind that is expressed in the fundamental East Asian Buddhist scriptures, the *Awakening of Mahāyāna Faith*, *Sutra of Perfect Enlightenment*, etc. That is, the mind is originally pure, but when it moves into activity, it has the potential to be distorted. Gihwa opens the *Hyeonjeong non* by saying:

> Though its essence neither exists nor not-exists, it permeates existence and non-existence. Though it originally lacks past and present, it permeates past and present: this is the Dao. Existence and non-existence are based in nature and sentiency. Past and present are based in life-and-death. Nature originally lacks sentiency, but when you are confused about nature you give rise to sentiency; with the production of sentiency, wisdom is blocked—thoughts transform, and the essence is differentiated. It is through this that the myriad forms take shape and life-and-death begin. (HBJ 7.217a)

In this way, Gihwa starts off by grounding his argument in an essence-function view of the mind and its activities. The mind is originally pure, but as it engages in situations, it can become entangled and enmeshed. As Zongmi had well-clarified more than five centuries earlier, for the purpose of recovering the original mind, Buddhism has a wide spectrum of practices, which range from the most expedient and superficial, to the most profound. In outlining the teaching starting from the most profound and extending to the most superficial teachings, Gihwa ends with the teaching of the law of cause-and-effect. As it was stated in the *Inquiry*, this teaching, however, no matter how superficial, is one level above the typical application of the Confucian teaching, which Gihwa defines as the mere conditioning of people through reward and punishment on the part of the state. But he later shifts his position and shows how the true, correctly understood Confucian teaching, when applied with the right understanding, can also extend to profound levels. Thus, Gihwa's validation of Confucianism extends considerably beyond that of Zongmi in his *Inquiry*.

The *Hyeonjeong non* is markedly conciliatory in tone compared to the *Japbyeon*. Gihwa has no intention of entirely discrediting the Confucian tradition. Rather, his aim is to point out the underlying unity of the three teachings and to see them as varying expressions of a mysterious unifying principle. What Gihwa will say, mostly, is not that the Confucian teachings are wrong, but that they serve an important purpose. Unfortunately, however, they have been incorrectly understood and practiced by even the most important figures of their own tradition.

Gihwa refutes the charges made against Buddhist practices that are seen to be antisocial, such as the abandonment of family relationships, by showing how they are actually helpful to society, rather than harmful, when practiced correctly. Responsibility for excesses indulged in by saṃgha members is laid upon the offenders as individuals making their own decisions, rather than upon the tradition as a whole. Jeong's criticisms of the Buddhist doctrines of karma and causation are dealt with by logical argumentation, by showing that the law of cause-and-effect cannot but be universally valid; criticisms of the doctrine of rebirth are defended with anecdotes of people who have memories of past lives.

The core of Gihwa's argument lies in the presentation of what he takes as common denominator of all three traditions (Confucianism, Daoism, and Buddhism): a doctrine of *humaneness* (K. *in*; 仁), based on the ubiquitously expressed assertion that the myriad living beings of the universe are deeply interlinked with one another. While the notion of the mutual containment of the myriad things is ostensibly Buddhist in origin, it ended up being one of the central tenets of the most influential of the Song Neo-Confucian founders, including Zhou Dunyi and the Cheng brothers, and especially Cheng Hao, who declared that "the myriad things and I form a single body."[27] With this being the characteristic and seminal Neo-Confucian development of the Confucian/Mencian "humaneness," Gihwa finds an inconsistency between what Confucians say and what they do, and makes this point the central issue of his essay.

Buddhism and (Neo-)Confucianism share the view that it is fundamentally wrong to harm others. Since others are intimately connected with oneself, harming others is the same as harming oneself. Buddhists have the doctrine of *ahiṃsā* (non-injury) at the core of their practice of moral discipline, and this is observed completely in all Buddhist practices. Confucians, on the other hand, take humaneness as the most fundamental element to their path of cultivation. Confucius himself continually referred to humaneness as the source of all forms of goodness. Mencius made it clear that humaneness was innate to all people, explaining its function through a variety of metaphors, the best known being that of the stranger who automatically rushes to prevent a toddler from falling into a well.

However, Gihwa says, the Confucian corpus is riddled with inconsistencies on this matter. For example, although Cheng Hao has told us that humaneness means that we form a single body with the myriad things, Confucius himself only went halfway in his practice of single-bodiedness, as he still enjoyed the sports of hunting and fishing.[28] For Mencius, the taking of the life of an animal was not problematic for the humane man, as long as he didn't hear the animal's screams in its death throes.[29] And, in general, the Confucian tradition fully endorsed the practices of ritual sacrifice. Gihwa says:

> Since animals share with people the sense of aversion to being killed, how do they differ from human beings? With the sound of ripping flesh and the cutting of the knife, they are in utter fright as they approach their death. Their eyes are wild and they cry out in agony. How could they not harbor bitterness and resentment? And yet people are able to turn a deaf ear. In this way human beings and the creatures of the world affect each other without awareness and bring retribution to each other without pause. How could a humane person, observing such suffering, continue to act as if nothing was wrong? (HBJ 7.220a–b)

As Gihwa goes on to tell us, it was precisely the difference on this point that turned him toward Buddhism during the time when he was weighing the two systems in the balance.

> One time, during the period when I still had not yet entered the Buddhist order, a monk named Haeweol 海月 was reading the *Analects* to me. He reached the passage that says:
> [Zi Gong asked:] "Suppose there were a ruler who benefited the people far and wide and was capable of bringing salvation to the multitude; what would you think of him? Might he be called humane"? The Master said, "Why only humane? He would undoubtedly be a sage. Even Yao and Shun would have had to work hard to achieve this" (*Analects* 6:28).
> He commented: "The humane man forms a single body with heaven and earth and the myriad things." With this, he put the scroll aside and asked me: "Was Mencius a humane man?" "Yes," I replied. "Are 'fowl, pigs, dogs, and swine' to be counted among the 'myriad things?'" "Yes," I replied. [Haewe-

ol continued, citing Cheng Hao:] "The humane man forms a single body with heaven and earth and the myriad things." If this statement is to be taken as a true expression of the principle, how are we supposed to see Mencius as humane? If "fowl, pigs, dogs, and swine" are to be counted among the "myriad things" then how could Mencius say: "If, in the raising of fowl, pigs, dogs, and swine, their breeding times are not missed, then people in their seventies can eat meat" (*Mencius* 1A:3). I was completely stymied by this question, and could not answer. I pondered over all of the classical transmissions, and could not come up with a single text that could support a principle that condoned the taking of life. I inquired widely among the brightest thinkers of the day, but not one of them could offer an explanation that could resolve my perplexity.

This doubt remained buried within my mind for a long time without being resolved. Then, while traveling around Samgak-san in 1396, I arrived at Seunggasa 僧伽寺, where I had the chance to chat with an old Seon monk throughout the night. The monk said: "In Buddhism there are ten grave precepts, the first of which is to not take life." Upon hearing this explanation, my mind was suddenly overturned, and I recognized for myself that this was indeed the behavior of the truly humane man. I was hereupon able to deeply embody the teachings of the Way of humanity. From this time forth, I was never again to be confused regarding the differences between Confucianism and Buddhism. I subsequently composed a verse, which went:

Up till now, knowing only the teachings of the classics and histories
And the criticisms of the Chengs and Zhu,
I was unable to recognize whether the Buddha was wrong or right.
But after reflecting deep in my mind for long years,
Knowing the truth for the first time, I reject [Confucianism]
And take refuge in [the Buddhadharma]. (HBJ 7.220a3–18)

The charge, then, that Gihwa will lay on the Confucians, is strikingly similar to that which Jeong wants to apply the Buddhists, in that both want to show the other side to be guilty of inconsistency. The difference, however, is that Jeong wants to point out inconsistencies in the Buddhist doctrine in itself, where Gihwa centers his argument on showing inconsistencies between Confucian doctrine and practice. That is, Confucians say one thing, but do another. Gihwa's final pronouncement of his treatise, however, is the conclusion that the three teachings should be understood as three types of expression of the same reality. Here he no doubt had in mind the concluding chapter of the *Bulssi japbyeon*, "Criticism of the Differences between Buddhism and Confucianism" ("Yuseok dong-i ji byeon"; 儒釋同異之辨). There, Jeong gives a final summation of all the ways that the Buddhist teaching is vacuous and nihilistic and thus inferior to Confucianism, which is substantial and consistent throughout. Jeong says:

> Prior Confucian scholars have [already] shown that the Confucian and Buddhist paths differ with every single phrase and every single situation. Here I will elaborate based on these. We say voidness, and they also say voidness. We say quiescence, and they also say quiescence. However, our voidness is void yet existent. Their voidness is void and non-existent. Our quiescence is quiescent yet aware; their quiescence is quiescent and nihilating. We speak of knowledge and action; they speak of awakening and cultivation. Yet our knowledge is to know that the principle of the myriad things is replete in our own minds. Their awakening awakens to the fact that the mind is originally empty, lacking anything. Our action is to return to the principle of the myriad things and act according to it, without error. Their cultivation is to sever connection with the myriad things and regard them as unconnected to one's mind. (SBJ 1.84a)

Gihwa, in obvious reference to Jeong's summation, also concludes his own argument by focusing on these two concepts of voidness and quiescence (and this section provides the most solid evidence that Gihwa was most certainly responding to Jeong when he wrote this piece) by showing instead that the connotations of these terms are basically the same throughout all three traditions and that at their most fundamental level, the three are equally valid approaches to the same reality.

> If you can grasp this, then the words of the three teachers fit together like the broken pieces of the same board—as if

they had all come out of the same mouth! If you would like to actually demonstrate the high and low among these teachings, exposing their points of similarity and difference clearly in their actual function, then you must first completely wash the pollution from your mind and completely clarify your eye of wisdom. Then you can study all of the texts contained in the Buddhist, Confucian, and Daoist canons. Compare them in your daily activities, at the times of birth and death, fortune and misfortune. Without needing words, you will spontaneously nod in assent. How strong do I need to make my argument to get the prince to listen? (HBJ 7.225b)

The much softer stance of Gihwa can be attributed to various factors. Throughout all of East Asia, it had never been part of the Buddhist agenda to expend energy in debunking the Confucian tradition, which had been so deeply a part of the fabric of Chinese and Korean society[30] Although Gihwa, who had taken his literary training in a Confucian academy, eventually opted for Buddhism to complete his spiritual quest, he never lost his deep respect for the more profound aspects of both Confucianism and Daoism. Indeed, he cites from the Chinese classics with regularity in his Buddhist commentaries. We might even imagine that it may have pained him considerably to be forced into the position of having to criticize Confucianism in the *Hyeonjeong non*.

Some Philosophical Observations on the Background of the Debate

The two texts that we have looked at above together represent a pivotal moment in Korean intellectual history, and thus their titles and authors are quite often known to modern-day Korean intellectuals from many areas in the humanities—not only specialists in philosophy and religion. But they are also important for the degree in which they encapsulate, to some degree, much of the history of East Asian thought in general. They can also be seen as important from the perspective of world philosophy and religion in general, in the sense that they constitute a rational, sustained, and substantive debate between members of different religious or philosophical systems. This kind of debate between members of different religious traditions does not happen all that often in the world;

interactions between religious traditions are more often typified by outright fighting, even war. Or superficial attempts at simple coexistence.

This is because the phenomenon of interreligious debate necessarily includes certain conditions. One is basic physical proximity—the fact that the traditions are forced to compete with each other for adherents within the same society. This forces them to deal with each other, whether or not it is in an amiable manner.

But more important, for such debate to occur, is the existence of a shared worldview, a shared vocabulary, and some sharing in basic values. We can see one of the best examples of such a situation in ancient India, where Buddhists, Jainas, Sāṃkhyas, Vedantists, and members of other Indian philosophical traditions engaged with each other in public debate. They were able to do this based on the fact that they shared a number of important principles in their worldviews: belief in the eternal return of the soul; belief in the liberation of the human being through the practice of a path (*mārga*) and the following of a proper set of beliefs (*darśana*). They even went as far as to agree upon some ground rules of debate, known as *nyāya*.

In similar fashion, the Confucians and Buddhists—as well as the Daoists in East Asia—clearly shared in some important principles. And perhaps it takes someone who comes from outside of the tradition to see it from a removed vantage point, but this reader at least, picks up in this discourse a clear sharing of a principle, that of *ti-yong*, or essence-function.

Essence-function is a characteristic traditional East Asian way of interpreting the world, society, events, phenomena, and the human being, that understands all things to have two contrasting, yet wholly contiguous and mutually containing aspects: (1) an underlying, deeper, more fundamental, hidden aspect, called in Chinese *ti* (體 K. *che*) usually translated into English as "essence," or "substance," and (2) a visibly manifest, surface aspect, called *yong* (用 K. *yong*) translated into English as "function," "activity," or "manifestation." This pair has many analogs in East Asian thought, one of the earliest and most readily recognizable being the "roots and branches" paradigm taught in the *Great Learning* (*Daxue* 大學), epitomized in the line that says "Things have their roots and branches, affairs have their end and beginning. When you know what comes first and what comes last, then you are near the Way." It can also be seen in Confucianism in the pair of "nature" (Ch. *xing* 性) and "emotions" (Ch. *qing* 情) which are foregrounded in the opening passage of the

Doctrine of the Mean, as well as the relationship between "humaneness" and "propriety" 禮 (Ch. *li*; K. *ye*) taught in the *Analects*.[31]

In the *Daode jing*, analogous pairs abound that express the dynamic relation of inner/outer, or fundamental/superficial, most prominent among these being the notions of the Way 道 (Ch. *dao*) and its power 德 (Ch. *de*), as well as the "white" 白 (Ch. *bai*) and the "black" 黑 (Ch. *hei*),[32] the uncarved block 樸 (Ch. *pu*) and the implements carved from it 器 (Ch. *qi*), etc. Later on, when Buddhism becomes thoroughly Sinicized, the same paradigm finds expression in a general manner in the pairs of nature 性 (Ch. *xing*)/aspects 相 (Ch. *xiang*), and in specifically in Huayan Buddhism, principle 理 (Ch. *li*) and phenomena 事 (Ch. *shi*).[33]

If we reflect on the two treatises presented above, we can see that although their positions differ regarding practice and interpretation of the doctrine, both Jeong and Gihwa fully agree on the basic essence-function structure of the human being, human development, and practice. Both assume the existence of a good mind that can be developed to a high level of purity and wisdom by engagement in a given set of practices. And they both must operate within the basic vocabulary of roots and branches, nature and emotions, principle and material force, or—essence and function. Neither proponent says that the other's *categories* are wrong—the categories themselves are accepted. It is in their interpretation and practice that they are wrong. Jeong accuses the Buddhists of being inconsistent in their definitions of these terms. Gihwa accuses the Confucians of being inconsistent in terms of doctrine and practice. But they are functioning in the same worldview, and thus they can argue.

Conclusion

Modern scholarship in both Korea and the West has long gotten past the mistaken perception that Buddhism was entirely suppressed during the Joseon Dynasty, as political leaders as well as ordinary people openly engaged in Buddhist practice.[34] The Confucian arguments had been pretty much exhausted in the *Bulssi japbyeon*, and no major polemical publications appeared from the Confucian side afterward. Buddhists, on the other hand, fully adopted Gihwa's "essential unity of the three teachings" approach. The most important representative work of this type is Hyujeong's *Samga Gwigam* 三家龜鑑 [35] which takes the three teachings as fitting together to form a large system of spiritual cultivation. Buddhism is taken as a more essential (*ti, che*) teaching, Confucianism as a more functional (*yong*) teaching, with Daoism occupying the place in between. It can be said that this general view of the three teachings has prevailed down to the present day.

Notes

1. The extensive mutual influence that occurred between Buddhism and Daoism is examined in depth in Sharf, *Coming to Terms with Chinese Buddhism*.

2. Charles Hartman's *Han Yü and the T'ang Search for Unity* (Princeton, 1986), provides an excellent study of Han's life and works.

3. A translation by Bryan Van Norden is online at http://faculty.vassar.edu/brvannor/Phil210/HanYu/On the Origin of the Way.pdf.

4. Translated in many anthologies. See for example, de Bary, *Sources of Chinese Tradition*, 583–585. Jeong Dojeon makes extensive use of these two essays in the final passages of his *Bulssi japbyeon*.

5. See Gregory, *Inquiry into the Origin of Humanity*, 35–36.

6. See *Message of the Mind*, 17.

7. The point is often made in present-day Chan historical scholarship that despite Chan's anti-textual rhetoric, Chan adherents ended up composing a voluminous literature that would be studied by succeeding generations. While this is true, we must still pay due consideration to the actual message of this literature, which points to a Buddhist teaching that emphasizes simplicity, intuitiveness, and directness in daily activity and which invariably casts "sutra-lecturers" in an inferior role to Chan masters of the "great function" 大用.

8. The four books of Confucian learning selected by Zhu Xi 朱熹 (1130–1200) as a core curriculum during the Song period. These are the *Analects* (*Lunyu* 論語), the *Mencius* (*Mengzi* 孟子), the *Great Learning* (*Daxue* 大學), and the *Doctrine of the Mean* (*Zhongyong* 中庸).

9. This canon was authorized by the emperor in 51 BCE and included the *Book of Poems* (*Shijing* 詩經), the *Book of Documents* (*Shujing* 書經), the *Book of Changes* 易經 (*Yijing*), the *Spring and Autumn Annals* (*Chunchiu* 春秋), and the *Record of Ritual* (*Liji* 禮記).

10. For a study of Zhou Dunyi, especially in the all-important context of his relationship to Zhu Xi, see Adler, *Reconstructing the Confucian DAO*.

11. It must be kept in mind here that when we say "Buddhism," we are referring specifically to the Chan Buddhism of the Song, which is a distinctive form of Buddhism.

12. The works of these two scholars are available in Chinese, but so far we do not have any translations of their works, other than small selected portions

contained in anthologies. The largest is that contained in Wing-tsit Chan's *Source Book*, 518–571.

13. See ibid, 554–555.

14. In using the term "exclusivism" here, I refer especially to the landmark work done on this topic by John Goulde in his 1984 PhD dissertation, "Anti-Buddhist Polemic in Fourteenth and Fifteenth Century Korea: The Emergence of Korean Exclusivism." In this work Goulde traces the developments of the Neo-Confucian polemic from their Chinese roots, through their failures and successes in Korea, to their final culmination in the creation of the Joseon Dynasty (1392–1910).

15. See Goulde, "Anti-Buddhist Polemic," 166–192, for a detailed description of the lives and works of the five above-mentioned figures, and others.

16. For a comprehensive treatment of Jeong Dojeon, see Han Yeong-u, *Jeong Dojeon sasang ui yeon-gu*. In English, see Chai-shik Chung, "Chŏng Tojŏn: 'Architect' of Yi Dynasty Government and Ideology." Also see the discussion of Jeong in the chapter "The Ideology of Reform" in John Duncan, *The Origins of the Chosŏn Dynasty*.

17. My English translation of this text is available in Muller (2015) in the Korean Classics Library. Muller, A. Charles. *Korea's Great Buddhist-Confucian Debate: The Treatises of Chŏng Tojŏn (Sambong) and Hamho Tŭkt'ong (Kihwa)*. Honolulu: University of Hawai'i Press, 2015.

18. Translated into English a few times, most recently and masterfully by Peter Gregory in 1995 with the title "Inquiry into the Origin of Humanity."

19. The *Sutra of Trapuṣa and Bhallika*. Not extant, but cited in many old texts. It is a Chinese indigenous sutra composed by Tanjing 曇靖 of the Northern Wei Dynasty during the reign period of Emperor Xiaowu of the Liu-Song Dynasty (453–464) in two fascicles. The text takes its name from its two main protagonists, merchants called Trapuṣa and Bhallika. These merchants are known elsewhere in the tradition. In the *Diwei Boli jing*, the two are described as well versed in knowledge of *yin* and *yang*, divination using tortoise-shells, and the *Yijing*. They meet the Buddha immediately after his awakening, and he teaches them that those who keep the five precepts will be reborn as human, while those who do the ten good deeds will be reborn in a heaven as a god (hence the name of the teaching, *rentian jiao* 人天r, for which the text was known in the doctrinal taxonomies of the period; see below); persons who commit various misdeeds will be born into the unfortunate destinies. The ten good deeds are correlated with the five Confucian virtues 五常; they are also correlated with various other sets of five, after the manner of the tradition of correlative cosmology native to Chinese culture.

20. The present-day Seongyun'gwan University in Seoul traces its roots to this academy.

21. A reference to Zhou Gongdan 周公旦 and Shao Gong 召公, two worthies who are said to have cooperated in the establishment of the Zhou Dynasty.

This passage is from the biographical sketch of Gihwa, entitled "Hamheo tang Deuktong hwasang haengjang," HBJ 7.250c6–11.

22. Gihwa's extant writings are contained in volume seven of the *Hanguk Bulgyo Jeonseo*. One of his major works, his commentary on the *Sutra of Perfect Enlightenment*, is translated and published by Muller with the same title, and his *Hyeonjeong non* is translated in Muller together with the *Bulssi japbyeon*. In terms of Gihwa's connection with Zongmi, the *Sutra of Perfect Enlightenment* is of great significance, as it was Zongmi's favorite text, which he commented on extensively. In Korea, it was Gihwa who wrote the definitive commentary on the sutra. Thus, Gihwa and Zongmi are closely linked in terms of mutual interest.

23. I stress this point in view of the fact that Han Yeong-u explicitly stated that "the *Hyeonjeong non* is *not* a refutation of the *Bulssi japbyeon*." See Han's *Jeong Dojeon*, 53, note. I see Han's view as being accurate only in a very strict sense. It is no doubt true that Gihwa did not sit down upon the publication of the *Japbyeon* and write an immediate, point-by-point rebuttal. In 1398, when Jeong wrote the *Japbyeon*, Gihwa would have been twenty-two, a mere novice in Buddhism. Yet even though Gihwa never directly names Jeong or his treatise, the fact that Jeong was a faculty member of the Seongyun'gwan at the time that Gihwa was a student would make it a virtual impossibility for Gihwa not to have read the text. Furthermore, in the *HJN* Gihwa directly replies to all of the *Japbyeon*'s accusations, using mimicry that directly alludes to Jeong's text.

24. In Zhu Xi's *Chuanxilu* 體用一原、顯微無間 is identified as a citation from Cheng Yi, but I have not yet located it.

25. "Correcting the internal with reverence, correcting the external with due-giving." is a repeated aphorism found in the texts of the Cheng brothers, Zhu Xi, and many other Neo-Confucianism writers, originally drawn from the *Yijing*: in the text of *kun* 坤, the second hexagram. See Wilhelm, 393.

26. Note that unlike the *Bulssi japbyeon*, the *Hyeonjeong non* does not have its own section headings supplied by its author. The heading titles below are my own suggestions.

27. *Henan Er Cheng yishu*, 15. Also see Wing-tsit Chan, *A Sourcebook in Chinese Philosophy*, 530, sec. 11. No doubt Gihwa focuses on this particular citation partly because it comes from the same section of Cheng Hao's *Yishu* that contains most of the philosophical arguments that form the basis for Jeong's arguments in the *Japbyeon*.

28. *Analects* 7:27 says: "When fishing, the Master would not use a net; when hunting, he would not shoot at a perched bird."

29. *Mencius* 1A:7 says: "The Superior Man keeps his distance from the kitchen, for if he hears the screams of slaughtered beasts, he cannot stand to eat their meat."

30. A good example for this point is the *Inquiry*, which includes an important chapter on the relationship of the three teachings. While Zongmi includes

Confucianism and Daoism in the status of a lower order than the Buddhist teachings, they are nonetheless taken to be part of a continuum of ultimately valid teachings. Like Gihwa, Zongmi was noted for the depth of his Confucian learning prior to his entering the Buddhist order.

31. Those who are familiar with the influential little book *The Secular as Sacred*, written a generation ago by Herbert Fingarette, will recognize that I am here disagreeing with the central tenet expressed in that work—that it is the concept of propriety that is most fundamental to the worldview of the Confucian classics, with *ren* having only secondary significance. Fingarette was duly praised for his interesting and profound analyses regarding the pervasiveness of the unconscious uses of propriety, not only in ancient Chinese society, but society in general. But in his prioritization of *li* over *ren*, he ignores a mountain of evidence in the Confucian classical texts that belies his position, as the textual evidence in the *Analects* that points to a greater "psychological interiority" for *ren* than the other virtues of the sage or *junzi* is overwhelming. And to merely state that *ren* is more internal, deeper than the other virtues is to stop short—as the relation between *ren* and the other virtues is quintessentially *tiyong* in its nature.

32. It is notable that in traditional East Asian thought, the relationship of black and white markedly distinguished from the common association seen in the West where black tends to be associated with evil and white with good. From the earliest periods of East Asian history, black (also written with the ideograph *xuan* 玄) has the connotations of depths, profundity, mastery, etc., while white tends to be associated with superficiality.

33. On the role of *li* in Chinese thought, see Ziporyn, "Coherence."

34. A recent solid treatment of this issue can be seen in Sem Vermeersch, "Yi Seong-gye and the Fate of the Goryeo Buddhist System."

35. English translation by Lee Yong-ho (1993).

Bibliography

Abbreviations

HBJ = Hanguk Bulgyo Jeonseo 韓國佛「全書
SBJ = Sambong Jip 三峯集
T = Taishō Shinshū Daizōkyō 大正新脩大藏經

Digital Texts

All Citations from the Thirteen Classics and Chinese Histories were found in the Academia Sinica on line Text Database at http://hanji.sinica.edu.tw.

All Citations from Zhou Dunyi, Zhang Zai, and Zhu Xi were located in the texts distributed by the Chinese Philosophical Etext archive at http://sangle.web.wesleyan.edu/etext/index.html.

All Citations from the Taishō Canon were found in the SAT Daizōkyō Text Database at http://21dzk.l.u-tokyo.ac.jp/SAT/ddb-bdk-sat2.php/.

Classical Texts

3.1. BUDDHIST

Gihwa 己和. *Daebanggwang wongak sudara youigyeong seorui* 大方廣圓覺修多羅了義經「誼 (Commentary on the *Sutra of Perfect Enlightenment*). HBJ 7.122–169.

Dafangguang yuanjue xiuduluo liaoyi jing 大方廣圓覺修多羅了義經 (Sūtra of Perfect Enlightenment). T 842.17.913a–922a.

Dasheng qixin lun 大乘起信論 (Treatise on Awakening of Mahāyāna Faith). T 1666.

Hamheo tang Deuktong hwasang eorok 涵「堂得通和「語「 (The Record of the Teachings of the Reverend Hamheo Deuktong). HBJ 7.226–250.

Hamheo tang Deuktong hwasang haengjang 涵「堂得通和「行「 (The Life of Reverend Hamheo Deuktong). HBJ 7.250–252.

Gihwa. *Hyeonjeong non* 顯正論 (Exposition of Orthodoxy). HBJ 7.217–225.

Zongmi. *Yuanren lun* 原人論 (Inquiry into the Origin of Humanity). T 1886.

3.2. NON-BUDDHIST

Er Cheng ji 二程集 (Collected Works of the Two Chengs). Beijing: Zhonghwa shu ju, 1981.

Henan Er Cheng yishu 河南二程遺書 (The Remaining Writings of the Two Cheng brothers of Honan). Taipei: Guoxue zhiben shu-cong si bai zhong, Taiwan shangwu yinshu kuanvol, 45.

Xunzi dong shi. Taipei: Guoxue zhiben shu-cong si bai zhong, Taiwan shangwu yinshu kuanvol, 34.

Yijing. Academia Sinica Text Archives, http://hanji.sinica.edu.tw.

Zhuzi yulei. Confucian Etext Archive, http://sangle.web.wesleyan.edu/etext/song-qing/song-qing.html.

Modern Works

Adler, Joseph A. *Reconstructing the Confucian DAO: Zhu XI's Appropriation of Zhou Dunyi*. Albany: State University of New York Press, 2014.

An Gyehyeon. *Han-guk bulgyo sasang sa yeon-gu*. Seoul: Dongguk University Press, 1982.
Chan, Wing-tsit, ed. *Neo-Confucian Terms Explained*. New York: Columbia University Press, 1986.
———. *A Source Book in Chinese Philosophy*. Princeton, NJ: Princeton University Press, 1969.
Ch'en, Kenneth. *Buddhism in China: A Historical Survey*. Princeton, NJ: Princeton University Press, 1964.
Ch'ien, Edward T. "The Neo-Confucian Confrontation with Buddhism: A Structural and Historical Analysis." *Journal of Chinese Philosophy* 15 (1988): 347–348
Choe Yeongseong. "Jeong Dojeon, Gweon Geun ui haksul sasang gwa yuhak sajeok wi chi." *Han-guk yuhak sasang sa, vol. II (Joseon jeongi pyeon)*, 19–53. Seoul: Asea munhwasa, 1995.
Jeong Dojeon. *Sambong jip*. 2 vols. Seoul: Gyeong-in munhwasa, 1987.
———. *Sambong jip*. Seoul: Minjok munhwa ch'ujinhoe, 1997.
Chung, Chai-shik. "Chŏng Tojŏn: 'Architect' of Yi Dynasty Government and Ideology." In *The Rise of Neo-Confucianism in Korea*, edited by Wm. Theodore de Bary. New York: Columbia University Press, 1985, 59–88.
de Bary, Wm. Theodore. *The Message of the Mind in Neo-Confucianism*. New York: Columbia University Press, 1989.
———, ed. *The Rise of Neo-Confucianism in Korea*. New York: Columbia University Press, 1985.
———, ed. *The Buddhist Tradition*. New York: The Modern Library, 1969.
———, ed. *Sources of Chinese Tradition*. New York: Columbia University Press, 1960.
Duncan, John B. *The Origins of the Chosŏn Dynasty*. Seattle: University of Washington Press, 2000.
Fingarette, Herbert. *Confucius: The Secular as Sacred*. New York: Harper and Row, 1972.
Fu, Charles. "Morality or Beyond: The Neo-Confucian Confrontation with Mahayana Buddhism." *Philosophy East and West* XXIII(3) (1973): 390–391.
Goulde, John Isaac. "Anti-Buddhist Polemic in Fourteenth and Fifteenth Century Korea: The Emergence of Confucian Exclusivism," PhD diss., Harvard University, 1985.
Gregory, Peter N. *Inquiry into the Origin of Humanity: An Annotated Translation of Tsung-mi's Yuan jen lun with a Modern Commentary*. Honolulu: University of Hawai`i Press, 1995.
Han Yeong-u. *Jeong Dojeon sasang ui yeon-gu*. Seoul: Han-guk munhwa yeon-gu so, 1973. Han-guk munhwa yeon-gu chongseovol.
———. "Jeong Dojeon ui ingan gwa sahoe sasang." *Jindan hakbo* 50 (1980): 123–135.

———. *Jeong Dojeon sasang ui yeon-gu*. Seoul: Seoul National University Press, 1985.
Hartman, Charles. *Han Yü and the T'ang Search for Unity*. Princeton, NJ: Princeton University Press, 1986.
Gim Jangdae. "Jeong Dojeon ui byeokbullon gwa gyeongse non." *Hanguk yuhaksa ui yihae*, 18–24. Seoul: Minjok munhwa sa, 1994.
Lee, Peter H., ed. *Sourcebook of Korean Civilization*, vol. I. New York: Columbia University Press, 1993.
Lee, Young-ho (Jinwol). "The Ideal Mirror of the Three Religions (Samga Kwigam) of Chŏnghŏ Hyujŏng." *Buddhist-Christian Studies* 15 (1995): 139–187.
Morohashi Tetsuji. *Dai kanwa jiten*. Tokyo: Taishūkan, 1930.
Muller, A. Charles, trans. *The Analects of Confucius*. http://www.acmuller.net/con-dao/analects.html, 2012.
———, trans. *Daode jing*. http://www.acmuller.net/con-dao/daodejing.html, 2009.
———, trans. *Doctrine of the Mean*. http://www.acmuller.net/con-dao/docofmean.html, 2012.
———, trans. *The Great Learning*. http://www.acmuller.net/con-dao/greatlearning.html, 2012.
———. *Hamhŏ Kihwa: A Study of his Major Works*. Stony Brook: State University of New York Press, 1993.
———. "Essence-Function (*t'i-yung*): Early Chinese Origins and Manifestations." *Bulletin of Toyo Gakuen University* 7 (1999): 93–106.
———. "The Buddhist-Confucian Conflict in the Early Chosŏn and Kihwa's Syncretic Response: The Hyŏn jŏng non." *The Review of Korean Studies* 2 (September 1999): 183–200. Seoul: Academy of Korean Studies.
———. *The Sutra of Perfect Enlightenment: Korean Buddhism's Guide to Meditation*. Albany: State University of New York Press, 1999.
———. "Tiyong and Interpenetration in the *Analects* of Confucius: The Sacred as Secular." *Bulletin of Toyo Gakuen University* 8 (2000): 93–106.
———. "The Centerpiece of the Goryeo-Joseon Buddhist-Confucian Confrontation: A Comparison of the Positions of the and the." *Journal of Korean Buddhist Seminar: Memorial Edition for the Late Professor Kim Chigyŏn* 9 (2003): 23–47
———. "The Great Confucian-Buddhist Debate." Buswell, Robert E., ed. *Religions of Korea in Practice*, 177–204. Princeton, NJ: Princeton University Press, 2007.
Sasaki, Ruth Fuller, et al. *A Man of Zen: The Recorded Sayings of Layman P'ang*. New York/Tokyo: Weatherhill, 1976.
Sharf, Robert H. *Coming to Terms with Chinese Buddhism: A Reading of the Treasure Store Treatise*. Honolulu: University of Hawai`i Press, 2002.
Shimada Kenji. *Shushigaku to Yōmeigaku*. Tokyo: Iwanami shoten, 1967.

Vermeersch, Sem. "Yi Seong-gye and the Fate of the Goryeo Buddhist System." *Korea Journal* 53(2) (2013): 124–154.
Wilhelm, Richard. *The I-Ching*. Princeton, NJ: Princeton University Press, 1973.
Wu, Joung-Sang. *Joseon jeongi bulgyo sasang sa yeon-gu* [Studies of the Buddhist Thought of the Early Joseon]. Seoul: Dongguk University Press, 1966.
Yun Sasun. "Jeong Dojeon seongnihak ui teukseong gwa pyeongga munje." *Jindan hakbo* 50 (1980): 151–160.
Ziporyn, Brook. "Li (Principle, Coherence) in Chinese Buddhism." *Journal of Chinese Philosophy* 30(3–4) (2003): 501–524.

Part II

Confucianism and Catholicism
Conflict and Assimilation

4

Catholic God and Confucian Morality
A Look at the Theology and Ethics of Korea's First Catholics

Don Baker

One of the most intractable questions for those who study the history of Christianity in Korea is "why did a group of young Confucians become Catholics before they had even met a Catholic missionary?" The religious answer is "the grace of God led them to belief in Him and His Church." However, that answer will not satisfy secular scholars. They expect an answer grounded in historical documentation. Therefore, in order to find an answer the broader world of scholarship will find acceptable, it is incumbent on us to delve deeper into the historical records of the first couple of decades of Catholicism in Korea to find out what those early Catholics tell us about their specific reason or reasons for leaving the non-theistic moral philosophy of Neo-Confucianism for the theistic religion of Catholicism.

Unfortunately, those records don't tell us very much. The most explicit explanation of the appeal of Catholicism to late eighteenth-century Confucians comes from Chŏng Yagyong, who provided that explanation after he had apostatized and needed to explain to his king what he described as a youthful error. Those who stayed faithful to Catholicism, and were literate enough to tell us about their faith, did not leave many written records behind before they were executed for their beliefs and religious practices. The primary exceptions are Chŏng Yagyong's brother Yakchong, who wrote a catechism from which we can deduce his reasons for becoming a Catholic, and the *Silk Letter* of Tasan's nephew-by-marriage Hwang Sayŏng, who provided an account of the first decade of Catholicism in Korea in which he touches briefly on what drew those first Catholics to their faith. There is a third text, believed by many to have been written by Tasan's friend and brother-in-law Yi Pyŏk, that also promises a glimpse of the beliefs of Korea's first Catholics, but the authenticity of that text is doubtful, as I will show later.

To understand the motivations behind the first Korean conversions to Christianity on Korean soil (this paper will not discuss the Korean Catholics in Japan in the early seventeenth century), it is necessary therefore to search for indirect evidence. In particular, it is necessary to identify different concepts of the ultimate ground of morality in pre-Catholic Korea and examine how that may have paved the way for the birth of monotheism in Korea in the 1780s. Since Korean intellectual life in the eighteenth century was dominated by Neo-Confucianism and its emphasis on questions of morality rather than questions of existence, we also need to look at the moral concerns of those first Catholics and how their ethical orientation may have led them to accept the notion of the existence of a Supreme Being.

Korea before Christianity

Korea has been transformed so much over the last century by urbanization, industrialization, and modernization, accompanied by the widespread adoption of Christianity, that it is difficult to conceive how different Korean beliefs, values, and fundamental assumptions were two and a half centuries ago. As a result, the radical nature of the break with tradition made by the first Christians is often underappreciated. It is important, therefore, to detail exactly how different Korea's religious culture was in the eighteenth century so that we can give the first Christians the credit they deserve for starting Korean cultural history down a new path.

First of all, we have to recognize that, contrary to a common misconception today, there was no monotheism in Korea before Catholicism arrived. Koreans back then either believed in the existence of many gods or they didn't believe in any God. The Neo-Confucian scholarly elite, out of whom the first Christians emerged, should not be labeled atheists, since they didn't take the question of the existence of God seriously enough to debate whether there was a God or not. Rather, they were non-theists who subscribed to a worldview in which God was irrelevant. The other residents of the peninsula, with the exception of some philosophical Buddhists, were polytheists. They believed that there were many supernatural personalities with whom they could interact, but none of those gods had the characteristics we associate with the Supreme Being.[1]

Nor was there a clear concept of the immortal human soul, or of life after death. There were vague notions in Confucianism that the vital energy (*ki*) of the dead lingered for a while after their death (hence the need for ancestral memorial services), and there was a vague belief in shamanism that the dead were in some sense still alive, at least to the extent that we could interact with them, but neither assumption was clearly formulated. Even the Buddhist doctrine of reincarnation did not have a very strong grip on the religious thinking of the majority of Koreans, especially the thinking of the Confucian scholar elite. Koreans may have gone to temples after the death of a loved one to pray for their rebirth in a better form of existence, but the concept of what that better form of existence might be was nebulous. Despite the persistence of Pure Land strands in Korean Buddhism, we don't find in pre-Christian Korea precisely articulated notions of what awaited us after we die, unlike the frequent and detailed references to Heaven and Hell we find in Christianity.

Not only was the religious orientation of pre-Christian Korea quite different from the monotheism and belief in an afterlife that is central to the religious beliefs of many in Korea today, the very notion of religion, and of a religious community, was radically different as well. Religion today, both Christian and non-Christian, tends to be defined as congregational and confessional. Groups of people form communities (congregations) to affirm their shared beliefs through communal participation in ritual affirmations of their common faith.

It would be appropriate to label such groups faith-based communities. In pre-Christian Korea, however, instead of faith-based communities, we find ritual-based communities. First of all, there was no notion of separate and distinct groups of laypeople who identify with one, and only one, religious community. Except for religious professionals such as Buddhist monks, Confucian officials, and shamans, the average Chosŏn-era Korean could call upon a shaman for help, pray at a Buddhist temple, and even participate in a Confucian ritual all on the same day with no sense of self-contradiction.

That is because, first of all, we do not see in pre-Christian Korea the emphasis on doctrine we see today. What you believed was less important than what you did. In certain situations, customs and social pressure required people to engage in ritual behavior. But such behavior was usually on an ad-hoc basis for specific purposes, such as honoring an ancestor or asking a supernatural being to cure a disease. Participation in a religious ritual was not seen as an affirmation of the religious beliefs underlying that religion, for a couple of reasons. First of all, the religious beliefs that justified such rituals were not usually clearly articulated. Second, many of the lay participants were not particularly concerned about whether those beliefs were true or not. Much of the time, their participation was of the "just-in-case" variety. To fail to engage in the expected ritual behavior was seen more as a failure to conform to behavioral norms than as a deliberate rejection of the religious assumptions shaping the ritual.

This does not mean that, in pre-Christian Korea, doctrine was irrelevant. There are many instances of Korean Confucians criticizing Buddhist belief in reincarnation, for example. However, the primary criticism of Buddhism was behavioral, not doctrinal. Buddhism was accused of encouraging people to neglect their obligations to society. The most important obligations were those linked to filial piety and loyalty, values that dominated ethical discourse under the hegemony of Confucianism that prevailed during Chosŏn times. Both of those values, as well as the other ethical values found in Confucianism, are directed toward interactions within the human community (including deceased members of that community). This is quite different from the Judeo-Christian-Islamic approach in which obedience to the will of God is a core ethical imperative.

There are two important implications of the anthropocentrism (rather than theocentrism) and relative lack of interest in doctrine in pre-Christian Korea. First of all, when encountering new philosophical, religious, or ethical assertions, pre-Christian Koreans tended to ask not whether those ideas were logically true but whether or not belief in those ideas led to appropriate behavior. When appropriate behavior was defined along Confucian lines, this emphasis on the behavioral rather than the logical implications of truth-claims raised barriers to the acceptance of Christianity, which is firmly grounded in such truth-claims as the existence of God Above and that He sent His Son to dwell among human beings on earth and to be crucified in order to save us from our sins.[2]

Second, the lack of communities of lay believers with a strong sense of forming a separate and distinct community within the larger society meant that there was no demand for a strict separation of church and state. Because of the blurring of boundaries within society, there was also a blurring of the boundary between society and the state. As a result, the state was accepted as the prime authority in matters of religious ritual, though it tolerated some differences in religious beliefs. This led to the ritual hegemony of the state to which even Buddhists and shamans had to acquiesce.[3] No one was allowed to refuse the ritual demands of the state on the grounds of their own personal religious beliefs.

This is a religious culture with defining assumptions so different from what we see in Catholicism that, at first, it is difficult to see how Catholicism managed to take root on Korean soil. It is especially difficult to see how it began with members of the non-theistic Confucian scholar elite, and did so without the benefit of nurturing from missionaries on the ground in Korea itself.

The Soil on Which the Christian Seed Fell

There were two features of eighteenth-century Korea that may have made one small group of Korean scholars more open to the radical shift toward belief in an actual God above. Both created a sense of crisis, of a failure of the traditional worldview to provide guidelines for dealing with the world as they experienced it at the end of the eighteenth century. One such feature is demographic—a rising death rate may have given them a vague sense of unease that there was something wrong.[4] There may have also been a rising sense among a small group of Confucian scholars from the *namin* (Southerner) philosophical-political faction that the Confucian promise of self-perfectibility may be flawed. That particular segment of the Korean Confucian community, the group out of which Catholicism emerged, appears to have developed a growing sense of human moral frailty, which may have been heightened by their recognition that the world around them was not the way Confucianism told them it should be if they were properly virtuous.[5]

The traditional explanations for those conversions to Catholicism among the yangban elite in the last quarter of the eighteenth century are unconvincing. One common explanation, enshrined in such popular textbooks as Yi Ki-baik's *Korea, Old and New*, is that conversions to Catholicism were a form of protest against the oppressive "feudalism" of the Chosŏn Dynasty. As that textbook puts it, "what they sought from

Catholicism was a means to grapple with the host of evils that then beset Chosŏn's social and political order. . . . [they] took fresh hope for creating a heavenly kingdom on earth through belief in the new religion."[6]

However, aside from the issue of whether or not the Chosŏn Dynasty can be accurately characterized as "feudal" (in non-Marxist historiography in the West, feudal is a term reserved for decentralized government in which the military is in control), an examination of statements made by Catholics under interrogation by government authorities, of the earliest Korean Catholic publications and Catholic libraries, and of the behavior of Korean Catholics well into the twentieth century uncovers no evidence of any hidden political agenda. Catholics were not secret modernizers. They accepted the patriarchal and stratified structure of traditional Chosŏn society. Moreover, they recognized the authority of the state, with one exception. Their one challenge to the existing political order was their demand that they be allowed to practice their religious beliefs as they best saw fit, with no interference from the state. That was a radical demand,[7] but it was not a rejection of the entire political, social, and economic system that governed Chosŏn Korea.

Another explanation we can dispense with is that Koreans were drawn to Catholicism by the appeal of Western science and technology.[8] Though we find a few examples of people reading Jesuit-authored books of natural philosophy as well as Western books on theology, with the conspicuous exceptions of Yi Pyŏk (1754–1786), Yi Kahwan (1742–1801), and Chŏng Yagyong (1762–1836), all of whom left the beleaguered Catholic community, most of the people who were involved with Catholicism when it first entered Korea did not show any particular interest in books on mathematics, astronomy, or medicine.

Nor do we see Catholicism in the late eighteenth century using modern medicine and education to attract people to the church. In their first decades on the peninsula, Catholics established no medical clinics or modern schools, and, even if they had, the medicine in those clinics would not have been any more effective than the Hanŭi (traditional Chinese-style medicine) Koreans had access to at that time; and the education in those schools would not have had much appeal, since it would not have helped them navigate the shoals of modern life (which had not yet reached Korea at that time, anyway.)[9]

If neither political dissatisfaction nor the appeal of Western science and technology explains those eighteenth-century conversions to Catholicism, what does? I would like to suggest that the motives of those first

Catholics were moral and religious. They turned to Christianity for a solution to a perceived moral crisis.

What was this moral crisis and why was it so strong that it gave Catholic proselytizing publications, which had been circulating in Korea since the early seventeenth century, new persuasive power? And why did the religious message of those missionary publications from China strike a responsive chord in only one small group of Confucian scholars, while most of the rest of society found Catholicism not only unappealing but appalling as well?

The answer to the first part of those questions lies in some demographic changes in eighteenth-century Korea. Most students of Korean history are unaware that Korea entered into a demographic crisis in the second half of the eighteenth century. Pre-industrial societies normally grow at a rate of 0.5 to 1 percent a year, except for those years when they are decimated by war, serious epidemics, or widespread famine. Before 1750 the Korean population usually had been able to rebound from such demographic setbacks with a healthy growth rate of 0.5 percent or more. That is not the case after 1750, however. After a series of famines and epidemics between 1747 and 1765, the Korean population between 1765 and 1777 was able to rebound at an annual rate of only 0.38 percent. From 1780 through 1799 the record is even worse. The growth rate is only 0.20 percent a year.[10]

The official census figures on which I base those percentages probably should not be taken literally. However, the trends they show probably are an accurate reflection of whether the Korean population was growing or shrinking and how fast or slow it was doing so. Kwŏn Taehwan and Shin Yongha estimate that the actual population in Korea may have been 18,657,000 in 1750, 18,443,000 in 1800, and 16,476,000 in 1850.[11] Whatever the figures, the trend is the same. Sometime in the second half of the eighteenth century the Korean people began to lose the capacity to reproduce themselves at a healthy rate.

What caused this sharp drop in Korea's population growth rate? The weather may have been one factor. In the early part of the sixteenth century Korea entered into a little ice age from which it did not emerge until the end of the nineteenth century. Kim Yŏnok and Kim Chaeho have argued that this drop in the average temperature in Korea brought an increase in the number and the severity of droughts and floods on the peninsula, which had a negative impact on agricultural productivity.[12] Moreover, the cooling of the Korean climate may have had an even more insidious side effect. A drop in the average temperature may have provided a more favorable environment for the survival and spread of viruses, particularly those viruses that cause smallpox and measles.[13] There is evidence that both measles and smallpox, which had long been present on the peninsula, became much more deadly in the seventeenth and eighteenth centuries.

Why did they suddenly become more deadly? An earlier growth in the population of the peninsula may have finally given both viruses the population density they needed to move from one human host to another easily enough to produce an epidemic, in the case of measles, or to become firmly entrenched and endemic, in the case of smallpox.[14] In addition, Korea may have had encountered a more virulent strain of the measles virus in the seventeenth and eighteenth centuries than it had encountered in the past. Tasan Chŏng Yagyong reported that in 1613 a new rash-producing fever reached Korea, created a deadly epidemic, and then started reappearing at fairly regular intervals fifty years later. Tasan may have been wrong about the 1613 epidemic. The disease that took so many lives that year was probably scarlet fever.[15] However, the virus that attacked Korea in 1668, and reappeared in 1680, 1692, 1706, 1718, 1729, 1752, 1775, and 1786 probably was the new virulent strain of measles that Tasan and other observers said it was.[16]

Both diseases are seen as childhood diseases now, but in the eighteenth century they were quite deadly. Another disease that may also share in the responsibility for the declining rate of population growth was a less visible killer. Malaria did not strike in epidemics, but it killed nonetheless, especially in the southern provinces where flooded rice paddies provided favorable conditions for mosquitoes. Besides smallpox, measles, and malaria, famine may also have adversely affected population growth in the eighteenth century. From the middle of the seventeenth century through the nineteenth century, Korea was hit by a famine on average every 3.6 years, with the famines of 1696–98, 1718, 1732–34, 1742, 1757, 1763, and 1784 having a particularly noticeable adverse impact on the size of the population in the eighteenth century.[17] Epidemics were even more frequent, averaging one every 2.6 years.[18]

This deadly combination of measles epidemics, endemic smallpox, malaria, and frequent famine is probably the reason Korea suffered such a sharp decline in population growth rates in the latter half of the eighteenth century. After growing, according to official census figures, from 5,922,510 in 1702 to 7,340,318 in 1747, a gain of around 1.4 million in 45 years, Korea added only 105,938 more to the census roles over the next 52 years, growing to a population of only 7,412,686 by 1799.[19] That steep decline in the annual population growth rate in Korea means that, in the last half of the eighteenth-century, more and more Koreans were witnessing the deaths of more and more family members and friends. Under almost constant assault by disease and famine, grieving the untimely death of children, spouses, relatives, and neighbors, made fearful of the future, unsure of whether they or their loved ones could survive for another day, month, or year, many Koreans did what people the world over have done in times of mental distress when the world turns incomprehensible, unpredictable, and uncontrollable. They turned to religion.

The Confucian yangban ruling elite believed that they shared some of the responsibility for suffering caused by disease and famine, since their Neo-Confucianism taught that such disturbances in the natural order were a reflection of moral failings among the ruling elite. That connection between moral and cosmic order was enshrined in the official prayers offered to placate the spirits of pestilence, prayers that explicitly stated that epidemics were caused by human immorality rather than by misbehaving spirits.[20]

In 1775 Ch'ae Chegong (1720–1799), a prominent politician under Kings Yŏngjo (r. 1724–1776) and Chŏngjo (r. 1776–1800), echoed that moral explanation in a prayer he offered in the hope it would end a measles epidemic raging while he was governor of P'yŏngan province. He prayed:

> The measles epidemic that started this summer is killing 2 or 3 out of every ten it attacks. Grandmothers are mourning their grandsons, and mothers are grieving over the loss of their sons. There is so much crying heard in the streets that men want to stop up their ears to block out that sorrowful sound. More have died than even in the terrible epidemic of 1752. Is this the will of the Lord Above? How could such an august spirit wish us such harm?
>
> I know I have not been perfect. Even since I have been in charge of this district, I have not been diligent enough and have failed to take proper care of those I have been given responsibility over. I have lacked virtue and have failed to carry out my duties properly. Instead, I have just sat back and made myself comfortable. That must be why you are so angry with

me, oh Great Lord Above. That must be why you have inflicted this plague on my charges. You have done this as a warning to me to insure that I do not stay this lazy and self-assured. So I can understand why you would punish me. But why must you make others suffer as well?

You are the loving parent of humanity. Do you not feel their suffering? Do you not hear them crying? Can you not take pity on them?

I pray to you, oh Lord Above, quickly expel those evil spirits which are bringing so much pain to the people and help me become a better shepherd for my charges. Let us have no more epidemics and no more suffering inflicted upon the people.[21]

Ch'ae Chegong was a *namin*, a member of a political faction whose philosophical beliefs were such that his feelings of personal moral guilt for natural disorders were probably even stronger than they would have been if he had belonged to another faction. As a *namin*, Ch'ae had inherited the philosophical stance of T'oegye Yi Hwang (1501–1570) and Sŏngho Yi Ik (1681–1763), a stance which placed stricter ethical demands on Confucian scholars than other Korean interpretations of Neo-Confucian did and thus made its adherents unusually sensitive to personal moral frailty and exceptionally aware of the difficulties they faced in meeting their moral responsibilities, despite the Neo-Confucian assumption that human beings were innately virtuous.

T'oegye Yi Hwang (1501–1570) and his *namin* disciples based their Neo-Confucian philosophy on an awareness, acquired through attempts to cultivate sagehood, of how difficult it was to consistently adhere to demanding Confucian standards of selflessness and self-control. (We can see this tendency toward concern over human moral frailty in T'oegye's philosophical stance in which he expressed distrust of the *ki* of the human body and the emotions it generated and emphasized instead *li*, the immaterial moral organizing force in the cosmos.)[22] The result was an ethical orientation that, over the centuries, came more and more to resemble a form of asceticism, with a strong stress on the control of desire.

Sŏngho Yi Ik (1682–1763) was part of this increasingly ascetic Neo-Confucian tradition. Sŏngho asked, "[W]here did evil come from then? What led the intrinsically good human nature astray?" Man's desire to avoid hunger and cold and to be comfortable was Sŏngho's answer. In other words, it was the human body, and the desires of that body for personal pleasure, which kept men from becoming sages. Sŏngho's deep suspicion of the body and its temptations led him to advocate severe restraint on the exercise of even those normal human desires for food and sex which are necessary to the survival of the human race. For example, he encouraged husbands and wives to sleep in separate rooms in order to make it easier for men to resist the pull of the flesh. He also suggested that men eat less than one full bowl of rice at every meal so that they would be accustomed to leaving physical desires less than completely satisfied.[23]

Sŏngho's ascetic attribution of human moral frailty to the fact that men inhabit physical bodies struck a responsive chord among many of the *namin*, who were searching for an explanation for the fact that, though they were all trying hard to become sages, none of them had succeeded in doing so. Yi Pyŏk, who never met Sŏngho but considered himself his disciple nonetheless, was a staunch supporter of his argument that the human body was the root of everything that is evil. In a conversation with his friend Chŏng Yagyong in 1784, Yi argued that all that is good in human thought and action is produced by our immaterial human nature, and thus comes from *li*, but everything that is generated by our physical form comes from *ki* and thus is untrustworthy.[24]

This *namin* tendency toward moral frustration and guilt was reinforced by the political situation in which the *namin* found themselves in the second half of the eighteenth century. The *namin* were a political as well as a philosophical faction. They wanted to share the reins of power with the king. As orthodox Neo-Confucians, they believed that those who were the most moral, the least selfish, were the most qualified to serve the king as his top officials. However, since the 1680s they had lost a series of political battles in Seoul and were forced for most of the eighteenth century to stand on the sidelines as important political decisions were made. The most important decision in which they had no effective input was the decision by King Yŏngjo in 1762 to have his son and heir killed.[25]

According to Neo-Confucian reasoning, there could be only one underlying explanation for the *namin*'s political impotence. They must have lacked the virtue necessary to win the confidence of the king. The only solution was to work even harder than before at eradicating all selfish thoughts and deeds and all improper attitudes and actions from their lives so that a tragedy such as the death of Crown Prince Sado would not occur again. In other words, they had to strive for moral perfection. Since that is a goal unobtainable to mere mortals, the *namin* were doomed by the standards they set for themselves to never-ending moral frustration.

Beset by repeated pangs of guilt for failing to achieve the sagehood Neo-Confucianism told them they could and should achieve, they were ready to listen to suggestions of new approaches to moral cultivation or even to a new interpretation of Confucianism which could offer them a way out of their dilemma. In the last quarter of the eighteenth century, some *namin* found themselves facing a psychological, spiritual, and moral crisis brought on by the rising death rate among their family and friends, by the increasing ethical demands made on them by the increasing asceticism of T'oegye Neo-Confucianism, and by the continuing political frustration of their political impotence. It was the search for a solution to this ethical crisis that made them receptive to the Catholic message they encountered in books written by Jesuit missionaries in China.

Catholicism Takes Root in Korea

The first person we know of to be attracted to the religious message in Jesuit-authored books was Yi Pyŏk. The *Silk Letter*, written by the early Catholic Hwang Sayŏng (1775–1801) to provide details to the bishop in Beijing of the fervor even unto death of Korea's first Catholics, tells us that Yi had been secretly reading some Catholic religious works from China and wanted to learn more about Catholicism. He learned that his friend Yi Sŭnghun (1756–1801) was traveling to Beijing in 1783 as part of a diplomatic mission and asked him to try to bring back books. We are told that Yi Pyŏk said to Yi Sŭnghun, "There is a Catholic church in Beijing and in the church is a Western missionary. Go and see him and ask for a guide to Catholic teachings. In addition, you should ask to be baptized. The Western missionaries will certainly be pleased to see you and will treat you well. Then you will be able to get a lot of interesting and enjoyable things from them. You must not come back empty handed."[26]

Yi Sŭnghun took Yi Pyŏk's advice. He visited a Catholic church several times while he was in Beijing, was instructed in the essentials of the Catholic faith and was baptized, and then returned to Korea as Peter Lee, a fervent Catholic. Soon he and Yi Pyŏk began sharing their faith with friends and relatives. Among those friends and relatives was Tasan Chŏng Yagyong, a brother-in-law of Yi Pyŏk's sister.

Tasan and his brother Yakchŏn (1758–1816) joined Yi Pyŏk at a memorial service for Yi's sister in April (by the lunar calendar) of 1784. (She had been married to Chŏng Yakhyŏn (1751–1821), another Chŏng brother, but had died in 1780.[27]) During a boat ride on their way back to Seoul from that traditional Confucian ritual in the countryside, Yi Pyŏk shared with Tasan and his brother what he had learned from the Catholic books Yi Sŭnghun had brought back from Beijing. After they reached Seoul, Yi showed them some of his collection of Catholic works, including the introduction to Catholic teachings by Matteo Ricci (1552–1610) *Tianzhu shiyi* [*The True Significance of the Lord of Heaven*] and a guide to Catholic ethics, *Qike* [*Seven Victories*] by Diego de Pantoja (1571–1618). Tasan later confessed that he and his brothers found the conversation on the boat fascinating and those books a pleasure to read. He wrote that they were intrigued by the information Yi said those books contained about the creation of the universe, about the difference between material and spiritual beings, and about life and death.[28] Tasan was only twenty-two years old at that time.

Later that year Tasan and his brother Yakchŏn were baptized by their brother-in-law Yi Sŭnghun (he was married to their sister) and became some of the first members of Korea's nascent Catholic community. Yakchŏn went on to convert his cousin Yun Chi-ch'ung (1759–1791), and his younger brother Yakchong (1760–1801).[29] In 1790, however, Korean Catholics, who still were without a missionary or a priest, learned via a letter from the bishop in Beijing that Catholics were not allowed to use a spirit tablet (a tablet on which were inscribed the names of the deceased being honored) in an ancestral memorial rite. Since that tablet was an essential part of that ritual display of filial piety and was mandated by the government, upon learning this news Yi Sŭnghun withdrew from active leadership of the Catholic church, turning his responsibilities over to someone Yi Pyŏk had converted, Kwŏn Ilsin (1742–1791).[30] Chŏng Yagyong and his brother Yakchŏn also withdrew from further participation in Catholic activities after the announcement of the ban on Confucian ancestor rites, although their brother Yakchong, the last one of the three to convert to Catholicism, remained an active leader of the Church until his execution in the 1801 persecution.[31] Yi Pyŏk was saved from having to choose between his Confucian ritual obligations and his new faith, having passed away four years earlier.[32]

Because of the conditions under which Catholicism emerged in Korea, because of the hostility it endured from both the government and society at large, Korea's first Catholics did not leave us much written evidence of what precisely they believed and why they came to believe it. Most of the information we can glean on the motivations and beliefs of Korea's first Catholics come from anti-Catholic documents such as government interrogation records and statements by apostates. That information has to be supplemented by the catechism that Chŏng Yakchong wrote, the *Jugyo yoji* [*Essentials of the Lord's Teachings*], and statements smuggled out of prison by Yun Chich'ung and Yi Suni (1782–1802), along with letters Yi Sŭnghun sent to the priests in Beijing. Those are about the only pieces of authentic writing by those Catholics themselves.

A few decades ago some scholars claimed to have discovered a text Yi Pyŏk composed sometime during the two years between when he became a Catholic believer and when he died.[33] However, that text, known as the *Sŏnggyo yoji* [*Essentials of the Sacred Teachings*], is probably not authentic. It was never mentioned in Catholic discussion of Yi Pyŏk's life in the years after his death, not even in the *Silk Letter* of Hwang Sayŏng or the discussion of Yi Pyok in Dallet's magisterial survey of the early history of Korean Catholicism.[34] Moreover, the oldest version we have appears in a collection of Catholic writings attributed to Yi Sŭnghun that was written (some say copied from an earlier source) in the 1930s.[35] We can therefore dismiss the *Sŏnggyo yoji* as a trustworthy guide to the thinking of Korea's first Catholics.

We can, however, turn to an anti-Catholic source for information on what those first Catholics believed, even if it doesn't tell us why they believed it. In 1785, right after the birth of Korea's first Catholic community, An Chŏng-bok (1712–1791), one of the leaders of the *namin*, wrote down his version of a conversation with one of those early Catholics. His conversation partner was probably based on conversations he had with his son-in-law Kwŏn Ilsin, although An doesn't name him. However, in An's version of their conversation, Kwŏn was convinced to return to the Confucian fold, which didn't happen. Instead, Kwŏn was arrested in 1791 for his role in creating a Catholic community. He was beaten so severely during his interrogation that he died on his way into exile.[36]

In this fictionalized conversation, called *Chŏnhak mundap* [*A Conversion on Heavenly Learning*], An reveals that he is aware that Catholics believed not only in one God above who is the Creator of the universe but also that God rewards the virtuous with eternal life in Heaven after they die but punishes the wicked for eternity in hell. He also reveals awareness of Christian belief in Jesus, the messiah, who is God but lived among human beings in Judea, as well as of Christian belief in Satan. He even refers to the Christian belief that Adam and Eve were the first human beings and that it was to wash away the stain of their original sin on their descendants that Jesus descended from Heaven to earth and was crucified on our behalf.[37] An could only have learned this much detail about Catholic beliefs from the younger Catholic *namin* he knew well.

Despite Yi Sŭnghun's confession in a 1789 letter to a priest in Beijing that he had only a limited knowledge of Catholic doctrine when he was baptized in 1784,[38] it is clear that Yi and those he converted were aware of such basic doctrines as the Incarnation and the Atonement. Yet we do not find detailed explanations of such Catholic doctrines when Catholics tried to explain their faith to government interrogators. In fact, it is hard to find any mention at all of Jesus, or of Adam and Eve, or of Satan in the answers Catholics gave when they were asked what they believed. Instead, we find those early Catholics referring to God not so much as the Creator than as God the Father to whom we owed the traditional Confucian virtue of filial piety.

The First Confirmed Martyr

The first interrogation records we have are those of Yun Chich'ung. Paul Yun (he is known to Catholics by his baptismal name) was raised to the status of Blessed Paul Yun, one step below full sainthood, by Pope Francis when he visited Korea in August, 2014. Yun earned that honor by his fidelity to Catholic beliefs even at the cost of his own life. Before he was beheaded in December, 1791, he was given many opportunities to renounce his faith but instead explained why he could not do that.

Yun was arrested, tortured, and then executed because he had obeyed the directive from the bishop in Beijing to forgo the mandated spirit tablet in mourning a deceased ancestor. The bishop had sent a letter to the small Catholic community in Korea informing them that the Pope had determined that placing a spirit tablet on a memorial altar was a form of idolatry and therefore was forbidden by the laws of God. Soon afterwards, Yun's mother passed away, making him the first in the Catholic community to have a parent die after that message was received. When he mourned his mother without that spirit tablet, he discovered how seriously the Confucian government of Chosŏn Korea took its responsibility to ensure that all its subjects performed the rituals in the manner the government expected them to be performed.

Confronted by the magistrate of Chinsan County, in which Yun lived, and later by the governor of his province of Chŏlla, he insisted over and over again, despite strong urging from both of them, that even though he preferred not to disobey a command from his king, he had no choice. He had to continue to refuse to erect a spirit tablet for his mother. He admitted that virtue required people to be obedient to their rulers and to display filial love toward their parents. However, he argued those ethical values were not absolute in themselves. Instead, "the basis of loyalty to the ruler is the laws of God, and the basis of filial piety toward one's parents is also the laws of God."[39] This was a radical contradiction of the core of Confucian thought. Rather than accepting the virtues of filial piety and loyalty as the standards by which all else was to be judged, Yun claimed that filial piety and loyalty were themselves only conditional obligations, binding on human beings only because God, the source of all value, had so willed. This granted primacy to doctrine (the belief that God existed) over the Confucian focus on proper behavior.

Paul Yun did not completely escape the behavioral orientation of the Confucian world that placed concern for what should be done ahead of concern for what should be believed. When told to provide a short summary of Catholic teachings, he replied, not with an account of the divinity of Jesus Christ and His power to redeem men from their sins, but with the statement that "What we practice can be reduced to the Ten Commandments and the Seven Virtues."[40] Catholicism is thus reduced by Yun to its moral commands and is presented as essentially a collection of guidelines for ethical behavior

Nevertheless, Yun's view of Catholic morality placed him in fatal conflict with his Confucian society, since he placed man's obligations to his God ahead of his duties to his fellow man. Yun was asked by his interrogator to state the Ten Commandments by which Catholics regulated their conduct. The governor immediately noticed that there was no specific mention of the relationship between subjects and their rulers and demanded an explanation of this lack from Yun, who replied that the king was the father of his realm and his subjects owed him and his officials the same respect and loyalty they owed their parents as enjoined by the Fourth Commandment. Yun was ordered to write down in greater detail the Catholic principles of morality and was warned to "emphasize the principles of loyalty to the king and filial piety so that you might be able to save your life."[41]

Yun responded with a written statement in which he declared that the Lord of Heaven was the Creator and Father of all men. Since he recognized God as his Father, he could not disobey any of His orders. God had forbidden His children to have ancestral tablets in their homes or to offer meat and wine to the spirits of the dead as represented by such tablets. He could do nothing but obey.[42] Why should those who are only obeying the commands of their God in the privacy of their own homes be threatened with capital punishment and charged with defying the laws of the land?[43]

Yun sealed his fate when he thus defied the ritual hegemony of the traditional Korean state. He failed to convince the government officials with whom he argued that the state should recognize limits to its own reach by refraining from interfering in the private ritual and religious practices of its subjects. Yun was ahead of his time with his call for a separation of church and state.

Of note is that Yun never mentions Jesus in his exchanges with his interrogator. Yun must have known of the core Catholic doctrines of the Trinity, the Incarnation, and the Atonement. Yun may have felt it would be too difficult to get his interrogators to understand those Catholic beliefs or, it may be that, for him, as someone raised in the Confucian ethical tradition, the most important feature of Catholic teachings was the requirement to show respect for, and obedience to, God the Father in heaven—just as Confucians were required to show respect for, and obedience to, their parents and rulers on earth. Whatever reason Yun had for focusing in his interrogation on God the Father, since he never mentions Jesus we do not know if he was drawn to Catholicism by the pull of God the Father as the object of supreme filial piety, if he was attracted by the promise of eternal life (which he doesn't mention to his interrogator), or if he converted to Catholicism because of the powerful example of love for humanity shown in the life and death of Jesus.

The Apostate

The absence of any mention of Jesus is more understandable in the case of Tasan Chŏng Yagyong. Even though Tasan had become a Catholic (with the baptismal name of John) before his cousin Yun had, Tasan left the church when he learned of the prohibition against spirit tablets and saw the price that had to be paid to obey that church directive.[44] However, even after he left the Catholic community in 1790, if not earlier, Tasan continued to believe in God and inserted God, whom he called Sangje (the Lord Above) rather using the Catholic term Chŏnju (the Lord of Heaven), into the commentaries on the Confucian Classics he wrote over the next forty years. It is unclear, however, how much Tasan's concept of God had in common with the Catholic understanding.⁴⁵

As Tasan used the term, Sangje does not appear to be the Christian God. Sangje did not send his only begotten Son to earth to die for the sins of humanity. Sangje did not threaten sinners with the eternal fires of hell or promise eternal happiness in heaven to the virtuous. Sangje did not provide sacred texts human beings could read to learn the will of God. Sangje did not demand that human beings praise Him in sacred song and ritual. And Sangje did not create the universe out of nothing.

At times, Tasan depicts Sangje as responsible for the normative principles that define and generate appropriate interactions in the natural world as well as within the human community. And Sangje is said to have given human beings the inclination toward the good that defines them as human beings. But those are roles Heaven, in the guise of *li* (normative principles), had assumed in traditional Confucianism. Tasan simply added to those traditional attributes of Heaven an insistence that the Lord Above was an actual supernatural personality.

Tasan insisted that Sangje was a personality rather than an impersonal principle for a couple of reasons. First of all, he believed that the traditional Confucian virtue of "reverence" had been misinterpreted by Neo-Confucians as mindfulness, an inner state of mind. Reverence, he insisted, needed to be directed outward, toward an object for that reverence. *Li* could not provide such an object. Sangje could.⁴⁶

Second, steeped in the Confucian moral vision as he was, Tasan defined morality in terms of interpersonal interactions in which the common good rather than individual benefit was the guiding intention. Such an interpersonal morality, in his view, should be grounded in a personality who always and everywhere was motivated by the common good. In other words, Tasan's ethical vision required a being who was the personification of virtue by being nothing other than objective subjectivity (a personality who was always objective) and subjective objectivity (objectivity rooted in a personality). That being was Sangje.

That is the full extent of Tasan's theology, if it is acceptable to use that term for a rather limited discussion of the attributes of Sangje. What is important to note here is that Sangje's attributes are not what Tasan is primarily concerned about. Rather, he is concerned with the practical implications for human beings of belief in Sangje. True to his Confucian roots, Tasan prioritized human behavior over human beliefs. He determined whether ideas and assertions were true or not by whether or not they encouraged appropriate behavior. He believed that belief in Sangje had precisely that effect. He noted:

> There is no human being born on this earth without base desires. What keeps us from following those desires and doing whatever we feel like doing? It is the fear that our misbehavior will be noticed. Noticed by whom? Whose gaze keeps us in a state of constant caution and apprehension? We are cautious and apprehensive because we know there are enforcement officers responsible for making sure rules are followed. We are cautious and apprehensive because we know our sovereign can punish us if we behave improperly. If we did not think there was someone watching us, would we not simply abandon all sense of moral responsibility and just do whatever we felt like doing? . . .
> But what makes us behave properly even in the privacy of our own room and make sure that even our thoughts are proper thoughts? The only reason a superior person is watchful over his thoughts and behavior even in the privacy of his own room is that he knows that there is a Lord Above (*Sangje*) watching him.[47]

In a letter Tasan wrote to King Chŏngjo in 1797, several years after he had abandoned his youthful involvement with Korea's Catholic community, he tried to explain why he had made what he, after the fact, called a mistake.

> When I read Catholic writings, I was still a young man, barely out of my teens. . . . I was entranced by their promises of life after death and was impressed by their calls for rigorous self-discipline. The twists and turns of their fancy rhetoric fooled me into thinking that what they were offering was just another form of Confucianism.[48]

Even though Tasan is speaking here as an apostate, not as a devout Catholic, it is still possible to extract from this letter and his use of the notion of Sangje in Confucian contexts why he was a Catholic for a while:

Tasan was drawn to belief in God as a means to an end. He believed at first that belief in God would help him become a better human being, with a "better human being" defined in terms of behavior in accordance with such important Confucian values as filial piety and loyalty.

It is reasonable to assume that others among the yangban elite who were the first Korean converts to Catholicism had the same motivation Tasan had. They were frustrated at their own inability to achieve the state of perfect virtue Confucianism told them was possible to achieve through their own efforts. Catholicism, with its doctrine of original sin, seemed to offer an explanation for their moral frailty, and with its doctrine of God's saving grace seemed to offer a way to overcome that frailty. However, those who turned to Catholicism as a means to a Confucian end, such as Tasan, abandoned it when it appeared to interfere with their pursuit of a life in conformity with Confucian moral and ritual demands.

Pursuing Eternal Life

Others among the first Catholics, however, came to see God not as a means to an end but as an end in Himself. One such person was Tasan's own brother, Chŏng Yakchong. Yakchong may have adopted that different approach because he approached Catholicism from a different angle. He was searching for a way to gain immortality, not for a way to be a better Confucian. The promise of eternal life, not the promise of a helping hand on the path to secular virtue, was the primary appeal of Catholicism for him. That is why he and many of the other early Korean Catholic martyrs were willing to give their lives for their new faith. They believed that God was real and He would reward them for fidelity to Him. That reward would be to bask in the presence of God in Heaven for all eternity.

> When Yakchong was young, he wanted to learn about the immortals and their techniques of prolonging life.[49] At that time, he believed in the false theory of the Great Transformation: the end of this universe and birth of another. But, realizing there was a problem with that theory, he sighed and said, "When the cosmos undergoes this great transformation, even the immortals will not be able to escape destruction. In the end there is no way to live in this body forever. It's not worth studying those techniques." Then he heard of Catholi-

cism and gained new hope for eternal life. He became a sincere Catholic.[50]

Yakchong was not alone. In fact, many of Korea's early Catholics made clear when they were being interrogated that they had joined the Church because they wanted to go to Heaven when they died, and were willing to hasten that transition by refusing to renounce their Catholic beliefs even though that meant they would be executed. The Confucian prosecutors noticed that this unusual attitude was characteristic of Catholics. The official statement summing up the persecution of 1801 noted that "Those Catholics are deluded into believing in heaven and hell. . . . Though it is normal for human beings to love life and fear death, when they are brought to the execution ground they look on it as a comfortable place to lie down and take a rest!"[51] Some recent observers have even described early Korean Catholics as "in pursuit of martyrdom."[52]

Not only was Yakchong's motivation for becoming a Catholic different from his brother Tasan's, the way he approached Catholic teachings was different as well. Unlike Tasan, he did not incorporate Catholic monotheism into a philosophy that remained fundamentally Confucian. Instead, he delved deeply into Catholic doctrinal writings and produced, probably with the help of the first missionary to Korea, Father Zhou Wen-mo (1752–1801), who have been smuggled into Korea in 1794, a catechism that, in standard Catholic fashion, placed primary emphasis on doctrinal issues.[53] Yakchong, who had been baptized as Augustine, clearly believed that correct knowledge was a prerequisite for correct behavior, unlike Tasan, who assumed that the correct behavior provided the standard by which knowledge claims were to be evaluated

Chŏng Yakchong begins his catechism, not with the usual Confucian exhortations to the cultivation of virtue but with logical arguments for God's existence. Even the trinitarian doctrine of three persons in one God is introduced early in this text, long before the ethical implications of the assertion of God's existence are addressed.[54] The first moral principles Chŏng Yakchong specifically mentions are the need to worship the one true God and the related sin of worshipping false gods.[55] Worship of the true God is thus given clear priority over loyalty to political rulers or filial piety to parents, a sharp break with Korean tradition.

The rest of the Ten Commandments are not ignored but, as this is a work of theology rather than ethics, they clearly take a back place to the demands of monotheism. The only commandments to which Chŏng devotes much attention are the ones that impose ethical obligations not found in Neo-Confucianism. The relationship of human beings to God, the obligation to worship the one true God and to refrain from worshipping false gods, is given much more emphasis than those commandments which echo Confucian concerns about relations among human beings. The other commandments are given only a glancing mention, showing how much the *oryun* [the five moral principles which govern the five basic human relationships] have retreated into the background in this theological conception of orthodoxy.

Chŏng fills most of his pages with theological issues such as God's omniscience and with details of the life of Jesus. He even discusses at length the crucifixion of Jesus, a topic Jesuit publications downplayed in their efforts to present Catholicism as compatible with Confucianism. Chŏng also devotes more attention to attacking Buddhist beliefs that contradict Catholic doctrine than he does to pointing out any overlap of Confucianism and Catholic moral principles. As a result of this subordination of morality to theology, of orthopraxy to orthodoxy, when Chŏng was later arrested during a widespread anti-Catholic persecution in 1801, he was condemned for moral perversion, accused of promoting an evil philosophy that undermined the ethical foundations of society.[56] For his theological and moral challenge to his Confucian state, he was beheaded on April 8, 1801.[57]

In his final days, when he was undergoing interrogation, he made a statement that reveals much about what Catholicism meant to him. When asked why he did not seem to fear death, since he would not renounce his Catholic beliefs even though that might allow him to escape capital punishment, he responded, "It is only natural for human beings to want to live and to hate the thought of dying. So how can I not dread the thought of dying? However, I cannot go against my moral principles just to stay alive. The Lord of Heaven is the Supreme Ruler and the Supreme Father of the entire universe. Those who do not realize that they have to serve the Lord of Heaven are the real criminals, since they have sinned against heaven and earth. So in my case it is better to die than to live."[58]

Augustine Chŏng Yakchong was recognized for this devotion to his faith unto death by being raised to Blessed status by Pope Francis in August, 2014. Elevated along with him to that step toward full-fledged canonization as a saint were not only Paul Yun Chich'ung but also fifty-two other martyrs from the 1801–02 (sinyu) persecution.[59] Among those fifty-two other martyrs were two more examples of Catholics who believed so strongly that fidelity to God would win them the reward of an eternity with Him in heaven that they were willing to be tortured and executed rather than renounce their faith: Luthgarde Yi Suni (1782–1801) and Kollumba Kang Wansuk (1761–1801).

We know of Yi Suni's strong faith and thirst for eternal life because of a letter she sent to her mother from prison on the eve of her execution. Telling her mother not to be sad about her imminent demise, she wrote, "Regard this world as a dream; view eternal life as truly home. When your life of obedience to the will of the Lord in this world comes to an end, your worthless child, crowned with eternal blessing, girdled in everlasting joy, will greet you, take you by [the] hand, and lead you into eternal happiness. News reached me that my older brother [Yi Kyŏngdo] has received the verdict of capital punishment. What a great blessing from the Lord!"[60]

Unlike Yi Suni, Kang Wansuk did not leave any of her own writings. All we know of her comes from the *Silk Letter* as well as the official records of her interrogation. In both sources, we are told that she withstood the leg-screw torture because of her belief that, as long as she remained faithful to the Lord of Heaven, she would soon be in heaven.[61]

Conclusion

This short study has shown that there were two different reasons Koreans were drawn to Catholicism in the late eighteenth century. A few Koreans had begun reading Catholic books from China in the seventeenth century, but it wasn't until the last quarter of the eighteenth century that some among them began taking the religious message of those books seriously. The first Catholics in Korea were members of the Confucian scholar *yangban* elite. It appears that a heightened sense of crisis in the second half of the eighteenth century, caused by a combination of a growing death rate and by centuries of growing frustration at their inability to achieve through their own efforts the moral perfection Neo-Confucianism told them was possible, made them more receptive to the Catholic promise of help from God in overcoming their moral frailty. The few records those Confucian converts to Catholicism left behind suggest that in many, though by no means all, cases, they adopted belief in God Above as a tool for achieving their Confucian moral goals. It would be appropriate to label them Catholic Confucians. In such cases the priority they gave to Confucianism over Catholicism led them to abandon Catholicism when those two different approaches to understanding the place of human beings in the universe came into conflict.

Others, such as Chŏng Yakchong, abandoned Confucianism completely, though their moral perspective still tended to be influenced by the Confucian emphasis on filial piety and loyalty, and became fully Catholic, even accepting torture and execution rather than apostatize. We also find Catholicism spreading to women and others not as deeply immersed in the Confucian worldview as the yangban were. This group of early converts appear to have been drawn more to the promise of eternal life in heaven above than they were to the possibility of obtaining help from God to become better Confucians in this life.

Both groups of early Catholics reveal that they were still operating within an ethical worldview largely shaped by Confucianism. God to both groups appears primarily as God the Supreme Father and God the Supreme Ruler. Except in the catechism of Chŏng Yakchong, which was a presentation in Korean of ideas borrowed from books published by Catholics in China, we do not find much discussion of Jesus in early Catholic writings. That does not mean they did not know about the Trinity, the Incarnation, or the Atonement. Rather, they expressed their newly adopted theology in terms that resonated with the filial piety and loyalty that were the core ethical values of their culture. Love of, and obedience to, the Son seemed to them less of an ethical imperative than love of, and obedience to, the Father. In other words, these first members of the Korean Catholic Church, despite being drawn to an approach to understanding the role of human beings in this life that was very different from that of their ancestors, remained Korean. That is why they are honored by millions of Korean Catholics today as forebears who did not abandon their Korean culture but instead tried to transform it. That is why they are seen as the founders of the Korean Catholic Church.

Notes

1. Don Baker, "Hananim, Hanŭnim, Hanullim, and Hanŏllim: The Construction of Terminology for Korean Monotheism," *Review of Korean Studies* 5:1 (June, 2002), 105–31. There were a few cases of people worshipping Heaven, but

such rituals were both illegal and quite rare. Moreover, before the emergence of Tonghak, such rituals do not appear to be evidence of monotheism. We do not see any articulation of a belief in one, and only one, God. Rather, Heaven was worshipped as a particularly powerful spirit but not as the only God. Ch'oe Chongsŏng, "Chosŏnjo yugyo sahoe wa minjung ŭi ch'ŏnje" [Confucian society during the Chosŏn Dynasty and the ritual of worshipping Heaven among the masses], Seoul National University Chonggyo Munje Yŏn'guso, ed. *Yugyo wa Chonggyohak* [*Confucianism and Religious Studies*] (Seoul: SNU Press, 2009), 216–32.

2. Don Baker, "The Martyrdom of Paul Yun: Western Religion and Eastern Ritual in Eighteenth-century Korea," *Transactions of the Royal Asiatic Society, Korea Branch*, 54 (1979), 33–58.

3. Don Baker, "The Religious Revolution in Modern Korean History: From ethics to theology and from ritual hegemony to religious freedom" *Review of Korean Studies* 9: 3 (Sept. 2006), 249–75. For an example of the sorts of laws that were used against those who violated the state's behavioral demands, see Pierre-Emmanuel Roux, "The Great Ming Code and the Repression of Catholics in Chosŏn Korea," *Acta Koreana* 15:1 (June 2012), 73–106.

4. Don Baker, "Diseases and Deities in Eighteenth-century Korea," *Papers of the Fifth International Conference on Korean Studies* (Republic of Korea: Academy of Korean Studies: 1988, I), 188–204.

5. Don Baker "Danger Within: Guilt and Moral Frailty in Korean Religion" *Acta Koreana* 4 (July, 2001), 1–25.

6. Eckert, Carter J., and Ki-baki Lee, et al. *Korea, Old and New: A History* (Cambridge, MA: Harvard University Press, 1990), 170.

7. Don Baker, "Rituals and Resistance in Chosŏn Korea," *Sungkyun Journal of East Asian Studies*, 7: 2 (October, 2007), 6–13.

8. Don Baker, "Jesuit Science Through Korean Eyes," *Journal of Korean Studies*, 4 (1983), 207–39.

9. For a look at traditional medicine in Chosŏn Korea, and how it compared to Western medicine, see Don Baker, "Sirhak Medicine: Measles, Smallpox, and Chong Tasan," *Korean Studies*, 14 (1990), 135–66.

10. I took my population figures from Paek Rin, ed. *Hogu Ch'ongsu* [*An Overall Survey of Population Statistics*] (Seoul: Seoul National University Press, 1971). This work contains population figures from a 1789 work of the same name and supplements those figures with figures taken from the *Chosŏn wangjo sillok* [*Annals of the Chosŏn Dynasty*].

11. Kwŏn T'aehwan and Shin Yongha, "Chosŏn Wangjo sidae in'gu ch'ujŏng e kwanghan ilsiron" [An Attempt at Estimating the Population during the Chosŏn Dynasty], *Tonga munhwa*, 14 (1977), 289–330.

12. Kim Yŏnok, "Han'guk ŭi sobinggi kihu" [Korea's Little Ice Age], *Chirihak kwa Chiri Kyuyuk*, no. 14, 1984, 1–16; Kim Chaeho, "Chosŏn hugi Han'guk nongŏp ŭi t'ŭkching kwa kihu saengt'aehakchŏk paegyŏng" [Climatic Conditions

and the Distinctive Characteristics of Korean Agriculture in the Latter Half of the Chosŏn Period], *Pigyo minsokhak* 41 (2010), 97–127.

13. Both measles and smallpox viruses prefer cold and dry weather (Ann Bowman Jannetta, *Epidemics and Mortality in Early Modern Japan* [Princeton, NJ: Princeton University Press, 1987], 64 and 111), which Korea would have had in the winter and early spring months during the little ice age.

14. Hochol Lee, "Rice Culture and Demographic Development in Korea, 1429–1918" in Erik Aerts, ed. *Economic and Demographic Development in Rice-Producing Societies: Aspects of East Asian Economic History (1500–1900)*, proceedings of the Tenth International Economic History Congress (Leuven: Universitaire Pers Leuven, 1990), 68, provides evidence for growing population density, particularly in the southern provinces, from 1550 through 1875.

15. Miki Sakae, *Chōsen igakushi oyobi shippeishi* [*The History of Medicine and Disease in Korea*] (Osaka, Japan: privately printed, 1962), II, 52.

16. Chŏng Yagyong, *Yŏyudang chŏnsŏ* [*Complete Works of Yŏyudang Chŏng Yagyong*] *Magwa hoetong* [*A Comprehensive Survey of Pox-Related Diseases*] VII: 4:2b–3b.

17. Chin Tŏkkyu et al., *19 seigi han'guk chŏnt'ong sahoe ŭi pyŏnmo wa minjung ŭisik* [The changes in traditional Korean society in the nineteenth century and the consciousness of the populace] (Seoul: Minjok munhwa yŏn'guso, Koryŏ University, 1983) provides the estimate for the frequency of famines and epidemics. The *Sillok* records major famines for the specific years mentioned.

18. Chin Tŏkkyu, 198.

19. These figures are much smaller than the figures demographers have calculated. It is likely that the Chosŏn government undercounted its population, since many Koreans had good reasons to avoid being counted in the census, which was also the tax roll. Nevertheless, I believe these figures reveal changes in the size of the Korean population even if they do not show us the exact number of inhabitants on the peninsula at that time.

20. Miki, II, 25.

21. Ch'ae Chegong, *Pŏnamjip* [*The Collected Works of Pŏnam Ch'ae Chegong*], 37:38b–40b (Seoul: Kyŏngmunsa, 1976). I am grateful to Boudewijn Walraven for pointing out this document to me.

22. Don Baker, "Sinyuhak-ŭi Todŏk kwa Hyŏngisanghak" [Morality and Metaphysics in Korean Neo-Confucianism], *Chosŏn hugi yugyo wa ch'ŏnjugyo ŭi taerip* [*The Confrontation between Confucianism and Catholicism in the Latter Half of the Chosŏn Dynasty*], (Seoul: Iljogak, 1997), 1–26.

23. Yi Ik, *Sŏngho saesŏl* [*The Classified Writings of Sŏngho Yi Ik*] (Seoul: Minjok munhwa ch'ujinhoe, 1977–78), 26:15b–16a.

24. Chŏng Yagyong, "Chungyong kangŭi" [Discussing the Meaning of the Doctrine of the Mean], *Yŏyudang chŏnsŏ*, II, 4, 65b.

25. For more on this tragic incident, see JaHyun Kim Haboush, trans. *The Memoirs of Lady Heygyŏng: The Autobiographical Writings of a Crown Princess of Eighteenth-Century Korea* (Berkeley: University of California Press, 1996).

26. Hwang Sayŏng baeksŏ [*The Silk Letter of Hwang Sayŏng*], lines 43–44. See Yŏ Chinchŏn, *Nuga chŏhŭirŭl wirohae chusigessŭmnigga?* [*Who Will Comfort Us?*] (Seoul: Kibbŭn sosik, 1999), 83.

27. Cho Kwang, "Sinyu kyonan kwa Yi Sŭnghun" [Yi Sŭnghun and the 1801 Anti-Catholic Persecution], *Kyohoesa yŏn'gu*, 8 (*1992*). Ki Sŭngje, *Tasanŭl ch'ajasŏ* [*Searching for Tasan*] (Seoul: Chungang Ilbosa, 1995), 22.

28. Chŏng Yagyong, "Sŏnjungssi myojimyŏng" [An Epitaph for my Older Brother] *Yŏyudang chŏnsŏ*, I, 15:42a.

29. Charles Dallet. *Histoire de L'Église de Corée* (Paris: Victor Palmé, 1874), I:38; Kang Mangil, et al. ed. *Ch'uan kŭp Kugan* [*Records of Special Investigations by the State Tribunal*], vol. 25 (Seoul: Asea munhwasa, 1978), 51.

30. Ch'oe Sŏgu, "Han'guk kyohoe ŭi ch'angsŏl kwa ch'och'anggi Yi Sŭnghun ŭi kyohoe hwaldong" [Yi Sŭnghun and His Church Activities during the Founding of Early Years of Catholicism in Korea], *Kyohoesa yŏn'gu* 8 (1992), 29; Cha Kijin, "Manchŏn Yi Sŭnghun ŭi kyohoe hwaldong kwa chŏngch'ijŏk ipch'i" [Manchŏn Yi Sŭnghun's Political Stance and His Activities for the Church] *Kyohoesa yŏn'gu*, 8 (1992), 47; *Chosŏn hugi Ch'ŏnjugyo sinja chaep'an kirok: ch'uan mit kugan* [*Records of the Trials of Catholics in the Latter Half of the Chosŏn Dynasty: The Records of Special Investigations by the State Tribunal*] (Seoul: Kukhak Charyowŏn, 2004), 940–43; Dallet, I: 34–35.

31. *Ch'uan kŭp Kugan* vol. 25. 86–88. *Chosŏn hugi Ch'ŏnjugyo sinja chaep'an kirok: ch'uan mit kugan*, 937–40; Dallet, 24.

32. Dallet, I: 28–29.

33. Kim Ok-hŭi, *Kwangam Yi Pyŏk ŭi Sŏhak Sasang* [*The Catholic Thought of Yi Pyŏk*] (Seoul: Catholic Press, 1979); Yi Sŏngbae, *Yugyo wa Kŭrisŭdo: Yi Pyŏk ŭi Han'gukchŏk sinhak wŏlli* [*Confucianism and Christianity: The Korean Nature of the Theological Principles of Yi Pyŏk*] (Seoul: Pundo Publishing, 1979).

34. Yŏ; Dallet, *Histoire de L'Église de Corée*.

35. Yi Ihwa, "Yi Sŭnghun kwan'gye munhŏn ŭi kŏmt'o" [An Examination of Documents Related to Yi Sŭnghun] *Kyohoesa yŏn'gu* 8 (1992), 122–23.

36. Cho Hyŏnbŏm, "Kyohoe ŭi hwaldong kwa kyosae ŭi hwaksan," [The Activities of the Church and its Expansion], Han'guk kyohoesa yŏn'guso, ed., *Han'guk Ch'ŏnjugyohoesa 1* (Seoul: Han'guk kyohosesa yŏn'guso, 2009), 305–07; Joseph Ch'ang-mun Kim and John Jae-sun Chung, *Catholic Korea: Yesterday and Today* (Seoul: St. Joseph Publishing Co., 1984), 40–41.

37. An Chŏngbok, "Ch'ŏnhak mundap," *Sunam Chip* [*The Collected Writings of Sunam An Chŏngbok*], 17: 8a–26a.

38. Yun Min'gu, ed. *Han'guk ch'ogi kyohoe-e kwanhan kyohwangch'ŏng charyo moŭmjip* [*A Collection of Documents from the Papal Archives Related to the First Years of the Korean Catholic Church*] (Seoul: Catholic Press, 2000), 32–33.

39. Dallet, I:47. An English translation of Yun's account of his interrogation in Chinsan and Chŏnju and of his final statement is available in Joseph Ch'ang-mun Kim and John Jae-sun Chung, 58

40. Dallet, I: 43.

41. Dallet, 47.
42. Dallet 47–48. A version of Yun's statement similar to that found in Dallet can be seen in the *Chŏngjo sillok*, 15th year, 11th month, 7th day.
43. Dallet, 49.
44. Don Baker, "Tasan between Catholicism and Confucianism: A Decade Under Suspicion, 1791 to 1801," *Tasanhak* 5 (2004), 55–86.
45. Yoo Kwon Jong, "Dasan's Approach to Ultimate Reality," *Korea Journal* 53:2 (2013) 31–53; Pak Chonch'ŏn, "Chŏng Yagyong ŭi sin'gwan-e taehan chonggyosa chŏk haesŏk" [An Explanation from the Standpoint of Religious History of the Notion of God of Chŏng Yagyong], *Yugyo wa chonggyohak*, 3–43; Kim Yŏngil, *Chŏng Yagyong ŭi Sangje Sasang* [*The Lord Above in the Thought of Chŏng Yagyong*] (Seoul: Kyŏngin munhwasa, 2003).
46. Chŏng Yagyong, "Maengja yoŭi" [Essential Points in the Mencius], *Yŏyudang chŏnsŏ* II, 6:23b.
47. Chŏng Yagyong, "Chungyong Chajam" [Admonitions for Myself upon Reading the Doctrine of the Mean], *Yŏyudang chŏnsŏ* II:3, 4b–5a.
48. Chŏng Yagyong, *Yŏyudang chŏnsŏ*: I, 9:43b.
49. The pursuit of physical immortality is often associated with Daoism in East Asia. Daoism, unlike the other imports from China, Confucianism and Buddhism, never established much of an institutional presence in Korea. There was no Daoist religion per se, outside of a government Daoist temple that closed in the sixteenth century. However, throughout the Chosŏn Dynasty, there were a few scholars who practiced what may be called Daoist techniques of breathing and physical exercises in order to reverse the process of physical decay in their bodies. Chŏng Yakchong appears to have been one of those "Daoists" before he became a Catholic. Kim Nakp'il, *Chosŏn sidae ŭi naedan sasang: Kwŏn Kŭkchung ŭi Togyo Ch'ŏrhakchŏk sayu wa kŭ chŏn'gae* [*Internal Alchemy Thought during the Chosŏn Era; The Unfolding of the Daoist Philosophy of Kwŏn Kŭkchung*] (Seoul: Han'gilsa, 2000).
50. *Yŏ*, 74.
51. *Sunjo sillok*. Year 1, 12th month, 22nd day (kapcha)
52. Andrew Finch, "The Pursuit of Martyrdom in the Catholic Church in Korea before 1866," *Journal of Ecclesiastical History*, 60:1 (January, 2009), 95–118; Franklin Rausch, "Dying for Heaven: Persecution, Martyrdom, and Family in the Early Korean Catholic Church," Charlotte Horlyck and Michael Pettid, ed. *Death, Mourning, and the Afterlife in Korea: From Ancient to Contemporary Times* (Honolulu: University of Hawai'i Press, 2014), 213–35.
53. Chŏng Yakchong, *Chugyo yoji* [*Essentials of the Lord's Teachings*] (Seoul: Hwang Sŏkdu Luga sŏwŏn, 1984). This edition contains a complete modern Korean translation by Ha Sŏngnae. For an English-language translation and analysis of that work, see Hector Diaz, *A Korean Theology: Chu-gyo Yo-ji, Essentials of the Lord's Teaching by Chŏng Yak-jong Augustine (1760–1801)* (Immensee: New

Seitschrift für Missionswissenschaft, 1986). A more recent English translation is Deberniere J. Torrey, trans. *Jugyo Yoji* [*The Essentials of the Lord's Teachings*] (Seoul: KIATS Press, 2012)

    54. Diaz, 297–301.

    55. Diaz, 327.

    56. *Ch'uan kŭp Kugan* 25, 48–49; Yi Nŭnghwa. *Chosŏn kidokkyo kŭp oegyosa* [*A History of Christianity and Foreign Relations in Korea*] (Seoul: Han'gukhak yŏn'guso, 1977), 118.

    57. For more on Chŏng Yakchong and his Catholic faith, see Cho Han'gŏn, "Chugyo yoji wa hanyŏk sŏhak wa ui kwang'gye [The Relationship between the Chugyo yoji and Catholic Books Translated into Chinese] *Kyohoesa yŏn'gu* 26 (2006), 5–74; Kim T'aeyŏng, "Chŏng Yakchong ŭi Chŏnju kyori ihae" [Chŏng Yakchong's Understanding of Catholic Doctrine," *Yŏksa wa Kyŏnggye* 89 (2013), 109–147.

    58. *Ch'uan kŭp Kugan*, 50

    59. Han'guk Chŏnjugyo chugyohoe ŭi sibok sisŏng chugyo t'ŭkpyŏl wiwŏnhoe, ed, *Hanŭnim ŭi chong: Yun Chich'ung Paoro wa tonggyo sun'gyoja 123 wi* [*Servants of God: Paul Yun Chich'ung and 123 Fellow Martyrs*] Seoul: Han'guk Chŏnjugyo Chugyohoe ŭi Sibok Sisŏng Chugyo T'ŭkpyŏl Wiwŏnhoe, 2003).

    60. JaHyun Kim Haboush, *Epistolary Korea: Letters in the Communicative Space of the Chosŏn, 1392–1910* (New York: Columbia University Press, 2009), 364; Yi Suni's letter is reproduced in Dallet, I: 182–185. There is some question about whether all the letter attributed to Yi Suni by Dallet is by her or whether Dallet mistakenly combined portions of letters by her with parts of a letter from another martyr. However, even if the letter is not all Yi Suni's words, it still gives us a glimpse of the thought and motivations of some of the first Catholics. See Yi Yujin, "Yi Suni Lugalda okchung p'yŏnji hyŏnjŏn p'ilsabon ŭi charyojŏk kach'I wa hedok ŭi munje" [The value of, and problems interpreting, the extant hand-written version of Luthgarde Yi Suni's letter from prison] *Kyohoesa yŏn'gu* 40 (2012), 173–203.

    61. Ledyard, Gari, "Kollumba Kang Wansuk, an Early Catholic Activist and Martyr," Robert E. Buswell Jr. and Timothy S. Lee, ed. *Christianity in Korea* (Honolulu: University of Hawaii Press, 2006), 57; *Silk Letter*, line 69.

Bibliography

Baker, Don. *The Silk Letter of Hwang Sayŏng: Catholics and Anti-Catholicism in Chosŏn Dynasty Korea*. Translated by Don Baker and Franklin Rausch. Honolulu: University of Hawaii Press, 2016.

Cho, Kwang. *Chosŏn huge Chŏnjugyosa yŏn'gu ŭi kich'o* [*Preliminary Research into the History of Catholicism in the Latter Half of the Chosŏn Dynasty*]. Seoul: Kyŏngin munhwasa, 2010.

———. *Chosŏn hugi sahoe wa Chŏnjugyo* [Catholicism and Society in the Latter Half of the Chosŏn Dynasty]. Seoul: Kyŏngin munhwasa, 2010.

Choi, Jai-Keun. *The Origins of the Roman Catholic Church in Korea: An Examination of Popular and Governmental Responses to Catholic Missions in the Late Chosŏn Dynasty*. Norfolk: The Hermit Kingdom Press, 2006.

Chŏng Yakchong. Deberniere J. Torrey, trans. *Jugyo Yoji* [The Essentials of the Lord's Teachings]. Seoul: KIATS Press, 2012.

Chŏng Yagyong. *Chŏngbon Yŏyudang chŏnsŏ* [The Definitive Version of the Complete Works of Yŏyudang Tasan Chŏng Yagyong]. Seoul: Tasan Haksul Munhwa Chaedan, 2012.

Dallet, Charles. *Histoire de L'Église de Corée*. Paris: Victor Palmé, 1874. Reprinted Seoul: Royal Asiatic Society, 1975. An annotated Korean translation is available: Ŭng-nyŏl An and Andreas Choi Sŏgu, trans. *Han'guk chŏnju kyohoesa* [A History of the Korean Catholic Church]. Seoul: Han'guk Kyohoesa Yŏn'guso, 1996).

Kim, Joseph Ch'ang-mun and John Jae-sun Chung. *Catholic Korea: Yesterday and Today*. Seoul: St. Joseph Publishing Co., 1984.

Kim Yŏngil, *Chŏng Yagyong ŭi Sangje Sasang* [The Lord Above in the Thought of Chŏng Yagyong]. Seoul: Kyŏngin munhwasa, 2003.

Kŭm, Chang-t'ae. *Sirhak kwa sŏhak; Han'guk kŭndae sasang ŭi wŏllyu* [Practical Learning and Western Learning: The Origins of Modern Korean Thought]. Seoul: Chisik kea Kyoyang, 2012.

5

On the Family Resemblance of Philosophical Paradigm

Between Dasan's Thought and Matteo Ricci's *Tianzhu shiyi*

Young-bae Song

Introduction

The growing academic interests in and publications on Jeong Yagyong (Dasan, 1762–1836) exceed those on any other Korean thinker. This is mainly because his thoughts are complex enough to attract scholars from across many different disciplinary fields including philosophy, history, literature, and the history of Korean Catholicism.

In particular, recent studies on Korean philosophy and thought by Han Hyeong-jo and Yu Cho-ha have clarified the significance of Dasan's creative paradigm, which fundamentally transformed the normative Neo-Confucian philosophical paradigm.[1] The majority of existing studies have examined Dasan's thought only in relation to Toegye or Dasan's own ingenious readings of the Confucian classics. Scholars such as Yi Dong-hwan and Yu Cho-ha have considered Dasan's thought to have very little relevance to Catholicism,[2] whereas Kim Ok-hui and Yi Won-sun[3] have examined Dasan's thoughts in relation to Western Learning (Kor.: *Seohak*; Ch.: *xixue*). The studies of Kim Ok-hui and Yi Won-sun have mainly approached Dasan through analyses of the very few remaining historical documents. On the other hand, there are those, including Choe Seok-u, Kang Jae-on, and Geum Jang-tae,[4] who have compared Dasan's thought with Matteo Ricci's *Tianzhu shiyi* (*The True Meaning of the Lord of Heaven*) from a philosophical perspective. However, these studies, in my opinion, fall far short of explaining the formative process of Dasan's new paradigm.

I have recently analyzed Matteo Ricci's Chinese texts *Tianzhu shiyi* (Beijing, 1603), *Jiaoyoulun* (*On Friendship*) (1595), *Ershiwuyan* (*The Twenty-five Sayings*) (1600) and *Jiren shipian* (*Ten Essays of an Eccentric Man*) (1608) in order to publish annotated translations in Korean.[5] I have also examined Dasan's major works and commentaries related to Confucian classics in the past few years, and in this process have gained new insights into the striking structural similarities between Dasan's thought and the Western paradigm of Aristotle and Aquinas as seen in Ricci's *Tianzhu shiyi*. This paper will examine Ricci's rejection of the Neo-Confucian paradigm in *Tianzhu shiyi* as well as Dasan's shift away from Neo-Confucianism to his own synthesis, and disclose the family resemblance of philosophical paradigm between *Tianzhu shiyi* and Dasan's thought. Dasan's synthesis can be seen as an original work of mediation between Ricci's Western Learning and the prevailing Neo-Confucianism of his time.

The Rejection of the Neo-Confucian Paradigm in *Tianzhu Shiyi*

Duality of Spirit and Matter and the Definition of Man as a Rational Being

As the world has been viewed as a duality of corporeal matter and incorporeal spirit since Aristotle (384–322 BCE), Matteo Ricci (1552–1610) in his "Diagram of the Kinds of Being"[6] in *Tianzhu shiyi* also divides substances into spirits and bodies. He also notes that among the spirits, there are those which are good, such as angels, and those which are evil, such as demons.[7] Matteo Ricci classifies all things in the universe into those with life and those without life.[8] The fundamental difference between living or animate things and lifeless or inanimate things is the existence of the soul (*anima*); Ricci categorizes the soul, based on Aristotle's philosophy, on three levels:

> In this world there are three kinds of souls. The lowest is called the life principle—the vegetative soul. This kind of soul sup-

ports vegetation in its growth, and when the vegetation withers, the soul is also destroyed. The second class of soul is called the sentient soul. This soul is possessed by birds and beasts. It allows the birds and beasts to be born, to develop and grow up, and causes their ears and eyes to be able to hear and see, their mouths and noses to be able to taste and smell, and their limbs and bodies to be aware of things, though *they are not able to infer truth*. When these creatures die, their souls are destroyed along with them. The most superior of the souls is called the intellectual soul. This is the soul of man. . . . It enables people to grow to maturity; it causes people to be aware of things outside themselves, and it allows people to make inferences as to the nature of things and to distinguish between one principle and another. . . . But a thing which can infer and distinguish is not dependent on a fleshly body, and such a soul can, therefore, exist on its own. Though the body may perish, a man's soul still has its functions.[9]

Matteo Ricci introduces Aristotle's view, which considers the intellectual soul or the rational ability to discern and infer as human nature. He, therefore, deems "intellect" as the faculty differentiating men from animals.[10] Because the ability of inference (or intellectual soul) is not, like the perceptions of sight and hearing, dependent on a fleshly body, he states that the body of man may perish but his soul is eternal and inextinguishable.[11] This soul or intellect is seen as the characteristic that distinguishes human beings from all other things. He states, "The capacity to reason establishes man in his own category; it distinguishes man from all other things, and it is that which is called human nature."[12]

But if a man with a body can have awareness only through reason,[13] then those incorporeal spiritual beings, such as angels and demons, can have immediate and complete comprehension of all things without need for reason.[14] This fact, Ricci claims, distinguishes human beings from other intellectual beings.

The Completion of Self through Free Will and Moral Practice

Unlike the incorporeal spiritual beings (god, angel, and ghost), the human nature attached to a physical body contains both material and spiritual aspects,[15] and thereby both the animal soul and human soul coexist.[16] In this respect, man is distinguished in essence from all other beings that possess only "one soul" (that is, instinct),[17] for example, vegetation with the vegetative soul and the beasts with the sentient soul. They lack the intellect to act independently with reason, so all that remains are instinctive functions. Ricci explains the instability of the human mind stemming from this duality of human nature as follows:

> When a man is confronted by something, he can react toward it in two apparently opposing ways at one and the same time. A man misled by wine and women will simultaneously be obsessed with them and wish to pursue them, and be mindful of the unprincipled nature of his action. To follow [after wine and women] is to be "animal-minded," and in this, man is no different from birds and beasts. To follow [after the rational] is to be "human-minded," and, in this, man is the same as the angels. *Man cannot with only one mind simultaneously reduce two incompatible dispositions to one thing.*[18]

Here, the question of whether a human mind, which has both material and spiritual aspects (unlike the mountains, trees, and beasts, which have only the material), would follow the animal mind or the human mind, constantly places demands on a man to make a choice. In other words, "only the soul of man is capable of being the master of his body causing it to act or arresting it, in accordance with its [*free*] will."[19] By claiming that true human value lies in the principle that "although men may have selfish desires, it is impossible for [them] to defy the commands of universal reason," Ricci defends the free will as the prerequisite of self-perfection. With the claim of achieving virtue or vice only through free will and moral practice, he is directly challenging the Neo-Confucian belief, which considers man's ability to achieve virtue or vice to be predetermined by the inherited *qi* at birth or the "physical (human) nature."

Ricci does not, however, renounce the existence of "innate" goodness originally bestowed on man and beasts by the Lord of Heaven. In accordance with this innate goodness, "children love their parents, but so do animals." He claims, "When ordinary people suddenly see a child about to fall into a well, they will feel fear and apprehension about it whether they are humane or not." But this results from innate goodness, and this must be strictly distinguished from acquired goodness. It is because the former "innate goodness" is only a gift from the Lord of Heaven that man can claim no merit for it, whereas man can for the latter "acquired goodness" because it is accumulated through man's own efforts.[20]

Ricci, who advocates the ethics of Thomas Aquinas (1225–1274), explicates the three functions of the immaterial human mind:

> The *corporeal* body uses ears, eyes, the mouth, the nose, the four limbs and five senses to make contact with and to perceive the physical objects [in the world outside itself]. The *incorporeal* spirit [within man] employs memory, the intellect and the *will* to communicate with the outside world. The images of what I see, hear, taste, or feel enter the five portals of my body to reach the spirit [within my body], and the spirit employs the faculty of memory to receive these things and to store them, as it were, in a storehouse so that they are not forgotten. Later, should I wish to understand something thoroughly, I employ my intellect to weigh up the true nature of the things stored away in my memory in order to determine whether they are true or not. If they are good, my *will loves and desires* them; but if they are bad, my *will hates* and abandons them, for my intellect can thoroughly understand what is right and what is wrong, and my *will causes* me either to *love* what is good, or to *hate* what is evil. When the work of these three controlling factors has been done, there is nothing which remains unaccomplished.[21]

While animals do not have an intellect and only have one mind [instinct] to follow their innate nature and therefore without the capacity to choose moral actions, human beings are equipped with both intellect and will, and are able to distinguish good and evil through reason. Ricci emphasizes the *free will* as the precondition of moral practice or moral cultivation: it is impossible to expect moral goodness or evil from those beings without intellect and free will.

> Everything in the world which has a will can allow the will to achieve its end or can restrain it, and a distinction is thereby made between virtue and vice, good and evil. The will issues from the mind. Metal, stone and vegetations are devoid of mind and therefore of will. Thus, if a man is injured by a sword, his avenger will not break the sword in two. If a tile

falls and injures a man's head, the man who is harmed will not bear a grudge against the tile.... Because they have no mind and no will they are devoid of virtue and vice, goodness and evil, and one cannot reward or punish them.

As to animals, we can say that they have the minds and wills of animals, but that they have no intelligent mind with which to distinguish between right and wrong. They follow their senses, and are unable to regulate their reactions with reason. Everything they do, whether it be fitting or not, is done without their being able to be masters of their actions and without any self-awareness; how, then, can one speak of good and evil? Thus, of the laws enacted in the countries of the world, there is not one which punishes an animal for wrongdoing, or which rewards an animal for its virtue.

But man's conduct is quite otherwise. His actions are external, but his reasoning mind lies within him. Not only is he aware that his actions are right or wrong, correct or otherwise, but he is also capable of allowing them to run riot or of bringing them to a halt.[22]

In this respect, Ricci claims that "(free) will" is clearly the "source of good and evil."[23] He regards "sincerity" and the "rectification of the mind" as the foundation of Confucian teachings, especially the teachings in *Great Learning*.[24] He also insists that "the teaching in the *Great Learning* concerning the regulation of the family, the ordering of the state, and the bringing of peace to the world has sincerity of *will* as its most necessary ingredient, for, if there is no sincerity, nothing can be accomplished."[25]

If Ricci's contention is taken into consideration, then the long-standing controversy in Chinese philosophy, namely whether or not human beings have innate goodness, no longer holds any importance as a crucial issue of fundamental moral cultivation. Nature, according to Ricci, is "nothing other than the fundamental essence of each category of things,"[26] and the Lord of Heaven creates different "original nature" for each category of things. Therefore, the original nature of each thing can only be different from that of another. Ricci also claims that "if we let reason be the master of them, then they are lovable and desirable and are essentially good and not evil."[27] Therefore, this question is a matter of practice, of whether or how they use the original nature. When one comes to the uses to which these things are put, one finds that all depends on the individual; based on one's practice, one can be lovable, but one can also be loathsome.[28] Therefore, the Neo-Confucian theory equating "(human) nature (*xing*) as the principle (*li*)," which asserts that the goodness of human beings is *a priori* given independently of practices *a posteriori* accumulated by each, can *never* be accepted by Ricci. According to Ricci's philosophical perspective, the question is not how to grasp the transcendental principle itself, but rather how to independently put the principle into action. Therefore, individual conducts of putting principle into moral practice hold decisive importance. "Consequently, if I determine to follow what is right and rational, I am a superior man in my moral conduct" and "if, instead, I am dissolute, and determine to obey my animal mind, I am an inferior man."[29] In other words, "moral cultivation and completion" is not a contemplative and conceptual issue but a matter of man's actual practice.

Regarding this matter of moral practice, Ricci states the following:

> I can do both good and evil with my human nature, but one cannot say that human nature was originally evil. . . . [In contrast,] if men were unable to do anything but good from the moment of birth, how could one speak of anyone becoming good? There is no such thing in the world as unintentional goodness. I can refrain from doing good, and it is only when I decide to go and do good that I can be said to be a superior man who does good works. When the Lord of Heaven bestowed this nature on man, man was capable of doing both good and evil, and man was enriched thereby. Because man can take or reject goodness, not only is the merit of goodness increased, but that merit becomes man's own. . . . Although human nature is fundamentally good, one cannot for this reason say that all men are good. Only those who possess virtue can be called good. Virtuous conduct added to goodness is the expression [of that goodness]. This is how man perfects that which is fundamentally good.[30]

In this respect, moral goodness is the result of moral practice by human beings who have reason and free will. Therefore, this question of moral goodness cannot be raised for beings other than man since they lack moral elements in their "original nature."

According to Neo-Confucian presuppositions, however, the immeasurable transformations or changes of all beings including mankind are never a series of evolving and developing events or facts of nature beyond ideal values for human life. These transformations are considered to be the realization of the ontological basis of value and order such as humanity, righteousness, propriety, and wisdom. This may be described as a kind of moral metaphysical teleology. This Neo-Confucian paradigm of anthropo-cosmic teleology, which puts nature and man on the same level, cannot hold within Ricci's Western philosophical paradigm. According to Ricci's metaphysical perspective, the moral question cannot be directed toward plants or animals that lack intellect as well as free will. Only the path of human self-cultivation and practice, which is also termed the human *Tao* in Chinese thoughts, remains for Matteo Ricci.

The Supreme Ultimate (taiji) or Principle (li) as only Accidents and the Existence of the Lord of Heaven as a Rational, Spiritual Being

In the moral metaphysical world of Neo-Confucianism based on the *Heavenly Principle (tianli)*, *Supreme Ultimate (taiji)* or *principle (li)* is the origin of all things in the universe. The Christian concept of a personal God who created the universe is not readily accepted in Neo-Confucian culture.

However, for Ricci, who was accustomed only to the Aristotelian and Thomist worldview, the metaphysical framework of Neo-Confucianism was not at all properly comprehensible. As he believed in the one God who had created the universe, he could not accept the Neo-Confucian metaphysics, which claims that the *Supreme Ultimate (taiji)* is the origin of all things. He invoked the Aristotelian categorical distinction between substance and attribute, and declared that the *Supreme Ultimate* could not be the origin of all things, as follows:

> When we come to the *Supreme Ultimate* we find that it is only explained in terms of *principle* ("*li*"). It cannot therefore be the source of heaven, earth, and all things. . . . When men of letters and learned men of China discuss *principle*, they only speak of it in two ways: they either say that *principle* resides in the minds of men, or else they say it is to be found in things. They only say that things are real when their mode of being harmonizes with the *principles* in men's minds. When the human mind is able to study, penetrate and completely understand the *principles* inherent in things, this is called the

investigation of things [*gewu*]. It is clear, on the basis of these two ways of speaking about *principle*, that *principle* is dependent and cannot be the source of things.

Principles, whether in the human mind, or in things, are all subsequent to those things; and how can that which is subsequent be the source of that which exists prior to it?

Further, in the beginning, before anything existed, who said that there had to be *principles*? Where were those *principles* located and on what did they depend? Accidents cannot stand by themselves; if there are no substances for them to rely on, then the accidents are void and non-existent. If you say that they rely on *nothingness*, I am afraid I can only say that *nothingness* is not adequate to serve as their support. Thus, one can come to no other conclusion than that *principle* must *not stand*. Let me ask you: If *principle* existed prior to Pan Ku [the legendary creator of the universe in China], why did it remain at leisure and not move to produce things? Who later stimulated it into activity? If, as has been said, *principle* originally was neither active nor inactive, how could it possibly move of its own accord? If you say that *principle* at first did not produce anything but that later it wished to produce things, is this not tantamount to saying that *principle* possesses will?[31]

Here Ricci gives three reasons why *li* cannot be the source of all creation through his own understanding of the Neo-Confucian concept of *li*. In so doing, he relies on Aristotelian notions of the distinction between substance and accident, and the law of cause-and-effect based on the temporal sequence of the production of things.

First of all, *li* can only exist in the following two cases: *li* resides in the minds of men, or else in things. So in Ricci's view, *li* is not a real independent entity which exists in the empirical world, in other words, an independent substance. *Li* is no more than the formal cause of each individual object, existing within the substance and giving a name to (or defining) it as an existence. It follows, therefore, that *li* is not an individual object or a substance, but an accident dependent on such an object. Ricci then asks where this *li* exists and on what kind of existence it depends. By saying, "If you say that they rely on nothingness, I am afraid I can only say that nothingness is not adequate to serve as their support." Thus, he argues that one can come to no other conclusion than that *li* must not stand," that *li* cannot be the source of all things.

Second, Ricci criticizes *li* in terms of the law of cause-and-effect governing the production of things, by which an effect cannot temporally precede its cause. As *li* is dependent on temporally preceding substances, such as the human minds or things (outside the minds), *li* cannot be the source of all things.

Third, according to Ricci's comprehension of Neo-Confucian *li*, it has neither motion nor will. Therefore, he claims that as *li* is not a being who has the will to begin to move by itself and to create all things in the universe, *li* cannot be the origin of the creation of the universe, as is in the case of the Christian God.

Ricci interprets the concept of *li* as an immaterial being (*shen*), not a material thing (*xing*). Therefore, he contends that "if it has intelligence and consciousness and can comprehend the principle of righteousness, then, it must fall within the category of ghosts and spirits. In that case why should we call it the *Supreme Ultimate* (*taiji*) or *principle* (*li*)?"[32]

Here we cannot help but notice that Ricci's critique of *li* is based on the basic tenets of Aristotelian metaphysics, which differs completely from its Chinese counterpart. According to Aristotle and Thomas Aquinas, both the universality and unchangeableness, or the "form," which makes each individual object as it does exist, are embedded in each individual being within the changing empirical world. Aristotle's doctrine of the four causes states that each individual object in the empirical world is only comprised of the material component (*matter*) and its principle (*form*).

According to the medieval worldview, these objects—both animate and inanimate—composed only of matter and form are constantly being led to realize, regardless of their awareness, the "ultimate end" external to themselves. Therefore, the predominant teleological worldview explained the celestial movements of the sun, moon, and stars, the laws of universal gravitation, and the phototropism of plants, according to the teleological view that the ultimate end was actualized by the *Ultimate Being*.[33] Thomas Aquinas's teleological worldview, which is based on Aristotle's doctrine of the four causes, claims that the efficient cause which creates all things and makes them move, as well as the final cause which determines the purpose of motion in all things, cannot be internal to individual objects, but belong to an external being. Ricci explains this notion, as follows:

> Objects which lack souls and perception cannot move from their natural habitats by themselves in a regular and orderly

manner. If they are to move in a regular and orderly manner, it is necessary that an intelligence external to themselves should come to their aid. . . . When we come to the sun, moon, and stars, we find them attached to the heavens, each having the firmament as its natural habitat; but they lack *intellect* and perception. Without the slightest error, each thing follows the laws proper to it, and each is secure in its own place. If there were no Supreme Lord to control and to exercise authority [over these things], would it be possible to avoid confusion? . . .

If objects which are devoid of intelligence nevertheless possess order, there must be someone who imposes the order on them. . . . *Now we look at characters cast in metal [for printing] each of which has a separate meaning. How is it possible that they are to be joined together by themselves to form sentences and to be built up into an essay unless they have been arranged by an educated man who understands how to perform this task?* They are hardly likely to be able to come together by chance. Thus, it is obvious that heaven and earth and all things have a definite reason for their orderliness; that where there is matter there is form, and that things cannot increase or diminish of their own *will*. . . . If we consider the matter carefully we will conclude that the things on this earth are arranged and deployed in an orderly fashion, and that if there had not been a supremely intelligent Lord above at the beginning of creation to bestow various natures on things, they would not be able to exist in the world and each find its appropriate station. . . .

We must trace every kind of thing back to its first ancestor; and since nothing is capable of producing itself, there must be Someone who is both original and unique who is the creator of every kind of things and objects. It is this One whom we term the Lord of Heaven.[34]

Aristotelian metaphysics dictates that heaven and earth and all things in the universe are nothing more than objects without souls, perception,[35] or rational judgment. They cannot move by themselves and their motion can only be triggered by an efficient cause external to them. Therefore, if these objects, lacking the intellect, can still move rationally within the natural order and regulation of the universe, then this must clearly prove the existence of a transcendental Being who provokes and guides such order and movement into rationality. The Lord of Heaven is considered such a transcendental being. Taking the rational mode of lives and elaborate forms of all diverse creatures between heaven and earth into consideration, the existence of the Lord of Heaven, or the ultimate "final cause," who creates and assigns both purpose and use for each individual being, cannot be denied. In the creation process of the entire universe, including nature and everything living in it, God, the "unmoved mover" who initiated all movements, is the "efficient cause" external to all beings.[36] From this perspective, the absolute transcendental God, who creates and presides over the world, belongs to a completely different ontological category from those things created by him, and thereby Ricci strongly rejects the Chinese assertion that all things are one and the same.[37]

Transformation of Paradigm from Neo-Confucianism to Dasan's Thought

The Duality of Corporeal Qi and Incorporeal Mind and the Categorical Distinction of Humans and Things: Fundamental Rejection of the Neo-Confucian Notion of "The Same [original] Nature of Humans and Things"

As *Tianzhu shiyi* classifies all things in the universe into two different categories: visible "matter" and invisible "spirit," Dasan also asserts the duality of corporeal "bodies" and incorporeal "spirits." In the Western tradition, "matter" is understood as an entirely passive entity without the ability of autonomous motion, which simply has quantitative mass, that is, "extension." Dasan, on the other hand, considers the objects with corporeal body as being composed of *qi*, which engage themselves in motion through the oppositional as well as complementary interactions of *yin* and *yang*. This *yin* and *yang*, however, is not an actual entity in existence on its own.[38] He also believes that the incorporeal "immaculate intellectual being" ("虛靈知覺者," namely "pure reason"),[39] clearly distinguished from corporeal things contaminated by *qi*, must exist. This is because a "being with intellect" (有靈之物, namely "rational being")[40] is necessary to order and control the accidental and purposeless motions caused by *qi*. As an example of the fact that a being without intellect cannot preside over the world, he states: "If the head of a family is dim-witted, foolish and lacks wisdom, then all matters of the household cannot be regulated, and if the magistrate of a town is dim-witted, foolish and lacks wisdom, then all matters of the town cannot be ordered."⁴¹ From this perspective, Dasan clearly accepts the existence of a Rational Absolute, namely the Lord of Heaven, "dominating and raising all things"⁴² in the world, the idea of which is highlighted in the first chapter of *Tianzhu shiyi*. It is now easily deduced from the above description that in Dasan's thought the duality of corporeal *qi* without intellect and the incorporeal spirit with intellect is clearly imprinted, thereby categorizing all things in a hierarchy, as follows:

> All living beings in this universe can be categorized into three levels: plants that have life but lack perception, animals that have perception but lack the ability to make an inference, and man who has both life and perception and also a subtle intellect.⁴³

Dasan thus accepts the Aristotelian concept of "three levels of souls." The more fundamental issue, however, is the fact that Dasan embraces the image of humans possessing both incorporeal spirit and corporeal body,⁴⁴ and that he essentially differentiates humans from things. The rational inference of "immaculate intellect" humans possess is also defined by him as human nature.⁴⁵ If Mencius designates the "organ of mind" (*xinzhiguan*) as "one of greater importance"(*da ti*) and "the organ of perception" (*ermuzhiguan*) as "one of smaller importance" (*xiao ti*),⁴⁶ then Dasan terms "the corporeal body" (有形之軀殼) as the organ of lesser importance (*xiao ti*) and "the incorporeal intellect" (無形之靈明) as the organ of greater importance (*da ti*).⁴⁷ Therefore, the "incorporeal mind" (無形之心), or the spiritual reason, independent of the physical body, is considered as the human "originality" (*benti*) given by birth. With the help of its reason and will humans can grasp the subtle principles of all things in the world, and can also love and hate all things including their own behaviors.⁴⁸

Consequently, "man [with reason], when confronted by a robber, can chase him away by screaming, or can capture him through a strategic feat. A dog, which lacks reason, however, only barks and makes sounds, but is unable to [calmly] make plans [against the robber]. It can only do what has been determined by instinct. Human nature and animal nature are thus strictly distinguished."⁴⁹ In other words, humans with reason and animals without reason are fundamentally different kinds or categories of being.

According to Zhu Xi's moral metaphysical perspective, "the original nature and the *Tao* (or *Way*) are the same for humans and other things, but the *qi* is differently given to them by nature so that the qualities of *qi* must be different between them; some are unavoidably excessive or deficient. Therefore, the sages were able to determine the hierarchical order according to the differently given functions which both humans and other things respectively have to carry on."[50] Dasan critiques Zhu Xi's theory that the original nature for humans and other things is the same, as follows:

> The difference of excessiveness or deficiency exists among human beings, not among things. What human beings are able to do is truly flexible, whereas what animals can do is already predetermined. Once they have been predetermined, how can there be a difference of excessiveness or deficiency? The ways a rooster cries at dawn, a dog barks at night, a tiger devours animals, an ox ruminates and head-butts with its horns, bees protect their queen, and ants travel in a colony are the patterns of behavior over thousands of years throughout the world. How can there be a difference of excessiveness or deficiency? The fact that plants flower in spring and wither in the fall, and they flower before they bear fruits is their original nature without any variation. How is it possible to project the particular problem of human beings [i.e., the differences of their behaviors] onto animals and plants? Their behavior is in accordance with their Heavenly Mandate. Even if according to human measures man tries to determine their practices in a hierarchical order and to regulate them, they will never be changed. Zhu Xi always focuses on the [same] original nature and the *Way* for both humans and other things, and most of the illogical aspects of his arguments stem from such [stubborn] thinking.[51]

Man invariably delights in goodness, is ashamed of evil, and seeks the *Way* through self-cultivation following her/his original nature. A dog guards the night, barks at the robber, eats filthy food, and chases birds. All these come from the original nature [which is differently determined in each species]. An ox feeds on grass, ruminates and head-butts with its horns according to its original nature. What has been endowed by the Heavenly Mandate for each individual being cannot be changed. An ox cannot substitute for a man's deeds, and a man cannot take the place of an ox. It is not the difference of their bodies that makes such interchange impossible but the fundamental difference in endowed *li* [*principle*]. . . . However, the present-day Neo-Confucian scholars claim that "there is no difference, big or small, of *li*. Since purity and impurity lie in *qi*, the same original nature for humans and animals can differ just as water changes depending on the shape of a vessel: a round vessel shapes water round and a square vessel shapes water square." I cannot understand this viewpoint. Your thirst is equally quenched when you drink water from a round vessel or a square vessel, because the original nature [of water] is the same. Human beings, [however], cannot chase birds or bark at the robber [like a dog], and an ox cannot read or reason [like humans]. If animals share the same original nature with humans, as Neo-Confucian scholars claim, then how can they not be interchangeable? It is clear that animals and human beings do not share the same original nature![52]

Dasan also refutes such Neo-Confucian notions as "the same nature for humans and other things," or "the same *li* (principle) but different *qi* (material forces)," as follows:

If the fact that the original nature is the same for human beings and other things were so clearly true, then not only can humans become [sages like] Yao and Shun but all things possessing the [same] original nature can also become Yao and Shun. How can this assertion be acceptable?[53]

He continues to question Zhu Xi's notion of "the same nature for humans and other things: if such a notion means not only that humans and other things are 'the same in their original nature endowed by Heaven,' but also that 'because humans and things share the same remarkable *li* and only differ in *qi*, things have all four virtues so unbalanced that their virtues are excessive (or deficient) and one-sided,'" then, according to Dasan, this Neo-Confucian assertion cannot be accepted from the genuine Confucian perspective. He points out that Neo-Confucianism is influenced by Buddhism, especially the *Suneung-eom gyeong*, which considers all beings to be fundamentally the same and discusses the notion of *samsara* (cycle of birth and rebirth), but distorts the genuine

Confucian thoughts based on the teachings of Confucius and Mencius.[54] Dasan conceptually rejects the Neo-Confucian notion of "the same *li* but different *qi*."[55]

The Discovery of Man's Free Will and the Emphasis on Moral Practice: A Structural Rejection of Neo-Confucian Distinction of "Original Nature" and "Physical Nature"

Tianzhu shiyi asserts that human beings consist of body and spirit, claiming that because "his/her spirit transcends his/her body, the spirit is respected as the true self, and the body considered as a vessel in which his/her self is contained."[56] Dasan, likewise, speaks of human beings as a subtle combination of spirit and physical body,[57] where the incorporeal spirit (*mind*)[58] is considered the human "originality."[59] He defines the originality of human beings, which is fundamentally distinguished from that of animals and things without intellect, as "incorporeal intelligence" (無形之靈明),[60] "intelligent mind" (靈明之心),[61] in other words, "incorporeal intellect."[62] For Dasan, this intellectual ability is the "original self."[63] He analyzes such heavenly endowed reason in terms of three aspects:

> Heaven has endowed [humans with] "intellectual mind" (靈知 reason), so its "endowment," "situation," and "disposition" exist: 1) Endowment refers to the achievability and the deciding power of reason. A *qilin*, [Kor.: *gilin*, an imaginary animal symbolizing humanity], is predetermined to be good, so no merit accrues from its goodness; and a wolf and a coyote are destined to be evil, so their evil cannot be counted as vice. The endowment of human beings, on the other hand, can either achieve goodness or evil. The achievability depends upon self-practice and the deciding power rests on self-determination, so that when a man performs a good deed he is praised and when he performs an evil deed he is criticized. . . . 2) The situation means the circumstances and moments where reason is involved, in which it is difficult to do good and easy to do evil. Appetites for food and sex tempt us within, while reputation and profit lure us without. Innate traits of personal desires favor easy and comfortable practices over the difficult. Therefore, the situation makes it difficult [for humans] to follow goodness, like climbing heights, and easy to follow evil,

like (suddenly) lapsing. . . . 3) The Heaven-endowed disposition is fond of goodness and righteousness so it promotes self-cultivation.⁶⁴

Accordingly, Dasan concludes that in the incorporeal mind of human beings who have reason or the ability of inference, there is an "endowment" ("才"), or free will, to make a choice between good and evil. Animals are bound by their instinctive behaviors so their moral goodness or evil cannot be in question. This incorporeal human mind is also struggling in a "situation" ("勢") that makes it difficult to do good and easy to do evil. In this context, Heaven has endowed humans with the moral disposition "to delight in goodness and be shameful of depravity," thus prompting them to seek goodness over evil.⁶⁵

In *Tianzhu shiyi*, Matteo Ricci maintains that because human beings embody both spiritual and material aspects, "beastly desires" and "humane ideals" are in constant tension with one another within the human mind.⁶⁶ Dasan also recognizes two always conflicting and contradictory categories of the human mind: "the *Tao* (Way) mind (*daoxin*)" and "the human desires (*renxin*)." He claims that "if accepting a bribe is against justice, man tries to accept and not to accept the bribe at the same time. If in order to practice humanity one must deal with many troubles, he/she tries to avoid and not to avoid them at the same time."⁶⁷ Here, Dasan emphasizes free will, or the "autonomous decision" ascribed to the mind, as the basis for promoting moral cultivation:

> Heaven has endowed each human being with the ability to make autonomous decisions so that s/he can do good if s/he desires goodness and do evil if s/he desires evil. Human minds fluctuate and they are not constant. Because the capacity to make decisions is ascribed to man's mind, man is different from animals bound by preordained instincts. Therefore when a good deed is performed, it becomes her/his own merit and when an evil deed is performed, it becomes her/his own transgression. . . . Bees must protect their queen, but debaters do not consider this [an act of] loyalty because it is considered as an instinct. Tigers cannot refrain from harming other animals, but judiciaries do not reprimand them because [the behavior] is seen as an instinct. Human beings, [however], are different from these animals. Human behaviors are not fixed

or predetermined because the autonomous decisions to choose between virtuous and evil actions are ascribed to the doer him-/herself. Accordingly, good deeds become his/her merit and evil deeds become his/her own transgression.[68]

Moral affairs, for Dasan, are limited to human beings, as seen in *Tianzhu shiyi*. Morality only comes into question with free will, which follows rational judgment. The question of good and evil cannot be established or applied for all other beings which lack the intellect to discern between right and wrong, which have no free will to choose between virtue and vice, and the behaviors of which are in full reliance on their preordained instincts. This is the precise point for Dasan in rejecting the Neo-Confucian paradigm, which attributes the "moral nature" or "original nature" to both humans and all other beings. Dasan refutes Neo-Confucian moral metaphysics to distinguish the goodness ascribed to the "original nature" (or "moral nature") from the evil resulting from the "physical nature":

> The contemporary Neo-Confucian scholars ascribe "the immaculate intellect" to "the moral nature," and those resulting from the body to "the physical nature." They also consider all transgressions caused by the appetites for sex, food and comfort. Thus, all evil is connected with the body, while "the immaculate intellect" of mind is deemed to include all virtues, completely devoid of evil. [Such contention] is highly incorrect. If spiritual beings cannot do evil, then how can there be a differentiation between angels and demons among the incorporeal spirits? Neo-Confucians claim appetites for sex, food and comfort all stem from the body, but the insolent vice comes from the immaculate mind, and it is wrong to consider the mind to lack all evil. Some of those who intend to elevate themselves through studying the *Tao* (*Way*) are happy when praised, and are angered when criticized. What does this [spiritual] intention matter with the body! The logic that the immaculate mind is pure and devoid of evil is a Buddhist teaching.[69]

Dasan, accordingly, claims that without highlighting the human practices of morality through free will the dualistic Neo-Confucian discrimination between the original nature (derived from the pure mind) and the physical nature confused with good and evil (arising from the body) is meaningless. Because what is ascribed to the mind is neither necessarily good nor is what comes from the body necessarily evil, Dasan can no longer accept the Neo-Confucian moral metaphysics, according to which the original nature of the immaculate mind is considered an absolute and transcendental goodness—endowed by Heaven—without moral practices *a posteriori* accruing from the choice of free will. Dasan, therefore, fiercely rejects the moral determinism represented by Neo-Confucianism. According to Neo-Confucianism, whether all things, including human beings, are virtuous or not is dependent upon the purity or impurity of *qi* endowed by Heaven:

> Mencius, when discussing human nature, concluded evil as falling into the snares of temptation, and the Song Confucian scholars ascribed evil to the physical nature [given by Heaven]. If falling into transgressions originates from one's own self, then there is a way to salvage it. [But, as Neo-Confucians claim], if the physical nature is from Heaven, then there is no way of escaping it. If so, how can people not abandon themselves to despair and prefer to remain in the [morally] inferior situation? Heaven's endowment is originally uneven. It endows some people with beautiful and pure physical disposition, thus enabling them to become sages like Yao and Shun, and endows some with unsightly and turbid physical disposition making them like [Tyrant] Jie and Robber Zhi. How can the unfairness of Heaven reach such a point? As for Yao and Shun, I am not sure if their good acts were due to their pure physical nature. As for Jie and Robber Zhi, I wonder if their evil deeds were due to their turbid physical disposition. If Heaven had endowed Yao and Shun with the pure physical disposition and named them as sages, then why was Heaven so generous to them? Likewise, if Heaven had endowed Jie and Robber Zhi with turbid physical disposition and gave them the evil name, then why was Heaven so cruel to them? If we assume that Jie and Robber Zhi had intellect even after their death, then they would cry out every day and look up to Heaven to plead their unjust humiliation.[70]

If all moral goodness and evil are determined by the Heaven-endowed physical disposition, then people will be resigned to their fate and abandon their attempts to improve their morality. If Yao and Shun became sages only due to their endowed pure physical disposition and Jie and Robber Zhi came to bear evil names due to their endowed turbid physical disposition, then this is an irrationality on the part of an unjust Heaven.

> Therefore, if good and evil is determined because of the physical disposition, then Yao and Shun are naturally good and they are not worthy of praise. Likewise, [two vicious tyrants] Jie and Zhou are naturally evil and there is no need to keep one's distance from them. There is only a good or ill fortune with regard to the endowed physical disposition. . . . If one becomes the wisest man through the endowment of pure *qi*, then this is unavoidably predestined "goodness," and it cannot be counted "goodness." If one becomes the worst foolish man through the endowment of turbid *qi*, then this is unavoidably predestined "evil," and it cannot be considered "evil." The physical disposition can make a human being wise or foolish, but cannot make him/her good or evil.[71]

Dasan criticizes the Neo-Confucian discrimination between the "original nature" and the "physical nature" as being useless, if not harmful, in promoting moral cultivation. Similar to Ricci's recognition of man's "innate goodness" (*liangshan*) or moral potentiality in *Tianzhu shiyi*, Dasan highlights the moral "appetite" (*shihao*) or "disposition" (*xing*) endowed on the human mind by Heaven to "delight in goodness and be shameful of evil" as the point of departure for moral cultivation:

> Disposition is the appetite. The Heaven-endowed disposition is the appetite for goodness and righteousness. . . . It is pleasurable to have the will not to receive inappropriate goods, and it is shameful to be finally contaminated [by vicious desires], even while knowing that it is wrong. If one practices one good deed today and another tomorrow, and it accrues to virtue and to self-cultivation, then one's mind is at ease every day. . . . [On the other hand], if one commits a wrong against the mind today and shames the mind tomorrow, then one's mind is shameful. Barley's disposition prefers urine and it grows and becomes plump when given urine. If urine is withheld, then barley withers away. . . . Man's disposition delights

in goodness, and when cultivated in goodness, it becomes magnanimous and strong. [In contrast,] when goodness is withheld, it withers away. . . . This "disposition" (*xing*) is referring to appetites!⁷²

For Dasan, therefore, virtue and vice, or good and evil, are not predetermined or innately endowed by Heaven as the Neo-Confucian scholars claim. As seen in *Tianzhu shiyi*, moral goodness can only be *a posteriori* attained through the long processes of struggling with free will, strenuously practicing morality, and gradually expanding the moral disposition:

> The virtues of humanity, righteousness, propriety, and wisdom can be accomplished only after the [steady] practices [of morality]. Therefore, only after having loved someone can one talk about the virtue of humanity. The name of humanity cannot be established prior to loving someone. Only after having tried to make oneself better, can one talk about [the virtue of] righteousness. . . . How can the four virtues of humanity, righteousness, propriety and wisdom be [naturally] encased in the human mind like peaches or apricot pits?⁷³

Dasan asserts now that the four virtues are nothing more than the accomplishment through the gradual and steady expansion of the four innate dispositions or four moral minds, *a posteriori*.

> What Mencius meant when he said that "it is not that I am changed from the outside," refers to the act of attaining four virtues through the extraction of "four [inner] minds." It is not an act of pulling four virtues from the outside into [the inner mind] and to stimulate four [inner] minds. Consequently, [the virtue of] humanity can be attained if the [inner] mind of "compassion" is able to practice it into reality; and [the virtue of] righteousness can be attained if the [inner] mind of "shame" is able to practice it into reality. . . . These four [inner] minds are particular only to human nature, but the four virtues are accomplished only through expanding the four [inner] minds into reality. If the four [inner] minds are not expanded into reality, the four virtues cannot be attained.⁷⁴

If "one knows that serving one's parents is an act of humanity, then one must heat the room when it is cold and cool it when it is hot. [If they cannot digest food] then they must serve porridge and make efforts to provide meals in the morning and at night." But the Neo-Confucian scholars "simply sit with their eyes closed, claiming only that the spirit of Heaven and Earth that creates all things is benevolence itself."[75] Dasan believes that a transcendentally endowed "virtue" in itself, without any efforts of moral practice, cannot exist, and emphasizes concrete acts of practice to realize virtue. It is for this reason that he sternly rebukes the theoretical meditative attitudes of his contemporary Neo-Confucian scholars. "Morality," for Dasan—similar to the philosophical perspective of *Tianzhu shiyi*—is a particular domain for man with intellect and free will, and it is not—as Neo-Confucians claim—a transcendentally endowed nature within the human mind: human virtue can only be achieved *a posteriori* through actions or practices in the concrete situation. Dasan's philosophical interest, therefore, no longer lies in the Neo-Confucian moral metaphysics but in the social practice of human beings, especially intellectuals, and he dedicates himself to realizing the human *Way*. Dasan could only accept the anti-Neo-Confucian thought seen in the *Tianzhu shiyi* and embrace the philosophical message of self-fulfillment through moral practice.

The Emphasis on "Li" as a Mere Accident and the Sovereign on High as a Rational Ultimate Being

According to both *Tianzhu shiyi* and Dasan, all things of the universe, including human beings, are divided into corporeal matter and incorporeal spirit. Especially for Dasan, this world is a realm full of *qi*, which moves continually without any purpose, and changes and transforms without regularity. Does Dasan, then, regard this realm of *qi* as being transcendentally determined by *li* (or Heavenly Principle) as in the Neo-Confucian moral metaphysical paradigm? If not, how does Dasan think this realm of disorderly motion is regulated and maintained? Who, then, exercises authority over all things of the universe, including man? This section will closely analyze Dasan's position on the governor of the universe, especially in relation to the concept of moral cultivation. Dasan claims that it is easy for man to do evil and become a wrongdoer, but difficult for her/him to become a sage through moral cultivation. If this is the case, then how does Dasan accept the authority of the Lord of Heaven, or the transcendental being, over human actions, and His rewarding of the good and punishing of the evil?

We have earlier examined Ricci's rejection of the Neo-Confucian moral metaphysics, which consider the *Supreme Ultimate* (*taiji*) or "*li*" as the ontological basis of all things. In connection with Dasan's philosophical interests, two issues may be considered especially relevant for discussion: the Aristotelian categorical distinction between "substance" and "accidents" for all things in the universe, and the question of whether or not *li* is a rational substance (angels, demons, etc.) which moves and has the will through reason and perception.

According to Ricci's argument, *li* is not an independent substance even though it is categorized as belonging to the incorporeal realm. It is simply an accident attached to the substances like individual objects or their minds, and hence *li* does not autonomously exist. If this *li* is an entity with intellect and free will, then it will be the same as the heavenly spirits and therefore will not require a separate name of *Supreme Ultimate* (*taiji*) or *li*. Based on these two arguments, Ricci demonstrates that *li* cannot preside over all things in the universe. Two arguments contradicting the *li* as a substance—almost identical to Ricci's argument—can also be found in Dasan.

"*Li*" *is a mere accident.* Dasan compares *li* with the "veins" of jades. Freely interpreting the character *li* used throughout classical Confucian texts, Dasan proves that all the different meanings of *li* ultimately denote the veins inherent within all objects and all situations.[76] Therefore, he claims that *li* is not an independent substance that autonomously exists outside of all things. Only corporeal *qi* exists independently. Dasan echoes Ricci's argument that *qi* is a substance whereas *li* is only a mere accident, which must depend on the substance.[77]

"*Li*" *lacks intellect, influence, power, and free will, and hence it is not a rational substance.* According to the Neo-Confucian view *li* lacks intellect and influential power.[78] This *li* cannot love or hate, does not have joy or anger, and even has neither the [specific] "name" (*ming*) [for each separate *li*] nor "substance" (*ti*) because it is empty and ambiguous.[79] Hence, *li* is not a personified rational being capable of thinking and exercising authority or an entity with the capacity to love or hate, and to be joyful or be angry at all things. Therefore, *li*, unlike the Sovereign on High (Ch.: *shangdi*; Kor.: *sangje*) or the angels, cannot exercise authority or preside over things without intellect in this world.

Dasan even rejects the Taoist assertion that *Tao* or the *Way* presides over all things, including human beings.

> What, in fact, is the *Tao*? Is it a being with intellect? Does it have intellect but nullify it? If [*Tao*] has neither the mind nor the traces, then there also lack intellect and traces of the creation and transformation of this world. What kind of an entity, then, is the *Tao*?[80]

Dasan is convinced that only a rational being can preside over the universe:

> Is that blue and corporeal sky . . . a rational being? Or is it an entity without intellect? If it is empty and bare, how can it think or infer? In this world, an entity without intellect cannot preside over all beings. Therefore, if the head of a family is dim-witted, foolish and lacks wisdom, then all matters of the household cannot be regulated, and if the magistrate of a town is dim-witted, foolish and lacks wisdom, then all matters of the town cannot be ordered. If an empty and bare *Great Void* (*taixu*) [as seen in Zhang Zai] is considered as the presiding principle of all things, then how can the affairs of the world be accomplished?[81]

Dasan considers the blue and corporeal sky or Zhang Zai's empty and bare *Great Void* as being nothing more than corporeal entities without reason so that they cannot preside over the world. The ultimate being with authority over the universe, in Dasan's opinion, is an invisible rational being—categorically different from the blue visible sky.[82]

> What is invisible to man? It is the body of [the Lord of] Heaven. What is inaudible to man? It is the voice of Heaven. How can one know about this? It is said in the *Doctrine of the Mean*, "The virtue of spirits is great! It is invisible even when one attempts to see, and it is inaudible even when one attempts to listen. Spirits make bodies out of all things and compel people to make offerings with clean and clear mind. How vitally operating they are! Spirits seem to be on top of people's heads, and they also seem to be on people's either sides." That which cannot be seen or heard can only be Heaven. For people to live, desires surely exist and people seek after their desires. When their desires are filled, they become arrogant, fastidious, and perverse and forget their place. There is nothing they would not do. The reason these people cannot openly commit trans-

gressions, however, lies in the fact that they are on guard with care, and they tremble in fear. Why are they on guard? It is because there are officials implementing the legal codes. Why do they tremble in fear? It is because the king punishes and executes the offenders. If they know that neither the officials nor the king exist, who would not become arrogant, fastidious, perverse and forget their place in society? . . . People do not tremble in fear without reason. If they are taught [and forced] to tremble in fear by their teachers, then this is not a true fear. If the king orders them to tremble in fear, then this is also a false fear. People tremble, without being told to do so, when they pass by the cemetery at night because they know about ghosts, even though they are invisible. Likewise, when people walk through the woods at night, they tremble with fear because they know that the tiger or panthers are present even when they are not in sight. The gentlemen remain in dark rooms with fear and cannot commit transgressions because they know that the Sovereign on High (Ch. *shangdi;* K.: *sangje*) presides over them.[83]

If Ricci stipulates the Lord of Heaven (*tianzhu*) as a being without a body or sounds,[84] then Dasan also defines the Sovereign on High (*sangje*), who presides over the world, as an invisible and inaudible entity. This Being discourages human beings from doing evil and guides them to do good. Unlike the Neo-Confucians who reject the absolute authority of the Sovereign on High, Dasan claims that the ancient people believed that this invisible and incorporeal Sovereign watched over man's good and evil deeds like the sun, and worshipped this Sovereign on High, or Heaven, with a genuine heart.

People in the past wholeheartedly served Heaven and its [heavenly] spirits. Every time these people either moved or stayed, a thought was conceived, sometimes as the truth and sometimes as deceit, some as good and some as evil. People guarded against them and said, "Heaven watches over [us] like the sun." Therefore, the seriousness of their actions not to transgress Heaven and their trembling in fear, to even avoid [transgressions] while they were alone, was grave enough for them to be well versed in the virtuous behavior of serving Heaven.[85]

> The great Heaven has neither body nor material substance, yet He rules over humans and all other things of the universe like the bright sun. He is indeed the original ancestor of all things and the greatest among the [heavenly] spirits. The brightly shinning Heaven watches over us! The sages serve Heaven with care, and this is the reason "the sacrificial rite [to the Heaven] in the suburb" (*jiaoji*) has been established.[86]

Dasan's notion of Heaven is that He, as the absolute rational being, watches over human beings and their actions with numerous heavenly spirits at his sides. Therefore, Dasan recognizes the absolute rational being—as in *Tianzhu shiyi*—as an evident truth.

Conclusion

I proposed to discuss and show the family resemblance of the philosophical paradigm between the metaphysical framework of *Tianzhu shiyi* and Dasan's thought. I analyzed many of Dasan's writings as a way of comprehending his position on the issues in question.[87] Dasan (1762–1836) first encountered *Tianzhu shiyi* in 1784 at the age of 23.[88] The majority of his writings investigated in this paper, however, were written between 1812 and 1834, between the ages of 51 and 73, near the end of his life. Through my studies I've come to the conclusion that the following three agreements between Ricci and Dasan are the most notable:

1. All things of the universe are fundamentally divided into beings with intellect and beings without intellect.

2. Only human beings, above all others, can engage in moral behavior because they have the ability to discern between good and evil, and possess free will. Therefore, moral affairs are limited only to human beings. All other beings in nature cannot be asked to follow morality.

3. The invisible Rational Being, named "*tianzhu*" or "*shangdi*" (K.: *shangze*), presides over all things in the universe, whose function is rewarding the good and punishing the evil.

These characteristics common to *Tianzhu shiyi* and Dasan's philosophical thought can be compared with the Neo-Confucian paradigm, in the following two ways:

First, both reject the Neo-Confucian claim of "the Unity of Natural *Way* and Human *Ideal*" (*tianren heyi*). According to both *Tianzhu shiyi* and Dasan's philosophical perspective, there is no ontological basis for the moral metaphysics unifying the realm of Nature (Heavenly *Way*) and the realm of human values (human *Way*). They both argue that because only human beings are endowed with the ability to discern and infer, human value systems cannot be extended to the realm of nature. Accordingly, the Neo-Confucian belief in *li* as the ontological basis for all things in both realms is not acceptable to either *Tianzhu shiyi* or to Dasan because there is a clear distinction between the laws governing the realm of nature (Heavenly *Way*) and those of the human realm (human *Way*).

Second, morality can only be attained through man's practice. Human beings cannot attain virtues without free will or autonomous decisions because they can only seek good or evil according to free will. However, Neo-Confucian scholars understood *li* as the everlasting and objective moral law, in which the virtues can be attained through the meditative investigation of things even without moral practice through free will. Such a notion is not acceptable to Ricci or Dasan. Human beings, according to them, can accumulate virtues and only become sage-like when they continue to practice moral deeds before the Rational Being or God, who presides over the world and rewards or punishes human beings according to their actions.

In this respect, Dasan's notion of the human *Way* or the adoption of the philosophical paradigm centered on man's practical ethics, marked a turning point toward modern conceptions of nature and human being in eighteenth-century Joseon (Korea). It marked the beginning of a modern understanding of nature, which no longer measured nature according to the human value system. The creative encounter of traditional Confucian thought with modernity can be seen in Dasan's paradigm of practical ethics, which defines man as a rational being with the capacity of making autonomous decisions through free will.

Dasan claims that all of the metaphysical elements of Neo-Confucianism are the results of Buddhist influence, which distorted the original Confucian teachings. He, then, emphasizes that true Confucianism or "*zhusixue*" ("洙泗學") can only be recovered through a return to Confucius's teachings, which placed importance on social ethics through human practices along with a belief in a personal God.

Finally, we have to deal with a very controversial issue: whether Dasan should be considered a Catholic or not. Although many structural similarities exist between *Tianzhu shiyi* and Dasan's philosophy, as seen throughout this paper, this, in my opinion, cannot be interpreted as the two sharing the same philosophical rationale. Even buildings with the same structural principle differ in character based on the intention of each building's usage. If it is equipped with medical supplies and machinery and used to heal the sick, then it is a hospital. But if it is used to prepare and treat the dead, then it becomes a mortuary. Likewise, a mere structural similarity cannot be seen as having the same intention or philosophical rationale.

In this respect, Ricci's ultimate purpose in *Tianzhu shiyi* is to propagate Christianity among Confucian intellectuals through emphasis on the human conditions in the afterlife with the idea of heaven and hell. It is difficult, however, to attribute such a religious intention—an acceptance of religious belief through Christian notions of afterlife—to Dasan's philosophy. Rather, Dasan's philosophical purpose can be seen as an ambitious project to liberate Joseon intellectuals from the contemplative Neo-Confucian metaphysics on one hand and to encourage their moral self-perfection on the other. He sympathized with the plight of the Joseon intellectuals who were struggling in a social situation where it is difficult to do good but easy to do evil. At the same time, he firmly believed that it is necessary to recognize the authority of the invisible Ultimate Being or Sovereign on High, who presides over and rewards and punishes human beings in this present world. However, the notion of the Lord of Heaven, who rewards and punishes, is related to the afterlife in *Tianzhu shiyi*, whereas such a notion of afterlife is not significantly discussed in any of Dasan's writings.

Though Dasan does borrow the important Western philosophical framework from *Tianzhu shiyi*, he maintains the Confucian emphasis on self-perfection during one's present lifetime. The most significant elements of Dasan's philosophy lie in the realization of the human *Way*, which can be seen in the original thoughts of Confucius and Mencius. The philosophical achievement of Dasan, in which he transformed the Neo-Confucian moral metaphysics into a paradigm of man's socio-ethical practice, is highly regarded as the prototype of the creative synthesis of traditional Confucian philosophy and the Western philosophy introduced to Asia through Western missionaries in the seventeenth century.

Notes

1. cf. Han Hyeong-jo, *Chu Hui-eseo Jeong Dasan-euro: Joseon yuhak-ui cheolhakjeok paereodaim yeon-gu* [*From Zhuxi to Dasan: A Study on the Philosophical Paradigm of Korean Confucianism*] (Seoul: Segyesa, 1996); Yu Cho-ha, *Jeong Yak-yong-ui ujugwan* (*On the Cosmology of Jeong Yak-yong*), dissertation, Korea University, 1990.

2. Yi Dong-hwan, "Dasan sasang-e isseoseo-ui 'sangje'-ui munje" ["Issue on the Sovereign on High in Dasan's Thoughts"], *Minjok munhwa* 19 (1996); Yu Cho-ha, "Seongnihakjeok inmulseongdong-i ron-e daehan Jeong Yak-yong-ui bipan" ["Jeong Yak-yong's Criticism on the Debates on the Nature of Humans and Other Creatures in Neo-Confucianism"], *Taedong gojeon yeon-gu* 12 (1995).

3. Kim Ok-hui, *Hanguk cheonjugyo sasang sa II: Dasan Jeong Yak-yong-ui seohak sasang yeon-gu* ["The History of Korean Catholic Thought II: a Study on Dasan's Thought of Western Learning"]) (Seoul: Sun-gyo-ui Maek, 1991); Yi Won-sun, *Joseon seohaksa yeon-gu* [Study on the History of Western Learning in Joseon Dynasty] (Seoul: Iljisa, 1986).

4. Choe Seok-u, "Jeong Dasan-ui seohak sasang."["Jeong Dasan's Thought of Western Learning"], in *Jeong Dasan-gwa geu sidae* [*Jeong Dasan and his Age*] (Seoul: Mineumsa, 1986); Kang Jae-on, *Jeong Dasan-ui seohak gwan* [*Dasan's View of Western Learning*], in *Dasanhak-ui yeon-gu* [*A Study on the Learning of Jeong Dasan*] (Seoul: Mineumsa, 1990); Geum Jang-tae, *Dasan Jeong Yak-yong: Silhak ui segye* [*Dasan Jeong Yak-yong: The World of Western Learning*] (Seoul: Senggyunguan University Press, 1999).

5. Song Yeong-bae (Song Young-bae), trans., *Cheonju sileui* (Seoul: Seoul National University Press, 1999); Song Yeong-bae (Song Young-bae), trans., *Gyouron, Seumul daseot madi jameon, giin sippyeon* (Seoul: Seoul National University Press, 2000).

6. Matteo Ricci, *The True Meaning of the Lord of Heaven* (*Tianzhu Shiyi*), trans. Douglas Lancashire and Peter Hu Kuo-chen, S.J., 192–93. (St. Louis: The Institute of Jesuit Sources, 1985). Citations from the *Tianzhu shiyi* are based on this English version, but changes, if necessary, are marked in italics.

7. Ibid., 193.

8. Ibid., 193.

9. Ibid., 145–47.

10. Ibid., 69. The concept of 靈才 (intellect or intelligent nature) (as seen in 73, 105, 189, and 191) are usually termed 靈 and is used throughout the *Tianzhu*

shiyi. It is also interchangeably used with 靈心 (p. 293), 靈明 (p. 205), and 靈性 (pp. 75 and 81).

11. For the discussion of the immortality of the soul, ibid., 147, 149, 151, 159 and 171.

12. Ibid., 351.
13. Ibid., 351.
14. Ibid.
15. Ibid., 151.
16. Ibid.
17. Ibid.
18. Ibid., 151–53.
19. Ibid., 151.
20. Ibid., 357.
21. Ibid., 365.
22. Ibid., 291–93.
23. Ibid., 295.
24. Ibid., 285.
25. Ibid., 287.
26. Ibid., 351.
27. Ibid., 351.
28. Ibid.
29. Ibid., 293.
30. Ibid., 353–55.
31. Ibid., 111.
32. Ibid., 115.
33. Song Yong-bae, "Chunju Silui wa Tochakhwa ui uimi" ["On the Meaning of Tianzhu shiyi on the Enculturation"]) in *Gyouron, Seumul daseot madi jameon, giin sippyeon*, 489–90.
34. Matteo Ricci, op. cit., 73–83.
35. Ibid., 73.
36. For a summary of Thomas Aquinas's five ways to prove God's existence from his *Summa Theologiae* Ia.2,3, see Song Yong-bae, Chunju Silui wa Tochakhwa ui uimi, loc. cit., 490–92.
37. As to Matteo Ricci's argumentation, see *Tianzhu Shiyi*, ch. 4.
38. In Dasan's view, *yang* is simply considered as a phenomenon such as sunshine; in contrast, *yin* as that of shade, therefore *yin* and *yang* can never be substantial beings. Hence, it is impossible for him to accept *yin* and *yang* as the two origins of all things in the world. *Yoyudang Chonseo* (*The Complete Works of Chong Yangyong*, supplemented and revised), 6 vol., (reprinted, Seoul: Kyongin munhwasa, 1970. This voluminous anthology is in following quotations referred simply as *Chonseo*), *Chungyong chajam* 1, *Chonseo* II, 61a. In addition, Dasan asserts that the *Sublime Ultimate* (*taiji*) or the heavenly principle, is not

the ontological Ultimate Being, as Neo-Confucianism presupposes. To him, the *Sublime Ultimate* (*taiji*) is considered no other than as a chaotic original matter, even not yet divided into *yin* and *yang*: "太極者, 陰陽混沌之物," *Yeokhak seoeon* (易家緒言) 2, ibid. III, 517b and 505.

39. Chonseo II, Simkyong milhom, 36a.
40. *Chonseo II*, Maengja youi 2,144b.
41. Ibid.
42. Cf. especially the subject of the first chapter of *Tianzhu shiyi*.
43. *Chonseo II*, Noneo gokeum chu (論語古今注) 9, 338a.
44. *Chonseo II*, Simkyong milhom, 36a.
45. Ibid. According to Dasan, one word's *terminus* for the word-complex of "heryoung jigakja" (虛靈知覺者, "immaculate intellectual being") cannot be found in the ancient Confucian classics, but is differently expressed by later philosophers who keep in mind the diversity of its functions, for example, in "*xin*" (heart/mind), "*shen*" (spirit), "*ling*" (reasoning), "*hun*" (soul) etc.
46. Cf. *Mencius*, Book XI (Gaozi A, 11:14 and 11:15)
47. Chonseo II, Maengja youi 2, 140a.
48. Dasan first of all discriminates the meanings of "*xin*"(heart/mind) into two categories: the corporeal one and the incorporeal one. He designates the former as the organ of heart, while the latter is emphasized as the human originality. It is also asserted that this originality has nothing to do with the physical body of humans. *Chonseo II, Taehak kangui* 2, 25a.
49. *Chonseo II*, Maengja youi 2, 135a.
50. Ibid., Chungyong kanguibo 1, 62a.
51. Ibid., 1, 62b.
52. *Chonseo II*, Maengja youi 2, 135b.
53. *Chonseo II, Nono kogumju* 9, 339b.
54. Ibid., 339a.
55. For a more detailed exegesis on Dasans rejection of "the same *li* but the different *qi*" (理同氣異) theory, see *Chonseo II*, Maengja youi 2, 135b–136a.
56. *Tianzhu shiyi*, 361
57. *Chonseo II*, Simkyong milhom, 36a.
58. Dasan's terminus: "無形之心" (the incorporeal mind) is also found in *Tianzhu shiyi*, for example, ch. 3, 150; ch. 7, 362.
59. *Chonseo II*, Taehak kangui 2, 25a.
60. *Chonseo II*, Maengja youi 2, 140a.
61. *Chonseo I*, Simunjip·Seo, 410b.
62. The ability of rational inference as human originality is represented by the following words: "靈" (intellect), "靈性" (intellectual nature), "靈才" (intellectual ability), "靈明" (intelligence), "靈心" (intelligent mind) etc. in *Tianzhu shiyi*, while Dasan expressed the same intellectual ability with the following words: "靈" (intellect), "靈明" (intelligence), "靈知" (intellectual understanding), "大體"

(the organ of greater importance), "無形之心" (in corporeal mind), "虛靈之本體" (immaculate intellectual originality), "虛靈不昧者" (immaculate intellectual illuminator) etc.
    63. *Chonseo III*, Maessi sopyong 4, 202a.
    64. *Chonseo III*, Maesi sopyung 4, 203a.
    65. Ibid.
    66. *Tianzhu Shiyi*, ch. 7, 349.
    67. Chonseo II, Maengja youi 2, 135a.
    68. *Chonseo II, Maengja* 1, 111b–112a.
    69. Chonseo II, Maengja youi 1, 112ab.
    70. Ibid., 2, 138a.
    71. Chonseo II, Nono kogumju, 338b.
    72. Chonseo III, Maessi sopyong 4, 202b.
    73. Chonseo II, Maengja youi 1, 105b.
    74. Ibid., 2, 137a.
    75. Ibid., 1, 105b.
    76. Ibid., 2, 138b.
    77. Chonseo II, Jungyong gangui bo 1, 92b–93a.
    78. Chonseo II, Jungyong jajam (中庸自箴) 1, 47a.
    79. Chonseo II, Maengja youi 2, 144b.
    80. *Chonseo III, Juyeok seo-eon* 2, 504b.
    81. Chonseo II, Maengja youi 2, 144b.
    82. Chonseo I, Simunjip-mun 8, 164b.
    83. Chonseo II, Jungyong jajam 1, 46b–47a.
    84. The expressions of the Lord of Heaven or spirit as "a being without body or sounds" are very often found in *Tianzhu shiyi*, ch. 2, 104, 126, 128; ch. 3, 154, 156; ch. 5, 256; ch. 7, 362, 364, etc.
    85. Chonseo II, Jungyong gangui 1, 71a.
    86. Chonseo III, Chunchu gojeung (春秋考證) 1, 229a.
    87. Those works include: Jungyong gangui (1784), Yeokhak seo-eon (1808), Chunchu gojeung (1812), Noneo gogeumju (1813), Maengja youi (1814), Daehak gongui (1814), Jungyong gangui bo (1814), Daehak gangui (1814), Jungyong jajam (1814), Simgyeong milheom (1815), Maessi seopyeong (1834), Sangseo gohun (1834).
    88. Geum Jang-tae, op. cit., 35–36.

Bibliography

Chong, Yagyong. *Yoyudang Jeonseo* [*The Complete Works of Chong Yagyong*]. 6 volumes. Seoul: Kyonginmunhwasa, 1970. Vol. 2 contains *Maengja youi*

[孟子要义], *Jungyong gangui bo* [中庸讲义补], and Vol. 3 contains *Chunchu gojeung* [春秋考證].

Limadou [利玛窦 Matteo Ricci]. *Tianzhu Shiyi* [天主實義]. Taipei: Huagang Shuju [华冈书局], 1962.

Ricci, Matteo. *Cheonju sileui* [*Tianzhu Shiyi*]. Translated by Song Young-bae. Seoul: Seoul National University Press, 1999.

———. *Tianzhu Shiyi* [*Tianzhu Shiyi*] (*The True Meaning of the Lord of Heaven*). Translated by Douglas Lancashire and Peter Hu Kuo-chen, S.J. St. Louis, MO: The Institute of Jesuit Sources, 1985.

Part III

Protestantism and Korean Religions
Exclusion and Assimilation

6

A Genealogy of Protestant Theologies of Religions in Korea, 1876–1910

Protestantism as a Religion of Civilization and Fulfillment

Sung-Deuk Oak

This paper examines the development of the Protestant missionary theologies of East Asian religions in Korea at the turn of the twentieth century, which were the result of integrating three elements—Anglo-American, Chinese, and Korean. Pioneer North American missionaries in Korea accepted the contemporary Anglo-American theologies of East Asian religions as well as those from China adopted by senior missionaries for a generation. Korean Christian leaders, who learned these two sources through missionary studies of Korean religions, began to write their own comparative religious apologetics in vernacular Korean from 1897. Diagram 1 shows this process of circulation and mutual influence. Unlike other studies that included Japanese sources, this paper seeks to show the genealogy of specifically Protestant theologies of East Asian religions by tracing them to their American-Canadian and Chinese-Protestant roots.

In addition to tracing the theological sources of Korean-Protestant attitudes toward other religions, this paper has another aim: to provide a nuanced interpretation of the theology of religions prevalent among the first-generation Protestant missionaries and Korean Christians by rediscovering their fulfillment theory toward Confucianism, Buddhism, and shamanism, and by emphasizing their development from cessationism to continuationism. Contrary to widespread stereotypical images, this paper argues that early prominent Protestant missionaries and Korean Christian leaders were not militant fundamentalists determined to destroy traditional religions but moderate evangelicals who were open-minded enough to seek points of contact between Christianity and traditional Korean religions. A new form of Christian knowledge or episteme was produced through the synthesis of two ideas, the superiority of Western Christian civilization that crusaded against East Asian and Korean religions, and the superiority of Protestantism which was to "fulfill" Korean religions while also accepting congenial elements from them. As the early Protestant theology of Korean religions is a result of the civilizational and religious superiority of the Christian West, it is clearly based on the assumption that Korean religions were inferior and must learn from Christianity. It was open enough to integrate certain acceptable elements from Korean religions, but it was still a far cry from any sort of inclusivism and pluralism in the current sense.

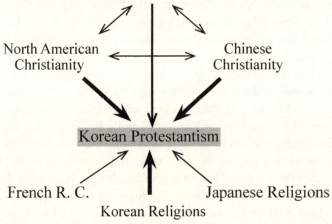

Elements in the Formation of the Korean Protestant Theory of Religions from 1876 to 1910

North American Contributions

When Rev. Henry G. Appenzeller (1858–1902), the first American Methodist clerical missionary to Korea, arrived at Chemulpo in April 1885, he brought about seventy books for his future work. Two books—James Clarke's *Ten Great Religions* (1871, 1883) and William Griffis's *Corea, the Hermit Nation* (1882)—contained information about Asian and Korean religions. In 1910 Horace G. Underwood (1859–1916), who came to Korea with Appenzeller in 1885 as the first American Presbyterian clerical missionary, published *The Religions of Eastern Asia*. The authorities Underwood cited were all missionary or Christian scholars like G. W. Aston, S. Beal, I. B. Bishop, R. K. Douglas, E. Faber, H. A. Giles, W. E. Griffis, S. Gulick, H. B. Hulbert, G. W. Knox, J. Legge, W. A. P. Martin, and T. W. Rhys Davids. These sources for Appenzeller and Underwood clearly indicate that the theories of East Asian religions of Anglo-American scholars and missionaries in China, Japan, the United Kingdom, and the United States of America were widely circulated among North American missionaries and Korean Christian leaders.

The earliest Protestant missions in Korea had a unique feature—the dominance of two North American denominations. Among 575 Protestant missionaries sent to Korea from 1884 to 1910, about 70 percent, namely 401 (230 Presbyterians and 171 Methodists) were Americans (Oak 2004, Appendix 1). When we include Canadians here—20 Presbyterians and 3 Methodists, who worked closely with Americans—North American Presbyterians and Methodists totaled 424 accounting for 73.7 percent of the first generation of the Korea Protestant Missions. And the majority of them were recruited by the Student Volunteer Movement for Foreign Missions (SVM) from colleges and seminaries. It is, therefore, crucial to investigate the theology of religions advocated by the American Presbyterians, Methodists, and the curriculum of the SVM.

This section examines five authors who represented the turn-of-the-twentieth-century theology of Asian religions of North American Presbyterians, Methodists, and the SVM leaders. A review of these representative authors and their books will shed light on the Protestant missionaries' framework for approaching East Asian religions and the changing missiological trend with which missionaries and Koreans interacted to form their own attitude toward Korean religions.

James Freeman Clarke, Ten Great Religions (1871, 1883)

James F. Clarke (1810–88) was a Unitarian minister, social reformer, and theologian in Boston. The first volume of *Ten Great Religions* (1871) compared world religions by describing them one by one, pointing out their inadequacies, and claiming the superiority of Christianity as measured by three criteria: racial catholicity, universality of truth, and historical development (degeneration or progress) (Clarke 1871, 15–31). These three became the standard criteria among North American scholars and missionaries in the late nineteenth century.

Clarke asserted that Judaism was fulfilled by complete Christianity, and that eight other world religions had good elements, which, however, were incomplete. By acknowledging the partial truths of non-Christian religions, Clarke criticized the belief that Christianity was the only true religion and all others were totally false. At the same time, he rejected the assertion of the equality of all religions. He opposed the old classification of religions into true and false religions, natural and supernatural, paganism and revealed religion, and spiritual religion and superstition. Instead he divided them into tribal, ethnic, and catholic (missionary or universal) religions. He concluded that Christianity could teach the supernatural element to Confucianism and justification by faith and faith in a Heavenly Father to Buddhism, while promoting the progress of civilization in non-Christian cultures (Ibid. 495–96).

In the second volume (1883) Clarke provided a comparative discussion of doctrines. He accepted two theories of the origin of religions: the sudden beginning of catholic religions by the prophets and the gradual and natural evolution of ethnic religions. He accepted the theory of religious evolution from animism to polytheism and then either progressively to monotheism or degeneratively to idolatry (Ibid. 214–21). The evolutionary framework of his thinking was evident in the declaration: "Christianity alone now keeps alive a steadily advancing civilization" (Ibid. 373). The idea that non-Christian ethnic religions had partial truth was a radical departure from the traditional view. Since the object of Clarke's new discipline, comparative religion, was to prepare the way for this universal religion, however, his comparative religion was the science of Christian missions.

Appenzeller was influenced by Clarke's conviction of the superiority of Christianity and Christian civilization. Clarke's language of "civilization" and "progress" replaced the old conservative "biblical" superiority of Christianity over non-Christian religions. For instance, when the first volume of James S. Dennis's *Christian Missions and Social Progress: A Sociological Study of Foreign Missions* was issued in 1897, Appenzeller and other pioneer Methodist missionaries—W. B. Scranton, F. F. Ohlinger, and G. H. Jones—praised the book, which became a textbook for Protestant missionaries in their work for Christian civilization as well as Christian evangelization. Clarke's book was used by Methodists in Korea from H. G. Appenzeller in 1885 to E. M. Cable in 1916 (Cable 1916).

William E. Griffis, Corea, the Hermit Nation (1882)

Before coming to Korea, North American missionaries collected information about Korea and Korean religions through several sources. *Corea, the Hermit Nation* (1882) by William E. Griffis (1843–1928) was one such source. It was praised as "the best work on Corea which has ever been published in English" (Noyes 1882). It remained the standard reference work on Korea for missionaries for several decades (A. Appenzeller 1928; Hunt 1980, 54). Although it used Japanese materials on Korean history as a major source, it also utilized available Western materials including Charles C. Dallét's *Histoire de l'Eglise de Corée* (1874) and John Ross's *History of Corea* (1881).

Griffis examined Korean religions through a doubly thick Orientalist lens, shaped both by American Protestantism and Japanese expansionist pan-Asianism. He supported Japan's colonial mission to civilize stagnant Korea and devalued Korean religions. He considered shamanism the basis of Koreans' faith and thought that "the fibers of Corean superstition" had not "radically changed during twenty centuries in spite of Buddhism" (Griffis 1882, 326). He regarded ancestor worship as a link between shamanism and Confucianism and anticipated that ancestor worship would be the greatest obstacle for the progress of Christianity. He defined Confucianism as a system of morality and philosophy (Ibid. 328–30). He dealt with Buddhism more favorably than Confucianism and was inclined to classify Korea as a Buddhist country. He emphasized Korean Buddhism's great influence on Japan, its tendency toward cultural accommodation, and its influence on political and social affairs. He was aware of contemporary Japanese Buddhists' missionary efforts in Korea, leading him to ask a challenging question about the future of Korea: "Shall Chosen [*sic*] be Buddhist or Christian?" (Ibid. 335).

Griffis had never seen Korea until 1927, and did confess that if he had had a Korean assistant in 1882, he could have written a much better book (A. Appenzeller 1928). His biased perspective was repeated in the literature of early North American missionaries to Korea until at least 1907, when the eighth edition of his *Corea, the Hermit Nation* was published.

Frank Field Ellinwood, Oriental Religions and Christianity (1892)

The Korea Mission of the Presbyterian Church in the USA was under Dr. Frank F. Ellinwood (1826–1908)'s leadership, mission method, and mission theory from 1884 to 1902. He was appointed a corresponding secretary of the Board in 1871 to represent the New School churches. For some years, he served as professor of comparative religions at New York University.

Ellinwood's book *Oriental Religions and Christianity* (1892) aimed to present the superior truths of the Christian faith to other religions considered futile systems of man-made self-righteousness. He maintained that Christian missions should conquer heathenism with weapons borrowed from its own philosophy and religions as well as with Christian truth (Ellinwood 1892, 39–72). The chapter on "the traces of a primitive monotheism" criticized the theory of evolution. Ellinwood said: "We cannot believe that fetishism and idolatry have been God's kindergarten method of training the human race for the higher and more spiritual service of His kingdom" (Ibid. 224). He concluded that every nation had some notions of a supreme god, but evidence also showed their decline into polytheism, for which Ellinwood cited Naville's statement, "Monotheism is primitive, but polytheism is derivative" (Ibid. 262).

In the 1890s when American Christians began to take interest in comparative religion, secretary Ellinwood categorically defended the superiority of Christianity over Asian religions. He believed that both the Bible and the missionary experience supported the theory of primitive monotheism and its degradation to polytheism, which should be corrected and replaced by universal Christianity. His practical missionary approach to comparative religions and conviction of the superiority of Christianity exerted a strong influence on Presbyterian missionaries in Korea. Methodist mission secretaries—John M. Reid, Charles Henry Fowler, and Adna B. Leonard—in New York at the turn of the century, like the Presbyterians, advocated an exclusivist view on the superiority of Christianity over "doomed" heathen religions (Reid 1884, Leonard 1907).

George M. Grant, The Religions of the World in Relation to Christianity (1895)

The Student Volunteer Movement for Foreign Missions (SVM) was dedicated to developing its programs to promote the scientific study of missions. In 1907, there were about 1,500 classes with about 18,000 students under trained leadership. Among the recommended textbooks, three discussed the relationship between Christianity and other religions—George M. Grant's *The Religions of the World in Relation to Christianity* (1895), Samuel H. Kellogg's *A Handbook of Comparative Religions* (1899), and several missionaries' *Religions of Mission Fields as Viewed by Protestant Missionaries* (1905). These books represented an official position of the SVM on the subject.

Dr. Grant, principal of Queen's University, Canada, advocated both the traditional theory of degradation and newly expanding fulfillment theory. He too was convinced of the superiority of Christian civilization. His book, *The Religions of the World* (1895), a revision of *The Religions of the World in Relation to Christianity* (1894), dealt with world religions from the Christian perspective. He reviewed the founders and the origins, the sacred books, the sources of the strength, and the causes of failure of these religions. Each chapter conclusively presented the defects of these religions and suggested how to commend Christianity to their adherents.

The three standard categories in comparing Christianity with other religions were the conception of deity (theism and Trinity), communion between the divine Spirit and the human soul (soteriology: salvation and spirituality), and the free will of humanity (morality and progressive civilization). When these categories—dependence, fellowship, and progress—were applied to Confucianism, it was found "even more defective than Mohammedanism" (Grant 1895, 87). The original monotheism of ancient China, argued Grant, deteriorated into polytheism and sorcery. Grant claimed that the intellectual horizon of Confucianism was limited to the past, and that once they believed in God, they could make progress in civilization.

Grant presented "prophetism" as the appropriate Christian attitude to world religions. His missionary prophetism meant that it stood on the common platform of brotherhood, spoke their language, understood their literature, sympathized with their ideals, respected their ancestors, appreciated their fundamental religious ideas, yet aimed to transform them with Christian truth. Grant insisted that missionaries in China should acknowledge the old Chinese schoolmasters just as St. Paul did the Greeks, barbarians, and Jews (Ibid. 91). Confucius, Buddha, and Laozi could be the schoolmasters to lead Asians to Christ. Christianity was presented as the fulfillment of the spiritual aspiration of the Asian people and as the religion that would establish all the three ontological orders of Heaven, human beings, and things—theology, morality, and civilization—for modern Asia.

In Korea, the Methodists—especially George H. Jones and Ch'oe Pyŏnghŏn—extensively used Grant's book between 1905 and 1910. The Methodists tried to build a prophetic kingdom of God by the sociological and holistic mission method on one hand, and to fulfill the traditional Korean religions by Protestantism on the other. Grant's book was well-suited to the Methodist missiological orientation in Korea.

Samuel H. Kellogg, A Handbook of Comparative Religion (1899)

Samuel H. Kellogg's (1839–1899) comparative religion exerted a great influence among the missionary circles and student volunteers. His chief works were *The Light of Asia and the Light of the World* (1885), *The Genesis and Growth of Religion* (1892), and *A Handbook of Comparative Religion* (1899). The SVM used them as textbooks for the mission study classes. The Presbyterian Church in Korea used the last as a textbook on the issue until the 1920s. Its summary was translated in the *Sinhak Chinam* (*Theological Compass*), a monthly of the Union Presbyterian Theological Seminary in Pyongyang, in 1925 (Kellogg 1925).

Kellogg was a premillennialist, and many Presbyterian missionaries were also premillennialists who affirmed absolute helplessness of the individual for self-redemption. Premillennialism had a melancholy view of non-Christians (Bosch 1991, 317). They hardly spared space for other religious traditions within salvation history, and denied the liberal idea of a saving element in all religious systems. As the practical bearings of premillennialist eschatology intensified the interest of the believers in the redemption of the world, he termed premillennialism a "missionary eschatology" (Kellogg 1888, 267).

In his second book, *The Genesis and Growth of Religion*, he provided a strong and comprehensive criticism of the modern naturalistic and evolutionary theories of the origin and development of religion such as Edward B. Tylor's theory of natural descent from fetishism and animism, Herbert Spencer's ghost theory of ancestor worship, and Max Müller's theory on the unbroken historical evolution from natural worship to polytheism and then from henotheism to monotheism. Kellogg claimed that there were two factors in the genesis of religion—the subjective factor was the nature of the human being, and the objective factor was the revelation of God. He insisted that the four characteristics of religious belief—spontaneity, universality, intensity, and persistency—were unaccountable without revelation. As the law of the tendency to moral depravation was universal, he argued, the evolutionary theory of religion was a wholly incredible hypothesis.

Kellogg elaborated a theory of degradation in his last book, *A Handbook of Comparative Religion*. After delineating various lines of decline from the purity of original monotheism to pantheism or materialism on the theoretical side, and into creature-worship, self-worship, and various forms of polytheism and idolatry on the practical side, he denied the existence of an innate evolutionary tendency toward monotheism and criticized the relativism of comparative religion. Kellogg opposed the tolerant attitude of comparative religion for practically undermining the need and urgency of Christian missions (Kellogg 1899, Preface). His fundamental belief was that beyond the superficial similarities between Christianity and other world religions, the contradictions far outweighed any real agreements.

Kellogg agreed with Robert K. Douglas and James Legge regarding original Confucian monotheism. Other religions had the remnants of revelation and parts of the divine truth. However, Kellogg compared "the elevating and reforming power of the moral teaching of Christ" with the practical morality of other religions. His main criticism was their degradation of women and children. He concluded that his theory of the degradation of religions was a historical truth, and that all religions other than Christianity must be regarded as false.

In sum, the mission theology of non-Christian religions of the SVM was mainly the theory of degradation up to 1905, and began to open up after that to a more liberal approach, fulfillment theory. The evangelical consensus on the absolute superiority of Christianity, especially Protestantism, over other religions was a non-negotiable conviction. Based on biblical passages, conservative mission scholars and many veteran missionaries advocated the theory of degradation, which denied the presence of truth in other faiths. More progressive mission scholars, mission promoters, and younger missionaries, armed with the language of social evolutionism and modernism, supported the superiority of Christian civilization and regarded non-Christian religions as inadequate for the modern world. However, they realized that the attitude of one-way proselytism did not work in Asia, where the traditional religions had preserved the societies for thousands of years. Influenced by mission scholars in England and Scotland and comparative religious studies, North American progressive evangelicals and some veteran liberal missionaries in India, China, and Japan supported fulfillment theory through the conventions of the SVM and its literature. Grant's *The Religions of the World* (1895), which advocated moderate fulfillment theory, was one of the most widely used books on the subject by the student volunteers.

For the conservative evangelical mission scholars and missionaries, the theory of degradation justified evangelism among non-Christians. On the other hand, the concept of the primitive monotheism and the idea of its survivals inspired some missionaries to search for its original forms in the past and its remnants among the contemporary people's spirituality. When they found the original monotheistic belief among the people, they used it as a point of contact with Christian monotheism. More progressive mission scholars accepted the concept of progress and fulfillment. They presented Christianity as the fulfillment of the aspirations of the ethnic religions. The religious fulfillment theory let the missionaries see East Asian religions as preparation for the Christian gospel. Christian civilization theory inspired them to develop the holistic mission method, which included educational, medical, literary, social, and women's work. At the end of the nineteenth century, the North American Protestant missionaries had a firm belief in the superiority of Christianity over East Asian religions. The concepts of "degradation" and "fulfillment" shaped their perspectives through which they understood "heathen" Korea religions. Their sense of superiority in race, religion, and civilization, however, had to undergo a process of adjustment and adaptation in the new context of the Korea mission field.

Chinese Contributions

The second element that influenced the formation of the religious ideas among Protestant missionaries in Korea and Korean Christians came from Chinese Christian literature and the General Mission Conferences held in Shanghai in 1877 and 1890. The writings of Protestant missionaries in China on Chinese religions from 1830s to 1890s became the sources and references of scholarly studies of Asian religions. These Chinese materials were also imported to Korea and used by the Korean missions from 1880s to 1910s. This section argues that the impact of the Chinese element (which was a mixture of British, Scottish, American, German, and Chinese elements) on Koreans was chronologically earlier, culturally more congenial, and theologically more influential than that of the North American elements.

The first-generation Korean Protestantism was under the strong literary and theological influence of Chinese Protestantism up to 1910. The classical Chinese language was a universal language in the Sino-centric East Asian culture in the nineteenth century. Moreover, at least up to 1904, Korean intellectuals understood modern Western civilization through Chinese books, as only a small number of Korean intellectuals could read Japanese or English. Likewise, Korean Christian leaders understood Christian civilization and Christian theology through Chinese books. As the official written language in Chosŏn Korea had been classical Chinese for centuries, and a mixed Chinese–Korean script was adopted in 1895, educated Korean Christians preferred Chinese or mixed-script books. One of the results of the influx of Chinese Christian literature through the Chefoo–Chemulpo or the Shanghai–Nagasaki–Pusan steamship lines and their Korean translations from 1883 to 1900 was that missionaries and Korean leaders, who were occupied with proselytizing works, did not write new evangelistic and apologetical books in vernacular Korean, with a few exceptions. Therefore, in using Chinese books or Korean books translated from the Chinese, early Korean Protestantism was under the theological influence of Chinese Protestantism up until at least 1910.

Moreover, the American Methodist and Presbyterian missions in Korea were guided by senior missionaries in China (John L. Nevius, William A. P. Martin, Alexander Williamson, and others) and Manchuria (John Ross) or those who were transferred from China to Japan (Robert S. Maclay and James C. Hepburn). Through these senior mentors, Chinese Christian Scriptures, hymnals, best-selling books, tracts, and catechisms were introduced to Korea. Their mission theories of religions were transferred to Korea through the books and tracts on the relationship between Christianity and Chinese religions. These evangelistic tracts or books of comparative religions took two different attitudes toward Chinese religions—confrontational iconoclasm and lenient accommodation, besides strong criticism of Roman Catholicism.

The former was based on the theory of religious degradation. It attacked the "superstitious" worship of ancestral spirits and idols and harmful customs such as smoking opium, foot binding, gambling, and polygamy. William Milne's *Zhang Yuan liangyou xianglun* [*Two Friends*] (1819), Ferdinand Genähr's *Miaiozhu wenda* [*Dialogues with a Temple Keeper*] (1856), and John Nevius's *Sixian bianmiu* [*Errors of Ancestor Worship*] (1859) belonged to this conservative majority. The latter, a progressive group, however, emphasized the congenial points of contact between Christianity and traditional religious heritage that originated from primitive monotheism, and accepted them as preparation for the gospel. William A. P. Martin's *Tiandao suyuan* [*Evidences of Christianity*] (1854) was representative of the liberal evangelical attitude.

In Korea both groups of books and tracts were used. Most translated vernacular Korean tracts, which targeted the ordinary people and women, had the iconoclastic attitude, whereas many not-translated Chinese books, which targeted the educated classes, had the accommodating attitude toward Confucianism (Oak 2005). These two were integrated in the common conviction of the superiority of Christian civilization.

John L. Nevius, Errors of Ancestor Worship *(1859)* and Demon Possession *(1893)*

An important source of the conservative attitude toward Chinese religions came from John L. Nevius (1829–93) of the Presbyterian Mission in Shandong and his Chinese tracts. He worked in China from 1854 to 1892. His writings on Chinese religions as well as his mission method of planting indigenous churches were widely used and adopted in Korea after his visit to Seoul in 1890. On the issue of ancestor worship, his *Sixian bianmiu* [社先辨謬 *Errors of Ancestor Worship*] was a required reading for Korean evangelists.

The book's main goal was to persuade people to "forsake idolatry, renounce spirit and ancestor worship, and wholly worship the only and one God." Nevius argued that the original ancestor worship served Heaven, yet that the post-Confucius practice had deteriorated into empty formalities and vanity. Thus the human principle, filial piety to parents and ancestors, although biblically sound, should be extended to and perfected by the worship of God, the heavenly principle. Nevius insisted that the original sacrifices offered to Shangdi for thanksgiving and atonement anticipated the redemptive sacrifice of Jesus Christ to come. As such, Nevius disapproved the necessity of ancestor worship in connection with Christology. He acknowledged the historical role of ancestor worship in

China but also dismissed it as a needless historical relic after the redemptive sacrifice of Jesus Christ. Here we can see at work the theory of degradation of primitive monotheism in China and a Protestant discourse of the reformation of Chinese religions by Christ-centered soteriology and liturgy.

Not only was the Nevius method and his Chinese tracts adopted by the Korean missions, but his theory of demon possession and Christian exorcism also influenced the missionaries in Korea. Nevius had experienced cases of "demon possession" from the beginning of his work in Shandong. He asked himself the question: "Is there such a thing as demon possession in the latter part of the nineteenth century?" He investigated these cases and gathered the facts and testimony of missionaries and Chinese Christians on the incidents in which they expelled spirits and set the victims free. The result was his posthumous book, *Demon Possession and Allied Themes*, published in 1896. Nevius argued that cases of demon possession actually existed in China. He described those supposedly cured by Chinese Christians, not by the old methods that exorcists had used, such as burning charms, frightening with magic spells and incantation, or pricking the body with needles, but by hymn singing and praying to God. Some missionaries testified that they felt themselves "transported back to the days of the Apostles" and were "compelled to believe that the dominion of Satan is by no means broken yet" (Nevius 1896, 71). Nevius insisted that the phenomenon of demon possession could be explained not by contemporary evolutionary and psychological theories but only by the Bible.

Nevius's theory of demon possession introduced continuationism to the Korea missions that were dominated by cessationism. The latter argued that the supernatural charismatic spiritual gifts like speaking in tongues, prophecy, and miracles ceased with the death of the last apostle. When North American missionaries and Korean Christians experienced the curing of demon-possessed patients by extended prayer meetings in the 1900s, especially around the great revival movement in 1907, some of them began to accept the continuationist view in miraculous healing.

William A. P. Martin, Evidences of Christianity (1854)

William Martin (1827–1916) worked in China for sixty-six years, first in Ningbo from 1850 to 1860 and then in Beijing until 1916. His lectures to educated people at Ningbo Presbyterian Church became the basis for

Tiandao suyuan [天道溯源 *Evidences of Christianity*] (1854). It was the most popular evangelistic book in China. Before 1912 it went through thirty or forty editions in Chinese as it did through many in Japanese. In Korea the book was read by educated Koreans and Korean Christians. Ch'oe Pyŏnghŏn translated a part of the book into Korean in the *Sinhak Wŏlbo* [*Biblical and Church Monthly*] in 1907.

Martin's *Tiandao suyuan* was similar to Matteo Ricci's *Tianzhu shiyi* [天主實義 *The True Meaning of the Lord of Heaven*] (1607). Chinese officials once regarded Martin as a second Ricci. Martin's book caught the attention of the reform-minded educated class, especially as verification through documentation became the preferred method of research on the classics among the Confucian intellectuals increasingly tired of traditional dogmatism and academicism. Ricci and Martin believed that Confucian morality was compatible with Christian ethics. They presented Christianity as a faith that could be adopted by Confucian scholars and asserted that God could be preached in the language of local culture. Both were, however, extremely critical of Buddhism. Their message of continuity and methods of accommodation showed that new missionaries had to train their minds to enter into the Confucian intellectual world. Both used the printed word and natural theology to access the educated.

Ricci was a product of the Italian Catholic humanism of the sixteenth century, so it was easy for him to relate Catholic humanism to Confucian humanism. He was influenced by his mentor Alessandro Valignano and his *Catechismus Japonensis* (1582) (Meynard 2013). In contrast, Martin related eighteenth-century English natural theology and Scottish commonsense philosophy to Confucian natural theology, realism, and morality. With their influence on Korea, both gained an audience among the Confucian intellectuals. Some minority Confucians accepted Ricci's interpretation of original Confucianism and converted to Catholicism in the 1780s. Likewise, in the 1880s and '90s some reform-minded Koreans accepted Martin's arguments that Christianity was the fulfillment of Confucianism. However, such an accommodating message was devalued by their successors, conservative French missionaries in the Catholic case, and American fundamentalist missionaries in the 1920s in the Protestant case.

Martin regarded the progress of Western civilization as a means for missions. He identified Christian faith with Western civilization and used the latter as proof of the legitimacy of the former. There was no doubt that the Enlightenment and Scottish commonsense philosophy had a profound impact on nineteenth-century missions and mission methods, to which Martin's work belonged. William Paley's natural theology had a valuable role in supporting the claims of biblical revelation. The Newtonian worldview declared the universe to be a harmonious system that operated according to the natural laws imposed by God. These laws were moral as well as physical, dictating the course of history as well as shaping the natural world. Martin's employment of the concept of divine providence was an illustration of the confluence of biblical and Enlightenment influences in fashioning his evangelical worldview.

Martin wrote the book in accordance with Chinese modes of thought and Chinese points of reference. He utilized Chinese terminology, illustrations, and concepts to gain points of contact. He expounded Christianity with a dialogic attitude, a classical Chinese style, and an accommodating method. He believed that God had already been at work in the Chinese ethical and religious systems, unlike the majority of the missionaries, who assumed that they brought a new God to China. Although he condemned idolatry and ancestor worship, and was partially critical of the theory of *yinyang wuxin*, Martin did not denounce other Chinese beliefs and customs—such as geomancy, opium smoking, and polygamy.

In chapter 5 of the second volume, Martin defined the relationship between Confucianism and Christianity with the images of a house and a necklace. Christianity was "like the foundation of a house, on which all the pillars and rafters should be built, and then the house becomes safe and strong. The five relationships are like precious pearls, which have no flaw. The primary relationship is like a golden string on which the pearls are threaded so as not to be lost. Christianity brought Confucianism to perfection; Christianity complemented the latter at critical points. What was important was the order of priority: worshipping God took precedence over filial piety and other human relationships.

Potential Chinese converts commonly asked: "If I follow this way, must I turn my back on Confucius?" Martin answered: "Confucianism and Christianity are different in terms of breadth and narrowness, but not in terms of heterodoxy and orthodoxy. Then, how can you talk about apostasy?" (Martin 1854, 57a–57b) Although Confucian teachings were good and beautiful, however, Martin added, they were imperfect and incomplete, for they vaguely or scarcely sought to establish a relationship with God. Christianity prioritized this primary relationship over the five human relationships. Worshipping God is the real way of filial piety. Christianity did not represent a destruction of Confucianism but its fulfillment. At the same time, Christian civilization would help China become a rich and strong nation. Christianity was the root of Western civilization. Accepting Western civilization without Christian religion (中體西用 *zhongti xiyong*) was like a tree without the root, which would not produce the fruits of civilization.

Shanghai Mission Conferences, 1877 and 1890

The above two attitudes toward Chinese religions were presented and debated at the General Missionary Conferences held in Shanghai in 1877 and 1890. Their official resolutions condemned ancestor worship as an idolatrous sacrifice and required all candidates for baptism to abandon it. However, there was a theological tension between the old-generation missionaries and the new-breed college-educated missionaries behind these decisions. Some liberal or open-minded evangelical missionaries emerged and appreciated the value of traditional religious customs. Both the official policy of Chinese Protestantism against ancestor worship and its changing theological openness to Chinese religions were imported to Korea.

In 1877, the Conference drew a line against Confucianism and ancestor worship. Matthew T. Yates, who had written *Ancestral Worship* in 1867, presented a paper in which he defined ancestral worship as "the direct worship of the dead" and argued that it was "the most formidable obstacle to the introduction of Christianity" (Yates 1875, 385). With some minor dissent Yates's view carried the day the Conference and remained a consensus among the missionary communities until at least the 1920s.

James Legge was not able to attend the Conference, but his essay, "Confucianism in Relation with Christianity," was published in a booklet for the Conference. Legge made three points. First, the Di and Shangdi of the Chinese classics was the true God. Second, the original Confucian anthropology taught that human beings were the creatures of heaven or God. Third, the teaching of Confucianism on human duty was wonderful and admirable. He concluded that Confucianism was in many important points defective rather than antagonistic to Christianity. He believed that Confucius and Mencius were raised up by God for the instruction of the Chinese people. Legge believed that Christianity was the fulfillment of Confucianism (Legge 1877, 10–12).

These two views of Confucianism—Yates's conservative view and Legge's progressive one—were introduced into Korea from the beginning of its missions. Yates and other conservative missionaries emphasized the points of conflict between Asian religions and Christianity, whereas Legge and some progressive missionaries were concerned with the points of contact between them. These two perspectives coexisted in the Korea missions in creative tension and controversy.

The second Shanghai Conference of 1890 emphasized social reform and higher education of the native leaders. Franklin Ohlinger, who was transferred from Fuzhou, China, to Seoul, Korea, in 1887, stressed the need to abandon all native idolatrous and cruel customs such as ancestor worship, opium smoking, drinking, gambling, fighting, polygamy, and foot binding (Ohlinger 1890). One of the most important resolutions adopted by the conference was to reject W. A. P. Martin's "Ancestral Worship: A Plea for Toleration" (Martin 1890). Martin had suggested that a wise adaptation of means would solve "the most serious impediment to the conversion of the Chinese." He emphasized its threefold good element in ancestor worship: (1) to strengthen the bonds of family union and stimulate active charity, (2) to nourish self-respect and impose moral restraint, and (3) to keep alive a sort of faith in the reality of a spirit world. He insisted that ancestor worship could be modified into harmony with Christianity. He interpreted the word "worship" as a respectful salutation, and after analyzing the essential elements of ancestor worship, such as posture, invocation, and offering, he maintained that these essentials did not necessarily imply idolatry. He believed that a tolerant position might be Protestantism's highway to success in China. After an exchange of opposing arguments by H. Blodget, E. Faber, W. Muirhead, C. F. Thwing, and J. Hudson Taylor, who declared that "toleration of idolatry is treason to Christianity" and supporting arguments by John Ross, Timothy Richard, and Gilbert Reid, the assembly rejected Martin's proposal.

Although the Conference of 1890 anticipated the time when more mature Chinese Christians would reform the system of ancestor worship, it did not adopt a wait-and-see policy. It clearly declared its opposition to ancestor worship. The majority affirmed their belief that idolatry was an essential constituent of Confucian and Daoist ancestral worship. This resolution exerted a crucial influence on the young missionaries in Korea. Soon after the Conference, Presbyterian missionaries in Seoul invited John Nevius and adopted his method as the guideline for the mission policy. They followed the official conservative approach of the Shanghai Conference to ancestor worship rather than the tolerant approach of Ross, Martin, and Richard. This did not, however, completely eliminate the influence of the minority opinion among the missionaries in either China or Korea.

Korean Missionary Contribution

When the Protestant missions started in Korea in 1884, there had already been a generation of theological discussions regarding the salvific significance of Confucianism, Buddhism, and Daoism in China. It is only natural that the pioneer missionaries in Korea would accept the emerging consensus from these discussions from either the English writings of missionaries in China or their Chinese books and tracts (which were given to Korean helpers for studying together or translating them into the Korean language) as well as from the decisions of the Shanghai Conference of 1890. As seen above, however, some missionaries in Korea supported the lenient attitude toward ancestor worship and polygamy as related to Confucian culture. On the other hand, young missionaries in Korea focused on the study of Korean shamanism, a people's religion. The barely explored terrain of Korean shamanism was mostly mapped by five missionary scholars of Korean culture, George Heber Jones, Eli B. Landis, James S. Gale, Homer B. Hulbert, and Horace G. Underwood from 1894 on.

G. Heber Jones, "The Spirit Worship in Korea," 1901

Starting in 1894, G. Heber Jones, a Methodist missionary in Chemulpo, and other Protestant missionaries began to use "shamanism" as a general term to describe all folk religions in Korea. In 1901 Jones published a paper, "The Spirit Worship of the Koreans," which was his full-blown study of the topic and made him an authority on Korean shamanism. He defined Korean shamanism technically as "spirit worship" and used "spirits" for *kwishin*, for their nature was not fixed but flexible between benevolent and malicious. He listed seventeen spirits from those enshrined outside of the house to the household gods dwelling in the fetishes inside of the house. He contended, "This is the religion of the Korean home and these gods are found in every house." He claimed, "Their ubiquity is an ugly travesty of the omnipresence of God" (Jones 1901, 63).

Jones's term of "spirit worship" for shamanism might have been influenced by Edward B. Tylor's (1832–1917) theory of animism and his definition of religion as "the belief in spiritual beings." Tylor asserted that the human mind and its capabilities were similar worldwide and that religions existed universally and evolved from primitive to higher ones. When a society evolved, certain customs were retained that were unnecessary in the new society, which Tylor called "survivals" of primitive culture. He argued that animism as a natural religion was the essence and foundation of all religions, and that the chief feature of animism was a belief in the existence of spirits. Jones identified Korean shamanism with animism in 1907 by saying that "the most universal belief among the Koreans is that of spirit worship, of Animism" (Jones 1907, 49). His use of animism was shared by other missionaries, including H. G. Underwood (Underwood 1910, 113).

George O. Engel's Tolerant Attitude at the Seoul Conference, 1904

When the missionaries in Korea had experienced Korean culture for a couple of decades, some senior missionaries began to propose that they should wait until Korean Christians could solve the issue of ancestor worship for themselves under the guidance of the Holy Spirit. In September 1904, at a conference marking the twentieth anniversary of the Presbyterian mission in Korea, George O. Engel of the Victorian Presbyterian Mission of Australia read a paper on native customs. After emphasizing the need for adaptation to the Korean context, he suggested that missionaries should take a more tolerant attitude toward Korean dwellings, food, clothes, and hair. Regarding the customs with religious implications, such as marriage customs and ancestor worship, he suggested the substitution of Christian ceremonies through the initiative of the Korean Christians, not through the interference of missionaries.

Engel believed that the Holy Word and Spirit would bring about the changes and that spiritually enlightened native Christians would truly become Christians, not Western Christians but Korean Christians (Engel 1904, 205). In discussion, J. Robert Moose remarked that "all Korean Christians pray regularly for their departed ancestors, this being the understanding on which they have given up Confucian worship." James S. Gale stated that "the question, what shall be our attitude toward mourning customs, confronts all of us. We must deal gently with the Koreans, who, as they grow in grace, will gradually advance in such matters." Samuel F. Moore felt certain that "such pernicious customs as lotteries, wine drinking, debt, usury, smoking excessively, grave-sorcery, would disappear as the light of God shines in." S. A. Moffett asserted that not all church members were in the habit of praying for their ancestors, and that he had found them willing to abandon it (Ibid. 205–06).

Missionary Conversion to Continuationism: Christian Exorcism, 1907–11

In 1907 Professor David Lambuth of Vanderbilt University completed a special study of the relationship between Korean spirits and Christian missionaries, based on the letters and reports from American missionaries in Korea. He maintained that "the missionaries in Korea display a sense of the presence of evil spirits markedly in excess of that manifested in other countries where demonology had no such popular hold. The spirit-saturated air has with insidious power waked in the missionaries all the dormant demonology with which the Christian religion was at some time furnished forth" (Lambuth 1907). He stated that the point at issue, which was "the unconscious and insidious tendency of the foreigner to accept the native point of view," was prevalent in the writings of the missionaries in Korea. North American missionaries were influenced by Koreans' shamanistic worldview (Oak 2010).

A typical case of such a missionary "conversion" was that of Rev. Charles A. Clark of the Central Presbyterian Church in Seoul. During his education at McCormick Theological Seminary in Chicago, he had belittled the idea of demon possession, attributing the symptoms to psychosis or a nervous temperament. In 1906, when he read an account of a missionary casting out demons in China, he regarded it as nonsense, maintaining that there had to be a medical or scientific explanation. But his experience during the 1907 revival changed his view. One man at the meeting disrupted the service with his raving and lashing out at anyone who tried to control him. Clark and Kil Sŏnju left the platform and led the disturbed man to an outer room. There he began to rage like a wild beast. He smashed his own hat, ripped off his coat, tore open his leggings, and started to tear down the room. He fell to the floor on his face and prostrated himself before the ancestral box. Finally, Clark became convinced that "it was a devil's manifestation," and that "the devil can work now in opposition to Him exactly as he did 1900 years ago." (Clark 2003, 39–40). Clark revised his views on the idea of casting out the devil and was convinced that the man was an agent of Satan and possessed by a demon.

His colleague Rev. James S. Gale also confessed that Koreans felt an immediate attraction to the stories of demons in the New Testament, regarding Jesus as the "wonder-worker" who is omnipotent. "Throughout the land prayers go up for the demon-possessed in his name, and they are delivered; prayers for healing, and the sick are cured; prayers for the poor, and God sends means" (Gale 1908, 88–89).

In 1911, after ten years of pastoral experience in Pyongyang, Rev. Charles F. Bernheisel confessed that he changed his cessationist view on miraculous healing after witnessing many cases of demon possession being cured by the prayers of Christians. The supernatural gift of miracle was considered to have been bestowed on the early church for providential purposes and to have ceased with the death of the apostles. But experiences in the mission field caused him to reexamine the biblical teachings on the subject and to harmonize what he had been taught at the seminary with what he saw and heard in Korea. He argued that Koreans distinguished between a *mich'in saram* (insane person) and a *magwi tŭllin saram* (demon-possessed person). He testified that all the characteristics of demon possession as recorded in the Gospels were present in Korea, and concluded that the gift of miracle was not confined to a few individuals and to a certain time period but a general power to be exercised, and that demon-possessed people were cured by the prayers of Christians (Bernheisel 1911, 9–10).

Not only did the missionaries introduce and represent Korean shamanism to the English-speaking audience, but their own initially rationalistic and modern worldview was transformed by shamanism. They accepted the premodern Korean view of spirits, which became a factor of the Protestant success in Korea. We need to examine their overall meanings in terms of the "conversion" of the missionaries. One missionary confessed that when he read of devil possession in the Bible in the United States, he knew how Christ had dealt with such cases, but he seldom saw a person possessed by demons. But when he came to a mission field, his doubts regarding "devil possession in the latter days" were completely vanquished. That the devil at times made his home in the bodies of men and women, especially in heathen lands, was "a matter of unmistakable evidence" (Cram 1905, 148).

Three elements—American Biblicism, Chinese Protestant exorcism, and Korean shamanistic healing ceremony—were combined to produce the Korean Protestant theology of spirits. The result of the power encounter between Protestant Christianity and shamanism was neither a wholesale destruction of the latter nor a unilateral conversion of Koreans to the former. The first-generation Anglo-Saxon missionaries to Korea condemned shamanism as a "primitive" and "superstitious" form of spirit worship. As most scholars have argued, missionaries attempted to destroy

Korean shamanism in the name of Protestant monotheism, iconoclastic rationalism, medical science (germ theory), and Western civilization. On the other hand, their field experience led them to embrace John L. Nevius's theory of demon possession and Christian exorcism as spiritual and supernatural phenomena in modern East Asia, not just in first-century Palestine. Protestant missionaries adopted the premodern Korean view of spirits, and thus they practiced Christian exorcist rituals—burning fetishes and offering communal prayers for the patients—in contradiction to their home churches' official doctrine on demonic possession and miraculous faith healing. Many of them abandoned cessationism and accepted continuationism.

Horace G. Underwood, The Religions of Eastern Asia, 1910

H. G. Underwood (1859–1916) arrived in Korea in April of 1885 as the first Presbyterian clerical missionary. He was the only opponent to the term *Hanănim* around 1900 among the Protestant missionaries in Korea. As it was a "name" of the supreme sky god of the Korean shamanic pantheon, he argued, it was inappropriate for the "term" for the biblical God. His conservative attitude was changed after a discussion with other missionaries like James S. Gale and Homer B. Hulbert, who insisted that the ancient Koreans were the worshippers of the monotheistic god *Hanănim*. Underwood accepted *Hanănim* as the Christian term for God around 1904 after his own research on ancient Korean mythology and religious history (Oak 2001, 42–57).

Since the controversy, Underwood shared an irenic policy with other Seoul missionaries in his attitude toward Korean religions. He wrote in 1908: "What religions are chiefly attacked by the missionaries? In reply I would state that I think no attack upon any religion is usually made. The missionary who goes to a foreign field has not the time to spend in attacking its old faiths. His work is simply to hold up Christ and Him crucified." (Underwood 1908a, 90–91). He clarified that the earlier success of the Christian mission did not come from missionary efforts but from the "miraculous" preparations of the gospel in the Korean religious culture (Underwood 1908b).

His concern for the possibility of monotheism in ancient Eastern Asia developed into a set of lectures during his third furlough in the United States from 1907 to 1908. The lectures were published in 1910 under the title *The Religions of Eastern Asia* as the fruit of his missiological study. It integrated many studies of famous Sinologists and Japanologists such as James Legge, Robert K. Douglas, E. Faber, H. A. Giles, W. A. P. Martin, S. Beal, G. W. Aston, W. E. Griffis, G. W. Knox, and S. Gulick (Underwood 1910, x.). It investigated five East Asian religions—Daoism of China, Shintoism of Japan, Shamanism of Korea, and Confucianism and Buddhism. Its main theme was the conception of God held by each of them.

The first thesis of the book was the theory of degradation. The polytheism of nature worship, fetish worship, and ancestor worship had never developed into monotheism "without the aid of a revelation." The ancient peoples had had purer and higher ideals of God, yet "the so-called evolution has been downward." Although there was a temporary uplift through the teachings of Confucius and Buddha, the constant tendency was downward rather than upward. Thus Underwood concluded that "religion is not a creature of civilization, nor of evolution worked out by a gradually developing animal, but a matter of inspiration, . . . the gift of God" (Ibid. 232–36).

The second thesis was the existence of primitive monotheism in ancient China and Korea, a common ground on which Christianity, Confucianism, and shamanism could meet. Underwood agreed with James Legge who identified the ancient Chinese Shangdi with the Jewish Jehovah. Underwood also agreed with Hulbert and Gale who insisted that the Koreans had held stoutly to the monotheistic Hanănim despite their polytheistic tendencies. Thus Underwood argued that the Chinese Tian or Shangdi, or the Korean Hanănim was the "One Supreme Ruler"; the ancient Chinese and Koreans worshipped this God; and the idea of this God came from divine revelation (Ibid. 245–46). Underwood thought that when the descendants of Noah's three sons moved to China and Korea, they brought the original monotheism, and that this ancient monotheism survived in the myth of Tan'gun, a theory which Hulbert held from 1904. Underwood regarded this concept of monotheism as the first point of contact of East Asian religions with Christianity.

Underwood's third thesis was the finality and fullness of revelation in Jesus Christ, as articulated in Hebrews 1:1–2. He did not totally reject natural revelation, yet his emphasis was on special revelation—Jesus Christ and the written Word of God. Underwood sharply contrasted the Bible with other religions' scriptures. The latter had "never claimed to carry such authority as does the Word of God" (Ibid. 247–48).

His final thesis was the superiority of the Christian concept of God over that of East Asian religions: the Christian God was a holy and just

Spirit and "a living father." He emphasized the fatherhood of God and his sacrificial love for human beings. And he argued that Korean shamanistic belief in spirits was a *praeparatio evangelica*. The original Korean monotheism was fulfilled by Christian monotheism. This fact was the greatest point of contact of Korean religions with Christianity.

Underwood's theology of religions was based on two theories—the theory of degradation and that of fulfillment. As a lifelong student of East Asian religions, he demonstrated "the inability of their existing systems to give the highest ideals of deity, as well as the absolute insufficiency of their religious and philosophies either to solve the problems of life, or to provide for the crying needs of man's nature." He was convinced that all religious systems would achieve completion in Christianity (Ibid. 262).

Korean Christians' Integration

The last topic is Korean Christians' integration of the various North American and Chinese theologies of other religions with their own understanding of Korean religions. Many editorials and articles of two vernacular Christian weeklies, inaugurated in 1897, were written by Korean Christian intellectuals in Seoul like Ch'oe Pyŏnghŏn and Hong Chŏnghu and were embedded with phrases and verses from Chinese classics. The other early sources through which we can see Korean Christians' understanding of traditional Korean religions include two Korean books written by Kil Sŏnju in 1904 and Ch'oe Pyŏnghŏn in 1907–09.

The Christian Advocate, *1897–1903*

From the beginning, the editorials of *Taehan K'ŭrisŭdoin Hoebo* [*The Christian Advocate*] argued that ancient Chinese and Koreans worshipped God (Shangdi or Hanănim) as did ancient Jews. As Jehovah was active in ancient Israel, so was Shangdi in ancient China, and just as ancient Israelites presented offerings of thanks and sacrifices of supplication to Jehovah, so the ancient Chinese sage kings presented theirs to Shangdi. The worship of Hanănim had been common in all nations. In the East, Shennong founded the sacrificial rite for Heaven and performed it at the end of the year, and Zhuanxu ordered Zhong Nan-zheng to offer a sacrifice to the Heavenly God. All the services to Heaven and Earth of Xia,

Shang, and Zhou Dynasties were offered to God. Emperor Shun offered a sacrifice to Shangdi, and Emperor Tang prayed to Supreme Shangdi. There was no sage emperor who had not worshipped God. This editorial argued that ancient Chinese and Koreans had not worshipped a mere national god or an ethnic deity but a God of the universe. Only Korean Methodist leaders like Ch'oe Pyŏnghŏn (1858–1927) and Ro Pyŏngsŏn (1871–1941), both of them converts from Confucianism, could write this kind of editorial with erudite references to many passages of Confucian classics and Chinese history books. In other words, Ch'oe and other Korean leaders had read the Chinese apologetics and evangelistic books of those "liberal" missionaries and extremist Shangdists like J. Legge, W. A. P. Martin, and Ernst Faber. Korean Christians accepted the idea of primitive monotheism of Shangdi and applied it to the Korean term Hanănim around 1897.

The Christian News, 1897–1903

Underwood's *Kŭrisŭdo Sinmun* [*The Christian News*] also emphasized in 1897 that there was no idol worship at all in ancient China and that the sage kings worshipped only the true God Shangdi and offered sacrifices to him for their sins. Yet the customs were gradually degraded into superstitions and idolatry. "The ancient sages revered Syangjyu who created heaven and earth, governs all things, and controls all blessings and punishment." "The ancient sages and saints worshipped Syangjyu sincerely." One editorial, "Confucianism and Christianity: Two Sides of the Same Coin," maintained that Confucianism and Christianity were two sides of the One Way, and that Christianity did not destroy Confucianism but fulfilled it. It depicted their relationship with an analogy of beautiful trees (Confucianism) and the sunny spring (Christianity). "As the beautiful trees become mature, they become more luxuriant and take more sunshine. . . . Who can ignore interdependence of the two religions?" Christianity would let Confucianism grow, blossom, and bear abundant fruit. The sunny spring needed the beautiful trees of Confucianism to produce flowers and fruits. The same interdependence existed in the grafting of a new branch of Christianity onto the stem of Confucianism. The editorial emphasized the partnership of two religions in religious life in worshipping heaven as well as in the educational and moral life of the nation. The church agenda of evangelization could coexist with the national agenda of nation building in the discursive public space of the church newspapers.

Kil Sŏnju, Haet'a-ron, 1904

Kil Sŏnju's (吉善宙 1869–1935) earlier theology of religions was a product of his conversion experience in 1896, his ministry as an elder of the Central Presbyterian Church in Pyongyang from 1901, and a theological study at the Presbyterian Theological Seminary in Pyongyang from 1901. His first book, *Haet'aron* [*On Sloth*], a short Korean version of the *Pilgrim's Progress*, was written in 1901 and published by the Korean Religious Tract Society in 1904, when Korean society was busy pursuing enlightenment and education for the building of an independent modern nation. Although the allegorical novel was not an apologetic treatise in nature, it revealed Kil's theory of religions to some extent.

Haet'aron, an eleven-page allegory, was a typical didactic enlightenment novel. It promoted diligence, can-do-spirit, temperance, morality, and an indomitable will to attain personal goals and accomplish great matters. The main character of the story made a pilgrimage from the Castle of Wishes to the Kingdom of Attainment and finally to the Kingdom of Eternal Life. He should avoid the roads of drunkenness, merriments, lechery, self-conceit, double-mindedness, and haste, and enter the Gate of Resolution, from which his journey again needed to avoid the roads of comfort-seeking, sloth, tobacco, opium, lethargy, and slumber. In Asian history, those who had entered this Kingdom of Attainment by diligence and overcoming suffering were great men—Emperors Yao, Sun and Yu, Dong Zhongshu (179–104 BCE), and Zhu Maichen (d. 116 BCE)—and religious leaders like Buddha, Confucius, Paul, and Jesus.

Kil put much emphasis on the seriousness of the sin of sloth, which was one of the seven deadly sins (wrath, greed, sloth, pride, lust, envy, and gluttony). Sloth was a lesser capital sin among the seven because it was a sin of omission rather than commission. However, Kil highlighted the sin of apathy and indolence in the figure of the "Beast of Sloth," a personification of Satan who attacked people, and the most serious enemy in the fulfillment of one's dreams and the modernization of Korea as well. In the time of the national enlightenment movement, Kil took an optimistic view of human efforts and secular enterprises, an evolutionary view of time, and an irenic attitude toward other Asian religions. However, Kil emphasized the help of faith in Jesus, assessed contemporary Korean society negatively, and set entering the Kingdom of Eternal Life beyond the mundane world as the ultimate goal of humanity.

In the personal and national projects, Kil argued that the traditional religious figures—ancient Chinese emperors, Confucian scholars, and Buddha—could become models and schoolmasters to teach Koreans the virtue of diligence in entering the Kingdom of Attainment. In this sense Kil's theology of religions was open-ended. But these sages had not entered the Kingdom of Eternal Life, the ultimate achievement. In this sense Kil's theology remained within the limits of the late nineteenth-century evangelicalism that advocated the superiority, uniqueness, and finality of Christianity in the issue of salvation.

Ch'oe Pyŏnghŏn, Syŏngsan Myŏnggyŏng, 1909

Ch'oe Pyŏnghŏn (1858–1927) began to write chapters of his first apologetic and allegorical novel, *Syŏngsan Myŏnggyŏng* [*The Bright Mirror in the Holy Mountain*] in *Sinhak Wŏlbo* [*A Biblical and Church Monthly*] in 1907 and published it as a book in March 1909. The book consists of a series of dialogue on religions between a young Christian evangelist named Sinch'ŏnong (Trusting-Heaven Bird) and three old religious leaders—Confucian scholar Chindo (True Way), a Buddhist monk Wŏngak (Primal Awakening), and a Daoist Paeg'un (White Cloud). Their meetings continue on "the spiritual hilltop" (heart-mind) of "the holy mountain" (a believer's body) for three days, which was the first occasion of religious dialogue in Korean literature. In the preface, G. H. Jones compared Choi's allegorical book with John Bunyan's *Pilgrim's Progress*.

In the dialogues of the book, each religious leader presented the essential tenets of his religion, pointing out its differences with Christianity, and discussing the Christian doctrines of creation, the after-world, anthropology, and the Trinity with the Christian evangelist. The Christian, Sinch'ŏnong, Ch'oe himself, argued for the superiority of Christianity over Daoism, Buddhism, and Confucianism.

The major sources of the book were George M. Grant's *The Religions of the World* (1895) and some Chinese Christian apologetics including W. A. P. Martin's *Tiandao suyuan* (*Evidence of Christianity*, 1854). As seen above, Martin's and some other liberal evangelical missionaries' Chinese tracts, which adopted the Riccian method of accommodation toward Confucianism and argued that Christianity was the universal Great Way, neither Western nor Eastern, became essential reading among Korean Christian leaders.

Ch'oe also translated and summarized George M. Grant's *The Religions of the World* into "Sagyo kyoryak" ("Comparison of Four World Religions") in *Sinhak Wŏlbo* in 1909 (Ch'oe P 1909b). Probably G. Heber Jones introduced Grant's book, *The Religions of the World* (1895), to Ch'oe. Grant's statement about Chinese Confucianism as schoolmaster (Grant 1895, 91) was fully accepted by Ch'oe and became the prevailing attitude of the Korean Methodist Church toward non-Christian religions in the decade of 1897–1906.

The Christian evangelist has a definite goal in the dialogue—proving the evidences of Christianity to the three men and leading them to the Christian truth. As Jones mentioned in the preface, the book showed "most conclusively the all-surpassing value of the Christian faith as compared with old faiths of the Far East, and prophecies of the ultimate and complete Christianization of his people." Ch'oe's final goal was making the Confucian *yangban* scholar a Christian.

Buddhist Reactions, 1910–13

The reaction to Ch'oe's book, however, came not from Confucian scholars, but from Buddhist monks who engaged in the reform movement of Korean Buddhism. Paek Yongsŏng's *Kwiwŏn chŏngjong* [*The Orthodox Religion that Returns to the Fountainhead*, 1913] was a direct reaction against Ch'oe's book. Paek compared Buddhism to Confucianism, Daoism, and Christianity, calling Buddhism the "religion of Great Enlightenment" (Taegak-kyo). He argued that Confucianism presented a complete moral doctrine, yet it lacked transcendental teaching; Christianity was closer to the Buddhist teachings on heaven (meritorious actions would lead to rebirth in heavenly realms), yet it was completely ignorant of transcendental teaching. Only Buddhism, he concluded, presented the complete teaching on morality and transcendental truth (Buswell 145).

A more liberal monk Han Yong'un's *Chosŏn Pulgyo yusillon* [*On the Reformation of Korean Buddhism*, 1910] called for radical changes of Buddhism to survive and evolve into a religion of salvation of the world and civilization in the modern and scientific age. He explained Buddhism in terms of two categories, an egalitarian "ideology of equality" as the "essence" of Buddhism and a salvific "ideology of saving the world" as the "function" of Buddhism. Han thought that the vision of the symbiotic interrelatedness of all things of the Hwa-yen school could provide a Buddhistic foundation for world peace and universal equality among individuals, races, and nations. Yet Han emphasized the functional side of

Buddhism, which was to save the world. As a way of activating this salvific function, he proposed that Buddhist temples move from mountains to cities. In order to accommodate the Western ideal of democratization, he proposed the popularization of Sutras and the rationalization and purification of rituals. He also advocated the promotion of self-supporting economic basis of the temples, the standardization of the Sŏn meditation method, and the freedom of monks to marry (Buswell 146–50). Han's worldview was not different from that of Korean Christians, for he too accepted the ideas of civilization and evolution without abandoning the traditional foundation.

Conclusion

This paper attempted to find the genealogy of the formation of the Protestant theology of religions in early modern Korea. Diagram 2 shows the network of the theological and theoretical influences in the making of the Protestant Christian understanding of Korean religions. First, Chinese books and tracts on Chinese religions written by senior Anglo-American missionaries in China directly influenced young missionaries and Korean Christian leaders in Korea. Second, some evangelical mission scholars' books of comparative religions were used by missionaries in Korea. Third, after the Sino-Japanese War, Protestant missionaries in Korea, who had now a decade's field experience, began to produce semi-academic studies on Korean religions in the periodicals like the *Korean Repository*. When they published vernacular Korean Christian weekly newspapers in 1897, it was also time for Korean leaders to produce their own discourses on Korean religions, influenced by Chinese and English missionary materials. Ch'oe Pyŏnghŏn's *Sŏngsan myŏnggyŏng* (1909) and Horace G. Underwood's *The Religions of Eastern Asia* (1910) were the first results of Korean Protestant Christianity's search for a theology of Korean religions.

By rediscovering the fulfillment theory as an important part in the development of early Korean theologies of religions, this paper tried to revise the mainstream understanding of the theories of religions of the first generation missionaries and Korean Christians. Christianity came to Korea to fulfill the longings and aspirations of Korean religions at the turn of the twentieth century, and a distinctive indigenous Korean Protestantism flourished. This seemingly simple thesis has been rejected by the scholars of the history of Korean Christianity for a long time. In 1912, however, G. Heber Jones wrote, "Korea has been called the surprise of modern missions. The rapid rise of a church community now approximating 300,000, the early naturalization of Christianity in the Korean environment, and its expression in distinctive and original national forms have challenged the attention of the Christian world" (Jones 1912, 412). His witness about the indigenization of Christianity in Korea needs to be rehabilitated and taken seriously today when contemporary "evangelical" churches in Korea are still groping for a relevant theology of non-Christian religions. The moderate inclusive fulfillment theory adopted at Edinburgh in 1910 has still something to say to the Korean Protestant Churches that have been under the shadow of fundamentalism since the 1920s. The first step for the conservative mainline Korean Protestant Churches to take in order to free themselves from the grip of an outdated and irrelevant theology of religions is to recover the legacy of the first generation's theological turn from the crusading mentality to the fulfillment theory which at least approached Korean religions with respect and hope.

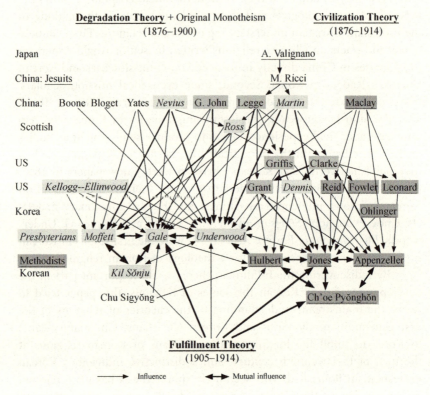

Genealogy of Protestant Theory of Religions: Network of Influence

Bibliography

Appenzeller, Alice R. "William Elliot Griffis, D.D., L.H.D.: An Appreciation," *Korea Mission Field* (April 1928): 78.

Appenzller, H. G. and Jones, G. H., eds. "Christian Missions and Social Progress," *Korean Repository* 5 (February 1898): 64–69.

Bernheisel, Charles F. *The Apostolic Church as Reproduced in Korea*. New York: Board of Foreign Missions, Presbyterian Church, USA, 1912.

Bosch, David J. *Transforming Mission: Paradigm Shifts in Theology of Mission*. Maryknoll, NY: Orbis Books, 1991.

Buswell, Robert Jr. "Buddhist Reform Movements in Korea during the Japanese Colonial Period: Precepts and the Challenge of Modernity." In Buddhist Behavioral Codes and the Modern World, edited by Charles Wei-hsun Fu and Sandra A. Wawrytko, 141–60. Westport, CT: Greenwood Press, 1994.

Cable, Elmer M. "종교비교학 Chonggyo pigyohak" [Comparative Religion] Sinhak segye 1:4 (October 1916): 51–62.

Ch'oe, Pyŏnghŏn, trans. 예수천주량교변론 Yesugo Chŏnju Ryanggyo Pyŏnnon [Protestantism and Roman Catholicism: Errors of the Latter]. Seoul: Ilhan Insoe, 1908.

———. 聖山明鏡 Syŏngsan Myŏnggyŏng [The Bright Mirror in the Holy Mountain]. Seoul: Chŏngdong Hwanghwa Sŏjae, 1909.

Clark, Donald N. *Living Dangerously in Korea: The Western Experience 1900–1950*. Norwalk, CT: East Bridge, 2003.

Clarke, James F. *Ten Great Religions*. Boston: Houghton, Mifflin, 1883.

Cram, W. G. "Rescued after Years of Bondage," *Korea Methodist* (September 10, 1905): 148.

Dallét, Claude Charles. *Histoire de l'Eglise de Corée*. Paris: Librairie Victor Palmé, 1874.

Ellinwood, Frank Field. *The Great Conquest: or Miscellaneous Papers on Missions*. New York: William Rankin, 1876.

———. *Oriental Religions and Christianity*. New York: Scribner, 1892.

———. *The Progress of a Generation*. New York: Board of Foreign Missions of Presbyterian Church in the USA, 1902.

Engel, George O. "Native Customs and How to Deal with Them," *Korea Field* 4 (1904): 205–06.

Gale, James S. *Korean in Transition*. New York: Young People's Missionary Movement of the United States and Canada, 1909.

Grant, George Monro. *The Religions of the World in Relation to Christianity*. New York: Revell, 1894.

———. *The Religions of the World*. New York: Anson Randolph; London: Adam & Charles Black, 1895.

Griffis, William E. *Corea, the Hermit Nation*. New York: Scribner, 1882.

———. *A Modern Pioneer in Korea: Henry G. Appenzeller.* New York: Revell, 1912.

Hunt, Everett N. *Protestant Pioneers in Korea.* Maryknoll, NY: Orbis Books, 1980.

Jones, George Heber. "The Spirit Worship of the Koreans," *Transactions of the Korea Branch of the Royal Asiatic Society* 2 (1901): 31–58.

———. *Korea: The Land, People, and the Customs.* Cincinnati: Jennings & Graham, 1907.

———. "Presbyterian and Methodist Missions in Korea," *International Review of Mission* 1:4 (1912): 412–34.

Kellogg, Samuel Henry. "Prof. Max Müller on the Origin and Growth of Religion," *Bibiliotheca Sacra* 41:161 (January 1884): 132–57.

———. "The Ghost Theory of the Origin of Religion," *Bibiliotheca Sacra* 44:174 (April 1887): 273–293.

———. "Premillennialism: Its Relations to Doctrine and Practice," *Bibiliotheca Sacra* 45:178 (April 1888): 234–74.

———. *The Genesis and Growth of Religion.* New York: Macmillan, 1892.

———. *A Handbook of Comparative Religion.* Philadelphia: Westminster, 1899.

———. "그리스도종교와다른종교에 ᄀᄀ관계 Kŭrisŭdo chonggyo wa tarŭn chonggyo e taehan kwangye" ["Relationship between Christianity and Other Religions"] *Sinhak Chinam* 28 (October 1925): 17–35.

Kil, Sŏnju. 懈惰論 *Haet'aron* [*On Sloth*]. Seoul: Korean Religious Society, 1904.

Lambuth, David K. "Korean Devils and Christian Missionaries," *Independent* (August 1, 1907): 287–88.

Legge, James. *Confucianism in Relation with Christianity.* Shanghai: Kelly & Walsh, 1877.

Leonard, Adna Bradway. *The Way of the Lord Prepared.* New York: Eaton & Mains, 1907.

Martin, William A. P. 天道溯原 *Tiandao suyuan.* Shanghai: American Presbyterian Press, 1854.

———. "Ancestral Worship: A Plea for Toleration," in General Conference of the Protestant Missionaries in China, *Records of the General Conference of the Protestant Missionaries in China*, 619–31. Shanghai: American Presbyterian Mission Press, 1890.

Meynard, Thierry S. J. "The Overlooked Connection between Ricci's *Tianzhu shiyi* and Valignano's *Catechismus Japonensis.*" *Japanese Journal of Religious Studies* 40/2 (2013): 303–22.

Mott, John R. *History of the Student Volunteer Movement.* New York: SVM, 1892.

———. *The Evangelization of the World in This Generation.* New York: SVM, 1900.

———. *The Decisive Hour of Christian Missions.* Edinburgh: Foreign Mission Committee of the Church of Scotland, 1910.

Nevius, John L. 祀先辨謬 *Sixian bianmiu* [*Errors of Ancestor Worship*]. Shanghai: Publisher not available, 1864.

———. *Demon Possession and Allied Themes*. New York: Revell, 1896.

Noyes, George C. "Review of Corea, the Hermit Nation," Dial 3 (1882): 167.

Oak, Sung-Deuk. Sources of Korean Christianity. Seoul: Institute of Korean Church History, 2004.

———. "Chinese Tracts and Early Korean Protestantism." In Christianity in Korea, edited by Robert E. Buswell Jr. and Timothy S. Lee, 72–93. Honolulu: University of Hawaii Press, 2005.

———. "Healing and Exorcism: Christian Encounters with shamanism in Early Modern Korea," *Asian Ethnology* 65:1 (July 2010): 99–135.

Ohlinger, Franklin. "How Far Should Christians be Required to Abandon Native Customs?" in General Conference of the Protestant Missionaries in China, *Records of the General Conference of the Protestant Missionaries in China, Held at Shanghai, May 7–20, 1890*, 603–09. Shanghai: American Presbyterian Mission Press, 1890.

Reid, John Morrison, ed. Doomed Religions: A Series of Essays on Great Religions of the World. New York: Phillips & Hunt, 1884.

Ross, John. History of Corea: Ancient and Modern. Paisley, Scotland: J. and R. Parlane, 1881.

Speer, Robert Elliot. *The Non-Christian Religions Inadequate to Meet the Needs of Men*. New York: Board of the Foreign Missions of PCUSA, 1906.

———. "A Missionary Statesman and Secretary: The Rev. Frank Field Ellinwood, D. D., LL. D.," *Missionary Review of the World* 31 (December 1908): 907–16.

———. *The Light of the World: A Brief Comparative Study of Christianity and Non-Christian Religions*. West Medford, MA: Central Committee of the United Study of Mission, 1911.

Underwood, Horace G. *The Call of Korea*. New York: Fleming H. Revell, 1908.

———. "Korea's Crisis Hour." *Korea Mission Field* 4 (September 1908): 130.

———. The Religions of Eastern Asia. New York: Macmillan, 1910.

7

What Can Christianity Learn from Korean Religions?

The Case of Ryu Yongmo

Young-Ho Chun

Ryu Yongmo, also called Daseok (多夕),[1] lived a long life (1890–1981), spanning one of the most turbulent periods of Korean history. His thought was formed by his national historical consciousness and his reflections on the dark events that deeply affected Korean people as a whole and him as a thinker. His thought and life are closely interwoven and inform his complex horizon, a product of the fusion with a number of worldviews and horizons[2] such as traditional Korean cosmology, Buddhism, Daoism, Confucianism, and Christianity. One should not abstract his thought from this symbiotic fusion of horizons. He is one of the most creative thinkers in modern Korean history, and yet he has been ignored as a thinker due to the general opinion that he was not "properly schooled" as a theologian and held "unorthodox" views of Christian doctrines. Lately a few scholars have begun paying serious attention to his writings. He was well-versed in Chinese literature, of which he offered a unique interpretation. He did not uncritically adopt ideas from the ancient Korean sources, but rather creatively constructed his own interpretation and synthesis. He refused to think in abstractions, but neither was he a mere pragmatist. In a quest for personal authenticity and holistic integration, he did not advocate a morality that he did not apply to himself. When he "became" a Christian, he read the Christian scriptures by giving his heart to them in the same manner he did to the Chinese and Buddhist canons. His knowledge of the Chinese language was unsurpassed even in his time according to expert opinion. His creative philological imagination was frequently expressed poetically, and that penchant for linguistic creativity resulted in the coining of new Korean words—pregnant with Chinese meanings—in order to convey emerging ideas for which there had been no appropriate expression.

Whenever there is a fusion of horizons in which a new meaning emerges, its expression can be difficult to understand. This was true for Ryu as well. His conceptualization was not merely predicated upon apparent reality but also upon the reality of the Void, the Unknown, the nonexistent—the reality upon which reason has not yet shed its light. He yearned for the reality that *is* without existence. Hence he called God the one who is "Being without existence."[3] His lectures were, for this reason, known to have been difficult to comprehend. However, responding to this perception, he said, his words are "useless." He does not try to talk about things conventional and *useful* to *this* world but rather about what is *helpful* to those who need to prepare well for death and the life after death—the eternal life, the life of *Eol* (얼).[4] To understand him properly, one must become acquainted with how he came to think what he thinks and why he says what he says. For this, it is crucial to pay serious attention to the historical context in which he lived.

This does not mean that he is to be treated as relevant only to his own context. He is a visionary thinker. This point was clearly expressed when he talked about the nature of faith: he understood faith/conviction (信) as comprising of two Chinese letters denoting "human" (人) and 'word' (言). It connotes a human being becoming word. In faith one becomes united with word. This is the way humans become what they are meant to be. It is the way of sincerity and authenticity. The authenticity and integrity of human life, therefore, is rooted in the "Word" given *from above* which *breaks through* the flatness of this world so we may *rise up* to *Heaven*, the realm of *Eol*.

Why should we be interested in *Ryu Yongmo*? Because he is one of the most significant Korean interpreters of the one God incarnate in Jesus Christ, a thinker who integrated indigenous Korean religious thought forms into his Christian theology. Unlike many other thinkers, he did not abandon his own world in receiving the ideas of others. He received them, reinterpreted them, and offered an alternative view to the orthodox interpretation of the Christian faith. In this essay I do not make any claim to be exhaustive in presenting his life and thought. There are other scholars who have reflected more deeply and more comprehensively on his thought. He still remains enigmatic as a religious thinker. My purpose here is only to introduce him to those who are unfamiliar with his profoundly creative synthesis.

There are three parts to this essay: (1) a short biographical background of Ryu Yongmo; (2) a select treatment of his thought; and (3) brief comments in terms of what we may learn from him.

The Life of Ryu Yongmo (柳永模), 1890–1981

Every Korean is born into a space where he or she existentially relates to the cultural ethos already deeply imbued with the three religious traditions and practices—Shamanist (*Mu*, 巫), Buddhist, and Confucian. Ryu Yongmo was born on March 13, 1890, in *Hanyang* (now Seoul), the eldest of thirteen children born to Ryu Myonggeun and Kim Wanjeon. His father, a leather worker, belonged to the *Jungin* class in terms of social status. They lived in relative poverty. Only two children out of thirteen—Yongmo and his younger brother Yongcheol—survived to adulthood.[5] His father achieved some economic success in later life in that he opened a small leather tanning business that enabled him to provide an education for his sons. Kim Heungho suggests[6] three stages of Ryu's life. The first stage (1890–1942) starts with his biological birth and includes the time when he was baptized into the Christian faith at the age of fifteen and received the Christian scriptures. The second stage (1942–1954) is the period in which he had a deep religious experience which led him to a life of extreme austerity, that is, adopting ascetical practices that break with conventional habits such as having one meal a day, abstaining from sexual relations, kneeling on his knees rather than sitting comfortably when studying, traveling on foot alone in an effort to offer to God a sacrifice of his bodily needs.[7] The third stage (1955–1981) is the period in which he predicted his date of death and commenced writing his diaries that captured his own inner voice. This is the voice that he heard from Heaven and is communicated through him to others. I basically agree with this division, but I would like to revise it by subdividing the first stage into 1890 to 1912 and 1913 to 1942, as will be shown below.

Ryu Yongmo's formal learning began at the age of five when his father introduced him to the Confucian classics through their simplified summary called *cheonjamun* (千字文). At six, he joined the regular school system of Joseon society called *Seodang* (書堂).[8] Ryu's *Seodang* education gave him a broad foundation for his intellectual development. It introduced him to the teachings of Neo-Confucianism on human propriety. It opened his eyes to the wider vista of the knowledge of the world of nature, humanity, morality, and social life. His education was abruptly interrupted at seven when he was infected by cholera, which forced him to stay at home for three to four years. It is said that his mother's devoted care saved him from certain death. He continued his education at Hasudong Primary School where he was exposed to physics and mathematics, at which he excelled, but, after completing two years of the three-year program, he returned in 1903 to *Seodang*, where he studied the thought of Mencius (371–289 BCE) for two years under the tutorship of Lee Insu.[9] This early foundation in traditional Confucian thought was to remain with him for the rest of his life. His adherence to Confucian values stimulated his youthful resistance to Japanese occupation, and remained as a defining frame of his existence. They were the sources of his thought and religious imagination.

Ryu's first encounter with Christianity came about as a result of his nationalist opposition to Japanese occupation. After the Japanese imposition of the 1905 Treaty of Protection, the Young Men's Christian Association (YMCA), protected as it was by the power of Western countries, became a sanctuary where Korean patriots could meet in relative safety. Both Ryu and his brother began attending YMCA meetings where they were soon steeped in nationalist thinking, one of the tenets of which was that the way to regain national sovereignty lay in education, which engages with the new learning of the West. Accepting this premise, Ryu also began to take an interest in Christianity. Under the guidance of Kim Jungsik, then YMCA director, Ryu began attending the Yeondong Church. Judging from his reminiscence of this time, it would appear that his introduction to Christianity came about primarily through his admiration of Kim's nationalism.[10] He began, however, to read the Christian Bible eagerly and attend Christian worship services.

This conversion involved a radical shift in his life since it stood for changing from a non-religious affiliation to a committed relationship with Jesus. During the same period, he enrolled himself at the Keongsung Foreign Language School, where he studied Japanese for two years and

What Can Christianity Learn from Korean Religions? 193

learned to speak it fluently. His motive was to strengthen the struggle for national sovereignty by knowing the enemy.[11] Through proficiency in Japanese, he was able to access the world literature that was being translated into Japanese at that time. Thus he extended his knowledge of Western civilization. He consolidated his studies from 1907 at Kyeongshin School, where he thrived in science as well as in the humanities. It was his proficiency in science, however, that enabled him to be hired in 1910 to teach at the Osan School. It was also science that he decided to study at an advanced level at the Tokyo School of Physics in Japan (1912-1913).[12]

In the autumn of 1910, Ryu was asked by Lee Seunghun (이승훈), the founder of the Osan School (1864-1930), to become a teacher at the school. There he read the works of Leo Nikolayevich Tolstoy (1828-1910).[13] This deepened his understanding of the Christian life, yet also stirred in his mind critical questions about the dogmatic and creedal expression of the Christian faith. At the school he taught physics, mathematics, and astronomy. He started his classes by praying and reading the Bible. The founder of the school was so impressed by Ryu's devout religious practices that he himself was converted to Christianity just three months after Ryu joined the faculty. The educational philosophy of the school was changed in line with the Christian spirit. The school built a chapel on its campus. As a result, the Osan School became a mission school! But personally, under the influence of Tolstoy's unorthodox Christian views that increasingly found an echo in his heart, Ryu began to distance himself from the "orthodox" element of Christianity. Ironically, he influenced others to become Christians, but he himself was taking leave of the traditional tenets of the Christian faith. This was the time when he turned to reading Lao-tzu[14] and the Buddhist canon. This started a period during which he unceasingly sought the assurance of his Christian faith, a voice from Heaven.

But on January 4, 1942, he attained "awakening" (*Kkaedaleum*).[15] Though he was baptized early, he did not have the assurance of truly having *faith*. He has long longed for it. On this day, however, he experienced it as *given*. He professed that, "I now finally enter the world of faith, thirty eight years after being called."[16] This is a point at which he returned, as it were, to the Christian faith—faith in Jesus. But it differed from the traditional Christian faith. After this point, he found his own voice (*Jesori*), expressing his own unique view of who Jesus Christ is and how believers/disciples are to follow him. From this point on, he took an ascetic turn, taking a cue from the cross of Jesus by taking one meal a day and abstaining from sexual intercourse though remaining in loving marriage.[17] In 1955, at the age of sixty-five, he predicted that he would die on April 26, 1956, and commenced writing diaries. This is the beginning of the *Daseok Ilji* covering twenty years. This is not a diary consisting of simple chronicling but rather a captured record of his *jesori*.[18] If anyone who hears the voice of God/Heaven calling, which is the core of the Gospel, follows Jesus as the example by means of grinding self-discipline, and is reborn in the Holy Spirit, then he/she is living a life of the New Birth (Rebirth). He taught the Bible, especially the Gospel of John, in 1928 at the YMCA in Seoul and continued for thirty-five years. The record of these lectures is *Daseok eorok*. Ryu Yongmo lived what he taught with integrity and sincerity.

The Thought of Ryu Yongmo: Salvation as Awakening

The theme of self-awakening is common throughout East Asian religions and philosophies. It denotes a fundamental awakening of the self through an intuitive realization of the truth, which is attained through a disciplined process of cultivation of one's spiritual, intellectual, and practical lives. Hisamatsu, a representative of the Kyoto School of Zen Buddhism, explicates self-awakening as *the way of seeking to overcome the 'absolute uncertainty' that physical death imposes on human life by re-centering life around the 'absolute death' of selfish appetites and 'rebirth' into relationship with the Absolute Nothingness (絶對無), which entails self-awakening to moral, ethical, and intellectual certainty.*[19]

In Korea, such self-awakening is known as *Kkaedaleum* (깨달음). Akin to the Japanese understanding, 깨달음 (awakening) seeks to overcome the crisis of "absolute uncertainty" that confronts each human being as long as death exists as the fatal "absolute uncertainty" of human life. It elevates death from a negative value to a positive realm of experience that transforms the very core of human consciousness. This "higher death" (大死) can be described as death of "absolute uncertainty" through a self-awakening that converts the uncertainties of death into the spiritual, cognitive, and ethical cultivation of life. It affirms that truth is apprehended through the cultivation of one's inner transcendence of physical death and the reorientation of one's life through the cultivation of one's spiritual faculties. This understanding of *awakening* as self-awakening can be likened to a journey by which a person incrementally progresses through ever more enlightened perceptions of the truth.

For Ryu Yongmo, the journey toward *awakening* started when he was teaching at Osan School. A critical stage of this journey was his acceptance of the Christian faith at the age of fifteen. It is clear from his diaries that this was a transforming moment in his life's journey. Unlike many for whom conversion entails a rejection of earlier beliefs, Ryu saw his conversion as a stage in his journey toward *awakening* of which Confucianism was also an essential part. He continued to appreciate the rationality of Confucianism as a valuable basis for social integration. He rejected the religious accretions of popular Confucian practices, but affirmed Confucianism's rational willingness to interact with other religious principles, especially those of Buddhism and Daoism. He held that Christianity should interact with other religions in ways that affirm what is good in them, and at the same time open itself to be influenced constructively by them. His view of *awakening* was fundamentally related to his openness toward other religious wisdoms and insights. The "self-cultivation" of each religion necessitates its being engaged in a dynamic relationship with other religious traditions for the sake of mutual learning and transformation. At the level of religious plurality, *awakening* is the way of overcoming the Christian exclusivism regarding the interpretation of death and joining with other religions for the purpose of the self-cultivation of human community. Thus viewed, awakening is his way of advancing to a higher truth. It provided Ryu with an important hermeneutical basis for receptive dialogue with other religions.

Eol (얼) and Christ

Christology traditionally refers to the consensus of the Christian community regarding who Christ Jesus (was) is and *what* Jesus Christ has done for the salvation of humanity. It deals with the *person* and *work* of Jesus as the Christ with regard to the redemption of humanity. Answers to who Jesus Christ is have varied throughout the history of Christianity. Diversities of Christology are evident in the New Testament itself and in the patristic period when central Christian dogmas were formed. *Faith* in Jesus Christ has been a constant feature of the Christian tradition, but that faith has never received a uniform intellectual expression in terms of Christian *belief*.[20]

Ryu Yongmo's relationship with Jesus was essential to his entire religious experience. It was this relationship that defined his self-identity as a Christian. Yet, his diaries reveal his struggle with the challenge of expressing his life-defining faith in Jesus in ways that also reflect the inescapable truths found in Korean cultural and religious traditions of which he was deeply convinced that Jesus was part, at least in spirit, if not historically.

What was Ryu's understanding of Jesus as Spirit? The key term that Ryu used in relation to Christ is *Eol* (얼), a genuinely Korean word that has no equivalent in the Sino-Korean vocabulary. It is therefore important to clarify the sense of this word in light of its general Korean usage, its particular usage in Ryu's own writings, and Ryu's view of Christ as *Eol*.

In its general Korean usage *eol* denotes "spirit" or "soul." It further refers to an invisible power that constitutes all things as they actually are. It typically appears in such phrases as "the *eol* of Korea" or "man's loss of *eol*," meaning the non-material "core" [substance] of a nation or a core identity of a person that makes who he/she is. Even though it is "real," it cannot be grasped by any sensory perception in terms of color, shape, or sound. It is the *substance* of a thing, person, or nation that holds diverse constitutive elements together into an integrated being.

In Ryu's specific usage *eol* has a dynamic power that gives reason and meaning to life. When a nation faces a collective crisis of identity, people appeal to this *eol* in order to reclaim their identity. *Eol* has played a very significant role in overcoming crises and bringing the nation and its people to the recovery of identity as a free people. Although *eol* is intangible and indefinable, its effects can be quite clearly evidenced in the spirits of Korean people regardless of their social stratification. This was never more emphatically the case than during the period of the Japanese colonial rule (1910–1945), when Korean social, cultural, and political identity was being systematically suppressed and eradicated. *Eol*, by virtue of its intangibility, could not be extinguished by the colonizers and proved to be the *spirit* that sustained the people and animated their determination to withstand and resist. These were the conditions in which Ryu's young mind was formed.

Ryu used the term *eol* as the equivalent of "spirit" (*pneuma*) in the New Testament. For example, in his commentary on the Gospel of John (6:63), he translated "spirit" as *Eol*: "It is the *Eol* who gives life; the flesh profits nothing."[21] How did he understand the relationship between *Eol* as spirit and the flesh? In his diaries, he explains,

The world of the beginning which leads to the end is that of the flesh. But the world of the beginning which starts from the end is that of *Eol*. To be born and to die is of the flesh, to die and to live is *Eol*. *Eol* is the life that starts from the death of the self.... There is no end in *Eol*. There is always and only the beginning.[22]

Ryu understood *eol* and flesh in relative terms. Flesh denotes physical appetite and desire. Both are essential to human life, but they have no benefit in and of themselves. They are beneficial only so far as they are used for God's purpose. He continues:

Human beings eat meals in order to fulfill God's will. Otherwise there is no point in eating.... Sexual desire is rooted in human energy. This energy should be used for profound reflection and reproduction. It should be used for others or God.[23]

Flesh is essential to human life and human relationships. He does not underestimate its importance. In fact, he wishes for three things in life and one of them is health.[24] He wishes to be healthy because it is necessary to have a healthy body in order to accomplish the responsibility of perfecting the whole human being. A healthy body enables us to live with a sound spirit. In order to accomplish our aim, we need to esteem our flesh.[25]

On the other hand, for human life to be fulfilled, the spirit must penetrate the flesh and all it entails. For it is *eol* that links the human person to the *real* existent which, though nonexisting existent, transcends the material or corporeal world of phenomena. This understanding of the spirit-flesh relationship returns us to issues discussed previously that underlie the importance of Confucianism and Buddhism as the background for Ryu's Christian theology. His view of Confucianism and Buddhism intensifies and clarifies the religious dimensions of *eol*, while the latter highlights the close relationship between *eol* and human beings.[26]

For Ryu the Neo-Confucian concept *Seong* (性) of itself refers to God. As a given thing, however, seong is spirit or *eol*. *Eol* is the very presence of God in nature and human life. The Chinese character, *Seong* (nature) is the compound word of two characters, 心 meaning "mind" and 生 meaning "life." Whereas this has led the Neo-Confucians to interpret

Seong as the mental desire for life in the body, Ryu disagreed and insisted on the identification of *Seong* and real life itself. Our breathing is life, but life, which needs breathing, is not real life. Life, which breathes with the spirit, is real life or Cheon Myeong (天命). If we live in this real life, there the eternal life emerges, for which we do not need bodily breathing.[27] The spirit is precisely like our mental breathing. Spirit is the *eol* of our mind. The spirit, or *eol*, is precisely the *real* me and eternal life. Some mistakenly believe that a great power through the Spirit enables us to cure disease and not to die even though we drink poison. But the great power through the Spirit does not mean such a thing.[28]

The defining characteristic of Ryu's understanding of *Seong* is that it is identified with life as such. All human beings share it. It affirms that every human being is inspired by the direct presence of God in his/her life.[29] Ryu also turns his attention to the Buddhist concept of *Bulseong* (佛性, Buddha-nature) for his elaboration of how *Eol* operates in terms of reaching perfect awakening. This term is also formed through a compound term of two ideas: *Bul* (佛), which is the Korean way of referring to Buddha, and *Seong* (性), which we have discussed above. Hence *Bulseong* means the original nature of Buddha and expresses the concept that every human being has the potential of becoming a Buddha, one who has achieved enlightenment. Ryu understands *Bulseong* not as an individual who is born or dies but as eternal life. Consequently, if the body of Buddha is born and enters nirvana, it is a temporary expedient of *bulseong*. This is a simple way for the ordinary person to acknowledge *bulseong*.[30] It is clear that Ryu broadly identifies the concept of *Bulseong* in Buddhism with the *Seong* of Confucianism. Both articulate the concept of truth, which is universal in the sense of being omnipresent within *nature*, and this is basic to the meaning that Ryu applied to *Eol*. It is from Buddhism, however, that Ryu derives his understanding of how this universal truth, the Buddha-teaching, is personified in the individual search for enlightenment.

Elsewhere Ryu identifies the "master" of the human being with a person's face or *eolgul* (얼골) in Korean. He draws attention to the fact that this is a compound of two words: *Eol*, meaning "spirit" and *gul*, meaning "valley (골, *gol*)." He says:

The valley, which exposes *Eol*, is *Eolgul*. The fact that everyone holds up his or her face seems to have the symbolic meaning that only the face is exposed. The fact that everyone tries to keep their faces comely and holds them up seems to show that the mind, which is more important than the body, is revealed in the face. The body is clothing, and *Eol* is the master. The face does not subsist under the body; on the contrary, the body subsists under the face. The face is the master and the body is the slave.[31]

Therefore, *eol* is not limited to the body, but surpasses it and connects it with the cosmos itself, the reality of which exists within a person's own self. Thus he writes,

> When we look into the face, its valley is so deep. The valley, the so-called *gol* (골), behind the face, has so many deep gullies. Beyond the cerebrum and cerebellum, unlimited mysteries of the cosmos connect with the face. Keep thinking deeply, and the stars and skies of the cosmos do not present a problem. Beyond the stars and skies, there is a sea of thought and the seat of God. In the deep and secluded place, there is the master of the face, my real self—*eol*.[32]

The face radiates the reality of *eol* within a person. It is the symbol of the presence of the spirit that links the human person with eternal life. He compares it with a rope (줄), "the rope of eternal life, which a human cannot help following, placed before a human fate. This rope of *eol* exists forever, and human beings cannot abandon it or leave it."[33] But this "rope" can be lost or broken since *eol* is damaged by sin to the point of being lost or being broken just as a rope can be severed. But elsewhere he expresses that *Eol* can never be lost or broken because it is the universal and omnipresent Spirit of God. For Ryu, Jesus Christ is this Spirit, this *Eol*.

Throughout his writings, Ryu identifies *Eol* as Christ. What then is Ryu's view of Christ? How does Ryu answer the question, "who is Jesus?" For him, Jesus was the human being in whose life the *Eol* of God was fully realized, making him therefore a man whom others can follow in their own search for self-cultivation. By insisting that Jesus was a human being, Ryu emphasized that Jesus was a man like all others. His humanity was real and subject to the same limitations and possibilities as any other human person. Like all human beings, Jesus's physical condition—his flesh—was subject to the frailties of the human condition. Ryu expressed these as three forms of defilement: *craving*, *anger*, and *delusion*, reflecting the Buddhist anthropology that diagnoses the human condition in terms of *dukkha* (suffering), caused by *tanha* (craving), resulting in *aniecca* (decay, impermanence).³⁴ As a consequence, Jesus as a human being has exactly the same body as other human beings. Like them, his body is prone to sin. He made no attempt to exclude Jesus from the influence of sin that infects the lives of all human beings.³⁵ Ryu, however, held that Jesus was able to overcome the effects of sin in his own life. To make this point, he did not use the orthodox Christian doctrine that Jesus's human nature, though real, was personally united with the divine nature (*hypostatic union*) that exempted him from original sin. As he rejected the notion of original sin, he also rejected the belief that Jesus's humanity was saved from the corrupting influence of sin by his divinity. He did not accept the orthodox doctrine of the Incarnation, at least in the metaphysical sense of Jesus being "begotten" of God. Ryu quite emphatically rejected such thinking as being tantamount to idolatry. He held that the fleshly nature of a human being cannot (should not) be divinized. He in fact warned:

> Do not make an idol of a person. The one to whom we can bow down is God, who is the truth. Religion does not mean to worship a person. If we do not acknowledge God correctly, we make an idol of a person. This is the cause of idolatry. This is the consequence of putting Jesus in place of God.³⁶

Flesh is, to Ryu's way of thinking, the "outer clothing" of humanity which will eventually be cast off. As long as it serves to clothe the body, it can be purified by the inner *Eol* that gives it life and therefore links it to the *real*, the nonexistent existence of Haneunim (하느님).³⁷ Though sharing the same corruptible body as the rest of humankind, Jesus succeeded in transforming his instinctual self into a spiritual self and by this means fulfilled the potentialities of the *Eol* that gave him life, as it gives life to all human beings. For this reason, he is the example for others to follow. The means by which Jesus achieved this fulfillment and by which others may follow his example was the practice of filial piety, known as *Buja yuchin* (父子有親).³⁸ He interprets the art of this in terms of self-emptying and altruism, and linked it ultimately to Jesus's death on the Cross in fulfillment of God's will.³⁹ Filial piety is the highest on the ladder of the Confucian virtues and lies at the heart of the Five Relations (오륜, 五倫).⁴⁰ It is an essential element of the Mandate of Heaven. Ryu criticized the tendency in Confucianism to interpret filial piety only in terms of natural relationships and social order. He argued that such an approach weakens its spiritual significance because it confines filial piety to the level of a natural relationship and has not yet broken through to the level of Heaven. His view is that, in the original Confucian view, filial piety transcended physical relationships and represented the way in which human beings felt themselves to be united with Heaven, reflecting in earthly terms the metaphysical state of harmony between Heaven, Earth, and Humanity. With this critique, he brought his understanding of the New Testament view of Jesus's relationship with God the Father and argued that this should be understood contextually as fulfilling the spiritual as well as physical demands of filial piety to perfection. Ryu argued that the perfect form of *buja yuchin* is found in the life of Jesus. In this sense, he saw the true nature of Christianity as manifested in Jesus's fulfillment of this relationship with the Father as the Son. This was the manner in which he interpreted the biblical language of "Father" and "Son," but he framed this in light of his understanding of the Confucian perspective on filial piety:

> The Absolute God opens a relative world by giving birth to a son, the *logos* of all creatures (the *logos* should be understood as *Eol*). The father gives birth to me as a son. That is why I certainly acknowledge my father. In this light, we have to acknowledge the father who is the Absolute. A father cannot forget a son. We call him father. There is no hurry. The relation between father and son cannot be sundered and divided. There seems to be a difference, but there is no separation.[41]

Reflecting Jesus's perfect filial piety toward the divine Father, Ryu characterized him as *gunja* (君子)—a person of virtue in Confucian thought. This denotes the quality of a sage (聖人), who Confucian scholars define as "the one who possesses a way which penetrates everywhere . . . [and] is in union with Heaven and Earth in his being."[42] There is no doubt in Ryu Yongmo's mind that Jesus is the perfect sage and that his powers of sagehood arose from his realization of the potentialities of *eol* that infused his being as a whole. The real Jesus, therefore, was the master of *eol* and, in this sense, the Son of Heaven.[43] This is a metaphoric rendition within the dimension of the *buja yuchin*. He says, "I called him [Jesus] *gunja*. *Gunja* is a son of a king or a son of Heaven. *Gunja* means 'one who longs for Heaven.' The one who longs for Heaven and attains Heaven is He."[44]

By means of the process of self-transcendence, Jesus, *gunja*, overcame the weakness of his fleshy body and became an *eol*—an inspired sage in the highest possible degree. From this hermeneutical angle, he interpreted the passage of John 14:6 thus: the way, the truth, and the life that Jesus sees are as follows: the way means to come from Heaven to earth and go back to Heaven; the truth means to walk this way; and the life means that father and the son become one through a great enlightenment. The son of a person—the Son of Man in terms of the Christian Bible—comes from Heaven and goes back to Heaven. To walk this way unswervingly is the truth. Consequently, to meet God is life. In terms of a railway, the rail is the way, train is the truth, and the arrival is the life. When this is followed, there is no difficulty in our life at all.[45]

It is through Jesus's passion and death on the Cross, self-sacrifice in Ryu's terms, that Jesus accomplished his mission as the "Son of Heaven," fulfilling in his own life the will of his heavenly Father. He writes: "Since a flower is red as *pi* (피, blood), we say flowers bloom ("pida," 피다)." [46] The blood that Jesus shed in his passion on the Cross is the blood of a righteous person that would help others in a *buja yuchin* relationship with the Heaven bloom (*pi-da, blossom*) fully as sons of God. When righteous blood is shed in the world, the glory of God is revealed. This is a symbol of maturity. Maturity means becoming a son of God. A son of God is myself as *eol* who overcomes the death of the flesh. To acknowledge the truth is the same as to overcome death. In order to overcome the defilement (three forms of sin), death delivers us from immaturity. Hence death is life. To move from the instinctual autonomous-ego (自我, 제나) to the *eol* ego (얼나) is *Kkaedaleum* or Awakening. Suffering that belongs to the fleshly body is transmuted into the serenity of the *eol*-filled self that is extinguished in the reality of nonexistence. This does not mean a flight into a mystical realm. It rather turns on the spiritual and moral power of a person who, in the act of self-sacrifice or self-overcoming, demonstrates him to be a righteous person who manifests spiritual maturity—being in fullness of the truth. At that moment, one becomes a "son of God." Jesus reveals the glory of God and stands as a symbol of righteousness for all others. Jesus's willingness to accept self-sacrifice was the factor that elevated Jesus above other sages as the one whose example was preeminently the way to fulfilling life through *Eol* (Phil. 2:5–11). By his death on the Cross, Jesus offered a perfect example of the master practitioner of filial piety and who thereby accomplished the completion of *Eol*.

Ryu is clear, on the one hand, that many can attain Christ's *Eol* and that hence there can be more than one Christ, since Christ is *Eol*. On the other hand, Ryu is also clear that Jesus Christ (*Eol-na* 얼나) is the only reliable one whom we must follow because he is the true master teacher who may be able to help us embody the true *buja yuch'in* by means of which we become one with the Heaven, Father, *true Eol*. *Eol* is what binds us to Haneunim, Heaven, the Void (invisible, not necessarily nonexistent but rather exists as nonexistent[47]), and the world of the *Eol* of Christ. Different words are used, but they point to the One. Hence *Eol* reconciles, harmonizes and unites. It possibilizes life in many forms.

Some Concluding Reflections

By way of concluding remarks, I would like to pose several questions regarding his Christology, his anthropology, his critique of reason, and his romantic view of traditional religions as well as the implications of his theology for interreligious relations and the methodology of indigenizing theology.

For Ryu, the same *Eol* as was present in Jesus's life animates all human beings. Jesus's realization of the Christic qualities of *Eol*, therefore, lies within the moral and spiritual capacity of all human beings. When human beings realize *Eol* in themselves, the individuals are not the naturalistic or instinctual *ego* anymore because it entails a relativization of the ego (the agential capacity of individuals) and its elevation to the *true self* (참나). This true self is Christ and the Son of God.[48] Different words are used, but they point to the same reality. Ryu's anthropology here seems to lessen the seriousness of the obstructive and destructive forces of sin and evil in the world that bring about the reality of suffering affecting all humans and other living beings. Ryu's position reminds me of the Greeks' basic assumption that "knowing the truth necessarily leads to doing it." But the Apostle Paul teaches, "I do not understand what I do. For what I want to do I do not do, but what I hate I do."[49] Perhaps, for Ryu, "sin" is ignorance, a lack or absence of "awakening." But the force that blocks and prevents one's awakening to the presence of *eol* is much more deeply rooted in us and in the world. He implicitly acknowledged this when he "cut" his physical relationship with his wife. But his theory of awakening lacks a serious reflection on this hindrance. He takes his connection to his body seriously enough to detach himself from it so as to ensure his *Eol* to be pure of taints from the body. Nevertheless, he regards the body to be superfluous. His negative view of the body is also reflected in his refusal to acknowledge the importance of the Incarnation of Jesus.

For Ryu, the purpose of Jesus's life and teaching is that he comes to this earth from God, Heaven, the Father, the Void in order to receive the *Eol*, the Spirit, the Word of eternal life, the power of life, or *Bulseong*, so as to reveal the truth that the true life of human beings is not lived in accordance with the flesh but solely in accordance with the *Eol* to which the flesh is to be subordinated and thereby transformed. *Eternal life* lies within the capacity of all human beings. This is to affirm the universality of God's relationship with humankind. To this purpose, Christ is constantly *coming* for our eternal life.[50] This view, however, eliminates any particular soteriological reason for converting to any other religious tradition and spiritual practice. Particularly in a multireligious context in which Koreans live, the approach to mission and evangelization calls for a certain discernment in deciding for a particular religious teaching and denominational affiliation. There are in fact differences among religions. This marks an existential condition that separates Koreans from the Westerners who believe that "all religions as leading to the same destination." Given this perspective, however, there is an existential and ontological difference that separates religions. The whole notion of "difference" takes a peculiar meaning. In Ryu's approach I seem to hear an echo of "the transcendent unity of all religions" advocated by Frijhof Schuon.[51] Do real differences of religions not matter then? Christians may say, "Buddha is Christ-like," but can they admit, "Christ is Buddha-like"? Would Buddhists agree with such a notion? Do all these notions matter to them? Does the cross signify what the lotus flower does? They may complement each other, but are they the same? Can one become Christian without acknowledging the unique Incarnation of Jesus? It is not clear on what ground Ryu preferred Jesus, as he in fact did, to the Buddha or Confucius.

One may characterize "theology" as a progressive articulation of the inner logics and belief systems inherent in the knowledge and confession of faith in God. This presupposes that a personal experience of faith in God precedes its theological articulation and thematization. Thus understood, any theological articulation without such religious experience becomes vacuous and subjectivistic to the extent that it is only self-referencing. Liberation theologians are right in insisting that theology is the

What Can Christianity Learn from Korean Religions? 205

second step—second to the experience and practice of faith. Theological indigenization is, therefore, inevitably predicated upon materials that are from particular religious worlds. Methodologically, norm and material form must be treated with discerning eyes on their particular cultural, religious, and linguistic experiential moorings that are distinct from those embedded in the "imported" already articulated theological body of knowledge (doctrine, ecclesial form, theological norms). An indigenous theology must give serious attention to an *indigenized* faith expressed in an indigenized linguistic form. Theological indigenization should not be viewed as an *indigenizing* theology but rather as a theology reflecting on the *indigenized faith*. When we allow an irruption of difference into our default form of faith, a new theological thinking may emerge. A difference provokes a critical rationality. This is akin to a "painting outside the lines." Ryu Yongmo offered an example of this.

Ryu Yongmo held a negative view of the role of reason. He was critical of the view that reason alone determines the category of existence in that whatever is knowable by reason is to be accepted as a real existent while whatever is unknowable by reason is rejected as nonexistent. He was convinced, however, that some things that are beyond the capacity of reason to comprehend might yet exist. The light of reason cannot be the sole criterion for the existence and nonexistence of things. What may not appear to our senses may yet exist. God belongs to this category. God exists outside the sphere of rationality. Hence God *exists* without existing. Ryu prefers darkness to the light, the shadow to the bright, the unknown to the known, the hidden to the revealed, the beneath to the surface. The "dark" is more encompassing, more embracing, and more inclusive. He exhorted intellectuals "to turn the light of reason off." This would liberate theologians from the shackles of the modern conception of rationality. Here we can hear the echoes of Meister Eckhart, Julian of Norwich, Blaise Pascal, Martin Heidegger, Thomas Merton, and others. The negative side of this, however, is that it can also justify religious fanatics in their claim to religious truth for all sorts of plainly absurd statements they are likely to make for less than sound psychological motives.

Ryu tends to romanticize the past and minimize the seriousness of the forces of evil in the world. Indigenous Korean religions were available to Koreans in the past as they are in the present, but they have certainly proven to be less than effective in combating historical evils, often instead collaborating with them. A certain ambivalence is unavoidable, therefore, when many thoughtful scholars desire to reclaim Korean religious heritages and resources for their own philosophical and religious theories without clear hermeneutical guidelines by which to discern what to preserve/conserve and what to discard in these resources. After all, these very resources were also responsible for some of the oppressive systems and abusive ideologies that perpetrated and justified economic inequality and injustice, and other social evils. What assures then that these reclaimed resources may become positive sources of transformation?

The Gospel of Luke[52] tells the story of a woman "bent over" for eighteen years until Jesus healed her and enabled her to *stand up straight* so as to live and flourish. Ryu Yongmo has been ignored for long and has only recently been acknowledged for his creative spirit and contribution. He is beginning to stand up and walk, as it were. In this light, I have restrained myself, albeit a few critical remarks made above, from making any substantial, critical comparisons of Ryu's thought with any Western and Christian theologies and philosophies. My restraint is further justified by the insight provided by Edward Said's *Orientalism*[53] in that I do not want to *level* the particularity and even the peculiarity of Ryu's thought *flat* with other thoughts or to *subjugate* him to "Western" knowledge, but to preserve the fragility of his offerings so that his considerable dynamic and substantial insights for transformation may be sustained. Hence I adopted more the hermeneutics of "nodding" than the hermeneutics of "disagreement." One advantage of this approach is to avoid the errors committed by other interpreters who rush to assess his thought by Western theological categories. Of course, we normally come to know new things through the established categories of our knowledge. Yet we must put our best efforts to *hear the other* as fully and as long as possible before we subsume *too quickly* others' words under our assumptions. Otherwise, we colonize them. To avoid it, *we need to patiently hear them into being.*

Ryu lived through the great challenge of many competing religious and philosophical claims, yet it is to his great merit that he did not lose his identity and language as a Korean, as so many others have. Rather, he was able to critically and imaginatively integrate these varying ancient sources into a profound religio-linguistic synthesis with the spirit of *Hwajaeng*[54] and the dialectics of Wonhyo. In his synthesis he was a thinker of reconciliation of differences. In his attempt to indigenize Christianity, he was a quintessentially Korean thinker. In both he proved to be indeed a great and original thinker.

Notes

1. This is a metaphoric literary rendering of his name in Chinese character and usually written as a prefix. It is composed of one Chinese word (夕) meaning "supper," combined creatively in a threefold manner. It denotes that he eats breakfast, lunch, and supper by taking one supper a day. This is an interpretation offered by Oh Jungsook. But Kim Heup Young offers a different interpretation, saying that this "literary name" denotes "so many nights" in his "The Word Made Flesh: Ryu Young-Mo's Christo-dao: A Korean Perspective," in *Word and Spirit: Renewing Christology and Pneumatology in a Globalizing World*, eds. Anselm K. Min and Christoph Schwobel (Berlin: Walter de Gruyter, 2014), 113–29: 114 I will follow Oh's view, even though Kim's view is plausible, but it is an interpretive over-reach based on Ryu's thought, rather than from his lifestyle he adopted after his *"awakening"* in 1942.
2. Hans Georg Gadamer argued that the understanding emerges out of the fusion of the horizons of the past and the present that are formed in a spatio-temporal, cultural, and linguistic existential situation; see his *Wahrheit und Methode: Grundzuge einer philosophischen Hermeneutik* (Tubingen: J. C. B. Mohr [Paul Siebeck], 1975), 282; 289–90.
3. God exists without existing.
4. Park Yongho, *Jinri ui saram Daseok Ryu Yongmo* (Seoul: Dourei, 2001), 305.
5. Park Yongho, 씨알 (*Ssial*) (Seoul: Hongikjae, 1994), 16.
6. Kim Heungho, "Thought of Ryu Yongmo—An Asian Perspective of Christianity," in *Wooweon Sasang Nonchong*, vol. 8 (Kangnam University), 194. Oh Jungsook accepts this division in terms of (1) 1890–1942; (2) 1942–1954; (3) 1955–1981. (See her "Ryu Yongmo wa Hankukjeok Kidogkyo," 41–45.) I am indebted to this division, except that I would insert an additional period of 1890–1912.
7. This was intended to be a way of bearing his own cross.
8. This institute taught most children regardless of rank. Even though it provided a kind of informal education, it played a significant role in terms of general educational formation initially directed to the children of five and six years of ages.
9. Park Yongho, 多夕 유영모의 생애와 사상 (*The Life and Thought of Daeok Ryu Yongmo*), vol. I (Seoul: Hongikjae, 1996), 42.
10. Park Yongho, 씨알—*The Thought and Life of Daseok Ryu Yongmo*, (Seoul: Honikjae, 1985) 30.
11. In his diary, Ryu wrote: "in order to take back our nation from Japan, we have to beat Japan. In order to beat Japan, we have to know them first." See Park Yongho, *The Life and Thought of Daseok Ryu Yongmo*, vol. I, 48. This statement is

based on a classic Chinese military strategy articulated in *Sun-Tzu Bingfa*, which is an account of the oldest military treatise in the world, authored by *Sun Tzu* (孫子) in *Ch'un Ch'iu* (春秋, 722–481 BCE) period. A famous phrase, "If I know the enemy first and know myself, there is no defeat," in this booklet.

12. At this time, there was no "college," or "university" in Korea. Therefore, anyone who desired to study at a university, had to go to Japan. This particular school is a "preparatory" school where one needs to obtain the prerequisites for entering the university in Japan. Ryu did not finish this preparatory school, so he could not enter the university in Japan, but returned home in 1913 with the hope of becoming a farmer.

13. Park Yongho, *The Life and Thought of Daseok Ryu Yongmo*, vol. I, 110. Lee Kwangsoo (1892–1950), a Korean poet and novelist, introduced Ryu to Tolstoy's ideas. They were colleagues at the Osan School, and Yi brought the works of Tolstoy in Japanese translation to Korea. Yi was critical of the exclusivist nature of the Christianity as interpreted by Western missionaries and wrote about "the tyranny of orthodoxy" in a journal *Cheongchoon* (November 1917). Having read Tolstoy, Ryu Yongmo allegedly proclaimed, "Both Tolstoy and I are unorthodox." [See Park Yongho, *Ssial*, 58. Tolstoy's independent thinking and his criticism of the orthodox theology of the Russian Orthodox Church led to his excommunication in 1901 (Henry Gifford, *Tolstoy*, Oxford, 1982, 46–48)]. After reading Tolstoy's works, he quit attending church worship services, and stopped singing hymns and praying in public. Reasons for Ryu's self-imposed estrangement from the church are several. First, he suffered a personal crisis of faith on the death of his younger brother, Yongmuck, in 1911, the year following Tolstoy's passing. His diary entry reads: "When I was twenty-one, my nineteen-year-old brother died. When he died, I lost my heart. After that accident, I thought that there is nothing complete in this world. This world is a relative one. . . ." (Park Yongho, *Ssial*, 62). His brother's death caused him deep personal grief and a spiritual crisis that led him to question the capacity of any religion to offer the assurance of absolute truth. The world and religions as part of it are *relative*. At best they offer *relative* ways of dealing with the "fatal uncertainty" of death. Second, he agreed with the nationalist criticism of the Western and colonial character of mission-founded churches. In this light, it would be incorrect to suppose that Ryu's distancing himself from orthodox Christianity was the direct influence of Tolstoy's thinking. He seems to have taken comfort from the fact that Tolstoy was also forced to abandon a church-affiliated Christianity. (See Park, Yongho, *Daseok Ryu Yongmo's Thought and Belief* [Seoul: Hyundai Moonhwa Sinmun, 1995, 97–99].) When the death of Tolstoy (Nov. 7, 1910) was reported, all the students and teachers of Osan School gathered and held a memorial service. This was shortly after Ryu's arrival at Osan School. Ryu attended it. Thereafter he began reading Tolstoy.

14. Ryu Yongmo was the first translator of Lao-tzu's *Dao De Ching* into Korean in 1959.

15. Kim Heungho, *Jesori: Ryu Yongmo Sunsaeng Malsseum* (Peungman, 1986), 354. This is also known as "keonseong" (見性) in Buddhism. Ryu called this "Ka-on-Jjiki." It is something akin to Christian experience of "conversion."

16. Kim Kyosin, *Sungseo Joseon*, No. 157 (Feb. 1942): 33–38. See also Kim Heungho, *Jesori*, 353–59.

17. One is here reminded of Gandhi who took the same vow and practice.

18. It denotes not voices of others, but *my own*. It is a *jesori* because it flows from the inner world where Heaven resides in union with *je-na* (the true self born of *Eol*; *Cham-na*).

19. See Shini'chi Himasamtsu, *Zen and the Fine Arts*. Translated by Gishin Tokiwa (Tokyo: Kodnasha International, 1982).

20. Christopher Tuckett, "Christology and the New Testament," in: *Scottish Journal of Theology*, vol. 33, 405–06. See for the distinction between *faith* and *belief*, Wilfred Cantwell Smith, *Faith and Belief*. Belief is the creedal expression of *faith*, and shaped by the influence of context. This implies that a belief is contingent upon faith's dialogical appropriation of a contextual particularity. What undergirds belief is a faith relationship with Jesus the Christ.

21. Kim Heungho, *Jesori* (제소리), 128.

22. 多夕語錄, 25.

23. Ibid., 138.

24. Ibid., 46.

25. Ibid.

26. In terms of Confucianism, Ryu draws a parallel between the concept of *Eol* and *Seong* (性, nature). Nature is the central concept of the Confucian classics, *The Doctrine of the Golden Mean* (中庸). To this doctrine, all that exists in the world is produced and maintained by *nature* and the goal of human life is to live in harmony with this *nature*. *Seong* means both *nature* and *truth* (see Lee Kidong, *A Lecture on the Great Learning and the Doctrine of Mean* [Seoul: Songgyunkwan University Press, 1990], 100). Therefore Ryu interprets this concept of *nature* in terms of God, in light of the theistic traditions of Confucianism and proceeds to apply this to his conception of *Eol*. For Ryu, "*Seong* (性) of itself is God. It, as a given thing, is spirit. This given thing can be more or less depending on the person it is given. God does not give *Seong* just once; God gives it all the time . . . things given by God are all called *Seong*, whether of the body or the mind." (See Park Yongho, *Daseok Ryu Yongmo ui Yukyosasang* [*The Confucian Thought in Daseok Ryu Yongmo*], vol. I [Seoul: Munhwailbo, 1995], 33.)

27. Park Yongho, *Daseok Ryu Yongmo ui Yukyosasang*, vol. I (Seoul: Munhwailbo, 1995), 20.

28. *Daseok orok*, 233. Ryu refers here to Mark 16:12.

29. Ibid., 383.

30. Park Yongho, *Daseok Ryu Yongmo ui Bulkyosasang* [*The Buddhist Thought in Daseok Ryu Yongmo*], (Seoul: Munhwailbo, 1996), 47.

31. *Daseok orok*, 24.
32. Ibid.
33. Ibid., 17.
34. Ryu borrowed these three forms of defilement from the Buddhist idea of the impermanence (*aniecca*) of an earthly life that is lived in suffering (*dukkha*). See Park Yongho, 多夕 유영모의 생애와 사상 [*The Thought and Life of Daseok Ryu Yongmo*], vol. I, 321.
35. *Daseok orok*, 308.
36. Ibid., 278.
37. Ryu took "Father" from the Confucian understanding of *Buja yuch'in* to denote "Heaven" in the personal terms of *Han'uhnim* as Father, the source of *Eol*. In metaphorical expression, the "Heavenly Father" begot His Son, not physically but in terms of *Ol*, and it was by living in harmony with *eol* that the Son achieved perfect filial concord with his Father.
38. See Kim Youngbok, *The Development of the History of Korean Christian Thought* (Seoul: Hankuk Kydogkyo Asia Yonkuwon, 1989), 18.
39. *Daseok orok*, 166.
40. See the footnote 38.
41. *Daseok orok*, 105.
42. See Julia Ching, *Confucianism and Christianity: A Comparative Study*, 80.
43. Ryu Yongmo occasionally allowed himself to use with regard to Jesus the expression "the only begotten son." Neither "Son of Heaven" nor "the only begotten Son" implies that Jesus himself is divine or that he participated in the divinity of God.
44. *Daseok Eorok*, 126.
45. Ibid., 167.
46. One can readily see that *pi-da*, to bloom, or to blossom has the same root as *pi* (blood) in Korean phoneme.
47. It echoes Paul Tillich's statement. To paraphrase, God does not exist, but God *is*. However, this may not mean what Ryu intended to convey.
48. Ibid., 108.
49. Romans, 7:15.
50. *Daseok Ilji*, vol. 1, 181.
51. (Wheaton, IL: Theosophical Publishing House, 1984).
52. Luke 13:10–17.
53. Edward Said, *Orientalism* (New York: Vintage, 1979). Also Homi K. Bahbah, *The Location of Culture* (London: Routledge, 1994), and Gayatri Chakravorty Spivak, "Can the Subaltern Speak?" in *Discourse and Post-Colonial Theory*, edited by Patrick Willaims and Laura Chrisman (New York: Columbia University Press, 1994): 66–111.
54. The principle of *Hwanjaeing* requires a substantive treatment which is beyond the scope of the present writing. A very brief reference to it is here suf-

ficient: during the time of the Unified Sila Dynasty, Buddhism reached its peak in popularity and prestige. Distinguished monks such as Wonhyo (617–86) and Uisang (625–702) made significant advances in re-interpreting Buddhism in the Korean context. Wonhyo's famous "East Sea Commentary" resolved problems of dating of the various Buddhist scriptures in their formation and thus helped overcome disputes about the relative authorities of individual scriptures. Thus he was able to harmonize different characteristics of Buddhism in an encompassing and syncretistic philosophy. His main philosophical idea was the principle of *Hwajaeng*, which means reconciling and harmonizing doctrinal disputes. With this, he sought to draw out the unifying principles that underlie the diversity of doctrines. This is what he meant by the "unfolding" and "sealing" (*Kaehap*) of meanings as the prelude to "reconciliation" of disputes. His desire to harmonize differences should not be interpreted as an attempt to suppress diversity. On the contrary, he affirmed diversity on the grounds that each theory expresses part of the truth and at the same time held that no single theory can embrace the fullness of truth in and of itself. The aim of *Hwajaeng* is, therefore, to harmonize these partial perceptions in light of a wider vision of the truth. Truth itself is best understood as *Void* (*gong*).

Bibliography

Daseok Ryu Yongmo. *Jugeume Saengmeongeul, Jeolmange Huimangeul: Daseok Eorok* [*Life to Death, Hope to Hopelessness: Daseok Eorok*]. Seoul: Hongikjae, 1993.

———. *Noja—Bicheuro Sseun Eolui Norae* [*A Study of Lao-Tzu—A Song of Eol Written in Light*]. Loosened in Korean Scripts by Park Youngho. Seoul: Moo-Ai Publisher, 1992.

Kim Youngbok. *Hankuk Gidokkyo Sasangjeonkae* [*The Development of the History of Korean Christian Thought*]. Seoul: Hankuk Gidokkyo Asia Yeonkuwon, 1989.

Kim Heungho. *Jesori: Ryu Yongmo Seonsaengnimui Malsseum* [*Jesori: Voices of Ryu Yongmo*]. Seoul: Peungman Publisher, 1986.

———. "Ryu Yongmo—Gidokkyoui Dongyangjeok Ihae," [Ryu Yongmo—An Asian View of Christianity] in *Daseok Ryu Yongmoui Dongyang Sasankkwa Sinhak* [*Daseok Ryu Yongmo's Asian Thought and Theology*]. Seoul: Sol Chulpansa, 2002. 15–28.

Lee Jungbae. "Hangeul gwa Gidokkyo—Munhwa Sinhakui gwajeroseo Hangeullo Sinhakhagi—Ryu Yongmo wa Kim Heunhoui Hangeulpurireul Jungsimeuro" ["Hangeul and Christianity—theological work in Korean language as a task for Theology of Culture: Focusing on Hangeul Usage of Ryu Yongmo and Kim Heungho"], in *Hankuk Gidokkyo Sinhaknonchong* [*The Journal of Korean Christian Theology*], vol. 22. (Seoul: Hankuk Gidokkyo Hakhoe, 2001): 407–44.

Oh Jungsook. "*Ryu Yongmo wa Hankukjeok Gidokkyo*" ["Ryu Yongmo and Korean Christianity"], in *Hankuk Munhwa Sinhak* [*Theology of Korean Culture*], vol. 9. (Seoul: Hankuk Munhwa Shinhakhoe, 2006): 38–73.

Park Youngho. *Daseok Ryu Yongmoui Gonkja Sasang* [*The Confucian Thought in Daseok Ryu Yongmo*]. Seoul: Munhwailbo, 1995.

———. *Daseok Ryu Yongmoui Saengae wa Sasang* [*The Life and Thought of Daseok Ryu Yongmo*], vol. I. Seoul: Hongikjae, 1996.

———. *Daseok Ryu Yongmoui Bulkyo Sasang* [*The Buddhist Thought in Daseok Ryu Yongmo*]. Seoul: Munhwailbo, 1996.

———. *Jinriui Saram Daseok Ryu Yongmo* [*Man of Authenticity: Ryu Yongmo*]. Seoul: Dourei, 2001.

Ryu Tongshik. *Hankuk Mukyoui Yeoksa wa Gujo* [*A History and Structure of Shamanism in Korea*]. Seoul: Yonsei University Press, 1975.

Part IV

Confucianism, Christianity, and the Challenges of the Modern World

8

Resurgence of Asian Values
Confucian Comeback and Its Embodiment in Christianity

Namsoon Kang

> Who determines the standards of conformity with cultural values and "national" objectives?
>
> —Abdullahi A. An-Naim[1]

> The idea of Asian values derives its appeal from its anti-West-centric stance.
>
> —Inoue Tatsuo[2]

The debate on Asian values has expanded considerably in the last couple of decades. At the core of Asian values lies Confucian familism, with its emphasis on human-relatedness. Feminists have exposed the oppressive potential of the resurgence of Confucian familism and challenged the Confucian concept of family. In this essay, I first will juxtapose Confucian and Christian familism and critically reevaluate them from a feminist perspective. In the process, I will explore the similarities and differences between the two concepts of familism. Second, I shall put Confucian familism under scrutiny, and show how people in Korea have practiced it in a concrete reality, and how Koreans misunderstood familism under the guise of the noble Asian values, emphasizing the importance of human-interrelatedness. Third, I shall carefully examine the social/religious embodiment of Confucian familism and its creation of male homosocial reality in Korean society and Christianity.

Confucian Comeback: The Rise of *Asian Values*

Since the 1970s, numerous East Asian countries have experienced rapid economic and national developments, especially with the emergence of the Four Asian Dragons: Singapore, Korea, Japan, and Taiwan. People have referred to this phenomenon as the "Asian Miracle" and attributed it to Asian values. Dynamic emerging markets, rapid economic growth, increased economic power, and rising standards of living have characterized these Asian countries. People often regard Asian values as family values. Therefore, one of the simple descriptions of Asian values involves the connection of the individual to the family; the family to the whole society; and these links to the basis of the society. When Asian leaders stress the importance of Asian traditional virtues, most of them directly or indirectly refer to the traditional Confucian virtues. In this context, Asian leaders highly exalt Confucian familism and often attack feminism for its allegedly antifamily nature. And such statements as "Confucian tradition is highly compatible with capitalism" or "Asian values are the alternative to the Western values" are increasingly being expressed in Asia.[3] In this era of globalization, people who do not want to lose their national/cultural identity tend to cling to the traditional values and customs in order to differentiate themselves from the West. Under the propaganda statement, "The most Korean is the most global," mass media and a group of allegedly progressive people in South Korea, for instance, have begun to emphasize the revival of Korean indigenous values and cultures. People even say that Asian values are universal, while Western values are only Western. Asians seek out local attachments to recover a sense of belonging and try to come to grips with a postcolonial identity while at the same time identifying, ironically, with larger, global movements.

Kuan Yew Lee, the first Prime Minister of Singapore (1959–1990), provoked the Asian values debate, and Prime Minister Mahathir of Malaysia further advocated for it. Those who advocate Asian values assert that a certain set of values, such as hard work, discipline, thriftiness, family solidarity, and a stress on the community rather than the individual, are uniquely Asian. Kuan Yew Lee argues that Asians have "little doubt that a society with communitarian values, where the interests of society take precedence over that of the individual, suits to them better than the individualism of America." They use Confucius as a weapon for their own purposes. People often refer the contemporary resurgence of Confucianism as the "Confucian comeback."[4] Interestingly, until recently, China has never attempted to revive Confucius, even though he was Chinese. Rather, socialist leaders in China believed Confucius was holding China back. Since the new cultural movement of May 4, 1919, revolution has meant rejecting traditional Chinese culture, especially Confucianism, in modern China. And one of the most important aims of Mao Zedong's Cultural Revolution was to get rid of Confucianism. However, the Chinese regime has recently attempted to revive Confucianism in order to protect itself from the "influx of Western notions like universal suffrage" and hopes to mix Chinese nationalism and Confucian thoughts. Yet, the Chinese regime's attempt to revive and reinsert Confucianism into the lives of the Chinese people has encountered huge criticism from those who contend that this is nothing but "cynical nationalism" and that Confucius promotes a "social hierarchy in which roles are strictly defined: students defer to teachers, kids revere elders, wives serve husbands, and citizens obey rulers."[5]

In the course of developing a postcolonial sensitivity, not only political leaders but also many scholars in Asia began to claim their cultural/national identity by clinging to their own past tradition and values. Those Asian nationalist scholars tried to overcome their cultural, political, and intellectual dependence on the West by especially emphasizing so-called unique Asian values and Asian unity. There are also Asia admirers—both specialist and amateur—among both Asians and Westerners who tend to attribute to Asia absolute differences from the West. They believe that the "Wisdom of the East" and its spirituality offer a deep, ancient, penetrating wisdom that will overcome the destructive materialism and individualism of the West. In such a form of anti-West-centrism, they merely change the evaluative connotation of this Oriental essence from negative to positive while keeping its cognitive content unchanged. For a unique Asian identity, they take the stereotype that orientalists imposed on Asia to establish a superior Western identity, and shift it to their newly revived identity as Asian in a positive sense. By upholding so-called Asian-owned cultural traditions, those who hold Asian values want to claim their right to self-determination. Furthermore, the conversion strategy can play the role of healing a people's wounded self-respect more powerfully than the strategy of destroying the stereotype, as one can see in some of the strategies among radical feminist groups.

Such rhetoric about Asian values versus Western values as the opposite, however, is not only an oversimplification but also a gross misrepresentation. Furthermore, the underlying assumption that Asia has a cultural essence fundamentally different from the West is, in fact, a view originating from Western intellectual imperialism, what Edward Said calls "orientalism." As Said puts it, orientalism operates in the service of the West's hegemony over the East primarily by producing the East discursively as the West's inferior Other. It does so principally by distinguishing and then essentializing the identities of East and West through a dichotomizing system of representations embodied in stereotypes. Orientalism is, therefore, a collective notion identifying us-Westerners as against all those-non-Westerners, and "a Western style for dominating, restructuring, and having authority over the Orient."[6]

The West-centrism guides and misguides those arguments for Asian values by Asian political leaders and scholars, which Asians have criticized because their dualistic assumptions are the products of the Western intellectual and discursive imperialism that those who hold Asian values are supposedly attacking. Furthermore, the sharp dichotomy between an individualist West and a communitarian Asia distorts Asian reality and promotes Asians stereotyping themselves. The tendency to overvalue the East produces dangerous problems of neglecting and distorting the materiality of the daily life of contemporary Asian people. In this imagined East, invented by an orientalist mentality, people eternally freeze and fix the real people of Asia to the timeless past. In the logic of Said's argument about orientalism, both the *Asian debaser*, describing Asia in an extremely negative way characterized by backwardness, inequality, or degeneracy, and the *Asian admirer*, simply admiring and glorifying Asia as a space of beauty, virtue, and wisdom, alike follow the orientalist logic by defining the Orient only as different from the West. Both groups are, wittingly or unwittingly, re-Orientalizing Asia, and these overvalued qualities are as distorted as their negative counterparts. Furthermore, establishing Asian identity based only on its difference from the West makes Asians a more true subaltern group, establishing their identity only in a limited form of an "identity-in-differential."[7] One of the serious problems with this *identity-in-differential* is that it requires always a constitutive other to address who one is.

Here is a dangerous trap in the rise of Asian values that Asian politicians and scholars propose as the potential remedy for the disease of Western egoism and destructive individualism, especially when it exalts Confucian values as the basis of the ideal virtues of Asian culture. The rise of the Asian-values discourse is dangerous because, first, it overlooks not only the vices of communitarianism, such as the hierarchical and patriarchal communitarianism, but also the virtues of individualism, such as the ethical individualism that highlights the dignity and value of an individual human being, which are fundamental in promoting human rights. Second, it tends to blur the root causes of women's oppression under Confucian patriarchy by idealizing traditional patriarchal family structure and values that rigidly and hierarchically distinguish between women's and men's places and their respective roles. As a result, it freezes women in the patriarchal past, the traditional images, and the premodern reality. Third, it justifies and perpetuates classist sociopolitical structures that relegate the lower-class people, the commoner, to being second-class citizens. The Confucian culture theory seems to respect women by emphasizing the harmony of *yin*, the female, and *yang*, the male, the two interacting universal elements. In its discourse, however, people tend to glorify patriarchal authoritarianism as a driving force of Asian economic development, and revive neo-conservatism in which people justify gender discrimination under the name of the noble Asian values.

In this Asian-values emphasis, culture is often more than a convenient excuse to ignore women's issues as neither urgent nor relevant. Here people use culture as a *culturalist alibi* that takes culture as an excuse for violating the human rights of women and sexual minorities, for instance. As Gayatri Chakravorty Spivak relevantly points out: "The new cultural alibi, working within a basically elitist culture industry, insisting on the continuity of a native tradition untouched by a Westernization whose failures it can help to cover, legitimizes the very thing it claims to combat."[8] In this context, people often dismiss the demand for women's rights on the grounds of its *foreign* origin and blindly accuse feminists of ignoring their own culture and national identity and as being too Westernized. In this rhetoric of Asian values, rooted in Confucianism, people mystify, obscure, and conceal the real inequalities between different classes, genders, sexuality, and ages. The long tradition and history of Confucianism show that improving women's status in Confucianism has never succeeded. Confucianism did not bring about counter-systemic transformation in women's conditions. On the contrary, it has perpetuated and reinforced women's oppression and inequality.

The rise of Asian values, therefore, is the rise of the spirit of antidemocracy because of its emphasis on the hierarchical human connection and community and because of its lack of the principle of actualizing and practicing universal human values, that is, justice, equality, power equity among different genders, classes, sexuality, and ages. It tends to silence depowered groups, especially women, minors, the poor, and the uneducated, which is unjust.[9] The rise of Asian values also is antifeminist because of its male-centeredness. It tends to disregard feminist issues as Western, not authentically Asian. Accordingly, it neglects the material praxis of women's lives in Asia today, and ignores how sexism and androcentrism distort, lessen, and marginalize women's lives under the Confucian patriarchal value system and its institutions.

People refer to Confucianism on different levels such as philosophy, political ideology, state politics and institutions, or religious practice. In this sense, Confucianism covers a broad spectrum. It is necessary, therefore, to make clear that I take Confucianism primarily as an ethical and religious discourse and practice which informs people about ways of life in their daily lives. Whether or not one regards Confucianism as a religion would depend on one's definition of religion. I take Confucianism as a religion and I believe religion is not just about philosophical frameworks and discourses, abstract cosmological principles, or doctrinal beliefs and confessions. Rather, "religion is, in reality, 'living.' . . . one's religion, then, is one's life, not merely the ideal life but life as it is actually lived. . . . All that we do and are is our religion."[10] In this regard, religion is about living together—with oneself and with others in dignity, equality, justice, and peace.

Views on the Family: Confucian and Christian

Patrilineal Biological Familism: Confucian View on the Family

If one asks Koreans what their religion is, only 2 percent of the population answers "Confucianism." But when one asks whether they practice or follow Confucian teachings in their daily lives, then 90 percent of Koreans answer "yes."[11] Confucian tradition in contemporary Korea is significant. While their adherence to Confucianism differs in intensity, most Koreans remain strongly influenced by Confucian values. In modern times, even though Confucian texts are not read and the rituals are becoming simplified or abandoned, Confucian values and ethics still guide Koreans' concrete lives. One can find the continued presence of Confucianism in Korea in how individuals respond to family, school, community, workplace, and the state. Contemporary Koreans obviously are not Confucians in the sense that their ancestors were, but Confucian values have deeply permeated and guided Korean people's daily lives. In this sense, Confucianism probably has more influence on Koreans than does any other of the traditional religions or philosophies of Asia. Confucianism was the official state ideology, philosophy, and religion of the Yi Dynasty (1392–1910) in Korea, and the Korean regimes and institutions have continued to thoroughly institutionalize and systematically diffuse the Confucian code of conduct and ethics to the Korean people. This long-standing implementation of the Confucian way of life and practice contributes to making Korea the most Confucian society in the world today. Because of the strong influence of Confucianism on Korean people's everyday lives, I regard Christianity in Korea as ethically Confucianized Christianity.

In Confucianism, people enshrine the family as a sacred community, and an important aspect of Confucianism is the rational justification or theoretical explication of this family system. People under Confucian influence consider the family the natural basis for all moral and political behavior and the most biologically rooted of all human institutions. Mencius states that "the root of the empire is in the state, and the root of the state is in the family."[12] This statement resembles Aristotle's argument that the earliest form of political organization was an extension of the family.[13] People under Confucianism consider themselves, therefore, to be a model for all human social organization, including government. Thus, in the Chinese and Korean languages, people use more than one hundred terms for various family relationships,[14] none of which have any equivalent in Western languages. People differentiate those terms according to whether they relate to the father's side or the mother's side, bestowing and denoting a more authentic status to the father's side.

Because of the emphasis on the family system in Confucianism, continuing the family lineage is the most significant duty of the family, which only the male child can perform. According to Mencius, therefore, "there are three things which are unfilial, and to have no posterity is the greatest of them."[15] Here posterity refers exclusively to a male child, not a female child. People often consider only the male child as a countable family member. Sons are still of overwhelming importance to the family because of their potential role as providers of the family income. Moreover, only sons can glorify the family through official appointment or perpetuate the family name. Even after death it is the sons, as sole performers of the ancestor worship, who are responsible for the welfare of their departed parents in the spirit world. Daughters cannot offer ancestral sacrifice. So, from the day of her marriage, a married woman is under pressure to conceive and bring forth a healthy male child because people acknowledge the clan lineage only through the male line. Without a son, there would be no head of the household to offer the ancestral sacrifices and the clan would acquire a secondary status, existing only along the female line. People regard the marriage as a sacred event in Confucianism, registered in the cosmic order and with the ancestral line, and people thereby consider it something that one should not dissolve. Yet, the importance of sons is so great that if a wife fails to bear a male child, according to Confucian teaching, the husband has the right to divorce her and send her back to her family.[16] A wife, however, never has any grounds for initiating a divorce against her husband under any circumstances.

Theoretically, the duty of the Confucian male child is to devote himself to the welfare of his parents. The duty of a son's wife is to share in this complete devotion to her husband's parents, not to her own parents. Here, the concept of filiality is of the most significance for understanding the Confucian family. The term *hsiao* (filiality or filial piety) presents one of the most basic social and religious concepts of Confucian society. The written symbol in Chinese for *hsiao* consists of the graph for the old supported by the graph for son placed underneath. Confucius gave this virtue of filiality a primacy in human moral development. Filiality, as the root of familism, is praised in all the Confucian classics. In fact, the Book of Filiality (or *Hsiao Ching*), one of the Confucian classics, is exclusively dedicated to this topic. The Book of Filiality describes filiality as follows: "while [the parents] are living, serve them with *li* [principle]; when they die, bury them with *li*, and sacrifice for them with *li*."[17] Confucians consider filiality as the virtue of all virtues and the source, measure, and form of all the virtues and direct sons toward their ultimate end in ultimate aim of piety toward heaven.

The center of the Confucian family is found in the relationship between father and son. Consequently, the teaching of the filiality is mainly focused on the relationship between fathers and sons. Since the family lineage is patrilineal, people exclude the family of the wife from the family lineage. This aspect is the most significant flaw in Confucian notion and practice of familism.

Because of its significant emphasis on filiality, ancestor worship or rite is the oldest and most basic Confucian tradition. One should note that "ancestor" primarily means a male ancestor of the husband. The ancestor in Confucian ancestor worship is not a universal category that evenly includes the ancestors of both husband and wife. A woman born into a family will not be an ancestor at all, for she is born to join herself to another family's ancestor worship. Confucian exaltation of the authority of father and son made the unequal treatment of women appear natural. Society can see the subordination of wives to husbands and daughters to all men in the family, the denial of inheritance rights, the inequitable marriage laws, and the unequal treatment in genealogical records as proof of the sexual inequality fostered by Confucianism in a Confucian society such as Korea. In sum, the Confucian view of the family is inevitably patriarchal, patrilineal, and patrilocal.

Critical Familism: Christian View on the Family

Focusing upon family discourse is significant for understanding a particular society because such discourse not only gives meaning to social life but also controls it. A monolithic image of family serves, as one can see in the conception of the Confucian family, not simply as an accurate reflection of reality but as an ideology prescribing one type of family as normative. People in a society take one's commitment to that type of family as evidence of one's normality and morality. In this sense, the family discourse "provides an important and ubiquitous social control rhetoric."[18] Unlike in Confucianism, for instance, Christianity offers no single concept of family. Within Christianity, different views on family coexist: from the fundamentalist view to the Christian feminist one, and from the Catholic view to the Protestant one, for instance. Most of the traditional Christian teachings on the family tend to suggest only one normative model for the family, which sometimes seems incompatible with feminism. From this traditional view of family, conservative Christians regard feminism as an antifamily ideology that would destroy so-called Christian family values. Conservative Christian groups such as the Christian Coalition in the United States use the term *antifamily* as a slogan. Conservative Christians have used such an understanding of family as a "conceptual and institutional fortress of patriarchy, sexism, and heterosexism."[19]

One of the more progressive Christian responses to the fundamentalist Christian view on family is an emphasis upon the formlessness of the family. According to John Platton and Brian H. Childs: "There is no ideal form for the Christian family toward which we should strive. There is, however, a normative function: Care."[20] For them, any form of family is acceptable as long as it comes with redemptive care, which one can characterize as a combination of appreciation, respect, compassion, and solicitude. Some argue that the Christian family should not be a haven of private separation from the public. In rejecting the public–private split that is typical of the modern bourgeois family, Rodney Clapp attempts to recover the notion of the Christian home as a mission base crossing over the split between the private and public, a concept that is consistent with the pattern of home churches explicit in the process of the formation of early Christianity.[21]

Christian feminists also began to challenge the patriarchal understanding of family in fundamentalist Christianity, and to redefine the family and marriage based on gender equality and justice. Family is not only a biological but also "a social institution, affecting and affected by other social institutions in which it is located."[22] In this sense, the public–private split cannot adequately characterize the complexity of family and interconnectedness between the two spheres, as addressed in the well-known feminist slogan, "The personal is the political." Emphasis on the family only as a biological unit and confining it to the private sphere has reinforced and justified the male headship of the household and sexism. Jesus relativizes both the biological reality and the sociological reality of the family in his claim, "Whoever does the will of God is my brother and sister and mother" (Mark 3:35; Matt. 12:50; Luke 8:21). Jesus's nonbiological conception of family is important because it puts priority on the theological reality, not biological reality, of family. This theological and spiritual relativization of the traditional family as a biological or sociological unit can be a Christian principle of the renunciation of patriarchal value and the male-centered structure of family. The theological principle of family, of course, does not deny the biological and sociological families, but puts all other relationships in the service of a community that exists for the purpose of enabling and enhancing each person's relationship to God.

In this context, Christians need to evaluate the Christian concept of family in a new way to understand how the family provides for people's relation to God in a concrete reality. Christians can judge the biological or sociological family as good, for example, only if it enhances the God-relation of its members and the community. Otherwise, one may need to rearrange or leave the family behind in light of the theological principle of family. Theologically speaking, Jesus's claim that only those who do the will of God are his family is a characterization of the demands of justice and equality in family. It deconstructs the patriarchal and homosexist family that has justified the subordination of women to men and the opposition to the civil unions or marriages of same-sex couples. It can also be a Christian feminist principle that criticizes the patriarchal aspects in the biblical and Christian tradition because practicing sexism or other forms of discrimination would not be the will of God. Jesus's view on who counts as family breaks from traditional social definitions and understandings of family, and especially contrasts with the Confucian understanding of family that people base exclusively on a male biological connection. Christians can therefore define family in terms of God-relation and doing the will of God—the deeds of justice and love, grounded in Jesus's teaching. Here, family as biological unit loses its status as family when it justifies unjust family relations, because such does not follow the will of God.

Christians have defined love in various ways, some associating it more with self-sacrifice (*agape*), and others with self-fulfillment (*eros*). But primarily, love means equal regard (*caritas*) that includes elements of both sacrifice and fulfillment. The Christian notion of family thus advocates "the committed, intact, equal-regard, public-private family" as a new family ideal in which both husband and wife respect each other and participate in both public and private realm. This Christian notion of family promotes not a narrow familism that endorses only one type of family but a "critical familism" that respects and supports those who live outside of a conventional family structure. A "love ethic of equal regard"[23] grounds this Christian family and places its value on mutuality, self-sacrifice, and individual fulfillment.

Critical Reevaluation of Two Familisms

On the surface, both Confucianism and Christianity seem to have one thing in common: an emphasis on the relationship of father and son. Sung Bum Yun, a Korean theologian who initiated Korean indigenous theology in 1960s, contends that the relationship of Jesus Christ with the Heavenly Father resembles Confucian filiality, that is, the father-son relationship.[24] According to Yun, both in Judeo-Christianity and in Confucianism, the father-son relationship is the essential norm for an integral approach to what it means to be human. He contends, "both Christianity and Confucianism are religions of the East, and the ethics of both begins with the family."[25] He goes on to argue that Christianity emphasizes the primary importance of the father-son relationship in the creation story and treats the husband-wife relationship as secondary. God first made Adam, and God was the Father and Adam was God's first-born son. After God established the father-son relationship between God and Adam, God made Adam a wife, Eve. Accordingly, the father-son relationship is primary and inevitable, while the husband-wife relationship is contingent.

Second, in the New Testament, the relationship of God the Father and God's Son, Jesus Christ, is likewise primary. The essence of the relationship of the Father to Son is clearly manifested in the New Testament's Christological thinking, which denotes that the triune God is grounded upon the Father-Son relationship.[26] In this sense, Yun argues, a similarity between Christian and Confucian ethics is obvious, because filiality is the essential norm in both. Yun regrets that the Western Christian tradition lost the meaning of authentic family that is the essence of Christianity by its adoption of individualism. Thus he unreservedly concludes that the most essential factor in both Judeo-Christianity and Confucianism is the father-son relationship.

However, Yun, as well as other scholars who share similar views on the relationship of Confucianism and Christianity, overlooks some critical differences between the Confucian notion of family and that of Christianity. First, Confucianism and Christianity have crucial differences in their understanding of what it means to be human, an understanding on which people have based the idea of human rights and equality. The idea of human rights requires "a certain level of individualism, wherein the individual person would be valued for her/his own sake, and not just as a relationship to others."[27] In Confucianism, unlike in Christianity, one can hardly find a sense of individuality because the family as a group precedes an individual person. In the Confucian tradition, no conception of individuality existed, and the underlying idea of Confucianism is "not individual liberty or equality but order and harmony, not individual independence but selflessness and cooperation, not freedom of individual conscience but conformity to orthodox truth" and "the purpose of society was not to preserve and promote individual liberty but to maintain the harmony of the hierarchical order."[28] In this vein, the feminist claim of woman as an individual, singular human being, not simply as a role or function, has no place in Confucian perception of human being. A number of Confucian scholars endorse the following understanding of human being and morality and use it as a rationale for rejecting universal human rights: "For the early Confucians there can be no *me* in isolation, to be considered abstractly; I am the *totality of roles*. I live in relation to specific others. I do not *play* or *perform* these roles; I am these roles. When they have all been specified I have been defined uniquely, fully, and altogether, with no remainder with which to piece together a free, autonomous self."[29]

In this Confucian context, therefore, the relationship between the family members is more important than the individual. The problem here is the fact that the relationship is hierarchical according to gender, age, and social status in a way that is anti-democratic and androcentric. Many regard Confucianism as a true humanism. But this idea is misleading because the human being in Confucianism has rights only if she or he has a certain position in a family. The individual person has rights not as an individual, singular person, but as a brother, son, or father. There is no place for a woman to claim her human rights as an individual person, especially in the public sphere—not even as wife, daughter, or mother. This asymmetrical status among family members—between husband and wife, son and daughter, senior and junior—is not seen when one argues that Confucianism is a true humanism because of its exaltation of human relationship within a community.

Even though the Fifth Commandment in the Ten Commandments says, "Obey your parents," the place of filial piety in Christianity and Confucianism is critically different. Paul teaches Christians, for instance, to obey parents *in the Lord* (Eph. 6:1) and if the biological parents instigate Christians to any transgression of God's law, such Christians may justly consider their biological parents not as parents, but as strangers who are attempting to seduce them from obedience to God.[30] In Confucianism, however, it is not possible for one to disobey one's parents, especially the biological father, in any circumstance. The concept of father as a symbol of God and of priest within the Christian community did not derive from the natural family as it is in Confucianism. Christianity claimed a higher right to be an authentic family than the natural/biological family. Christianity weakened people's loyalties to their traditional patriarchal clans by encouraging competing loyalties to Christian communities and Christian marriage ("A man shall leave his father and mother and be joined to his wife," Gen. 2:24), a fact that non-Christian Confucians may view as dangerous to the existing patrilineal social order.

In Confucianism, such a conception is not possible because a son never should leave his father.[31] From the Confucian view on family, the absence of a biological father in Jesus's birth, for instance, can be a serious problem because Jesus is a misbegotten child who does not have any biological father with a direct blood relation. Furthermore Jesus, as an unmarried man, is an unfilial son because he does not carry on his biological family line. Furthermore, Jesus relativizes the family, as the biological unit, by the claim that those who do God's will are his mother, brothers, and sisters, strangely omitting fathers. Therefore, one cannot bind Jesus's notion of family to the Confucian biological, patriarchal, and heterosexual notion of family. With its radical inclusivity, one can find some guiding principles not only for the heterosexual family but also for all forms of family today, for instance, a homosexual family, a single-parent family, a mixed-race family, a family with adopted children who have no biological connection to their parents, a family with no children, and so on. By contrast, the Confucian notion of family makes those people in allegedly nonstandard family forms marginal, abnormal, and deficient, thereby depriving their rights to be happy as normal citizens. Divorced women and their children, for instance, are among the most deprived people in Confucian society, not only legally but also socially and culturally, for they have no male head of household, which is the ideal of the Confucian family that people have legally practiced through various forms of institutions in Korea.

If one employs the method of reflection on praxis in examining a religion, then one ought to take a look at the concrete praxis of how each individual has rights as a human being under the particular religious/philosophical teachings in her or his everyday life. Academic discourse on Confucianism must take into account the serious violation of human rights in women's lives under Confucian teachings. Romanticizing and idealizing Confucianism as a true humanism will only blur the root causes of women's oppression under Confucianism and its practice, and will likely simply ignore the present problem of an extreme male-centeredness in Confucian culture and society. It is hard for one to find both the concept and the reality of human rights, especially for women in Confucian teachings and their practices in a concrete reality. Rather, widespread violations of the basic rights of women and children under Confucianism have prevailed even today.

One should also note that the Confucian concept of the person as a center of relationships, rather than merely an isolated individual, and its emphasis on family-centeredness and human-relatedness, have resulted in nepotism, favoritism, and provincialism in private and public sectors of Korea such as church, family, workplace, and politics. People establish most political and social relationships based on one's family relationships, one's hometown, or one's alma mater. Thus, people highly recommend and widely practice hiring someone because of personal ties and relations based on one's hometown, alma mater, personal acquaintance, and so forth. Confucian scholars have not fundamentally challenged the injustice resulting from these problematic social relations and values, which have raised major barriers to Confucian society's achieving a more advanced, mature form of democracy. Confucian scholars and practitioners should address not only the virtues but also the possible vices of Confucian communitarianism, especially in Confucian family discourse. The absence of the notion of individuality in Confucianism has exaggerated the vices implicit in egoistic family-centeredness and human-relatedness because of the lack of a sense of common justice and fairness, which one should apply to every single member of society regardless of age, gender, social status, natal origin, or similar factors.

The notion of individualism is in fact very complex. Generally speaking, one can view individualism in two ways. One view holds that individualism is destructive to an individual and to one's social interaction. People regard individualism as negative and destructive because it ignores the notion of human beings as social, communal, and interdependent beings, which has resulted in unscrupulous competition, an understanding of humans as self-contained and self-sufficient, and an alienation from self and society. Most contemporary feminists have criticized this negative view and practice of individualism. The other view of individualism maintains that this destructive individualism is a Hobbesian notion and is incompatible with true ethical individualism. The positive aspects of this ethical individualism are self-actualization, freedom of choice, personal responsibility, and universality, which involves respect for the well-being and rights of others because denying the rights of others would implicitly endorse the idea that one does not possess such rights for oneself as well.[32]

Despite the potential vices of individualism that many, including feminists, have pointed out, the initial stage of feminist consciousness nevertheless requires this positive notion of ethical individualism in order for women, the powerless, or the marginalized to acknowledge themselves as responsible and free agents not dependent on men, and to reject the patriarchal construction of men, the Subject, and women, the Other.

Failure to achieve sufficient autonomy, for instance, which is one aspect of individualism, can be a block to achieving a mature relationship and thus a full understanding of interdependence. Autonomy, in this feminist context, is not absolute self-sufficiency, as many too readily claim, but one's capacity for independent survival, thinking, and judgment. Autonomous persons recognize others' needs for freedom and their own lives. I do not see any inevitable dichotomy between individualism and communitarianism, or I-ness and we-ness. What we need is neither a total rejection of nor a blind acceptance, but an ongoing reconceptualization of the notion of individualism that requires a critical perspective.

Christian understanding of the human being implies a strong sense of ethical individualism on which people base the modern concept of human rights and equality in the name of natural rights. The Christian claim that God created each and every human being in God's image gave rise to the idea that we should treat all humans with the same reverence and respect because they equally bear God's image. All human beings are to have dignity and rights as humans created equal, regardless of their sex, class, or race. This ontological principle of human equality in Christianity became the conceptual framework for the nineteenth-century women's movement in the United States. When the first National Women's Right Convention in the United States took place in 1848 in Seneca Falls, New York, the delegates approved the Declaration of Sentiments, modeled on the Declaration of Independence. The following part of the declaration shows how the principle of ontological equality in Christianity became the vital force for the rise of the modern feminist movement in the United States, even though women activists harshly criticized patriarchal teachings and practices of Christian tradition at that time: "We hold these truths to be self-evident: that all men and women are created equal; that they are endowed by their Creator with certain inalienable rights; that among these are life, liberty, and the pursuit of happiness."[33] Following from this principle of human equality, justice becomes the necessary context for normative claims about the family and the norm of right relations both within and outside of biological and sociological family units. Because many feminists define justice as right relations, we have to ask how the members of the family, whether they are husband or wife or son or daughter, are relating to one another and to the context of their lives. When there are right, fair, just, equal relations among family members, one can judge the family as good. So, one should evaluate the family not just by a biological relationship but by deeds in accordance with God's will—justice and love.

People under the Confucian influence have used the lack of the concept of individuality in Confucianism, and the Confucian view of family as an exclusively biological unit, to justify the violation of women's basic human rights in the name of harmony and filiality. So many women have suffered because of its principle of agnation, which made men alone the structurally relevant members of family and society and relegated women to social/familial dependence. Most people have not seen women and the powerless as individual persons. Idealization of the Confucian concept of relatedness between humans without a reflection on the praxis of how women have actually lived under this Confucian concept of relatedness has resulted in the perpetuation of women's suffering under extreme androcentric values and institutions in Confucian society.

Researchers show that there had been not much discrimination of the paternal line against the maternal line dating back from the ancient times down to the mid-Yi Dynasty. The patrilineal system took shape later in the Yi Dynasty (*Choson*), which adopted Confucianism as its founding ideology. When the Yi Dynasty firmly entrenched Confucianism in the period from 1486 to 1636, systemic control and subjugation of women started. So, the ideal Confucian family system made Korean women legally subordinated to men in accordance with the prevalent Confucian ethic. One can characterize the Confucian family system as follows: (1) people regard only the paternal line relatives as primary relatives; (2) society transmits social class and rights only from fathers to sons; (3) the sole authority in the family rests with the father who holds control over the children; (4) society allows marriages only with those outside the blood clan; and (5) first-born males held the right to lineal succession.[34]

Here, one can see the fundamental ironies and problems in Confucian familism. The ironies of Confucian familism are as follows: first, it absolutely requires the male to carry on the family lineage, which results in female infanticide and the extreme imbalance in the ratio between female and male children in Korea[35]; second, the ancestors for filiality are primarily the ancestors of the husband's family, which thereby disregards the wife's family. The system of family lineage (*chokbo*) and the male headship of the family have been the most powerful operating social system in Korean society, and they have influenced the androcentrism in Korean Christian churches today.

Homosocial Reality: Embodiment of Confucian Familism in Christianity

In a patriarchal society, the relations between men, not between men and women, are the most important. Especially in Confucian culture, relations between men, both in the private and the public spheres, have been the center of all human relationships. The relations between men establish a firm solidarity among male members of society that enables them to dominate and hold power over women. Women isolated from the close-knit public relations among men cannot find their place except in small private sectors. To work in the public sphere, women must enter the exclusive network of men. However, it is extremely difficult for women to relate to men as coworkers because the Confucian tradition has defined the relationship of women to men as that of a life spouse suited only for marriage. Furthermore, men easily exclude women from the shared information among male workers, which information women would need for proper promotions and so on.

Various social/religious institutions also embody the Confucian emphasis on the homogeneity of the family lineage. For example, people neither encourage nor commonly practice adoption in Confucian cultural societies such as Korea. Since an adopted child has no homogeneity in terms of bloodline with the father, people would not consider the adopted child to be an authentic family member. So, most families try to hide the fact of the adoption and pretend so that people outside the family see the child as their real birth-child. In this context, it is not unusual that people extend this negative attitude toward interracial marriage and its offspring as well, for they also embody an impure marriage because of its lack of homogeneity in blood.

Another, initially paradoxical, example of the social embodiment of the Confucian emphasis on the homogeneous family line is that Korean women retain their maiden name even after marriage, which might seem to imply equality until one comes to understand the underlying androcentric view of family. Women after marriage still retain their maiden names not because their husband's family members respect women's independence but because they cannot accept women as a full member of their husband's household. Since the married women do not have a direct blood connection with the husband's family, women after marriage become absolute outsiders both in their natal family and husband's family: married women are in-between and belong nowhere. It is only when women give birth to a male child that they are able to claim their status as family members in their husband's family. So, it has been a survival issue for Korean women to give birth to sons, which has resulted in the extreme ratio imbalance between male and female children even today in Korea.

Christians have extended Confucian familism, with its emphasis on the homogeneity of family blood, to the religious sphere. Korean Christianity emphasizes a denominational homogeneity among Christians, which has resulted in a lack of ecumenical spirit. Because of this, one can hardly find a mutual interaction between denominations; instead, they are highly competitive and even hostile to one another. Consequently, mutual interaction among faculties and students of seminaries of different denominations is hardly possible or desirable. Faculties and students in denominationally affiliated theological schools are exclusively from the same denomination. Furthermore, among faculty members in a particular seminary, homogeneity also prevails, not only in terms of the denomination but also in the schools from which faculty members have graduated. Denominational or institutional nepotism creates an anti-ecumenical and anti-democratic ethos in theological educational bodies and practices.

Confucianism in Korea is not the only force for promoting the patriarchal reality in Christianity, but it justifies, reinforces, and finally perpetuates a strong patriarchal ethos in Christianity. Confucianism has tended to be extremely conservative, supporting the ruling elite and the status quo, providing theoretical justification for authoritarianism, and justifying inequality between the sexes and age groups. It strives to maintain the existing social hierarchical structure, and it reinforces and justifies women's subordination to men in family, society, and church in the name of harmony and peace of community. It has strongly influenced the contemporary patriarchal construction of Christianity in Korea. Of course, this has not taken place automatically, for men have been the primary social and religious engineers of Christianity, too. Yet, we should not overlook the fact that women also contributed to the development of early Christianity, and they were even equal partners with men.[36] Despite these problems, including the patriarchal tradition, Christianity—even Christianity in Korea—also has an egalitarian tradition that can engender a vital force for criticizing the patriarchal factors in Christianity and for fostering women's leadership in church and society. A large number of feminist theologians have attempted to recover the egalitarian principles and practices in Christianity and reconstruct Christianity as a more just religion.

I wonder, however, if there is any possibility for the emergence of feminist theologians within Confucianism who could recover a Confucian egalitarian tradition and practice within the Confucian community in the same way that Christian feminists try to do within the Christian community and its institutions. I wonder about this issue because it is hard to find any historical trace of egalitarian community for different sexes, age groups, and social classes in the long history of Confucianism. I regret that Christians in Korea have made Christianity ethically Confucianized and armed with a stronger patriarchy than that of the Christianity practiced in the countries from which missionaries introduced Christianity to Korea. This combination of Confucianism with Christianity in Korea has resulted primarily in the exclusion of women from leadership roles in theology and the ministry. Ai Ra Kim, a Korean feminist theologian and minister, argues that most Korean Christian women accept women's inferior status in the church, which has been shaped by Confucian teaching of gender hierarchy in terms of the ideology of namjon yobi (men should be respected; women should be lowered). The Confucian ideology of namjon yobi, she maintains, continues to operate even in the Korean immigrant churches in the United States. Pyong Gap Min also points out that one of the major factors for the underrepresentation of women in church leadership is the "influence of Korean Confucian patriarchal traditions."[37] The severe absence of women's leadership both in churches in Korea and immigrant churches has been a long-standing reality.

Furthermore, the Confucian exaltation of homogeneity in family lineage has resulted in a spirit of anti-ecumenism and exclusive denominationalism and has fostered a homosocial reality in the spheres of theology and ministry. As a result, Christianity in Korea is becoming more and more conservative and fundamentalist and is losing its prophetic voice and the possibility of transformation toward a more just and inclusive religion.

Confucian values, which people generally list as attachment to the family, respect for elders and authority, commitment to education, thriftiness, belief in order and stability, valuing consensus over confrontation, and so on, are likely to fail as political norms in the contemporary world, especially from a feminist perspective. Being *duty-oriented* rather than *rights-oriented* in people's relation to their communities, Confucian family-centeredness and human-relatedness force women to stay in private sectors, for Confucian teachings make a strict distinction between women's places and men's places, between women's work and men's work, between women's roles and men's roles, a distinction that limits equal opportunities for jobs and justifies this limitation. Almost all social institutions in Korea presuppose women to be housewives and often fail to count the female labor force as a real economic factor.

Whenever someone attempts to defend Asian or Confucian values, one must ask: *Who* is defending the values, for *what* purposes, for *whose* benefits, and *from what* perspective? This is especially the case with regard to women's issues. Emphasizing a respect for authority and elders often serves as a road to underpinning established social and political hierarchies and as a ground on which people in power force women, minors, and the lower social class to endure an authoritarian community, in terms of family, school, religious community, and the nation. When Asians try to utilize resources from Asian traditions, the consequence of these efforts should be to enhance the quality of our lives. If the traditions do not provide the better lives for which contemporary women aspire, women should make use of other cultural and religious traditions and learn from them. The geographical origin of democracy or feminism is, in this sense, pointless. What matters here is whether the idea or the tradition can contribute to promoting the rights of women and the marginalized and to opening a new horizon for the good life to both men and women, not only in their metaphysical or spiritual world but also in their concrete material world. Therefore, when one makes judgments about certain values, such as Asian values or Confucian values, one should make the judgments on the ground of whether those values would contribute to betterment of the lives of the marginalized, not the lives of the already privileged. One can direct feminist criticism of Asian or Confucian values at the tendency of men to use those values to justify women's subjugation to men in all forms of social and religious institutions.

When people criticize the concept of individualism in the modern West, they should also problematize the concept of communitarianism and human-relatedness in Asia. The chain of corruption in many forms in contemporary Korea, for instance, has deep roots in the distorted notion of human interconnectedness, which has led to the social injustices of nepotism, favoritism, provincialism, and male dominance. Attempts to argue that the Confucian notion of *Jen*, which is often translated as benevolence, love, kindness, charity, compassion, humaneness, humanity, perfect virtue, goodness, true humanity, and so on, is compatible with a feminist ethics of care[38] are misleading because the Confucian concept itself is characteristically patriarchal and therefore has persistently and deeply served as part of a patriarchal ideology for antifeminist traditions. Confucian scholars and practitioners have hardly implemented the concept of *Jen* for promoting the status and well-being of women, lower-class people, and the minor in Confucian society. Before glorifying Asian or Confucian human-relatedness as the alternative to the Western individualism, one needs to ask first whether these philosophies base the notion of human-relatedness on the ideal of justice and fairness among its members, regardless of one's gender, age, social status, and so on. In so doing, one can point out not only the vices of individualism but also those of communitarianism. Discursive binarism of individualism versus communitarianism or of I-ness versus we-ness does not lead one to a proper reflection on what we need to preserve as a universal value for a more egalitarian, communal, and just society, for those two are neither indivisible nor identical. Individualism and communitarianism have both vices and virtues, when people practice and implement them in human reality. Suppression of either, however, will result in a greater oppression. What we need is a critically scrutinized balance of individualism and communitarianism that contributes to maximizing the interest and well-being of the marginalized and to establishing a healthy society of justice, equality, peace, and solidarity.

Notes

1. Abdullahi A. An-naim, "The Cultural Mediation of Human Rights: The Al-Arqam Case in Malaysia," in *The East Asian Challenge for Human Rights*, ed. Joanne R. Bauer and Daniel A. Bell (Cambridge, MA: Cambridge University Press, 1999), 149.

2. Inoue Tatsuo, "Liberal Democracy and Asian Orientalism," in ibid., 29.

3. For the rise of Asian values, see Kuan-Yew Lee, "In Defense of Asian Values: Singapore's Lee Kuan Yew," *Time*, March 16, 1998; Fareed Zakaria, "Culture is Destiny: A Conversation with Lee Kuan Yew," *Foreign Affairs* 73, no. 2 (March–April 1994): 109–127; Marc F. Plattner and Larry Jay Diamond, "Hong Kong, Singapore, and 'Asian Values,'" *Journal of Democracy* 8, no. 2 (1997): 9–10.

4. Melinda Liu, "Confucian Comeback: China Remains Divided Over Reviving its Ancient Sage," *Newsweek*, September 10, 2012.

5. Ibid.

6. Edward Said, *Orientalism* (New York: Vintage, 1978), 3.

7. Gayatri Chakravorty Spivak, "Can the Subaltern Speak," in *The Postcolonial Studies Reader*, eds. Bill Ashcroft, Gareth Griffiths, and Helen Tiffin (New York: Routledge, 1995), 26.

8. Gayatri Chakravorty Spivak, "Who Claims Alterity?" in *Remaking History*, ed. Barbara Kruger and Phil Marian (Seattle: Bay Press, 1989), 281 (italics mine).

9. Cf. Won-Shik Choi, "Experiences of Non-Western Colonies and the Ghost of Asianism," paper presented at the International Conference on Toward a New Global Civilization—The Role of Activists of People's Movement, Nationalist Movement, and Local Activism, in honor of the 30-year anniversary of Creation and Critique, April 24–26, 1996, Seoul.

10. Jack Forbes, *Columbus and Other Cannibals: The Wetiko Disease of Exploitation, Imperialism, and Terrorism* (Brooklyn, NY: Automedia, 1979), 26–27. Quoted in Sharon D. Welch, "Beyond Theology of Religions: The Epistemological and Ethical Challenges of Inter-Religious Engagement," in *The Oxford Handbook of Feminist Theology*, ed. Mary McClintock Fulkerson and Sheila Briggs (New York: Oxford University Press, 2012), 353.

11. Choon-Sik Choi, *Han-Kuk Chongkyo Ijaki* [*A Story of Korean Religions*] (Seoul: Han Wool, 1995), 92.

12. *Mencius*, trans. James Legge, *The Four Books: Confucian Analects, the Great Learning, the Doctrine of the Mean, and the Works of Mencius* (New York: Paragon, 1966 [1923]), Bk. IV, Pt. I, Chap. V.

13. Aristotle, *Politics*, 1252b, 1259b.

14. Fung Yu-Lan, *A Short History of Chinese Philosophy* (New York: Free Press, 1948), 21.

15. Legge, trans., *The Four Books*, 725.

16. There were seven traditional grounds for divorce by husband—disobedience to a husband's parents, failure to bear a son, promiscuity, jealously, having an incurable disease, talking too much, and stealing. See Theresa Kelleher, "Confucianism," in *Women in World Religions*, ed. Arvind Sharma (New York: State University of New York Press, 1987), 137.

17. *Analects*, trans. James Legge, II. 5.3. The word *li* ("principle") originally has the meaning of order or pattern. There are various views on this concept in accordance with some different perspectives within Confucian philosophy. For further explanation, see Wing-tsit Chan, *A Source Book in Chinese Philosophy* (Princeton, NJ: Princeton University Press, 1963), 766–68.

18. Jaber F. Gubrium and James A. Holstein, *What Is Family?* (Mountain View, CA: Mayfield, 1990), 143.

19. Sally Purvis, "A Common Love: Christian Feminist Ethics and the Family," in *Religion, Feminism, and the Family*, ed. Anne Carr and Mary Stewart Van Leeuwen (Louisville, KY: Westminster John Knox, 1996), 112.

20. John Patton and Brian H. Childs, *Christian Marriage and Family: Caring for Our Generations* (Nashville, TN: Abingdon, 1988), 12.

21. Rodney Clapp, *Family at the Crossroad: Beyond Traditional and Modern Options* (Downers Grove, IL: InterVarsity, 1993).

22. Purvis, "A Common Love," 115.

23. Don S. Browning, et al., *From Culture Wars to Common Ground: Religion and the American Family Debate* (Louisville, KY: Westminster John Knox, 1997), 2, 3.

24. Sung Bum Yun, *Ethics East and West: Western Secular, Christian, and Confucian Traditions in Comparative Perspective*, trans. Michael C. Kalton (Seoul: Christian Literature Society, 1977 [1973]), 16.

25. Sung Bum Yun, *Sungeui Sinhak* [*Theology of Sung*] (Seoul: Sungkwangsa, 1973), 125.

26. Yun, *Ethics of East and West*, 23–25.

27. Leonard Swidler, "Human Rights: A Historical Overview," in *Concilium* ("The Ethics of World Religions and Human Rights"), ed. Hans Küng and Jürgen Moltmann (London: SCM, 1990), 12.

28. Louis Henkin, "The Human Rights Idea in Contemporary China: A Comparative Perspective," in *Human Rights in Contemporary China*, ed. R. Randle Edwards, Louis Henkin, and Andrew J. Nathan (New York: Columbia University Press, 1986), 21.

29. Henry Rosemont, "Why Take Rights Seriously? A Confucian Critique," in *Human Rights and the World's Religions*, ed. Leroy Rouner (Notre Dame, IN: University of Notre Dame Press, 1988), 177.

30. Robert Bellah, *Beyond Belief: Essays on Religion in a Post-Traditionalist World* (Berkeley: University of California Press, 1970), 93.

31. Ibid., 91.

32. Cf. Alan. S. Waterman, *The Psychology of Individualism* (New York: Praeger, 1984).

33. Elizabeth Cady Stanton, "Declaration of Sentiments," in *The Feminist Papers: From Adams to de Beauvoir*, ed. Alice S. Rossi (New York: Columbia University Press, 1973), 416.

34. Yung-Chung Kim, ed., *Women of Korea: A History from Ancient Times to 1945* (Seoul: Ewha Womans University Press, 1976), 84–89.

35. A study shows that in South Korea, the birth ratio of baby boys to girls was 107:100 in 1983. It increased to 112:100 in 1988, 115.4:100 in 1994, thereby setting the world record. This imbalance of birth ratio between boys and girls implies the world's highest abortion ratio of female fetuses. Among these abortions are some cases of terminating unwanted pregnancies from rape, but most of the abortions done are of female fetuses following a sex test. The Korean *Sisa Journal* magazine reported in 1993 that some 620,000 babies were born every year in South Korea, while 1.6 million fetuses—or 2.5 times the number actually born—were aborted. According to the *Journal*, one can now estimate the number of abortions at two million per year, which averages to six thousand per day. The balance of male vs. female babies began to shift in the mid-1980s with the introduction of ultrasonography, which doctors use as a means to find out the sex of the baby. The ratio of boys to girls is 106:100 if the baby is the firstborn; 113:100 if it's the second child, and 196:100 if it is the third child.

36. Cf. Elisabeth Schüssler Fiorenza, *In Memory of Her: A Feminist Theological Reconstruction of Christian Origins* (New York: Crossroad, 1983). Here Schüssler Fiorenza focuses on the important leadership role of women in the formation of the early church.

37. Cf. Ai Ra Kim, *Women Struggling for a New Life: The Role of Religion in the Cultural Passage from Korea to America* (New York: State University of New York Press, 1996); and Pyong Gap Min, "Severe Underrepresentation of Women in Church Leadership in the Korean Immigrant Community in the United States," *Journal for the Scientific Study of Religion*, vol. 47, no. 2 (June 2008): 225–41.

Bibliography

Bauer, Joanne R. and Daniel A. Bell, eds. *The East Asian Challenge for Human Rights*. Cambridge. MA: Cambridge University Press, 1999.

Bellah, Robert. *Beyond Belief: Essays on Religion in a Post-Traditionalist World*. Berkeley: University of California Press, 1970.

Kim, Ai Ra. *Women Struggling for a New Life: The Role of Religion in the Cultural Passage from Korea to America*. New York: State University of New York Press, 1996.

Kim, Yung-Chung, ed. *Women of Korea: A History from Ancient Times to 1945*. Seoul: Ewha Womans University Press, 1976.

Li, Chenyang. "The Confucian Concept of Jen and the Feminist Ethics of Care: A Comparative Study." *Hypatia* 9 no. 1 (Winter 1994): 70–89.

Swidler, Leonard. "Human Rights: A Historical Overview." *Concilium*. In *The Ethics of World Religions and Human Rights*, edited by Hans Küng and Jürgen Moltmann. London: SCM, 1990.

Mencius. *The Four Books: Confucian Analects, the Great Learning, the Doctrine of the Mean, and the Works of Mencius*. Translated by James Legge. New York: Paragon, 1966 [1923].

Rosemont, Henry. "Why Take Rights Seriously? A Confucian Critique." In *Human Rights and the World's Religions*, edited by Leroy Rouner. Notre Dame, IN: University of Notre Dame Press, 1988.

Said, Edward. *Orientalism*. New York: Vintage, 1978.

Spivak, Gayatri Chakravorty. "Can the Subaltern Speak." In *The Post-colonial Studies Reader*, edited by Bill Ashcroft, Gareth Griffiths, and Helen Tiffin. New York: Routledge, 1995.

9

Korean Confucianism and Women's Subjectivity in the Twenty-First Century

Un-sunn Lee

This article will explore ways to revitalize Confucian values in order to offer the Confucian tradition as a source of inspiration for developing women's subjectivity in the twenty-first century. It will also examine what implications Confucianism might offer in response to neo-liberal utilitarianism, competitionism, and the collapse of concern for the public spheres of life. The essay first pays attention to the current phenomenon of *Hallyu* (Korean Wave, or the enthusiasm for Korean pop culture) in the world, and asks what characteristics of Korean culture draw such a universal response from peoples of the world. This article finds an answer in Korean women's *saengmul* (生物, life-giving and caring) spirituality which has been nurtured in the long process of their household-making experiences in the Confucian tradition. Their virtues can be summarized into the practice of "giving up one's own way to follow that of others" and "seeking humanity and accomplishing sagehood." This article recognizes that these virtues aren't simply nonsubjective; rather, as the essence of Confucian spirituality, they have a positive meaning in our postmodern world as an alternative postmodern spirituality which is "least religious and yet richly spiritual." These virtues offer constructive resources today for healing the decline of the public spheres of life that seem to be a result of an excessive application of the modern principle of subjectivity.

Hallyu (Korean Wave), the Confucian Tradition, and Korean Women's Spirituality of Life-Giving-and-Caring (生物)

This paper explores ways of revitalizing Confucian ideals and values as inspiring resources for developing Korean women's subjectivity in the twenty-first century. The influence of Confucianism on Korean culture is well known. It is still very pervasive in everyday Korean life to a greater degree than in any other Asian country. In 2011, on his return from an official visit to Bulgaria, the South Korean Prime Minister, Hwang Gyeong-sik, expressed in a television interview his great amazement and excitement at the enthusiasm for Korean pop culture that he saw even in an Eastern European country like Bulgaria. As prime minister, he was deeply moved by seeing young people in the countries he visited singing the songs of Korean pop music stars, learning the Korean language, and listing Korea as the country they most want to travel to. Along with Prime Minister Hwang, most Koreans would have the same feelings about the current Korean wave sweeping through many countries in the world,[1] especially the older generation of Koreans who lived through the Korean war.

I want to call attention to the fact that Korean women are playing a prominent role in this wave of enthusiasm for Korean culture, known as *Hallyu* (Korean Wave or Trend). For example, Sin Gyeongsuk, a Korean female novelist, has excited the American readership with her novel *Please Look after Mom*. As a woman, she showed how the universal experience of motherhood could be expressed in the experience of Korean women. She once compared the publication of her novel to "the first snow falling in America for both herself and Korean literature."[2] This comparison sounds very symbolic, in that it makes one think of the spirit of Korean women and Korean motherhood blanketing American society like snow but also with the excitement of the first snow.

What, then, is the meaning and substance of this *Hallyu* that we are observing in many areas of the world? What is it about Korean culture that gives it such a universal appeal? How can we understand the Korean women's outstanding role in this trend? Generally speaking, the global dynamic of the twenty-first century can be described as the encounter between the Christian civilization of the United States and the Confucian civilization of China. More and more, we see a growing interest in Confucian values, and the revival of Confucianism is taking place even in Communist China. However, there is little interaction between Confucianism and feminism. This is because of Confucianism's doctrine of *namjonyeobi* (男尊女卑, honoring men and debasing women) and its founding principle of respecting *Yang* and repressing *Yin*. Nevertheless, Confucian women in many parts of the world have wrestled with the question of how to reconstruct the Confucian tradition in the light of the challenges of twentieth-century feminism. The dialogue between Confucianism and feminism has also been going on in Korea, the land that has most preserved its Confucian tradition, even to today.³

In this chapter, I will search for the lessons that Korean Confucianism can give to twenty-first century women for building up healthy subjectivity. It is an undeniable fact that Christian civilization had made a great impact on the liberation of Korean women, and that Western feminism brought a big change into the lives of Korean women in the late twentieth century. But today Christianity is criticized for not playing any further constructive role for Korean society. Likewise, contemporary feminism is not free from the harsh criticism that its goals should be reexamined in light of the current threats to communal life, including family life. In this context, I will discuss, from a Korean feminist perspective, what we can learn from the Confucian tradition and how we can have a constructive dialogue between Confucianism and Christianity.

Confucian Religiosity as a Way of Sanctifying Everyday Human Life

Most people in the world today are suffering from the collapse of *public realms*, while they are busy working for the benefit of their own private lives without concern for the public. This is also true for the people of South Korea, a nation which has accomplished its industrialization with unprecedented speed. By contrast, Confucianism has been consistently stressing the importance of the public, as it is shown in the *Book of Rites* saying, "All affairs are pursued for the realization of the public (天下爲公)."⁴ Even though it did not actually accomplish much in its concrete history of practice, the core of Confucius's idea lies in his saying, "Overcoming one's self and returning to propriety is true humanity (克己復禮爲仁),"⁵ and "When you see profits, think first of what is right (見利思義)."⁶ Menzius also repeatedly said "[on] letting life go, choosing righteousness (捨生取義)."⁷ As these teachings show, the Confucian tradition has considered the accommodation of human plurality and the harmonious integration of such individual desires to be the most important issue in maintaining human life. Confucian teachings such as "inwardly sagehood and outwardly kingship (內聖外王)" and "learning from the bottom and thereby reaching the top (下學而上達)"[8] can be understood as ways to harmonize the contradictions of modern life from which many are suffering today, including women. This harmonization is accomplished in a very practical and this-worldly way, as the divisions between the public and the private, the spiritual and the material, self and others are healed.

However, I will go further and call attention to Korean women's unique experiences within the Confucian tradition. In spite of the hostile conditions of life legitimized by the doctrine of respecting *Yang* and repressing *Yin*, Korean women have invested all of their practical efforts in giving birth to life and taking care of it. I think Korean women's life experiences contain the wisdom necessary to resolve the conflicts between the private and public realms. Korean women's lives in the age of the *Joseon* Dynasty have often been characterized as passive and miserable. But this view is too one-sided because it neglects the religious aspect of the Confucian tradition. Confucianism is generally known as a sociopolitical system or as a purely ethical doctrine. This popular view overlooks the profound religious aspect of Confucianism, failing to notice the unique Confucian way of learning to become a sage, an authentic person (聖人之道). I think this way of learning to become a sage is important for understanding not only the lives and historical achievements of Joseon men but also those of Joseon women. Unlike Buddhism, which sharply distinguishes the sacred from the profane, Confucianism does not make such a distinction. Instead, Confucianism attempts to realize the sacred in this profane world and carry out this project according to the doctrine of *li-i fen-shu* ("The principle is one, but its manifestations are many 理一分數").

Confucianism aims at making the whole world sacred. To accomplish this goal, however, it must have a starting point. In the past, the patriarch played that role in the family. So, although the Confucian doctrine of *li-i fen-shu* considers every person and everything in the world to be equally qualified for sagehood, everything still requires a starting point on the way toward sagehood. Thus the patriarch's or the eldest son's role can be regarded as the same one that the priest plays in other religious traditions. Of course, Confucianism, which intends to sanctify the whole world, could not abandon the area of women's lives and thus tried to regulate every corner of ordinary family life by its particular orders and arts (家禮). This process of the Confucian transformation of Joseon society has been already characterized as "a civilizing process."⁹ I think that Korean Confucian women's lives also went through the process of refining life-manners more fully than we used to think, and that they were able to cultivate the capacities of *self-control*, *literacy*, and *sense of time* to a more advanced degree than in other periods. It was really a ritualizing process of their lives (禮化).¹⁰

However, I want to go further in interpreting this process. In my view, it is not just a secular process of civilization or ritualization but also a spiritual sanctifying process of sagehood (sanctification, 聖化). I think that the religiosity of Korean Confucian women was expressed well in these efforts to make their whole lives sanctified by propriety and *sallim* (life-giving) actions. In the later period of the *Joseon* Dynasty there were many vivid examples of Korean women living their lives with the clear self-consciousness of sagehood, unifying self-cultivation and housekeeping, personal learning and social service. They had a strong sense of gender equality in the pursuit of the way of sagehood. Of many possible examples of "woman *seonbi*" (woman scholar or learned woman), two women stand out: Im Yeon-ji-dang (任允摯堂, 1721–1793) and Gang Jeong-il-dang (姜靜一堂, 1772–1832). They were very conscious of the way of sagehood in their performance of ancestral service, sincere hospitality, child caring, and everything that housewives do. Although they were restricted in their family life, they performed all these obligations with a strong sense of public responsibility and a sense of justice.¹¹

The lives of Confucian women were not purely passive and without subjectivity, as they are usually imagined to be. In fact, they were active in their consistent efforts to practice the Confucian way of "*giving up one's own way to follow that of others* (舍己從人)"¹² and "*cultivating oneself to give peace to others* (修己安人)."¹³ They concentrated all their energies on efficiently managing the whole household, taking care of it, and making it beautiful. These efforts can be understood as the best example of practicing the Confucian way of "*pursuing the highest and yet following the middle way of everyday life* (極高明而道中庸)"¹⁴ suggested in *The Doctrine of the Mean*. I think that the increasingly prominent roles that Korean women play in the current trend of *Hallyu* are connected to this Confucian spirituality and leadership, which they have nurtured in the process of making households.

Korean Confucian Spirituality of "Giving up One's Own Way to Follow That of Others" and Twenty-First-Century Women's Subjectivity

Although Korean women have long practiced the Confucian spirituality of life-giving and caring, the most difficult part for them has been the way of *giving up one's own way to follow that of others* (舍己從人). According to Mencius, who is considered to express the mentality of Koreans well, this practice shows the essence of the great sage-king *Shun* (舜)'s personality of beauty, goodness, and piety. Mencius said,

> When any one told *Tsze-lû* that he had a fault, he rejoiced. When *Yü* heard good words, he bowed to the speaker. The great *Shun* had a still greater delight in what was good. He regarded virtue as the common property of himself and others, giving up his own way to follow that of others, and being delighted to learn from others to practice what was good.[15]

From the perspective of modern feminism, with its emphasis on women's subjectivity, the doctrine of giving up one's own way to follow that of others is vulnerable to the criticism that it drives women into the ghetto of non-subjectivity, passivity, and non-self. After all, Confucianism does have a history of such practices. But, first of all, I want to call special attention to Mencius's explanation of why the great *Shun* was willing to give up his own way to follow that of others. Mencius says that the great *Shun* did so in order to "practice goodness together with others (善與人同)." It means that he was primarily trying to build up communal life rather than focusing on his own purposes. According to this explanation, the great *Shun* went beyond the concern for the goodness of his own life and tried to help others practice goodness; when they did not care about practicing goodness but only about themselves, the great *Shun* realized that he should sacrifice his own welfare and follow their way, in order to guide them toward virtuous living. The way that the great *Shun* took here seems to be very passive, but Mencius's interpretation is that it is an example of a great person's way of transcending the self (understood narrowly) and living the life of an authentic self. By interpreting the greatness of *Shun* in this way, Mencius once again confirms that the Confucian way is to focus on the job of building the public. Once again, one is reminded of the saying in the *Book of Rites*: "All affairs are pursued for the realization of the public."

Similarly, the renowned scholar of comparative culture, Hesung Chun Koh (1929–), of the East Rock Institute, New Haven, Connecticut, has identified "role dedication," as an important quality of leadership nurtured by the Korean tradition and a living expression of the Confucian leadership through *giving up one's own way to follow that of others*. Koh had immigrated to the United States and harmonized Western Christian and Confucian spirituality in her own life and work. She has dedicated her life to laying a groundwork for Korean studies in the Unites States, while at the same time raising six children—highly accomplished leaders in their own fields. Her two sons, Harold Hongju Koh, 54, dean of the Yale Law School and Howard Kyongju Koh, 57, associate dean of the Harvard School of Public Health, were both nominated to high positions in the Obama administration. She described "the role dedication as an excellent value that stands out of the tradition of Korean culture," and suggested it as a template for Korean women's leadership, adding: "Whereas self-growth or self-development is considered important in the West, in Korea one comes to succeed in self-accomplishment while performing one's role even though one does not necessarily pursue her own self-growth."[16] "Role dedication" can be understood as being the result of the embodiment of the virtue of *giving up one's own way to follow that of others* long practiced by Korean women. And today it offers hope for healing the lack of concern for the public, which is caused by the excessive emphasis on the modern principle of subjectivity and the disease of *worldlessness* or *world-alienation*, which have been causing people to be increasingly alienated from each other and become isolated selves.

In 2008, there was a heated controversy among Korean women about which person should be selected as the first female figure to be placed on the face of a new Korean bill. The controversy was eventually settled with the selection of Sin Sa-im-dang (申師任堂, 1504–1551), the mother of Yi Yulgok (李栗谷, 1536–1584), the renowned Confucian scholar of the Joseon Dynasty. Korean feminists strongly opposed her selection because she was known primarily as the mother or wife of someone in the Confucian tradition. However, in my view, there is no reason for devaluing the roles of mothers and wives in the name of women's subjectivity, especially when we consider the seriousness of the degree to which people now suffer uprootedness, anonymity, and atomization in Korean society. It is all the more compelling to take steps to build up the family and future generations beyond the narrow limits of "the individual self."

Of course, gender roles today are much freer from biological determinism than before. Accordingly, people now refer to motherhood as a *general human experience* or about the *womb of the mind* rather than the womb of the body. Today there is also the possibility of surrogate motherhood. However, no matter what kind of motherhood we are talking about, we cannot deny that the act of giving up one's self in her role to build up her family and future generations is always necessary to sustain human life and the public world.

We all know that today's world (including Korean society) is suffering from the ongoing deconstruction of family communities; the original foundation of human communal life is collapsing. It is not simply a matter of the dwindling numbers of the population but rather a serious question of whether we can sustain the foundation of human life that nurtures *jen*—the *ability to relate*. This ability to relate is an essential condition for the possibility of the existence and maintenance of the human community. Since humanity's ability to relate cannot grow without a communal life, and because this ability is acquired only through reliable, long-lasting relationships in intimate circles, the contemporary deconstruction of family communities is even more troubling.[17] Modern feminists have up to now criticized the Confucian tradition for confining and enclosing women within their private realm. I think, however, that contemporary women working in the public world, in the name of their own subjectivity, are actually more enclosed within their private world since they are working mostly for the sake of their own private profit.[18]

In the chapter on politics in *The Essentials for the Study of Sagehood*, Yi Yulgok, the son of Sin Sa-im-dang, stressed the importance of "practicing goodness together with others (善與人同)," and repeatedly mentioned Mencius's sayings that practicing goodness together with others is "learning from others to practice what is good" and that "there is no greater attribute of the superior man than that of helping men to practice goodness."[19] What is made clear here again is that in order to build the public world, which is essential for the maintenance of human communal life, someone should give up one's self. This act of giving up one's self is "the great act of sagehood."

I am here reminded of Hannah Arendt, a Western political philosopher who, in a way similar to Yi Yulgok, stressed the importance of building and taking care of the public realm in human lives. She argued that the authentic work of human subjectivity is related to throwing oneself into the public realm. On the concept of *freedom* as the symbol of human subjectivity, she pointed out that human freedom is not a matter of the "will" within persons but rather is a matter of political *acting* and *doing* in relation to a plurality of persons in the public sphere. According to Arendt, freedom does not emerge except in the area of the public sphere that requires the existence of others. However, Western thought has reduced freedom to being a matter of the inner world of human beings, identifying it with sovereignty. This understanding is what brought about Western individualism according to which "perfect freedom can never be compatible with society."[20]

Arendt seems to indicate that the modern feminist conception of women's subjectivity is vulnerable to a similar critique. In spite of severe criticisms from feminists at the time, she expressed in her story of the life of Rosa Luxemburg her subtle point of view with the words, "*Vive la petite difference!*" (Let the small difference live!). It was Arendt's conviction that a woman's subjectivity is not simply attained by removing the *difference* between women and men; instead, it is performed in freedom through public action.[21] In this sense, we can understand Korean Confucian women's acts of giving up themselves to follow that of others as the action of subjectivity that they performed on their own in order to give life to the public world of the family and future generations.[22]

Family life and motherhood are being denigrated today, and yet these are indispensable elements of human life that require sacrifices such as *giving up one's own way to follow that of others*. Such an act of self-sacrifice might seem like an impossible thing to expect in our age of subjectivity, but Korean women today are making the impossible possible. This practice of giving up one's own way to follow that of others could be seen as an alternative religion in John D. Caputo's sense.[23] It is fair to say that the religiosity of this action may very well be the kind of the "postmodern religiosity," "secular religiosity," or "postsecular religiosity" that we need today, a religiosity that is "least religious and yet fully spiritual."[24] Unlike traditional Christianity or Buddhism, Confucian religiosity tries to reach the Ultimate through work in the secular world and thus seems to be an example of "minimal religion."[25] It can be understood as an expression of authentic subjectivity insofar as it expresses sincere devotion. It makes the public world possible by giving and caring for life. Korean women's life-giving spirituality can be understood as an excellent example of postmodern religiosity.

Korean Confucian Religiosity of "Seeking Humanity and Accomplishing Sagehood" and Women's Leadership in the Twenty-First Century

Another example of Korean Confucian spirituality is "seeking humanity and accomplishing sagehood (求仁成聖)." In the chapters on "Western Inscription (西銘)" and "Explanation of Humanity (仁說圖)" of *The Ten Diagrams on Sage Learning* (聖學十圖), Master Yi Toegye (李退溪,1501–1570) explained that the human being is charged with the responsibility of the life-long work of "seeking humanity."[26] What, then, is humanity? Following Chu Hsi's answer given in the words of *The Doctrine of the Mean*, "heaven-and-earth's mind-and-heart of giving life to things (天地生物之心)," he answered that humanity is "for heaven-and-earth, the broad and open mind-and-heart of giving life to things," and "for humans, the warm mind-and-heart of loving other human beings and benefitting all things."[27]

According to a contemporary Korean Confucian scholar, Lee Kidong, the letter *jen* (仁) takes its form after "the shape of a mother having a baby in her womb," "the shape of two persons hugging each other," or "the shape of one person supporting another," which also seems to represent the nature of Koreans' mind-and-heart well.[28] As these shapes indicate, *jen* represents the work of feminine aspects of nature such as *life*, *love*, and *relationship*. In his *Korean History through a Biblical Point of View*, Ham Suk-hun also listed the "goodness" of *jen* and "a mind which cannot bear to see the sufferings of others" as the qualities with which Koreans can contribute to the world.[29] He found support for such a Korean quality in the fact that the letters "*Jen* (仁 humanity), *Ui* (義 justice), *Ye* (禮 propriety), *Ji* (智 wisdom), *Sin* (信 faith), *Sun* (順 obedience), *Sun* (淳 purity), *Hwa* (和 harmony), *Myeong* (明 brightness or clarity), *Yang* (良 goodness), *Suk* (淑 chastity)" are used frequently by Koreans as part of their names, which represent their ideal of becoming good persons.[30] He thus stressed that this very *jen* is the essential nature of human beings or their *Almaengi* (kernel), *Ssiat* (seed), or *Aljjam* (essence) in the Korean vernacular. For him *jen* is also the acting vital force within animals. He argued that it is the "hope for humanity" with the promise of bringing life to the nation of Korea and to the world as well.[31]

The Confucian doctrine of *jen*, as the foundation of the cultivation of authentic human nature and the construction of a humane world, has made a great impact on Korean culture for generations. Master Toegye emphasized in his "Diagram of the Western Inscription (西銘圖)" that "being one with all things in the universe" (the ultimate goal of sage learning) is accomplished through the learning of compassion, care, and concern, while sincerely seeking humanity. Along with these teachings, he offered an important diagnosis of and a remedy for his time, which are also relevant to our age: he pointed out that people in his time suffered from "an illness of recognizing things on their own (or as they please themselves)" and argued that the work of "seeking humanity and accomplishing sagehood" could cure that illness.[32] "Recognizing things on their own" refers to the same thing that Hannah Arendt described with the words *worldlessness* or "world-alienation," into which our age of excessive emphasis on subjectivity can easily fall. As she pointed out, the nineteenth-century English imperialist Cecil J. Rhodes (1853–1902) revealed his unlimited desire for the whole earth, wishing, "I would annex the planets if I could." It was an illness that showed the extreme self-centeredness willing to exploit all things in the world for the satisfaction of one's own greed.[33]

In response to this illness, and against such totalitarian subjectivism or egotism, quoting Chu Hsi, Master Toegye said, "The public is the way to embody humanity; that is to say, to overcome one's self and return to propriety is to make humanity."[34] In other words, although humanity is "what we humans obtained as our mind-and-heart," the way to realize and cultivate it is not simply to get it by oneself or to think about it in theory but rather to acquire it in relation with others, through acknowledging the plurality of life and thus in concrete acts of building relationships. If we really want to cultivate our humanity, we must show ourselves in public, get into relationships with others, and continue to do the work of building relationships with others in both words and actions. Only through such a public, relational, and humane way of life can we grow our human ability (*jen*) to give life, love, concern, and care for all things.

According to Arendt, human freedom and the capacity for action are nurtured only by "acting in concert," in recognition of the plurality of life. Freedom, as the meaning of politics, is "the great capacity of men to start something new" in spaces that are made by a plurality of human beings. Reminding us of Montesquieu, who identified "love of equality" as the political principle of republican government and stressed it as a "virtue," Arendt sums up the meaning of virtue by saying: "Virtue is happy to pay the price of limited power for the blessing of being together with other men."³⁵ The freedom and virtue described here by Montesquieu and Arendt are very similar to the virtues in the Confucian tradition, especially to the virtue of *jen*, which includes all four virtues of humanity, justice, propriety, and wisdom. *Jen* is "the essence of human uniqueness"³⁶ and "the nature of giving life and the principle of love,"³⁷ and includes the pleasant recognition and consideration of the existence of others; as Confucius said, "To overcome one's self and return to propriety is to make humanity." Arendt also added, in her criticism of totalitarianism, "people have lost contact with their fellow men as well as the reality around them; for together with these contacts, men lose the capacity of both experience and thought."³⁸

Regarding the great *Shun's* virtue of *giving up one's own way to follow that of others*, Yi Yulgok said: "If I take all eyes in the world as my eyes, there would be nothing I could not see clearly; if I take all ears in the world as my ears, there would be nothing I could not hear clearly; if I take all minds in the world as my mind, there would be nothing I could not think of wisely; that is why the sage emperors and the wise kings encourage the world without much efforts or concerns in their minds."³⁹ According to this explanation, Emperor *Shun* was able to become the great one because he did not boast himself to have all wisdom but relied upon those around him while acknowledging, trusting, and encouraging them. He thereby sought help from them and received their wisdom as his wisdom so that he could "make impartial judgments." Clearly, the virtue of *giving up one's own way to follow that of others* described here has the same implication for today as the virtue of *seeking humanity and accomplishing sagehood* by acknowledging the plurality and relationality of life.

Today, such virtues are being practiced in new ways on social media. The creative leaders of the twenty-first century live their lives as one of *multiple intelligences* or a part of *collective intelligence* while connecting with the wisdom of the multitude through such social media as email, Facebook, Twitter, and others. We can even call those people who are connected with me my *external brains* that are active outside of me as other brains of mine. I consider this phenomenon to be the Confucian way of *seeking humanity and accomplishing sagehood* reenacted in the twenty-first century. In this context, I do not believe it is a coincidence that South Korea has emerged as one of the powerhouses of information technology; it is internally connected with the Korean tradition of humanity. I also find postmodern wisdom in Yi Yulgok's explanation that humanity is to take plurality as its premise, that is, to know that all the people in the world have wisdom of their own, and thus to go together with them while encouraging and connecting with them.

There is a saying of wisdom in Mencius, "There are instances of individuals without humanity who have got possession of a single state, but there has been no instance of the whole world's being got by one without humanity."[40] The message for us here is that human leadership should be grounded upon a sensitively nurtured human mind-and-heart and that the power of this mind-and-heart should be the starting point of "the leadership for the world" that many people today are talking about and expecting from major CEOs. In a recent survey, which asked foreigners living in Seoul what makes Seoul attractive to them, the majority answer was Korean food—especially a wide variety of side dishes that are more generously provided than the main entrees on the table. The kindness and warm-heartedness of Seoul citizens was also listed as one of the main points of attraction. These spring from the Korean Confucian tradition of the virtue of humanity, seen especially in Korean women's virtue of life-giving hospitality to guests. In what other country in the world can we enjoy such a well-prepared meal with healthy food for a small amount of money? I think the meal is filled with Korean women's work of *giving up one's own way to follow that of others* and their sincere efforts of *seeking humanity and accomplishing sagehood*. Their virtues of leadership have been cultivated over a long period of time and with diligent practice. For example, there is the story of a Confucian wife giving hospitality to a guest in which she measured in advance the size of the guest's feet with her eyes through a small hole on the door of the building and later offered him a pair of socks exactly fitting his feet on his departure. This is an example showing how delicately those women of the Confucian tradition practiced the virtue of benevolence toward their guests.[41]

Bertram Müller, the director of Tanzhaus Düsseldorf, in a visit to Korea as part of a project introducing Korean dance to Europe, said that the traditional ritual dance of Korea has a delicacy that "Europe doesn't have," and so he hoped for Korea to have more opportunities to communicate with Europe.[42] All these examples suggest that the spirituality and leadership of seeking humanity and accomplishing sagehood can play an important role in revitalizing certain refinements and patterns of humanity which contemporary culture has increasingly been losing.

Implications of Korean Confucian Women's Spirituality and Leadership for the Twenty-First Century

A Korean political scientist pointed out, in his criticism of the Western concept of natural law, that the Western tradition has some limitations in that the law functions as an external power to regulate politics.[43] This echoes the often heard Confucian criticism of Legalism (literally, School of Law), but only recently did people start to take the criticism seriously. It sounds convincing again as we observe today that the whole civilization is suffering so much from the greed of modern financial capitalism, leading ordinary people to participate in demonstrations against Wall Street in the United States. The United States was once the richest country but now has become a malfunctioning one in which the top 1 percent of the population possess 23 percent of the national income, producing millions of homeless and unemployed people, and now reduced to the status of a Ghana or a Nicaragua in terms of the gap between the rich and the poor.[44] The ongoing financial crisis originating from the West clearly shows that no matter how good external laws may be, these very laws can easily turn out to be useless where the inner law of humanity is not operating.

The situation today in Korea is not much different from that in the United States. However, I want to ask: what is the operating mechanism of life by which suffering people in Korea or the United States feel that their lives are still worth enduring and thus can go on with their lives? Is it the power of a family life in which motherhood and relational concerns are still alive, or the legal system such as the unemployment allowance? I think the Confucian leadership of *seeking humanity and accomplishing sagehood*, based upon the belief in the inner natural law of human beings, has a great deal to offer human societies in taking care of the public as well as private realms. In opposition to the ideas of Yang Chu and Mo Tzu, which were very popular in the period of Warring States, Mencius presented the way of humanity and justice (仁義) as his alternative. He warned people that both extremes of Yang Chu's notion of *self-preservation* (爲我: "I would not pluck a hair from my body to benefit the world.") and Mo Tzu's notion of *universal love* (兼愛, which does not differentiate between those inside and outside of one's own family), could eventually turn humans into wild beasts, eating each other for survival.[45] Mencius called Yang Chu's idea of self-preservation "kingless" (無君) because it failed to recognize the sovereign, that is, the State. It fails to recognize the *public realm* because it reduces the whole of human life to the private realm. This is exemplified in the lives of government officials who abuse their public offices to make private profits. Mo Tzu's idea of *universal love,* which Mencius called "fatherless" (無夫), has been lauded as an idea that transcends narrow Confucian familism, and has often been compared to the Christian idea of universal love. But many in the East as well as the West are now confronting a common crisis of parentlessness. If no alternative form of communal life is available to replace the intimacy of family life, then, where can human beings acquire their consciousness of humanity and justice so essential to sustaining human life? There is no alternative, and thus we have now been witnessing instances of people "eating each other" as Mencius predicted: The richest 1 percent of the population is devouring the other 99 percent; a middle school student kills his mother for forcing him to get a good education for the sake of his later financial success. A father sexually violates his own daughter. Behind all these examples of people devouring each other, behind this fatherlessness and motherlessness, I detect an ominous, widespread deconstruction of the family.[46]

The Doctrine of the Mean repeatedly talks about *sincerity* (誠) with which one accomplishes not only the completion of one's self but also that of others and all other things. This means that one should not stop at self-completion but should extend the work of sincere concern and life-giving to all things. The book says, "Not ceasing, such an effort continues long; continuing long, it makes real change.... That is why long-lastingness of sincerity accomplishes the completion of all things."[47] I think Korean women of the Confucian tradition have continued to practice this principle of giving life to things and completing them in their lives. It was the role of being a mother, a daughter, or a wife that empowered them to survive despite all of their suffering. In other words, the action of completing one's role on the basis of *giving up one's own way to follow that of others* was the transcendental ground of making them what they were.[48] In this sense, the Ultimate was not the figure of a transcendent being in heaven (Christianity) or a god within one's self (Buddhism) but rather *the other,* who exists in the being of their child, husband, ancestor, guest, poor neighbor, or nation. Because of these others existing in their plurality, women also were able to not lose their hope and faith in the world. Transcendence for them was *life* existing before them in all its nakedness, asking for their help, their care, and their love. As they spent countless days and nights giving up themselves, listening carefully to the cry of life and responding to its voice, Korean women could continuously nurture their life-giving spirituality. If contemporary feminism is now searching for a new feminist ethic of care, consideration, and relatedness, it can also draw from these experiences of traditional Korean women.

Conclusion

I have examined the principles of *giving up one's own way to follow that of others* and *seeking humanity and accomplishing sagehood* as the core spirit of the Confucian mind and highlighted the fact that these were very well embodied in the lives of Korean women of the Confucian tradition. I have attempted to present these principles of life as an alternative spirituality and leadership for our age which is now undergoing severe global crises. However, I know how difficult such an attempt is; it seems to almost border on the miraculous and impossible. I can only respond with a quotation from the *Analects*:

> Someone said, "What do you say concerning the principle that injury should be recompensed with virtue?" The Master said, "With what then will you recompense virtue?" "Recompense injury with justice, and recompense virtue with virtue."[49]

We can notice here Confucius recognizing that human life has a level of unresolved feeling of injustice that should be recompensed with honest words and justice rather than with virtue. By saying so, I think, Confucius anticipated how much the practice of *giving up one's own way to follow that of others* and *seeking humanity and accomplishing sagehood* could be distorted in the harsh reality of the world in the twenty-first century, and how this way of virtue as the traditional way of life for women could catch them again in the trap of self-denial, submission, and repression. Therefore, he advised us to resolve injustice and the feeling of being injured with frank conversation, just compensation, and correction rather than with virtuous response. But in spite of all these, the reality of the world now is demanding the action of self-sacrifice from us and requiring us to show, in an exemplary way, what is the human thing to do. It is to rebuild our public realms and to heal human lives which have already fallen in the state of war of all against all. The human foundation such as the family that makes it possible for every human culture to exist is crumbling, and its harmful consequences are quickly becoming the reality of our age, just as Mencius warned. The important question here is how, as persons who practice the way of *giving up one's own way to follow that of others* and *seeking humanity and accomplishing sagehood*, we are going to rebuild the virtue of humanity (仁) and the public (公). I think this task involves recovering faith (信) in human beings and the world and finding a new ground for that faith. It is not a simple sociopolitical and economic matter but rather a question of *the ultimate* that is to be sought *ontologically* and *spiritually*. In other words, the issue of our age including that of feminism is the work of a "spiritual revolution" in the postsecular age.[50] Since the traditional way of division between the sacred and the profane, which was called the way of *religion*, is no longer convincing to our age, I suggest that we take seriously the Confucian way of sagehood, which is *the most this-worldly and yet other-worldly way* at the same time. The Confucian way as such is to see *plurality* and *multiplicity* premised in the virtue of *jen* and the public as the essence of human lives, with the central message that what really matters is not *independence* but *interdependence*. I think Korean women of the Confucian tradition have a lot to offer in this work, and hope to see Korean women, who were baptized also by modern Christianity and feminism, reconnect to this tradition to find an answer to the question.

Finally, I want to say that I do not think the Confucian virtue of *jen* belongs only to Asian or Korean women. Just as Professor Robert C. Neville suggested in his *Boston Confucianism*,[51] I hope for the Confucian tradition to become the common wisdom for all humanity and contribute to the solution of the problems of the world, just as we know that Plato is read not just in the universities of the West but worldwide, and that not only the Greek-knowing people but also other people can study Greek philosophy. I believe that just as Asian people in recent decades have spent so much time and energy in learning about the West and studying Western languages, now Westerners should take their turn in learning about the East or Asia and transmitting what they have learned from these traditions as the common heritage of all humanity. I do hope that as a part of this common heritage, the archetypal features of humanity that the women of the Korean tradition have nurtured with their delicate care with their own will make an important contribution to the common task of men and women as authentic subjects of life in the twenty-first century, that is, the task of giving life to all things in the world, rebuilding the public, and handing down the humane virtue of *jen*.

Notes

1. This article was written before the worldwide success of Korean singer Psy's "Gangnam Style" (the dance of horse). So I now point to Psy's case as a good example of my discussion of *Hallyu*.
2. MBN News, April 7, 2011.
3. Un-sunn Lee, "Confucianism and Christianity in Korean Women's Leadership in the Twenty-first Century," I and II, *Study of Eastern Philosophy*: 62, 63; Seoseria Kim, "Korean Women's Subjectivity Seen through the characters of *Silhak* of *Ganghwahag*," *Study of Yang-ming* (July, 2000): 221ff.
4. Sang-jun Kim, *Mencius' Sweat and King Sheng's Blood: Multiple Layers of Modernity and East Asian Confucian Civilization* (Seoul: Acanet, 2011), 270.
5. *Analects* 12.1.
6. *Analects* 14.13.
7. Chapter10 of the First part of Gaozi 告子 *Mencius*.
8. *Analects* 14.37.
9. Boudewijn Walraven, "The Confucianization of Korea as a Civilizing Process," Proceedings of the International conference on Korean Studies, The Academy of Korean Studies 1994: 535–56.
10. Un-sunn Lee, *Confucianism, Christianity and Feminism* (Seoul: Intellectual Industry Publishing Co., 2003), 133ff.
11. Un-sunn Lee, *To Acquire the Lost Transcendence: Reflections on the Religiosity of Korean Confucianism and Feminism* (Seoul: Hosting People Publishing Co., 2009).
12. Chapter 8 of the First part of Gon Sun Chou 公孫丑, *Mencius*.
13. *Analects* 14.45.
14. Chapter 27, *The Doctrine of the Mean*.
15. 孟子曰 子路, 人告之以有過則喜. 禹聞善言則拜, 大舜有大焉, 善與人同. 舍己從人, 樂取於人以 為善. Chapter 8 of the First part of Gong Sun Chou 公孫丑, *Mencius*.
16. Hesung Chun Koh, *Dictionary of Women's Ambitions* (Seoul: Jungang Books, 2007), 124–125.
17. Kyung-sup Chang, *Family, Life-development, Political Economy-Micro-Foundation of Compressed Modernity* (Seoul: Changbi Publishers, 2009), 15ff.
18. Un-sunn Lee, *To Acquire the Lost Transcendence*, 194ff.
19. 善與人同, 取諸人以爲善. 是與人爲善者也. 故君子莫大乎與人爲善 Yi Yulgoki, "Practice of Goodness," the Third Chapter on Politics IV, *The Essentials for the Study of Sagehood*, vol. 7.
20. Hannah Arendt, "What is Freedom?" in *Between Past and Future* (New York: Penguin Books, 1985).

21. Hannah Arendt, *Men in Dark Times* (New York: Harcourt Brace & Company, 1983), 44.

22. Jean Bethke Elshtain, "Antigone's Daughters," in *Feminism and Politics*, ed. Anne Phillips (New York: Oxford University Press, 1998), 363–67.

23. John D. Caputo, *On Religion: Thinking in Action* (London: Routledge, 2001).

24. Charles Taylor, *A Secular Age* (Cambridge, MA: The Belknap Press of the Harvard University, 2007), 533ff.

25. Ibid.

26. 求仁成聖 Yi Toegye, The Second Chapter of "Western Inscription" and the Seventh Chapter of "Explanation of Humanity" in *The Ten Diagrams on Sage Learning*.

27. 在天地則坱然生物之心, 在人則溫然愛人利物之心. Seventh Chapter of "Explanation of Humanity" in *The Ten Diagrams on Sage Learning*. In Michael C. Kalton's translation we see the expression of "In Heaven and Earth it is inexhaustible disposition to produce and give life to creatures," and "in men it is the warm love for others and the disposition to benefit all creatures." Michael C. Kalton, ed., trans., *To Become a Sage: The Ten Diagrams on Sage Learning by Yi T'oegye* (New York: Columbia University Press, 1988), 148.

28. Ki-dong Lee, *Three Elements of Confucianism and the Philosophy of Coexistence of Korean Confucianism* (Seoul: Dong-Yeon Press, 2010), 111.

29. Ham Suk-hun, *Korean History through the Biblical Point of View* (Seoul: Han-gil Press, 1986), 324.

30. Ibid., 68.

31. Ibid., 323.

32. 認物爲己之病. Yi Toegye, The Second Chapter of "Western Inscription" in *The Ten Diagrams on Sage Learning*.

33. Hannah Arendt, *The Origins of Totalitarianism*, (New York: Harcourt, Inc., 1973), 121.

34. 公者, 所以體仁, 猶言克己復禮爲仁. Yi Toegye, The Seventh Chapter of "Explanation of Humanity" in *The Ten Diagrams on Sage Learning*.

35. Hannah Arendt, "On the Nature of Totalitarianism," in *Essays in Understanding 1930–1954* (New York: Harcourt Brace & Company, 1994), 337.

36. 仁者人也 Chapter 20, *The Doctrine of the Mean*.

37. 所謂生之性, 愛之理, 仁之體也. Yi Toegye, The Seventh Chapter of "Explanation of Humanity" in *The Ten Diagrams on Sage Learning*.

38. Hannah Arendt, *The Origins of Totalitarianism*, 474.

39. 蓋以天下之目爲目, 則明無不見. 以天下之耳爲耳, 則聰無不聞. 以天下之心爲心, 則睿無不思. 此聖帝明王所以鼓舞天下, 而不勞心力者也. Yi Yulgok, "Practice of Goodness," the Third Chapter on Politics IV, *The Essentials for the Study of Sagehood* (聖學輯要), vol. 7.

40. 不仁而得國者有之矣; 不仁而得天下未之有也. The Second Part of *Tsin Sin* (盡心), the Seventh Book of *Mencius*.

41. Sun-hyeong Lee, *The Renowned Head Families of Korea* (Seoul: Seoul National University Press, 2000), 105; Un-sunn, *To Acquire the Lost Transcendence*, 185.

42. *Hangyeore Newspaper*, October 12, 2011.

43. Dong-su Lee, "Law and Politics in Korean Society—Seen in Terms of Republic Democracy," *Today's Eastern Thought*, vol. 17 (Fall and Winter 2007): 194.

44. "'I am scared, when I'll be unemployed.'—The Fear of American Middle Class," *Hangyeore Newspaper*, October 18, 2011.

45. Chapter 9 of the Second Part of *Tang Wan Kung* (藤文公), the Third Book of *Mencius*.

46. Hong Se-hwa, "We are all losers," *Hangyeore Newspaper*, November 26, 2009.

47. 故至誠 無息, 不息則久, 久則徵, . . . 悠久, 所以成物也. Chapter 26, *The Doctrine of the Mean*.

48. Un-sunn Lee, *To Acquire the Lost Transcendence*, 194f; Hannah Arendt, *Love and Saint Augustine*, (Chicago: University of Chicago Press, 1966); John D. Caputo, *On Religion: Thinking in Action* (London: Routledge, 2001).

49. 或曰, 以德報怨, 何如. 子曰, 何以報德. 以直報怨, 以德報德. Chapter 36 "Hsien Wen" (憲問) of *The Confucian Analects*.

50. Rosi Braidotti, "In Spite of the Times: The Postsecular Turn in Feminism," The 13th Symposium of the International Association of Women Philosophers, IAPh 2008; "Multiculturalism and Feminism," *Proceedings of the IAPh 2008*, Ewha Woman's University, Koran Association of Feminist Philosophy: 22–76.

51. Robert Cummings Neville, *Boston Confucianism* (Albany, NY: SUNY Press, 2000), xxi ff.

Bibliography

Arendt, Hannah. *The Origins of Totalitarianism*. New York: Harcourt Brace & Company, 1973.

———. *Men in Dark Times*. New York: Harcourt Brace & Company, 1983.

———. "What is Freedom?" In *Between Past and Future*. New York: Penguin Books, 1985.

———. "On the Nature of Totalitarianism." In *Essays in Understanding 1930–1954*. New York: Harcourt Brace & Co., 1994.

———. *Love and Saint Augustine*. Chicago: The University of Chicago Press, 1996.

Caputo, John D. *On Religion: Thinking in Action*. London: Routledge, 2001.
Chang, Kyung-sup. *Gajok, Saengae, Jeongchi-Gyeongje* [*Family, Life-development, Political Economy-Micro-Foundation of Compressed Modernity*]. Seoul: Changbi Publishers, 2009.
———. *South Korea under Compressed Modernity: Familial Political Economy in Transition*. New York: Routledge, 2010.
Chun Koh, Hesung. *Yeoseong Yamang Sajeon* [*Dictionary of Women's Ambitions*]. Seoul, Korea: Jungang Books, 2007.
Elshtain, Jean Bethke. "Antigone's Daughters." In *Feminism and Politics*. Edited by Anne Phillips. New York: Oxford University Press, 1998.
Ham, Suk-hun. *Tteutseuro bon Hangug Yeoksa* [*Korean History through the Biblical Point of View*]. Seoul: Hangil, 1986.
Kim, Sang-jun. *Maenja ui* Ttam *Seongoang ui Pi-Jungcheung Geundae wa Kongasia Yugyo Munmyeong* [*Mencius' Sweat and King Sheng's Blood: Multiple Layers of Modernity and East Asian Confucian Civilization*]. Seoul: Acanet, 2011.
Kim, Seoseria. "Ganghwahag ui Silhakjeog Teujing eyk Tonghae bon Hangug ui Yeoseong Jucheseong [Korean Women's Subjectivity Seen through the characters of *Silhak* of *Ganghwahag*]." *Yangmyeônghag* 20 (2008): 221–40.
Korean Association of Women Theologians. *Life Flowing through Korean Feminist Theology*. Seoul: Dong Yeon Press, 2013.
Lee, Ki-dong. *Yuhag ui Se Yoso Wa Hangug yuhag ui Sangsaeng Cheolhag* [*Three Elements of Confucianism and the Philosophy of Coexistence of Korean Confucianism*]. Seoul: Dongyeon, 2010.
Lee, Dong-su. "Hangug Sahoeesek ui Beopgwa Jeongchi-Gonghwaminjujug Gwabheineseo [Law and Politics in Korean Society—Seen in Terms of Republic Democracy]." *Oneul ui Dongyang Sasang* 17 (2007):194–210.
Lee, Sun-hyeong. *Hangug ui Myeongmun Jongga* [*The Renowned Head Families of Korea*]. Seoul: Seoul Daehakgyo Chulpanbu, 2000.
Lee, Un-sunn. *Yugyo, Gidokgyo geurigo Peminijeum* [*Confucianism, Christianity and Feminism*]. Seoul: Jisiksaneopsa, 2003.
———. *Ireobeorin Choowoeul Chajaseo-Hangugyugyo ui Jonggyojeog Seongchalgwa Yeoseongjuui* [*To Acquire the Lost Transcendence: Reflections on the religiosity of Korean Confucianism and Feminism*]. Seoul: Mosineunsaramdeul, 2009.
Lee, Un-sunn. "Eusibsegi Hangug Yeoseong Rideoswibeseoui Yugyowa Gidokgyo (I), (II) [Confucianism and Christianity in Korean Women's Leadership in the Twenty-first Century," I and II]." In *Dongyang Cheolhag Yeongu* (2010): 62, 63.
Neville, Robert Cummings. *Boston Confucianism*. Albany: SUNY Press, 2000.
Elias, Nobert. *Ueber den Proxess der Zivilisation: soziogenetische und psychogenetische Untersuchungen*, Basel: Haus zum Falken, 1939.

Taylor, Charles. *A Secular Age*, Cambridge, MA: The Belknap Press of the Harvard University, 2007.
Walraven, Boudewijn. "Yugyo Munhwa ui Bopeonseong gwa Teuksuseong [the Confucianization of Korea as a Civilizing Process]." *Proceedings of the International conference on Korean Studies, The Academy of Korean Studies* (1994): 535–56.
Yi, Toegye. *To Become a Sage: The Ten Diagrams on Sage Learning by Yi T'oegye*, Translated and edited by Michael C. Kalton. New York: Columbia University Press, 1988.
Yi, Yulgok. "Practice of Goodness," the Third Chapter on Politics IV, *Seonghakjibyo* [聖學輯要, *The Essentials for the Study of Sagehood*], vol. 7.

10

Confucianism at a Crossroads
Confucianism and Democracy in Korea

Young-chan Ro

Introduction

This paper is an attempt to examine the Confucian tradition in light of the social and political context of modern Korea. Confucianism was the ruling ideology during the Chosŏn Dynasty (1392–1910). In the process of the modernization of Korea, however, Confucianism lost this ideological prestige and privilege. Furthermore, Confucianism was blamed for all the ills and failures of the Korean society such as authoritarianism, nepotism, male chauvinism, conservatism, and many others. In fact, if anything went wrong during the time of Korean modernization, it was, they claimed, because of Confucianism.[1] In this respect, this paper will examine the role of Confucianism in the East Asian context, especially in Korea. Confucianism lost not only its official function as the ruling ideology but also its persuasive power to guide the Korean people. In modern Korea, social and political leaders and most elite groups of society are no longer Confucian scholars. While China now enjoys the revival of Confucianism, it would be hard to imagine that Korea will go back to Confucianism to find the wisdom to guide and build a future Korea. Korean Confucianism is facing a serious challenge to the point of wondering whether it will become a relic of the past. If Korean Confucian studies is simply concerned with and confined to the past of Korean history and becomes merely an object of professional Confucian historians, Korean Confucianism will become the sole interest of an intellectual archeology belonging to the museum to display the glory of the past.[2]

If we do not interpret or reinterpret our past, the past will become irrelevant to both the present and the future. Korean Confucian studies must acknowledge this critical task in order to revive and re-create the Confucian tradition as a vital source of inspiration for both the present and the future of Korea. What we need for Korean Confucianism is a creative hermeneutics: we have to reinterpret the basic assumptions of the Confucian worldview and values in light of the contemporary social, political, and philosophical discourse. With this task in mind, I am concentrating on one particular subject, Confucianism and democracy, in order to relate Confucian ideals to those of the modern West, especially regarding Confucian ideals and democratic institutions.

This paper's focus is on Confucian humanism[3] and Western democracy with a special reference to the perplexing historical question of why the Confucian tradition has not produced a Western-style democracy. What are the similarities and differences between Confucianism and democracy? What are the basic assumptions of the Confucian worldviews and Western democracy? This paper may not be able to answer all of these questions, but it does hope to raise some fundamental questions about the Confucian tradition in light of the many challenges of modernization facing Korea and East Asia.

Confucianism and Democracy

Modernization of Korea had little to do with Confucianism. Democracy in Korea was neither originated nor inspired by Confucianism. Modern Korea, especially during the last half century, has been shaped under the influence of Western culture, Christian ideas, Western science and technology, American style democracy, and Western capitalism. Korean democracy has undergone a unique historical process since Korean independence in 1945. Although the first President Rhee Syngman (李承晚, 1875–1965) introduced Western-style democracy, his regime (1948–1961) was dictatorial and fell as a result of the student revolution in 1961. The initial stage of Korean democracy (1948–1990s) experienced many difficult moments of struggle. Economically, however, Korea had a remarkable growth, especially under President Park Chung Hee (朴正熙, 1917–1979)

and his military regime (1961-1979). Korean democracy, however, had suffered during this time and the ensuing decades of military regime. Democracy in Korea was not fully realized until early 1990s. Economic growth during this period was phenomenal due to the unique form of government initiative and leadership. While the democratization process was slow, the economic success brought prosperity to the Korean people. This prosperity made the people desire political freedom, and eventually helped restore democracy in Korea.

Now, most Korean people believed that President Park, in spite of his dictatorial regime, was responsible for bringing economic prosperity and turning around the country to make Korea a modern industrial nation.[4] During his regime, he introduced some Confucian ideas and values for the foundation of national ethics, especially such as "loyalty" (*ch'ung/zhong*, 忠) and "filial piety" (*hyo/xiao*, 孝). Because of Park's use of these Confucian virtues, Confucianism again was blamed for providing and justifying Park's dictatorial rule. It is quite possible that Park simply used Confucian values such as *ch'ung* and *hyo* to support and justify his dictatorship and to counter the North Korean communist *chuche* (self-reliance) ideology rather than out of any genuine interest in Confucian values. It may also be true that as a visionary he might have believed that the process of transforming and modernizing Korea could not be achieved by Western scientific and technological knowledge alone. What he saw was the need of social values to transform the mind and heart of the people. He created the famous "*semaŭl undong*" or "new village movement" in order to inspire and motivate the people to transform themselves and build a new industrialized country. It is interesting to note that this "new village movement" is now attracting the attention of some of the underdeveloped nations in Africa and South Asia in their attempts to model the Korean success story.

During this critical period for both the economic and political development of Korea, Western capitalism, Christian sense of values and ideals, and scientific and technological knowledge had made significant contributions in modernizing Korea. Most Koreans, on the other hand, considered Confucianism an obstacle for modernizing Korea, especially in the political sense. Why, then, did President Park turn to Confucianism for an ideological foundation of his new regime in introducing two key Confucian concepts, "loyalty" and "filial piety"? President Park, since the fall of the Chosŏn Dynasty (1392-1910), was the first ruler of the nation who officially established an ideological foundation for modern Korea.

Although he was a Buddhist, President Park believed in the need for Confucian values in modern Korea. He transformed Korea from a pre-modern, economically poor and destitute nation to a modern industrialized and prosperous one. His ideological foundation for modern Korea, however, was from pre-modern Confucianism.

It may be debatable whether Park's attempt in introducing Confucian values for modernizing Korea was successful. Yet it would be fair to say that Park's attempt to transform Korea into a modern industrialized nation did involve heavy appeal to traditional Confucian values.

From the political point of view, Park's regime was dictatorial, not democratic. It is certainly true that democracy did not make much progress during his regime. For this reason, some Koreans grew resentful, blaming Confucianism for creating an obstacle to democracy. Indeed, it is debatable to argue whether or not Confucianism and democracy are compatible with each other, and whether or not Confucianism rather than Western-style democracy is more desirable for developing the underdeveloped Confucian-influenced countries. Some prominent political leaders of Confucian-influenced Asian countries such as the former Prime Minister Lee Kuan Yew (李光耀, 1923–2015) of Singapore and the former President Kim Dae-Jung (金大中, 1925–2009) of South Korea differed from each other on this issue: Lee Kuan Yew thought that Confucianism and democracy are simply incompatible[5] while Kim Dae-jung forcefully argued against Lee's view by stating the Confucian culture maintains a strong democratic spirit and principle by quoting the Confucian idea of "people" and "mandate of heaven" found in Mencius.[6] In fact, many Confucian scholars have argued, like Kim Dae Jung, for the compatibility of Confucianism and democracy by claiming that the "ideological" dimension of Confucianism has a democratic spirit and principle. For example, David L. Hall and Roger T. Ames developed the idea of "Confucian democracy" based on the idea of "communicating community" found in John Dewey also tried to relate Confucianism and democracy in terms of democratic values and principles in their discussion, "A Pragmatist Understanding of Confucian Democracy."[7] Trying to find some positive aspects or potentials of democratic ideals and spirits in order to advocate that Confucianism is pro-democracy is an attempt to defend that Confucianism is compatible with Western democracy in an *apologetic* way.[8]

On the other hand, Lee Kuan Yew and Park Chung Hee were neither anxious to defend Confucianism in terms of its compatibility with Western democracy nor did they try to expound Confucian traditional values from the perspective of Western democracy. Instead, they agreed that Confucianism and Confucian values are not compatible with the Western sense of democracy, but they also believed that Confucian values need not be interpreted from the perspective of Western democratic values. They simply believed that Confucian values would better serve the cause of developing economic prosperity and stabilizing social order in their nations. For this reason, some Koreans believe Confucian values are antidemocratic.

On the other hand, however, it is also debatable whether the Confucian traditional values introduced by the Park regime were entirely negative. Some Koreans believed that the introduction of Confucian values during the Park regime was no more than an ideological tool to control the people, and thus, Confucian values were distorted and manipulated by his dictatorial regime. It is true that the way Park advocated the Confucian ideas of *ch'ung* and *hyo* were very much manipulated as authoritarian concepts and had little to do with the democratic principle or spirit. They may not reflect the authentic sense of *ch'ung* and *hyo* as expounded in the Confucian tradition in expressing the genuine desire for building the Confucian family and society. In this sense, it was very unfortunate for Confucianism to be used and abused by a dictatorial regime. This may be yet one more reason for Koreans becoming disillusioned with Confucianism.

On the other hand, we may also have to look at the role Confucianism has played even in distorted ways, and how Confucian values may have contributed to providing an ideological basis for motivating and mobilizing the people in the process of modernizing Korea. As discussed above, Park was eager to follow the Western model to modernize Korea, but politically he did not embrace Western democracy. Instead, he felt that the efficient way to modernize Korea was to adopt a model that allows direct government initiative and intervention. This model was also found in the case of Singapore's Lee Kuan Yew. Both Park Chung Hee and Lee Kuan Yew felt that modernizing Asia, in terms of economic development, "Confucian values"[9] could be useful in emphasizing hard work, discipline, and loyalty to the nation and enhancing family values. Recently China is following a similar but more explicit way of promoting Confucian values in her modernizing process. Again, China has made a remarkable economic success in terms of modernizing, but politically China has not made much progress in transforming its government into a democracy. We may observe here that Korea, Singapore, Taiwan, and

China have shown rapid economic development and all these countries have revived, for good or ill, Confucian values in providing an ideological foundation for their success,[10] but they were highly reluctant to embrace democracy. In this respect, Korea has come much farther in democratizing itself compared with both Singapore and China. Confucianism or the Confucian sense of values certainly contributed to the development of the wealth of nations in the Asian context. The political progress of democratization, however, has not been so easy in these countries.

Democracy in East Asia, especially in Korea, was introduced by the modern West, especially America. Is Confucianism then incompatible with democracy? If not, why was Confucianism blamed for being an obstacle to democracy? If we take a look at Confucian ideals and democratic principles, we may be able to find some similarities between them. Humanism is deeply imbedded in the Confucian tradition as one of its central teachings. Furthermore, Confucianism has been characterized as "anthropocentric" in the sense that the human being is the most valuable being in the world and the universe. Recently, some Confucian scholars, especially Tu Weiming, expanded the notion of Confucian humanism to include the entire universe and make it "anthropocosmic."[11] In any case, it is an undeniable fact that the Confucian tradition has centered on the human in both the individual and collective sense. The Confucian concept of "learning" (hak/xue, 學) has to do with simply how to become a "human" in the sense that all human beings have the capacity to become a sage. Human beings have an innate disposition that makes it possible to become a sage, and thus, we must consider every human being a potential sage. One of Mencius's best known assertions is, "the mind of people is the mind of Heaven," as expressed in the following passage that Mencius is quoting from the "Great Declaration": "Heaven sees as my people see; Heaven hears as my people hear" (Mencius, 5A:5).[12] His egalitarian ideas clearly indicate the democratic ideals found in the Confucian tradition in designating that the people are the highest authority:

> Mencius said . . . "When all your immediate ministers say that a man is worthy, it is not sufficient. When all your great officers say so, it is not sufficient. When all your people say so, look into the case, and if you find him to be worthy, then employ him. When all your ministers say that a man is no good, do not listen to them. When all your great officers say so, do not listen to them. When all your people say so, look

into the case, and if you find him to be no good, then dismiss him." (Mencius, 1B:7)[13]

With all these Confucian ideals in mind, we may still ask why the Confucian tradition has not been able to produce democracy with such great democratic ideals and principles found in its own tradition. Democracy has a long history of development in the Western civilization: from the Greco-Roman period to the Enlightenment and the French Revolution, on one hand, and the Christian idea of human nature, on the other. Western democracy was deeply indebted to all of these ideas, systems, and movements in emphasizing individual right, human dignity, freedom, and self-fulfillment. In terms of political ideals, Confucianism and democracy may share similar values. As seen above, humanistic values found in Western democracy are also found in Confucianism in emphasizing human dignity and values. Why, then, is it that the West has developed democracy while East Asia has not?

We must acknowledge that the introduction of Christianity with Western culture and values has greatly facilitated modernizing Korea, providing a modern education system and healthcare, promoting gender equality, and elevating the status of disadvantaged people. The introduction of Christianity was one of the major events in the modernizing process of Korea. Korean Christianity has also made a critical contribution to the democratization of Korea. In this respect, we must acknowledge that Confucianism did not make much contribution to the democratization of Korea. Rather, it was blamed for being antidemocratic.

Democratic Ideology and Democratic Institution

Democracy requires two fundamental elements, democratic ideals and democratic institutions. Democratic ideology alone cannot produce democracy; it requires an institutional support system to allow democratic ideals be realized. Democratic ideals must be institutionalized in a concrete and tangible way. Democracy, in fact, is a form of an institution and system more than just an ideology. Unlike many political and social ideologies such as socialism, Communism, Marxism, Maoism, and others, democracy is not an "ism" but fundamentally an institution. While Western democracy paid much attention to the institutional dimension of democracy, East Asian Confucianism formulated the ideological foundation for making the people the supreme value in politics while neglecting to develop that politics with the institutional sophistication found in Western democracy.

Most East Asians in the process of democratization still believed in democracy as an ideology rather than as an institution. It is true that democratic institutions cannot be developed without democratic ideals, and thus it is important to ensure democratic ideals to be institutionalized. Confucianism has placed a heavy emphasis on the democratic ideals while neglecting the concern for how to institutionalize these ideals. It is interesting to note that many Korean activists who were engaged in the democratization process believed that democracy is the ultimate goal of humanity and made democracy an absolute and ultimate ideology. This is understandable because the political activists who had fought against the dictatorial regime needed to be armed with an ideology in order to fight against their enemy, the dictator. Now the dictators are gone, and the country has a democratic government, but these democratization activists are still longing for an ideal democracy as an ideology. Democratic institutions, however, are so vital for understanding the nature and limits of democracy.

Democracy as a form of an institution does not absolutize democracy as an ultimate goal we have to achieve. Rather, democracy fully accepts the fact that it is not a utopian dream or the perfect system. The beauty of democracy is in the fact that it resists becoming an absolute ideology by establishing a mechanism for constraining the power of government. This makes democracy different from an ideology, such as Marxism, Communism, or any other form of ideology. In this sense, democracy is fundamentally a "cracy" but not an "ism."

Some activists in Korea who fought for democracy with a strong ideological zeal were disappointed when the country became democratic and they realized that democracy in practice was far from the democracy as an absolute ideology. They then turned to nationalism that allows them to turn toward the North Korean dictatorial regime. Here is an interesting irony. Most democratization activists became more sympathetic toward the North Korean dictator in thinking that our next ultimate goal is the unification of North and South Koreas. Democracy is neither an absolute ideology nor a perfect system. In fact, democracy may appear to be inefficient and ineffective and sometimes even "messy." Democracy, however, understands itself to be imperfect and thus it allows being self-critical. This is the nature of democracy.

Confucianism, on the other hand, has served primarily as an ideology for centuries in Korea and East Asia. Although Confucianism did develop institutions, Confucian institutions were largely a bureaucratically structured meritocracy. Confucianism is based on the belief that human beings have an innate capacity to do good, and so highly emphasized "self-cultivation" (*susin/xuishen*, 修身). Due to this rather optimistic view of human nature, Confucianism developed the idea of education, of how to educate the people from the ruler to the commoner in order to realize the ideal Confucian state. Confucianism, while heavily emphasizing "learning" to produce the most desirable society, paid less attention to the institutional side in implementing how to prevent human beings, even if they are good in nature, from the tendency to fall into evil. Western democracy, on the other hand, has developed rather sophisticated democratic institutions to prevent human beings from falling into evil since all human beings are considered to have an inclination to do wrong. While Confucianism provided a strong ideological foundation for democratic ideals, it failed in producing appropriate democratic institutions. For this reason, for all its passionate commitment to humanism and the fundamental conviction that the "people" constitute the "foundation" of all government (*minbonjuŭi/ minbenzhuyi*, 民本主義), Confucianism was not able to realize demo-*cracy*. Democratic in its ideal, Confucianism was monarchical in its institution.[14]

Western democracy is deeply rooted in the Christian understanding of human nature. Unlike the optimistic Confucian view of human nature, the Christian view of human beings is a mixed one. On the one hand, the idea that human beings have been created in the "Image of God" has provided a positive and optimistic view of the human. On the other hand, however, Christians also believe that all human beings without exception inherited "original sin." These two powerful symbolisms reflect two sides of human beings, a good side and a bad side. These two conflicting ideas of human nature in the Christian tradition have influenced the shaping of social institutions in the West. However, this conflicting nature of human being has become the dynamic force in establishing democratic institutions, as nicely stated by one of the most influential American theologians and political thinkers, Reinhold Niebuhr, when he said, "Man's capacity for justice makes democracy possible; but man's inclination to injustice makes democracy necessary."[15] Niebuhr aptly summarized the relation between Christian ideas of human beings and democracy as a social institution in combining the "possibility" and "necessity" of democratic institutions based on the Christian understanding of human nature. Democratic ideals necessitate democratic institutions in order to fulfill their goal. More specifically, the two conflicting aspects of human nature understood by Christianity were reflected in social and political institutions in America as found in constitutional democracy: "Constitutional democracy is a form of politics that tries to combine two distinct values which are somewhat at odds with each other. One is based on an implicit trust in the people's capacity, while the other is related to an attitude of distrust toward government, be they democratic or not."[16]

Democracy, in this sense, is a form of "cracy" and institution, not a mere ideology. Confucianism, however, has not been able to develop democratic institutions due to its optimistic view of human nature in emphasizing "cultivation" and "learning" as the way to sagehood. Confucius, like Reinhold Niebuhr, understood the two sides of human beings, human *ability* to do "humanity" (*in/ren*, 仁) and at the same time human *unwillingness* to do "humanity" (*in/ren*, 仁):

> I have never seen one who really loves humanity or one who really hates inhumanity. . . . Is there anyone who has devoted his strength to humanity for as long as a single day? I have not seen any one without strength to do so. . . ." (*Analects*: 4:6)[17]

Here we see Confucius's ambiguity regarding human nature. Humanity as the most fundamental foundation for being a human is realizable, but the actual realization of humanity is not an easy task. We human beings are not likely to dedicate ourselves to and truly love "humanity" and truly hate "inhumanity" (*purin/buren*, 不仁). However, the reason for this human tendency of not liking "humanity" and not truly hating "inhumanity" is not because of the lack of the human ability to like "humanity" and dislike "inhumanity" but because of the lack of human "cultivation" and "learning." In general, human beings have an innate ability to like "humanity" and hate or dislike "inhumanity." It is, however, so difficult to find someone who "truly" likes "humanity" and dislikes "inhumanity," as Confucius said, "I have never seen one who really loves "humanity" or one who really hates "inhumanity." For this reason, the Confucian and Neo-Confucian tradition has always emphasized the role of "learning" and "cultivation." If we had a natural tendency for liking "humanity" and disliking "inhumanity" without any effort and "cultivation," we would not have any form of evil or injustice in the world. Thus, in reality, Confucius did recognize that it is so difficult to find someone who truly loves "humanity" and hates "inhumanity." For this reason, we need to develop and "cultivate" the strength or ability to love "humanity" and hate "inhumanity." Confucius even lamented, "Is there anyone who has devoted his strength to humanity for as long as a single day"? Thus, we see that the Confucian tradition has taken the view that humans have an innate ability to love "humanity" and hate "inhumanity" but that in reality, we do not see the full realization of this potential because of the lack of human "cultivation" and of the efforts to make our will sincere. As we see here, the Confucian tradition concentrates on "learning," "education," and "cultivation," and has created the institutions to develop and "cultivate" human nature, constructing the institutions based on the positive side of human nature as found in Western democracy.

Confucian institutions heavily relied on the *human ability* for the Confucian form of "learning" and "cultivation," which resulted in aristocracy and meritocracy at best but not in democracy. But why not in democracy? Why did Confucianism not pay attention to the establishment of democracy in the first place? Confucian assumptions simply did not allow the conception of even rudimentary democracy. The reason for this lack of interest in democracy was simple: the Confucian ideal was not to establish democracy but to create "sage-cracy" or rule by the wise. From the Confucian point of view, the most desirable form of society is a society governed by a sage-ruler, not a democratic government. The ideal ruler in the Confucian tradition is the ruler who treats his people as if they were "heaven" and respects the people as he respects heaven.[18] Furthermore, there is no ontological dichotomy between the human and heaven but only an unbroken continuity between them. From the Confucian perspective, heaven is an extension of the human through the process of self-cultivation, and humans are able to reach the state of being in correspondence with the universe. This is the state of being a sage.

The Confucian view of the human makes the following fundamental assumptions. The goal of human beings is to become a "sagely and superior person" (*sŏngin kunja/shengren junzi*, 聖人君子). In fact, every human being has the potential to become a sage due to the inborn human nature. Once we develop this inborn nature to the highest level, we are able to become a sage. For the ruler, it was necessary to cultivate the innate human nature and exemplify the Confucian ideal of sage-ruler, "inwardly sageliness and outwardly kingliness" (*nesŏng woewang/neisheng waiwang*, 內聖外王). The ruler must be able to possess the quality of sageliness inwardly and govern the people with the kingly way outwardly. The Confucian tradition distinguishes two different types of governing, the kingly way (*wangdo/ wangdao*, 王道) and the way of the despot (*p'edo/badao*, 霸道). The leadership based on the "kingly way" is an outward expression of the virtuous power coming from inner cultivation. Sage rule is based on the ruler's moral charisma. This is the model for sage-cracy.

The above discussion of "inward sageliness and outward kingliness" was not meant only for the ruler but for all human beings. This is the basic assumption of "Confucian humanism." Confucian humanism is not secular humanism or anthropocentrism that separates the human from the universe or earth from heaven. The Confucian worldview is not based on a dichotomy dividing heaven and human beings. On the contrary, the Confucian idea of being an authentic human being is to follow the heaven-imparted mandate in human beings: "What Heaven (*chŏn/tian*, 天) imparts to man is called human nature. To follow our nature is called the way (*to/dao*, 道). Cultivating the way is called education. (*Zhongyong* 1;1). Confucianism believes that human nature is from Heaven, and thus the way to fulfill human potentials and to achieve perfection is to follow the Heaven-endowed human nature. Education is vital in this process. Confucianism, in this sense, goes beyond a dualistic dichotomy of heaven and the human, of creator and creature. The Confucian anthropology is thoroughly "anthropocosmic." Unlike the Christian view, it is highly positive and optimistic, and thus education and "cultivation" of the Heaven-endowed nature is crucial in developing the human potential to the highest degree. Unlike Christianity, Confucianism sees no fundamental flaw in human nature. It has no concept of "original sin" or "sinner." Furthermore, it believes in human perfectibility as the goal for all human beings, especially for rulers. It is also true that there were not many perfect rulers or sage-rulers found in the Confucian tradition. Nonetheless, the Confucian tradition has never given up an optimistic view of human nature and the critical importance of education and "cultivation." For this reason kings, emperors, and rulers of the state must never abandon the learning process. With this emphasis on the education of rulers, Confucianism did not pay much attention to the shadow side of the human being that requires institutional measures to prevent human beings from falling into evil.

From the Christian point of view, however, even the most "virtuous person" or sage, like any other human being, is not exempted from the general category of being a "sinner," and thus needs a preventive measure, system, and institution. Democracy, in this sense, is an institution and a system providing precisely such a measure aimed at preventing human beings, including the sage, from committing evil. Constitutionalism in America, for example, is based on this idea. According to James Madison (1751-1836), the Father of the Constitution and the fourth President of the United States, "if humans were angels, we would need no government in the first place."[19] Democracy is a social extension of the two conflicting views of the Christian understanding of human beings. The Confucian tradition, however, holds a firm conviction of the goodness of human nature based on the orthodox Mencian line of the tradition. Due to this Mencian orthodoxy, the Confucian tradition had never given up the idealistic dream of the realization of "sage-cracy." The Confucian "sage-cracy," in spite of its unyielding commitment to and conviction of the ideals that consider the people as "heaven," has failed to develop the appropriate practical and institutional dimensions of such ideals. Nonetheless, the Confucian ideal was that of a virtuous sage-ruler governing the state with moral charisma or force because this is the most effective way to change society.

The Confucian "sage-cracy" can be a benevolent dictatorship. Confucianism, however, did not take issue with dictatorship in itself. The question was not the form of government but the person who was running the government. Confucianism rejected the government run by a despot but accepted dictatorship by a virtuous ruler. In this respect, Confucianism even at its best, cannot endorse democracy. In short, for Confucians democracy was not a vital issue. The central concern for Confucianism was whether the ruler and his leadership were based on the idea that the people were Heaven. The Confucian sage-cracy was, thus, deeply concerned with serving the people as the highest priority. In this sense, Confucian sage-cracy was definitely the government "for the people." The Confucian "sage-cracy," however, was neither the government "by the people" nor the government "of the people" in terms of Abraham Lincoln's formulation of democracy.

According to Lincoln's formula, democracy consists of three dimensions or elements. What is most important is "the government for the people," but it also requires the other two, "the government by the people" and "the government of the people." From the democratic point of view, the government for the people may not fulfill its goal without having "the government by the people" and "the government of the people." The Confucian tradition has rich resources for the government "for the people," but the dimensions of "by the people" and "of the people" were painfully neglected. The Confucian formula of sage rule "for the people" still contains the dichotomy of the ruler and the ruled. In this formula, the ruler and the people were clearly separated, and the people were not able to participate in ruling, which makes the system dualistic. The government "by the people," on the other hand, identifies the ruler with the ruled: the subject of government is also the object of government, and vice versa. Without the government "for" the people and "of" the people, however, the government "by" the people alone runs the risk of anarchism by simply identifying the ruler with the ruled, which makes the system monistic. The government "of" the people also has an importance of its own. It shows the two sides of democratic government: the government belongs to the people while the people belong to the government at the same time. In this formula, the relationship between the government and the people is neither dualistic nor monistic but non-dualistic. This relationship shows a delicate balance between the government and the people in terms of mutual interaction. The government and the people are clearly distinguishable but not separable. They are one yet two, and two yet one. The democratic institution defined by Lincoln brilliantly illustrated the Trinitarian nature of democratic government.

In its ideal vision Confucianism also possesses these three dimensions. A sage-ruler can be sympathetic and willing to listen to the voice of the people and develop the capacity to understanding the side of the ruled or the people. Furthermore, the Confucian principle of governing with virtue (*dŏk/de*, 德) also makes the people feel that they are part of the government, while the government is also part of the people. From the democratic point of view, however, Confucian idealism appeared to be vulnerable in two respects. First, it is not realistic to expect every ruler to possess the ideal Confucian qualities attributable to the sage-ruler.[20] It would be quite rare to find a ruler who is also truly a sage. Second, due to the lack of an appropriate institutional check, even the sage-ruler may still go astray.

The Confucian neglect of the institutional dimension of democracy is largely due to the Mencian line of thinking. Xunzi (荀子, c 298–c 238 BCE), another influential Confucian thinker, was keenly aware of this flaw in the Mencian tradition, rejected Mencius's (372–289 BCE) idea of the original goodness of human nature, and profoundly expounded his theory that "human nature is originally evil," advocating the necessity for "propriety" (*ye/li*, 禮) and "righteousness" (*ŭi/yi*, 義).[21] For Xunzi, "propriety" and "law" played an important role in controlling the people externally and functioned as a form of a social and legal institution.[22] It is unfortunate that the Xunzi line of the Confucian tradition was overshadowed by Mencian orthodoxy, resulting in the historical neglect of the shadow side of the human being. In fact, we have to understand that Xunzi never denied the human capacity for justice or good. The main thrust of his argument was not that human nature is evil in an ontological sense but that human beings, by nature, have an inclination or tendency to do evil. Xunzi fully recognized both the human faculty to know good and the capacity to do good:

> Every man in the street is capable of knowing the righteous relation between father and son at home and the correct relation between ruler and minister outside. It is clear, then, that the faculty to know them and the capacity to practice them are found in every man in the street.[23]

For Xunzi, "propriety" plays the role of social control that will help protect human beings against the tendency to fall into evil. Since the fall of the short lived Qin Dynasty (秦朝, 221–206 BCE), however, Xunzi has been put aside and forgotten because of the misfortune of having as his students the Legalist Hanfeizi (韓非子, 280–233 BCE) and Li Si (李斯, ca. 280–208 BCE) who later became a Chancellor of the Qin Dynasty; these two were later blamed for the fall of the Qin Dynasty. The brilliance and philosophical precision of Xunzi's arguments should be acknowledged and appreciated, not forgotten or buried. Fortunately, now some Confucian thinkers have made attempts to disclose the profundity of Xunzi's ideas. Boston Confucian thinker Robert Neville's attention to Xunzi, for example, must be recognized in this context. Robert Neville is one of the few contemporary thinkers who acknowledge and appreciate Xunzi's attempt to restore the social and ritual dimension of "propriety."[24] Although we may not be able find a full-fledged democratic "system" as a democracy in the Confucian tradition, we may be able to find a system that plays a role in restraining the absolute power of the ruler. In this sense, "ritual propriety" (*ye/li*, 禮) had played a prominent role during the Chosŏn Dynasty.

More specifically, there have been some attempts to focus on the significance of "ritual propriety" (*ye/li*, 禮) in relationship with the democratic element of Confucianism in the Chosŏn Dynasty. Chaihark Hahm, for example, explains that Confucianism used "ritual propriety" to play an important constitutional role in retraining the ruler's absolute political power through the office of Censorate.[25] Further, the office of Censorate consisted of two separate branches: "Office of Remonstration" (*saganwŏn*, 司諫院) and "Office of Inspection" (*sahŏnbu*, 司憲府). The role of the Office of Remonstration was largely advising and "lecturing to" the king while the Office of Inspection was in charge of surveillance and impeachment of the officials, including the king. The Chosŏn government had not one but two institutions whose constitutional function was to criticize the king according to the ideals of Confucian government.[26] However, overall, the goal of this system is to "educate," "cultivate," and "improve" the king to become a sage-ruler based on the optimistic view of human nature.

Confucianism in the Chosŏn Dynasty was based on the Mencius–Zhu Xi orthodox line. Korean Neo-Confucian discourses were largely shaped by Zhu Xi (1130–1200) more than by anyone else. The discussion of human nature in Korean Neo-Confucian circles was also shaped by the Mencius–Zhu Xi line emphasizing the optimistic side of human nature. Accordingly, the Chosŏn Dynasty, which took Confucianism as its official ideology, had to struggle to establish the Confucian state by educating the ruler to become a sage-king. Many brilliant and dedicated Confucian scholars made various attempts to educate and "lecture" their kings in order to produce an ideal Confucian sage-cracy but without much success. The two most prominent Confucian scholars during the Chosŏn Dynasty, Yi T'oegye (李退溪, 1501–1570) and Yi Yulgok (李栗谷, 1536–1584), were both totally convinced of the urgency to educate both the rulers and the people, and they wrote texts on how a ruler could become a sage-king. Yi T'oeye's *Ten Diagrams for Sagely Learning* (*Sŏnghaksipdo*, 聖學十圖), written shortly before he died at the age of 69, and Yi Yulgok's "*The Essentials of Sagely Learning*" (*Sŏnghakjipyo*, 聖學輯要) were two paradigmatic texts for education in sagely kingship, and became the most fundamental texts for Confucian learning for all, rulers and people alike.

Chosŏn Korean Confucianism was heavily invested in this idealistic wing of the Confucian tradition and did not pay much attention to Xunzi's ideas. The Chosŏn Confucianism was predominantly Zhu Xi learning, with the result that Korean Confucianism was not able to envision establishing democratic institution in its tradition.

Beyond Democracy

It is arguable whether Western democracy is the goal for everyone or every country on earth. Some may suggest that the Western form of democracy is the goal of all political systems and that history is moving toward that end as Francis Fukuyama is trying to argue.[27] What I have argued so far is not that democracy is the best institution and an absolute ideal for all. Nor do I wish to imply that democracy is the end of history and of humankind from the teleological and eschatological perspective of time and history. Although democracy or a democratic system is well fit to the Christian understanding of the two conflicting sides of human nature, democracy is not the Christian ideal.

Christians still pray that "Thy Kingdom come and Thy will be done on earth as it is in Heaven." "Thy Kingdom" is a symbolic expression of the reign of God. This, however, is an eschatological hope, and Christians are not about to practice this kind of theocracy for now. Historically, Christians have, at times, tried theocracy but failed. Meanwhile they accept democracy as a system or an institution that will prevent their rulers and leaders as well as the people from falling into evil. Confucianism, however, has not been able to take the dark side of human beings seriously and has been unable to create a well-developed social and political measure or system. In this regard, it is imperative for all serious Confucian scholars to pay special attention to the dimension of "propriety" and reinterpret its meaning as a way of reviving the Confucian tradition and providing a source of inspiration for now and for the future. A country like Korea, which has had a long history of the Confucian tradition and Confucian values, where the people still have a strong sense of their Confucian heritage, must seek wisdom from the Confucian idea of "ritual propriety" or "*ye/li*" as discussed above in order to complement the weak side of democratic institutions in Korea. On the other hand, the Confucian idea of relating the people with "heaven" and the Confucian concept of "ritual propriety" (*ye/li*) will greatly enhance the Western style democratic system.

If Western democracy and Confucianism can one day enter into a fruitful interaction, it may very well lead to the creation of a uniquely Korean form of the democratic system.

Notes

1. For more discussion of the negative impact of Confucianism on Korean society, see Kyŏng Il Kim, *Kongjaga Chukŏya Naraga Sanda* [*To Make the Nation Alive, Confucius Must Die*] Seoul: Pada Chulpansa, 1999. This book sold more than 300,000 copies.

2. For an assessment of the status of Confucianism in general, see Wm. Theodore de Bary, *The Trouble With Confucianism* (Cambridge and London: Harvard University Press, 1991), ix.

3. The term "Confucian humanism" differs from "secular humanism." The notion "secular humanism" is based on a dualistic thinking in dividing "humanism" and "theism." The concept "humanism" assumes a non-theistic, non-transcendental human attitude. "Confucian humanism," however, assumes the continuity between the human and the heaven. To become a genuine and authentic human being, one must have an intrinsic unity with "heaven." Once we lose this unity with "heaven," we lose the true nature of being a human. One of the Confucian Classics, the *Zhong-yong* or the *Doctrine of the Mean* begins with this assertion (中庸1:1天命之謂性, 率性之謂道, 修道之謂教), "what heaven endowed on human beings is called 'human nature,' cultivating this human nature is called the way, and following the way is called education." A leading modern Confucian scholar Tu Weiming has expounded the idea of "Confucian humanism" throughout his academic career from the early 1970s up to now. His commentary on the *Zhong-yong*, *Centrality and Commonality: An Essay on Confucian Religiousness* (Honolulu, Hawai'i: University of Hawaii Press, 1976) is a good example in this regard.

4. There are number of opinion surveys on Park Chung Hee's contributions to the economic development of South Korea. One survey conducted by Research and Research, and Korea Daily shows that Park Chung Hee was most accomplished president since the Korean independence in 1945 (*Chugan Hanguk*, 12/26/2014). Another survey conducted by Hanguk Jeongdang Hakhwe shows that 82.6 percent of Koreans show positive evaluations of his regime in developing the Korean economy ("A Survey in Commemorating 50th Anniversary of the 5.16 Military Revolution in South Korea" (*Chosun Ilbo*, 05/16/2011). See also the Gallup Korea survey in 2015, which shows 44 percent approving Park Chung Hee as the most successful president of all since Korean independence in 1945 (quoted from *Chŏsun Daily*, Aug. 7, 2015).

5. For a general discussion on the compatibility of Confucianism and democracy, see Francis Fukuyama, "Confucianism and Democracy," *Journal of Democracy*, vol. 6. no. 2 (April 1995), 20–33.

6. Tu Weiming has long been advocating that Confucianism and democratic values are compatible in its ideal, if not in the form of a democratic government. See Tu Wei-ming, *Confucian Ethics Today: The Singapore Challenge* (Singapore: CDIS and Federal Publications, 1984), pp. 23, 90; also *Confucianism in an Historical Perspective* (Singapore: Institute of East Asian Philosophies, 1989), 3. For the specific case of Korea, see Kim Dae Jung, "Is Culture Destiny? The Myth of Asia's Anti-Democratic Values," *Foreign Affairs*, n.p., Oct. 19, 2015. See also, Oct. 19, 2015, online at https://www.foreignaffairs.com/articles/southeast-asia/1994-11-01/culture-destiny-myth-asias-anti-democratic-values.

7. David L. Hall and Roger T. Ames, *The Democracy of the Dead: Dewey, Confucius, and the Hope for Democracy in China*, Chicago and LaSalle, IL: Open Court, 1999.

8. I am using the term "apologetic" in the sense of an attempt, in defense of Confucianism, to advocate that Confucianism is not antidemocratic by interpreting Confucianism from the perspective of the democratic "spirit" and "principle" rather than democracy as an "institution," a form of government.

9. One of the leading scholars on this topic, "Confucian values," Tu Weiming has been advocating Confucian values in East Asia. For more extended discussion on the topic, see Tu Weiming, "A Confucian Perspective on the Core Values of the Global Community," *The Review of Korean Studies*, The Academy of Korean Studies, vol. 2, September, 1999, pp. 55–70. Some scholars, however, disagree with the idea of "Asian values" based on Confucianism. See, for an example, Francis Fukuyama, "Asian Values in the Wake of the Asian Crisis," Ibid., 5–22. However, Korean values based both on Confucianism and Christianity have been influential in the process of Korean economic development, see Young-chan Ro, "Korean Worldview and Values: Economic Implications," Ibid., 45–54.

10. Ezra Vogel introduced the idea of "common values" in understanding the rapid economic growth of East Asian countries. For more extended discussion, see Ezra Vogel, *The Four Little Dragons: The Spread of Industrialization in East Asia* (Cambridge, MA: Harvard University Press, 1993). See also, Tu Weiming (editor), *Confucian Traditions in East Asian Modernity: Moral Education and Economic Culture in Japan and the Four Mini-Dragons* (American Academy of Arts and Science, Cambridge, MA: Harvard University Press, 1996). For more recent discussion Confucian values, see "Asia's Rise is rooted in Confucian Values" in the *Wall Street Journal*, Robert D. Kaplan, Feb. 6, 2015.

11. See Tu Weiming, "Confucianism, in *Our Religions*. Arvind Sharma, ed. (San Francisco: HarperSanFrancisco, 1993), 168.

12. Quoted by Wing-Tsit Chan (ed.), *A Source Book in Chinese Philosophy* (Princeton, NJ: Princeton University Press, 1969), 78. The original source is found in the book of *History*. Cf. James Legge, *Shoo King* (London: Truebner, 1865), p. 292.

13. Ibid., 61–62.

14. See Wm. Theodore de Bary, *The Trouble With Confucianism* (Cambridge and London: Harvard University Press, 1991), 2–3.

15. Reinhold Niebuhr, *The Children of Light and the Children of Darkness* (New York: Charles Scribner's Son, 1972; first published 1944), xiii.

16. Hahm Chaihark, "Constitutionalism, Confucian Civic virtue, and Ritual Propriety," in Daniel A. Bell and Hahm Chaibong, eds., *Confucianism for the Modern World* (Cambridge and New York: Cambridge University Press, 2003), 32.

17. Ibid., 26

18. There are ample evidences in Mencius that he believed the people are the subject of the government and the people are the deciding factor in terms of the succession of empire. [According to Mencius, the transfer of power from one ruler to another one as seen in the case of the legendary Emperors from Yao to Shun was done by Heaven, but Heaven could not do it alone without the acceptance of the people. Mencius used the metaphor "Heaven" in identifying with the people. For some examples see the *Book of Mencius* (1B:7, 4A:9, 5A:5, etc.). For the English translation of these passages, see Wing-tsit Chan, *A Source Book in Chinese Philosophy*, (Princeton, NJ: Princeton University Press, 1963), 61, 73–74, 77.

19. James Madison, "Federalist #51," in Alexander Hamilton, James Madison, and John Jay, *The Federalist Papers*, Clinton Rossister, ed. (New York: Mentor Books, 1961), 322.

20. The Confucian predicament regarding the idea of sage-ruler has been a persistent issue. For a contemporary discussion on this issue, see Wm. Theodore de Bary, *The Trouble With Confucianism*, 46–73.

21. Xunzi clearly and persuasively argued for the need to institute laws and structures. See his, "The Nature of Man is Evil" in Wing Tsit Chan, *Source Book*, 130.

22. See Wing-tsit Chan's comments on this subject, *A Source Book*, 129.

23. For Wing-tsit Chan's translation, see his *Source Book*, 134

24. Robert Cummings Neville, *Boston Confucianism* (Albany: State University of New York Press, 2000), 25–40.

25. For more discussion, see Chaihark Ham, "Constitutionalism, Confucian Civic Virtue, and Ritual Propriety," *Confucianism for the Modern World*, 34.

26. Hahm Chaihark, Ibid., 52.

27. From the teleological perspective based on a linear way of thinking, one can postulate democracy is not only the goal but also the end of history. For example, see Francis Fukuyama, *The End of History and the Last Man* (New York: Free Press, 1992).

Bibliography

Bell, Daniel A. and Hahm, Chaibong. *Confucianism for the Modern World*. Cambridge and New York: Cambridge University Press, 2003.

Chan, Wing-Tsit, ed. *A Source Book in Chinese Philosophy*. Princeton, NJ: Princeton University Press, 1969.

de Bary, Wm Theodore. *The Trouble With Confucianism*. Cambridge and London: Harvard University Press, 1991.

———. "Confucianism and Democracy," *Journal of Democracy* 6, no. 2 (April 1995): 20–33.

Fukuyama, Francis, *The End of History and the Last Man*. New York: Free Press, 1992.
Hall, David L. and Ames, Roger T., *The Democracy of the Dead: Dewey, Confucius, and the Hope for the Democracy in China*. Chicago and LaSalle, IL: Open Court, 1999.
Kim Dae Jung. "Is Culture Destiny? The Myth of Asia's Anti-Democratic Values." *Foreign Affairs*. November/December, 1994.
Neville, Robert Cummings. *Boston Confucianism*. Albany: State University of New York Press, 2000.
Reinhold Niebuhr. *The Children of Light and the Children of Darkness*. New York: Charles Scribner's Son, 1972.
Tu Weiming. "A Confucian Perspective on the Core Values of the Global Community," *The Review of Korean Studies*, The Academy of Korean Studies, vol. 2, (September, 1999): 55–70.
―――. *Centrality and Commonality: An Essay on Confucian Religiousness*. Honolulu, Hawai'i: University of Hawaii Press, 1976.
―――. *Confucian Ethics Today: the Singapore Challenge*. Singapore: CDIS and Federal Publications, 1984.
―――, ed. *Confucian Traditions in East Asian Modernity: Moral Education and Economic Culture in Japan and the Four Mini-Dragons*. Cambridge, MA: Harvard University Press, 1996.
Vogel, Ezra. *The Four Little Dragons: The Spread of Industrialization in East Asia*. Cambridge, MA: Harvard University Press, 1993.

11

Between Tradition and Globalization
Korean Christianity at a Crossroads

Anselm Kyongsuk Min

Introduction

Contemporary Korean Christianity faces a number of serious challenges, and these challenges are largely traceable to three sources or rather the interaction of three sources: (1) its tension with traditional Korean religions and cultures, (2) its exposure to the tidal wave of globalization, and (3) its relation to its own institutional, largely Western tradition with which it has been identifying and defining itself. The first refers to the long-standing problem of indigenization, the second to the more recent problem of globalization, and the third to the recurrent problem of reconstructing and reestablishing its own identity as authentic Christianity in the twofold context of indigenization and globalization.

There are, accordingly, three parts to this paper. In the first part I will discuss indigenization or Korean Christianity's relationship with traditional Korean cultures and religions. I will note certain characteristics of the prevailing relation between Christianity and Korean culture, the tensions inherent in that relation, and the possible causes of those tensions. I will also comment on current discussions of the methodology of indigenization and argue that the first task of all talk about indigenization is to examine the nature of the indigenization already actual and operative in the very fact that when Koreans become Christians, they bring with them into the church all the religious and cultural tendencies of the Korean tradition by which they have already been shaped and which reshape Christianity into a distinctly Korean Christianity without consciously intending to do so. When Koreans are baptized into Christianity, they do not suddenly cease to be Koreans as already shaped by Confucianism, Buddhism, and shamanism, and through them Korean Christianity is already indigenized into the basic orientation and character of Korean culture and religions. It is this *de facto*, unconscious indigenization that needs careful examination with regard to its complexity and authenticity before we move to the second step, that of consciously retrieving the best of the Korean traditions and incorporating them into the expanding identity of Korean Christianity.

This second step, however, cannot mean simply taking over certain congenial ideas or theories from the tradition. The hermeneutic of retrieval involves the bridging of the historical situation of the ancient culture in which those theories are rooted and the contemporary situation in which and for which they are meant to be retrieved so as to fulfill their constructive functions. This involves the need for doing an adequate social analysis of the contemporary situation in which we find ourselves today, a situation I would characterize as the phenomenon of globalization in all its ambiguities and challenges.

This leads to the second part of this paper, a characterization of globalization as the context in which Korean Christianity must become more indigenized and also more authentically itself. It is crucial to remember that indigenization must become effective precisely in the challenging context of globalization, just as it is in response to these challenges that Korean Christianity must prove its authentic identity as both Korean and Christian. There are many ways of characterizing globalization. It must be pointed out at the outset that by using the term "globalization," I do not mean to simply endorse a certain ideology of globalization, especially the neoliberal ideology that has been singing praises of globalization as a panacea for all human problems for more than two decades. I am simply taking globalization as an objective process that has been bringing different economies, nations, cultures, and religions of the world together into common space, with an increasing extensity, intensity, and impact, and then asking of that process what serious challenges it is posing to humanity, especially to human dignity and human solidarity with one another. Globalization is fraught with challenges and risks, which is all the more reason to take it seriously, as indeed the most central and most fundamental context and condition for *all* of human life today, and to discuss what we can do to humanize its challenges. Merely ignoring it because one does not like it is in fact to run away from the most serious problem facing humanity today. I will briefly discuss the economic/ecological, political/military, cultural/religious, and migratory dimensions of globalization and the ethical and theological challenges they pose.

In the third part dealing with the task of building authentic Christianity that is also authentically Korean, I will discuss first the problems facing Catholicism and Protestantism, respectively, and second the hermeneutic of retrieval in its methodological aspect. The problems I would like to highlight in Korean Christianity are fragmentation due to individualism in the case of Protestantism and passivity of the laity due to clerical authoritarianism in the case of Catholicism. I will argue that Protestantism needs to break out of its deeply entrenched tendency to fragmentation if it is going to deal with the multiple challenges of globalization that require a broadening of horizons and intellectual flexibility. I will argue that Catholicism, on its part, needs to be freed from its endemic clerical authoritarianism if it is going to liberate the enormous energy and potential of the laity for the tasks facing the church today and to meet these tasks with historical flexibility and adequacy. I will also outline three methodological steps in appropriating ancient Korean ideas for indigenizing Korean Christianity in the context of contemporary globalization.

The Challenge of Indigenization

The relation between Christianity and Korean culture has always been tense. The first encounter between Catholicism and Korea was accompanied by a century of persecution and conflict, based on differences in political and military interests between Korea and France and on philosophical/theological differences between Catholicism and Confucianism, a story well told earlier in chapters 4 and 5. Protestantism came into Korea only after the establishment of diplomatic relations between Korea and Western powers and the full legal recognition of Christianity, and the Korean encounter with Protestantism was spared political blood-letting, but it was socially and theologically no less conflictual, something hinted at in chapters 6 and 7.

Confucianism claimed to be the only true *Tao* or way for humanity to follow in order to become truly human. Christianity too claimed to be the only way for humanity to find their salvation. These exclusivist tendencies common to both were reinforced by the politics of preceding centuries. Political Confucianism did not mind enforcing its own rigid orthodoxy with all the political means at its disposal as the established religion of the nation. Christianity, no less political in its alliance with colonial powers, was compelled to reinforce its exclusivism theologically under the various threats and challenges from the secular world. Both Catholicism and Protestantism felt threatened by the increasing secularization of Western culture, especially the Enlightenment attack on the basic Christian dogmas such as the existence of God and the divinity of Christ. Catholicism felt threatened and besieged by the rise of hostile secular states eager to take away its traditional political privileges, as witness the revolutions in France and Italy. If Confucianism had plenty of reasons, both philosophical and political, to be exclusivist in relation to other religions and cultures, Christianity did not have any fewer reasons to be so. Both Confucianism and Christianity felt compelled to defend their own integrity by interpreting their respective orthodoxy in exclusivist terms and then by reinforcing that orthodoxy against each other.[1]

Today, deprived of the privileges of state power, neither Confucianism nor Christianity can oppose each other politically, but the ideological tension between Christianity and Confucianism, and for that matter, between Christianity and other Korean religions such as Buddhism and shamanism, remains in all its exclusivist rigidity. This tension is especially apparent in the relation between Protestantism on one hand and other religions on the other, such as Buddhism, various indigenous religions, and especially the cult of Dangun, the presumed ancestor of the Korean people. This tension often breaks out into the open in the form of violence and dismissal of or threats to theologians who advocate respect for other religions. Even when not violent, the tension forms the undercurrent of all relations between Protestantism and other religions. The basic ideological cause of this tension is the exclusivistic attitude still dominating the absolute majority of Korean Protestants, clergy and laity alike. Sorry to say, such exclusivism is not absent from the majority of other Korean religions either, whether Buddhism, Confucianism, or other indigenous religions. The only difference is that Protestantism shows its exclusivism in more aggressive, often violent ways.[2]

The case of Korean Catholicism is somewhat different. Although it had been just as exclusivistic as or perhaps even more exclusivist than any other religion until the Second Vatican Council, it has become inclusivist since then, not an insignificant progress from exclusivism. For half a century now Catholicism has been teaching the possibility of salvation for non-Christians and the corresponding respect for the elements of truth found in them. It is questionable, however, whether Korean Catholicism has been truly serious and active in teaching and promoting what official Catholicism teaches. It is true that the Catholic hierarchy exchanges greetings and visits with Buddhist leaders on important occasions, such as Christmas and the anniversary of the Buddha's birth, issuing statements of good wishes and mutual respect, but it is also true that such greetings tend to be pure formalities and never filter down to the pews so as to impact the consciousness of lay Catholics, which largely remains exclusivist in its relation to other religions.

The present relation between Christianity and other religions in Korea still remains one of tension, although somewhat mitigated by the introduction, however slow, of an ecumenical consciousness toward other religions and more significantly by the relativizing tendencies of contemporary secular education and public media. Despite the occasional cooperation of different religions on social issues, clearly, all the religions, not only Christianity, have a long way to go in educating their membership to greater tolerance and respect for one another with a less rigid, more flexible conception of orthodoxy and a gradual movement toward a more inclusive reception of other religions. It is important in this regard for Korean Christianity to realize that it has already received into itself, its own thinking and acting, so much of traditional culture and religion by the very fact that it draws its membership from Koreans already steeped in and shaped by Korean culture. Furthermore, it has to reflect on the positive elements in indigenous Korean religions and on ways of incorporating them into its own identity, in this way broadening, enriching, and Koreanizing its identity, while also reflecting on the negative elements which it perhaps cannot accept into its own identity at the present time and on which it may want to dialogue for the sake of greater mutual understanding and mutual acceptance. In any event, the need for engaging with traditional Korean religions is a compelling imperative for Korean Christianity. Korean religions remain the soil, the context, and the partner for the identity, operation, and task of Korean Christianity. Korean Christianity cannot remain closed in upon itself.

Let me dwell a little on a simple anthropological fact and its theological implications largely ignored by comparative religionists and comparative theologians. Our religious consciousness has many layers, all of which are internally related to one another in an impossibly complex hermeneutic circle. The first layer consists of things we know, will, and desire, which we can bring to reflective self-consciousness in the form of propositions. The second layer consists of more fundamental convictions, sensibilities, character orientations, and deep-seated longings particular to the person. The third layer consists of all the ontological, religious, and ethical assumptions particular to the culture that has nurtured and shaped the person. It is a complex combination of the second and third layers that provides the horizon and context from which the first layer arises and in terms of which it must be interpreted. When a person converts to a different religion, the person does not and cannot simply leave behind the whole content of the second and third layers and acquire a whole new content for them like taking off old clothes and putting on new ones. The person will indeed acquire a new religious content for the first layer of his or her consciousness, but how the three layers will then interact and give a new shape to a person's hermeneutic circle will constitute the concrete dialectic in the person's life to come. The simple anthropological fact here is that when Koreans convert to a new religion, they cannot simply leave behind what they have been in terms of their characters, sensibilities, and horizons shaped by their culture. They do not cease to be Koreans already shaped by their culture. Baptism into Christianity does not and cannot mean replacing the entire old content of the three layers of consciousness with something completely new. That is to say, Korean Christians bring what they have been into the church they enter, accepting a new content for the first layer of their consciousness but only interacting with the preexisting habits of thinking, willing, and feeling they have acquired from their culture.

This means that Koreans becoming Christians also means Koreanizing Christianity with the old cultural habits and horizons they bring with them. This is a simple anthropological fact. Korean Christians may no longer offer traditional Confucian rites of ancestor veneration to their deceased parents, no longer consult shamans about their fortune, and are no longer Confucians and shamanists in the formal sense, but their concrete attitudes toward the family, authority, and fortune remain much the same as their non-Christian compatriots. They remain thoroughly Confucian in their deference to their ministers and priests and thoroughly shamanist in their preoccupation with the fortune of their life, often turning their religion into a religion of good fortune and prosperity. It is no wonder that, as chapters 4, 5, and 7 clearly demonstrate, Korea's first

Christians conceived of their relationship to God in terms of filial piety, the chief Confucian virtue.

This fact also implies that Korean Christianity is already Korean or indigenized by the very fact that they are Korean Christians. Whether we like it or not, whether we are conscious of it or not, Korean Christianity is already indigenized into the traditional Korean ways of thinking, acting, and feeling when Koreans become Christians. This is no more strange than the fact that early Christians remained, despite their formal adherence to Christianity, deeply Greek and Roman in their concrete attitudes in many important matters of life. The only thing we can do, and I would say, the only thing we *should* do, is to examine this *de facto* indigenization already actual and operative in our concrete attitudes and ask ourselves which elements in these attitudes are compatible with Christianity, which are so positive as to deserve active incorporation into the always expanding identity of Christianity, and which are so negative as to be simply incompatible with the Christian faith and deserve critical purification. Prior to any self-conscious, reflective attempts to indigenize the theology of Korean Christians, it is far more imperative to critically reflect on the various positive and negative potential of the already indigenized existence of Korean Christians. As far as I know, this examination is something completely neglected by theologians of indigenization, who are more concerned with the Christian retrieval of ancient ideas and theories at the level of the first layer of reflective self-consciousness than with the Christian potential of the second and third layers that embody the deeper religious and cultural identity of Korean Christians.[3]

The Challenge of Globalization

The task of retrieving the tradition is critical and compelling. It is equally compelling to know the context in which and for which that task is to be fulfilled. We are not trying to retrieve the tradition for the end of the nineteenth century Korea or for the mid-twentieth-century Korea. We are certainly not trying to retrieve it for its own sake. We are trying to do so for the Korea of the twenty-first century, the century of globalization. It is essential to know something of this context and try to think of indigenization as indigenization *in* and *for* this particular context, not something else. Otherwise, we run the danger of abstract and irrelevant idealism as pure theories always tend to be when they are not related to concrete contexts. What are some of the characteristics of globalization especially relevant to the task of indigenization?

This is not the place for a comprehensive analysis of globalization.[4] Instead, I will simply sketch those characteristics of globalization that I consider most relevant to the contemporary Korean situation in which the indigenization of ancient ideas is to take place. I think there are six theologically relevant characteristics corresponding to the economic/ecological, political/military, cultural/religious, and migratory dimensions of globalization.[5]

Economically, globalization has been sharpening economic inequalities between different nations in the world and between different regions within nations. I do not deny that globalization has been increasing the wealth of the world in terms of its total absolute output, and that some nations such as China, India, Korea, Taiwan, Singapore, Thailand, and Vietnam have been significantly benefiting from the economic liberalization of trade barriers across the world. Still, it is a fact that in terms of comparative GDPs and distribution of wealth, globalization has also been creating an increasingly unequal world.

Furthermore, the global economic competition has been exploiting more and more natural resources and significantly worsening the ecological balance of nature. One only wonders, for example, what the world would be like twenty years from now when China and India, with almost three billion people between them, become consumer societies and add three billion more automobiles to the one billion already on the road, with all their demand for oil and with all their impact on air pollution.

Politically, globalization has been eroding the autonomy and sovereignty of small nations while increasing the power of big nations. More and more authorities of national governments over their own internal political and economic affairs are surrendered to the international economic agencies such as the World Bank, the World Trade Organization, and the International Monetary Fund, while the political power of big nations increases precisely through the economic and political clouts they exercise in these agencies as well as directly through their negotiating power in various free-trade agreements and through their long-standing status as global superpowers.

There is also a military aspect to globalization. Globalization increases the interdependence of nations and therefore also the master/slave struggle among nations, which is most concretely felt in the global arms race and the imperialist, military struggle for global hegemony. Nations compete for relative superiority of power in an increasingly interdependent world and use all the means at their disposal—political, economic, and military. There is a telling episode in recent times in this regard. China increased its defense budget by 17.8 percent for 2007,[6] and the United States has been asking out loud what is China's ultimate intention. It is very revealing to discover that the Chinese defense budget, even after all its increase, amounted to only 45 billion dollars, a mere 10 percent of the U.S. defense budget of 450 billion dollars! The world of economic globalization is increasingly also a world of military imperialism and the struggle for global domination, and therefore also a world in which wars are a constant possibility with all their potential for human disasters. Recent conflicts in Iraq, Afghanistan, and Syria are only the most recent, scandalous examples of this military aspect of globalization.

Culturally, globalization also means the free flow of ideas, values, and information across all the traditional barriers. No individual, group, nation, religion, or culture is immune from exposure to this flow or rather flooding, no matter how different, radical, demeaning, or enriching these ideas and values might be. Such a flow encourages a certain relativism in matters of moral and religious values. We become radically aware of how different the world is, how contradictory these ideas can be to our own traditional beliefs, and what a minority view my group is holding in important matters. The free flow of ideas and values thus relativizes and erodes our moral and religious convictions. By the sheer materialism of so much of the content traded on the mass media and the Internet, such free flow also cheapens and demeans human life and human dignity. Through its message of instant consumption and gratification it weakens our sense of moral and religious commitment, while also encouraging a completely materialist outlook on life, a radical challenge to all human cultures and religions except the modern Western capitalist culture.

In addition to relativizing and weakening our moral and religious commitments, the unrestricted flow of ideas and values also subjects the entire globe to the danger of cultural homogenization or at least that of culture war, a war for the soul of humanity. Those who are economically and politically powerful and thus possess the means to control the media and the Internet also seek to dominate the cyber space of the world and shape that space according to its own image. The tendency to cultural homogenization of the world is simply part of the dialectic of globalization. Or, at least a struggle for the cultural domination of the world is almost as much part of globalization as are struggles for the economic, political, and military domination of the world.[7]

Finally, globalization involves the free flow not only of goods and services, of ideas and values, but above all of human beings across all the national, cultural, and religious boundaries. It goes without saying that this massive migration of human beings is fueled and motivated by the search for economic opportunities. We have not only the migration of merchants, troops, and students but also and especially that of migrant workers. There are now some two hundred million people living outside the countries of their origin. In the Philippines, some 20 percent of the entire population live outside their country in faraway places such as Saudi Arabia, Taiwan, Japan, and Korea. It is well known that there are some thirteen million "undocumented" migrant workers in the United States, not to speak of many more millions who are there legally. With the migration of human beings from different nations and cultures we face two kinds of interrelated problems. One is the problem of difference: difference in culture and religion. What should we think of those who worship different gods? The other is the problem of divisiveness. How do we deal with these strangers in our midst? Migrant workers are routinely subjected to misunderstanding, discrimination, and exclusion that violate their basic human rights and condemn them to poverty and marginalization.[8]

Underlying the different dimensions of globalization is the constant temptation to imperialism or imperialist domination of the world. This is the very logic of capitalist-led globalization. Globalization does not simply mean harmless exposure to goods, ideas, and human beings from different parts of the world; it means joining global competition for the sake of survival. Increasing interconnection brings goods, ideas, and human beings into the common space of the globe. Increasing interdependence in a world where some are more dependent on others means unlimited competition in that common space and unlimited struggle to survive that competition by an increasing domination of an ever larger share of the world. Imperialism, therefore, is built into the very logic of globalization. Economic globalization involves the struggle to dominate the global market. Political globalization involves the struggle to manage the globe in the way most advantageous to one's own nation, even by means of military power if necessary. Cultural globalization involves the struggle to dominate global culture by imposing one's own culture on the rest. Whether any one nation or group of nations will completely succeed in this struggle for global domination is questionable; there is always the dialectic of unintended and unforeseen consequences that no nation can control or manage. What is unquestionable is the reality of global competition in all areas of life and the temptation to imperialist domination of the world by any means including war.

We may now ask how this globalization impacts the domestic situation of Korea. Economically, despite all the rapid progress Korea has made in the last half century that has made Korea, once an international basket case, the world's thirteenth largest economy, there has been a mounting concern over the increasing gap between rich and poor since the IMF crisis of 1998 but especially since the global financial crisis of 2008. This concern was recently expressed in the serious split of public opinion over the Free Trade Agreement reached between South Korea and the United States. The fear is that certain less competitive industries will suffer radical decline while other industries will be forced to restructure themselves for the sake of greater competitiveness. In either case, the chances are that there will be much unemployment and certainly the constant specter of unemployment for those who are lucky enough to hold jobs. The nation will be increasingly subjected to the antithetical pressures to be competitive, on the one hand, in the global market with all that this implies in terms of perhaps more and better jobs in the successfully competitive industries and firms and worse or no jobs for those in the failing, and to provide better social safety net, on the other, for those who are excluded and marginalized in the process. In recent years, increasing economic inequality and consequent polarization of society have become the hottest political issues. The demand for social justice will become louder as economic globalization proceeds.[9]

Culturally, South Korea has been, and will continue to be, at even an increasingly faster pace, subjected to the free flow of new ideas and values, mostly from the United States, and all the consequences of such a flow. Traditional religions and cultures will be severely challenged to respond to the intellectual questions they pose to the validity of tradition, to the relativizing and eroding tendencies of such questions, and to the enervating effect of sheer materialism so characteristic of the U.S. media. Will traditional religions and cultures simply retrench and close themselves to this radical challenge of diversity, suffer with resignation all the relativizing and eroding consequences of the free trade in ideas and materialism, or respond to them with determination and discrimination, with both loyalty and openness? We already know how South Korea suffers from the psychological chaos in which the remnants of tradition, still strong in the consciousness of the people, and the impact of new ideas on life, love, sex, the family, and religion, simply exist side by side without much critical and reflective ordering in the minds of the people, producing so much ambiguity and tension in social relations. Confucian family relations are still very strongly observed; just look at how all the major companies are run. Still, such Confucian relations have been suffering strong strains, tensions, and violations in myriad ways. There is an increasing ascendancy of materialistic consumer culture invading every area of the Korean mind, religious or not. Formally, they may be Buddhist or Christian or Confucian, but they tend to be materialistic in terms of the actual decisions they make.

In terms of migration, South Korea has been showing signs of becoming a multi-ethnic society, like so many other societies on the globe, and increasingly facing all the challenges endemic to such a society. It is not only that there are some seven million Koreans living outside Korea, many of their children increasingly marrying spouses of other ethnic groups; but more importantly, South Korea has been attracting, for over two decades now, hundreds of thousands of foreign workers from the Philippines, Bangladesh, Pakistan, Indonesia, and China. One recent report states that one of every eight marriages in Korea is interracial, one of every four marriages being interracial in the countryside, with 70 percent of these countryside marriages being with either Vietnamese or Chinese.[10] It is not only foreign ideas and values that are coming into the country; it is human beings from other parts of the world with their different cultures, languages, and religions that are now entering the country and posing all the human challenges to Korean society. Are Koreans ready to respect their different cultures, to treat them with dignity as fellow human beings, and to provide basic human needs as their human rights require? Or, are Koreans going to discriminate against them, violate their basic human rights, and marginalize them to the fringes of Korean society with all their human tragedies so often reported in the media? It is no longer just American society that is subject to the stresses and strains of a multi-ethnic society; Korean society too is now increasingly subjected to such challenges, and in fact these challenges may be greater in Korea than in America because these challenges are relatively new in Korea, which has long prided itself on being culturally and ethnically homogeneous.

Living in the age of globalization, especially as one of its important economic players, is also to face the challenge of imperialism. South Korea is not strong enough to be itself an imperialist nation, but it is not immune from the political necessity of aligning itself with one or the other of the imperialist nations. So far, it has been siding with the United States, sending troops to fight a war which has nothing to do with Korea, trading with the United States as its largest partner, sending most of its young students to the United States to get their advanced degrees, and visiting the United States as the most attractive tourist site. With the increasing emergence of China, which replaced the United States as Korea's largest trading partner since 2007,[11] the European Union, India, Brazil, and the resurgence of Russia as important players on the international scene, South Korea will be severely challenged to make prudent choices in the selection of its global imperialist partners with whom to align itself. As globalization proceeds at a faster pace and as the cutthroat competition increases in all areas of life, economic, political, military, and cultural, South Korea, like all small nations, will be increasingly and necessarily exposed to all the dangers and risks of the global politics of imperialism.

With all these economic, cultural, and imperialist challenges posed by globalization also comes *the* political challenge: How is Korea as a nation going to coordinate its responses to these multiple, complicating challenges of globalization so as to survive as a nation with a cultural identity of its own, to accumulate enough wealth to do social justice to the poor and marginalized in society, both Korean and non-Korean? Will Koreans be prudent enough to choose effective leaders who will be devoted to the common good of the nation, not to his own partisan interests, to learn to tolerate diversity of religious ideas to be able to cooperate as citizens of the same nation, to be faithful to the best of their own religions while also cultivating a sense of global human solidarity, the loyalty to humanity as such and their common good?[12]

Korean Christianity between Indigenization and Globalization

It is in the context of these challenges that Korean Christianity has to define itself and fulfill its mission as authentic Christianity, authentically Korean yet also open to God's call in this age of globalization. I would like to single out three tasks as especially compelling in that context. The task of overcoming individualism and fragmentation with a stronger sense of community for Korean Protestantism, the task of overcoming clerical authoritarianism by sharing power with the laity for Korean Catholicism, and the task of effective indigenization for both denominations. My claim is that Korean Protestantism cannot respond to the challenges of indigenization and globalization without overcoming its endemic tendency to fragmentation, just as Korean Catholicism cannot respond to the same challenges without liberating the resources and energies of the laity.

First, the task of overcoming individualism and fragmentation. From its inception Protestantism has suffered from its endemic individualism and fragmentation. This has been true of Protestantism worldwide, but it seems especially true of Korean Protestantism. Protestantism was founded on the theology that Scripture is the only source and principle of authority, whose interpretation, however, is left to the freedom of individuals, with no definitive institutional authority to arbitrate and rule in cases of dispute. The proliferation of denominations and the fragmentation of denominations into independent congregations each under the leadership of the pastor had already been the tendency of U.S. Protestantism even before it came into Korea; but this tendency has been exacerbated once it came into Korea through a variety of indigenous factors, such as personal loyalties, regionalism, narrow dogmatism, pastor's dependence on the local congregation, and above all the lack of a central authority that can define and rule.

The result over the years has been not only the multiplication and fragmentation of denominations but also the emergence of congregations solely based on loyalty to individual pastors without any sense of communion even with other congregations of the same denomination, still less with other Christian denominations. Korean Protestantism acknowledges no ultimate binding ecclesiastical authority, and whenever contentions arise, the contending parties simply separate from the denomination and found their own denominations and congregations. With no central authority to supervise and control and approve, poorly equipped seminaries proliferate and keep producing unqualified pastors in abundance. Pastors compete for followers in a field with a shrinking population and try to attach their congregation to their own personalities. Pastors depend on their own congregations for their livelihood, and it is imperative that they do everything to reinforce the congregation's personal loyalty to their pastors and to keep its membership from leaving for another congregation. Pastors compete with other pastors for sheer survival.

It is no wonder that Korean Protestantism has increasingly become a pathological scandal in the eyes of the Korean public in recent years, leading to decline in membership and positive social impact. Protestantism has ceased to command respect and credibility for a long time, certainly to be the sign of progressive modernism that it used to be during the first half of the twentieth century. People come to the churches because the pastors happen to be inspirational preachers, and leave the churches when pastors no longer inspire. In order to hold on to their followers, pastors are increasingly pressured to appeal to their immediate emotional needs. People forget that they should come to church because of their faith in God and Christ, not because of their purely personal loyalty and attraction to the pastor. They forget that they are above all Christians in fellowship with other Christians and other denominations, not primarily members of their own congregations. There is no sense of belonging to Christ over and beyond the pastors, of belonging to the larger communion of churches in the same denomination and in Protestantism as a whole. Each congregation is increasingly isolated into its own individual concerns, with no sense of communion even with other congregations of their own denominations, still less with the larger Korean society. Christianity is reduced to the internal dialectic of personal loyalties and interpersonal struggles on the local level.

The overall impression of Korean Protestantism, therefore, has been that of a group intensely self-absorbed, infinitely fractious and divisive, constantly involved in the scandalous struggle for power, control, and sheer survival, with no higher authority to acknowledge and respect than their partisan interests, and therefore also with no evangelical values to witness to with dedication and commitment. The result has been the struggle for wealth and power, increasing corruption, and the well-founded impression of sheer hypocrisy in the eyes of the Korean public. No wonder that Korean Protestantism is shrinking.[13]

If Korean Protestantism is going to respond to the challenges of globalization in an effective and credible way, it is imperative that it overcome its endemic individualism and fragmentation by learning to accept a structure of authority stable enough to endure, credible enough to inspire, and effective enough to rule. It desperately needs an institution of moral authority that can rule in matters of faith and morals, crack down on the sheer individualism of congregations and pastors, call the congregations to a sense of communion and fellowship with other congregations of the same denomination and eventually with all other Christians so as to be able to provide a common credible witness to the good news of Jesus Christ, and exercise effective control on the quality and number of seminaries. Without an institution of effective and credible authority Korean Protestantism is likely to dissipate all its energy in its purely internal domestic concerns and struggles, without doing its share in responding to the ever intensifying challenges of the globalizing world.

The problem with Korean Catholicism is just the opposite of that of Korean Protestantism. If Protestantism suffers from the lack of appropriate authority, Catholicism suffers from its excess, from its authoritarianism that concentrates all authority in the clergy and suffocates the dynamism and vitality of initiative and spontaneity on the part of the laity. Korean Catholicism is still perhaps the most respected religion in Korea, but this may be because Koreans are themselves authoritarian and prefer the stability, order, and unity authoritarianism inspires to the spirit of initiative and creativity. The other side of the image of stability Korean Catholicism projects is precisely the passivity and repression of the energy of the laity, now increasingly well-educated and conscious of their rights and responsibilities in the church. It is notorious how authority is concentrated in the hands of the clergy. All power, executive, legislative, and judicial, is concentrated in the hands of the clergy, of the pastors at the local level, of the bishops at the diocesan level, and of the pope at the global level. The ordained clergy totally control what the laity can do and should do in the church. The laity cannot do anything significant without the previous approval of the clergy. Centuries and decades of such practice have created a culture of authoritarianism and the authoritarian mentality in Korean Catholicism. The clergy enjoy their power and just take such power for granted, expecting automatic respect and obedience from the laity. Lay people too enjoy obedience and stability and take their obedience for granted. Those who are not content with such a passive role and are anxious to do their share in the common mission of the church feel alienated from the church that consistently stifles such initiative, and either grumble and despair or leave the church altogether.

It is safe to say that what makes Korean Catholicism more authoritarian than Catholicism elsewhere is the presence of Confucianism in the mentality and culture of the Korean converts. This has been pointed out many times. In popular Confucianism actually practiced by people, as distinct from the scholarly theories about the ideals of Confucianism, the emphasis has always been on obedience: obedience of children to parents, women to men, subjects to rulers, the young to the old, disciples to teachers. When Koreans join Catholicism, it is only a matter of transferring this habit of obedience to the ordained clergy whose status has already been theologically absolutized in Western Catholicism as "vicars of Christ" himself. Clerical authoritarianism, already inherent in Catholicism before its entry into Korea, has found only a fertile soil to nourish and reinforce itself in the Confucian culture when it came to Korea, and Korean Catholicism has been suffering from that authoritarianism ever since.

It is rather unfortunate that Korean Catholicism still persists in its authoritarian oppression of the laity. Increasingly the laity are now just as well-educated as the clergy, and provide immense resources of expertise, energy, and sense of mission for the church. If the Catholic Church is going to adequately respond to the challenges of the globalizing world, it will have to tap the resources of the laity it has been repressing, and thereby liberate and activate these resources for the mission of the church as a whole. It goes without saying that the clergy alone cannot do what the whole church is called upon to do. It cannot even do what it considers to be its own sphere, the sphere of doctrine and theology, because any kind of relevant theology will require sociological expertise and historical sensibility to make itself concretely responsive to the problems of our time, and such expertise and sensibility can only be provided by educated laity. The Catholic clergy must learn to let go of their often unedifying attachment to power and learn to share it with the laity so as to fulfill the mission of the church together. It is unfortunate that even half a century after the reform of the Second Vatican Council with its special call for an active role of the laity, the mentality of both the clergy and laity still largely remains preconciliar and authoritarian.[14]

The third compelling task facing both Korean Protestantism and Catholicism is the task of indigenization or coming to grips with their common Korean cultural and religious past. Here I return to the discussion of indigenization broached in the first section of this paper. In addition to examining the form of indigenization already operating in the mentality and culture of Korean Christians by the very fact that they are Koreans, it is now imperative to map out a methodology for the more reflective appropriation of the best of the Korean tradition. What are the important steps or points to remember in indigenizing Korean Christianity through such appropriation?

According to my reading of current discussions of indigenization, the foremost aspect of the Korean tradition singled out for appropriation by Christian theology is the emphasis of the tradition on a non-dualistic affirmation of unity, harmony, and solidarity in contrast to what is perceived—rightly or wrongly—to be a strong dualism characteristic of Western thought in general and considered responsible for the alienation and hostility between God and humanity, humanity and nature, Christians and non-Christians. Scholars typically try to retrieve the *han* (한, 韓) thought that says that reality is the mysterious harmony of what is two yet one, the emphasis on peace and harmony in Wonhyo, the unity of *li* and *chi* in Yulgok, the identity of the human and the divine in Donghak, the great identity of all things in which what is heavenly and what is human constitute unity in Park Eunsik, and the emphasis on mutual dependence in Kang Jeungsan. These are appreciated as responses to the problem of dualism and the principle of non-contradiction underlying that dualism in the Western tradition.

In trying to retrieve these ideas I suggest the following methodological steps, all of them based on the close relationship between ideas and their historical contexts. The first methodological step is to reflect on the historical origin and impact of such ideas. All human ideas arise in a particular historical context and fulfill their roles, positive or negative, in such a context. It is important to carefully review the historical circumstances under which those ideas originated and what kinds of roles they have played historically down the ages. Great ideas may transcend the ages, but they are hardly unconnected to them. They arise in response to certain historical needs, and continue to play certain roles, positive or negative, down through the ages. If those ancient ideas are now forgotten and no longer effective, it is important to also ask why they were forgotten, and how they perhaps failed to respond to certain challenges of the times.

In this respect, we may take a lesson from contemporary Western theology. Contemporary Western theology is in the process of reconstructing itself, often by returning to certain ancient ideas, but the first thing theologians do in returning to those ideas is to subject them to a hermeneutic of suspicion, to an examination of what ideological role they have played down the centuries and how they have negatively impacted our conceptions of God and one another. It is important to remember that many of these ancient Korean ideas were rejected by many progressive Korean reformers themselves at the turn of the twentieth century. It is generally recognized that they did serve as ideologies down the centuries, justifying hierarchism, patriarchy, fatalism, political indifference, and a culture of ambiguity. We cannot simply assume that ancient Western ideas need a critique and a hermeneutic of suspicion while ancient Korean or Asian ideas do not. Plainly, the first methodological step is to subject them to a critique of ideology and a hermeneutic of suspicion for the negative roles they have played and to purify them of such negativities before we try to make a positive use of them. Critical suspicion should precede positive retrieval.

The second methodological step in the contemporary theological appropriation of ancient Korean ideas is to know the contemporary historical context in which such appropriation is to take place. This will require interdisciplinary discussion among theologians, pastoral leaders, and social scientists with a view to the central characteristics and challenges of the contemporary world which are especially relevant to the identity of Christianity and the Christian mission in the world. I have outlined in the second part of this paper what I consider those challenges to be. The challenges include social justice, response to the relativizing and eroding impact of global culture, materialism of the media, respect for cultural diversity, and the political response to all these challenges as a nation and as a church. Korean society has always been a divided society, divided in terms of clans, regions, status, religion, gender, and other forms of exclusive identity. The pressures of globalization are going to further shake up Korean society and introduce different forms of division while reinforcing old forms such as ethnic diversity, economic inequality, nationalism and cosmopolitanism, and others. How do we actualize the ideals of harmony and solidarity and go beyond both affirmation and negation in such a divided society and divisive world? Much was said about restoring certain "Asian" or Confucian values in chapters 9 and 10. My concern is that we currently lack and do need creative reflections on how to modify those values today so as to make them concrete, effective, and relevant in the face of all the pressures of globalization.

The third methodological step is to produce a political theory of what society should be that will mediate and concretize ancient ideas in the contemporary context. The mediating theory presents a vision of a new social order that would provide a system of fundamental ideas and values about normative human relations and respond to the challenges of the contemporary world, a vision of human society possible and desirable under contemporary conditions. In Christianity, liberation theology, feminist theology, ecological theology, and political theology are examples of mediating political theories that concretize ancient religious ideals in the concrete context of today. Ancient religious ideas are abstract and general, and the contemporary world is concrete and differentiated; there is no way of directly transposing ancient ideas on the realities of the contemporary world. Such an attempt only results in ideology or despair or both. To impose a general idea on a society without knowing how that idea will operate in a concrete society struggling with divisive and opposed interests is to allow it to operate in favor of certain vested interests. To prevent this ideological use is to have an idea of what a society should be in terms of basic human relations and appropriate social structures, that is, to have a mediating political theory. One can only avoid ideologization of ancient ideas on the basis of a social analysis of the dialectic of powers and interests of a particular time and a normative theory of society rooted in the aspirations and possibilities of the time and which can also serve as a basis of ideological critique.[15]

Let me end with an illustration of what I mean. President Kim Dae Jung once wrote an essay titled "The Thought of *Chung Hyo* [忠孝] and Twenty-First Century Korea." His concern was how to concretize these central Confucian ideas in the rapidly changing Korean society of today. He pointed out that mere revival of these ideas would not work; what is necessary is to modernize them in a way appropriate to Korean society. *Chung* originally meant loyalty to the king, but there are no kings in contemporary Korea. The place of kings has been taken by the people. The loyalty to the king then must be translated into the respect for the people and their human rights. *Hyo* or filial piety originally meant piety to one's parents, but in a society where economic interdependence is growing, where children are no longer guaranteed stable sources of income as in agricultural societies, the support for the parents in their old age must be the shared responsibility of children and the state. Filial piety must be modernized into the social support of old age. Here let me point out that President Kim's arguments are based on a social analysis of the changes in the economic and political situation and a mediating political theory, that of democracy. My argument is that the same thing must be done to all ancient theories, whether Buddhist, Confucian, Christian, or shamanist, that we are trying to appropriate in the contemporary world.[16]

Thus far, I have tried to discuss three things: the problem of the tension between Christianity and Korean culture and religions, the problem of the context of globalization, and certain compelling tasks facing Korean Christianity in trying to fulfill its mission in that context, especially the problem of fragmentation in Protestantism, the problem of authoritarianism in Catholicism, and the problem of methodology in indigenization. It goes without saying that there are many other problems and issues facing contemporary Korean Christianity. It is my hope that I have brought some clarity at least to the problems I did discuss.

Notes

1. I give a brief analysis of the century-long persecution of Catholicism by the Confucian state during the Yi dynasty in terms of the factional conflict of the ruling class, the threat of French invasion, and the dogmatic opposition between the two worldviews of Confucianism and Catholicism; see Anselm Min, *The Spiritual Ethos of Korean Catholicism* (Seoul: Sogang University Social Research Institute, 1971), 70–77. See also Seogwu Choe, *A History of the Korean Catholic Church* (Seoul: The Institute for Church History, 1982), 1–162, a very detailed account of the conflict between Catholicism and Confucianism during the nineteenth century by the premier Catholic church historian.

2. On the Protestant exclusivist attitude, often violent, toward other religions, Anselm K. Min, "Between Indigenization and Globalization: Korean Christianity after 1989," in *Falling Walls: The Year 1989/90 as a Turning Point in the History of World Christianity*, ed. Klaus Koschorke (Wiesbaden, Germany: Harrassowitz Verlag, 2009), 209–12; Timothy S. Lee, "Beleagured Success: Korean Evangelicalism in the Last Decade of the Twentieth Century," in Robert E. Buswell and Timothy S. Lee (eds.), *Christianity in Korea* (Honolulu: University of Hawai'I Press, 2006); and Jingu Lee, "The Self-Understanding of Korean Protestantism," available online at: http://yesu.net/index.php?mid=data_theology_5&sort_index=title&order_type=desc&page=8&document_srl=223008.

3. This neglect of critical reflection on the *de facto* indigenization of Christians is so pervasive of current theological discussions of indigenization, contextualization, and mission where such reflection would seem most appropriate: they all talk about dialogue, reconciliation, and peace with other religions, and understanding and learning from them, but not about the presence of other religions already embodied in the life of Christian converts. Just two recent examples of this neglect: Simon Chan, *Grassroots Asian Theology: Thinking the Christian Faith from the Ground Up* (Downers Grove, IL: Intervarsity Press, 2014), and Jonathan Y. Tan, *Christian Mission among the Peoples of Asia* (Maryknoll, NY: Orbis, 2014). I give a detailed analysis of the functional harmony between Catholic and Confucian mentalities and the *de facto* indigenization of Korean Catholicism in this sense in Anselm K. Min, *The Spiritual Ethos of Korean Catholicism*, 92–119. An important study of the affinity of other religions such as Confucianism, Buddhism, Taoism, and popular religions with Christianity in the form of "syncretism" is found in David Chung, *Syncretism: The Religious Context of Christian Beginnings in Korea*, Kang-nam Oh (ed.) (Albany, NY: State University of New York Press, 2001), especially part IV (107–80). Chung believes that it is this affinity that accounts for the remarkable growth of Christianity in Korea during the twentieth century. This is the published version of Chung's doctoral dissertation originally presented at Yale in 1959.

4. The literature on globalization has been exploding. Three perspectives are generally recognized. Among the defenders of the first, optimistic perspective I include: Thomas Friedman, *The World is Flat: A Brief History of the Twenty-First Century* (New York: Farrar, Straus and Giroux, 2005); Martin Wolf, *Why Globalization Works* (New Haven, CT: Yale University Press, 2004); Philippe Legrain, *Open World: The Truth about Globalization* (Chicago: Ivan R. Dee, 2004); Jagdish Bhagwati, *In Defence of Globalization* (New York: Oxford University Press, 2004); http://www.polyarchy.org/essays/english/globalism.html. Among the defenders of the second, more critical but realistic view I include: Joseph E. Stiglitz, *Globalization and Its Discontents* (New York: W. W. Norton, 2003); David Held et al., *Global Transformations: Politics, Economics, and Culture* (Stanford, CA: Stanford University Press, 1999), Michael Hardt and Antonio Negri, *Empire* (Cambridge, MA: Harvard University Press, 2000), John Tomlinson, *Globalization and Culture* (Chicago: The University of Chicago Press, 1999). Among the defenders of the third, oppositional perspective I include: Zygmunt Bauman, *Globalization: The Human Consequences* (New York: Columbia University Press, 1998); Hans-Peter Martin and Harald Schumann, *The Global Trap: Globalization and the Assault on Democracy and Prosperity* (New York: Zed Books, 1997); Jerry Mander and Edward Goldsmith (eds.), *The Case Against the Global Economy and for a Turn Toward the Local* (San Francisco: Sierra Book Club, 1996); James Howard Kunstler, *The Long Emergency: Surviving the End of the Oil Age, Climate Change and Other Converging Catastrophes of the Twenty-First Century* (New York: Atlantic Monthly Press, 2005); Berch Berberoglu (ed.), *Globalization and Change: The Transformation of Global Capitalism* (Lanham, MD: Lexington Books, 2005); Tony Schirato and Jen Webb, *Understanding Globalization* (London: Sage Publications, 2003); Martin Steger, *Globalization: A Very Short Introduction* (New York: Oxford University Press, 2003); Richard J. Barnet and John Cavanagh, *Global Dreams: Imperial Corporations and the New World Order* (New York: Simon and Schuster, 1994); Bill Bigelow and Bob Peterson (eds.), *Rethinking Globalization: Teaching for Justice in an Unjust World* (Milwaukee, WI: Rethinking Schools, 2002).

5. My brief sketch here is based on my discussion of the different dimensions of globalization and the challenges it poses to theology in Anselm K. Min, *The Solidarity of Others in a Divided World: A Postmodern Theology after Postmodernism* (New York: T & T Clark International, 2004), 111–15 and 222–30; and "Christian Faith and Trust in the Age of Globalization," in Ingolf U. Dalferth and Simon Peng-Keller, (ed.), *Gottvertrauen: Die oekumenische Diskussion um die Fiducia* (Freiburg: Herder, 2012), 386–94.

6.   http://www.globalsecurity.org/wmd/library/news/china/2007/china-070304-voa01.htm.

7. I provide a relatively detailed analysis of what I call "the globalization of cultural nihilism" in Anselm K. Min, "The Deconstruction and Reconstruction of Christian Identity in a World of Differance," in Anselm K. Min (ed.), *The*

Task of Theology: Leading Theologians on the Most Compelling Questions for Today (Maryknoll, NY: Orbis Books, 2014), 38–45.

8. For a comprehensive treatment of the problem of global migration today, see "Migration in an Interconnected World: New Directions for Action," Report of the Global Commission on International Migration (October 2005), available online at: www.gcim.org.

9. https://www.google.com/?gws_rd=ssl#q=%EC%82%AC%ED%9A%8C+%EC%96%91%EA%B7%B9%ED%99%94.

10. *The Korea Times* (Korean edition), April 16, 2007, 1.

11. See the discussion of trading trends in recent years between Korea and China online at: http://cafe.naver.com/tradingb2b/397.

12. I elaborated on the political challenge facing Korea today in my essay, "From the Theology of Minjoong to the Theology of the Citizen: Reflections on Minjoong Theology in 21st Century Korea," *Journal of Asian and Asian American Theology* 5 (Spring 2002), 11–35.

13. The preceding assessment of present-day Korean Protestantism is based on a consensus found in the following material: Yu Hun, "Minjoong Theology as the Second Reformation," newsnjoy.com (September 25, 2006) available at http://www.newsnjoy.co.kr/news/articleView.html?idxno=18705; "Is Hereditary Pastorate a Disaster for Korean Christianity?" donga.com (June 27, 2007) at http://www.donga.com/fbin/output?f=total&n=200706270445&top20=1; "Has Korean Protestantism Entered into a Period of Decline?" chosun.com (September 10, 2007) at http://www.ohmynews.com/NWS_Web/View/at_pg.aspx?CNTN_CD=A0000755251&PAGE_CD=N0000&BLCK_NO=7&CMPT_CD=M0010&NEW_GB=; Park Ji Hoon, "The Fall of Korean Protestantism," ohmynews.com (November 2, 2007) at http://www.ohmynews.com/NWS_Web/View/at_pg.aspx?CNTN_CD=A0000755251&PAGE_CD=N0000&BLCK_NO=7&CMPT_CD=M0010&NEW_GB=; "Is Christianity a Religion That Should Disappear from Korea?" donga.com (November 23, 2007) at http://www.donga.com/fbin/output?f=total&n=200711230341&top20=1; Cho Yun Hyun, "Christianity Must Return to the Grammar of Its Original Faith," http://freeview.org/bbs/board.php?bo_table=d002&wr_id=76&page=; Kwon Sung Kwon, "Why Are Protestant Christians Leaving Their Churches?" ohmynews.com (December 28, 2007) at http://www.ohmynews.com/NWS_Web/View/at_pg.aspx?CNTN_CD=A0000800680&PAGE_CD=N0000&BLCK_NO=7&CMPT_CD=M0011&NEW_GB=; the whole January 2008 issue of *Pastoral Care and Theology* is devoted to the criticisms and responses of Korean Protestantism; "Eleven Reasons for Criticizing Christianity," joins.com (January 2, 2008), available at http://www.ohmynews.com/nws_web/view/at_pg.aspx?CNTN_CD=A0000384329; http://article.joins.com/article/article.asp?total_id=2998553&ctg=1703; Oh Myung Chul, "The Hope of Korean Protestantism Lies in Minority Churches Dedicated to the Narrow Gate," donga.com (March 24, 2008) at http://www.donga.com/fbin/output?n=200803240194&top20=1; all of these articles are in Korean.

14. I analyze clerical authoritarianism as a central issue for Korean Catholicism in my book, *The Korean Church 2000: Beyond Authoritarianism and Ecclesiocentrism* (Seoul: The Benedict Press, 2000) (in Korean), 197–269, and in my essay, "Korean American Catholic Communities," in David K. Yoo and Ruth H. Chung (ed.), *Religion and Spirituality in Korean America* (Chicago: University of Illinois Press, 2008), 28–38. That clerical authoritarianism is a central issue in Korean Catholicism has been well-recognized and was confirmed again in a recent survey of Catholics conducted by *The Catholic Times* (November 16, 2014), 10.

15. See further my *The Korean Church 2000*, 128–31.

16. See Kim Dae Jung, "The Thought of Chung Hyo and 21st Century Korea," *Shindonga* (May, 1999), 226–35.

Bibliography

Buswell, Robert E. and Timothy S. Lee, eds. *Christianity in Korea*. Honolulu: University of Hawai'i Press, 2006.

Choe, Seogwu. *Hanguk Cheonju Gyohoesa* [*A History of the Korean Catholic Church*]. Seoul: the Institute for Church History, 1982.

Chung, David. *Syncretism: The Religious Context of Christian Beginnings in Korea*. Edited by Kang-nam Oh. Albany: State University of New York Press, 2001.

Editorial Board of Gidoggyosasang, ed. *Hanguk Munhwawa Sinhak* [*Korean Culture and Theology*]. Seoul: Korean Christian Literature Society, 1993.

Held, David, Anthony McGrew, David Goldblatt, and Jonathan Perraton. *Global Transformations: Politics, Economics, and Culture*. Stanford, CA: Stanford University Press, 1999.

Je2 jonggyo gaehyug yunguso [Institute for a Second Reformation], ed. *Jonggyo gaehyugul pilyorohanun hanguk gidoggyo* [*Korean Christianity in Need of a Religious Reformation*]. Seoul: Gidoggyomunsa, 2015.

International Society of Korean Studies, ed. *Hanguk munhwawa hangugin* [*Korean Culture and Koreans*]. Seoul: Sagyejeul, 1998.

Lechner, Frank J. and John Boli, eds. *The Globalization Reader*, 2nd ed. Malden, MA: Blackwell, 2000 and 2004.

Min, Anselm K. *Hanguk gyohoe 2000* [*The Korean Church 2000: Beyond Authoritarianism and Ecclesiocentrism*]. Seoul: The Benedict Press, 2000 (in Korean).

———. *The Solidarity of Others in a Divided World: A Postmodern Theology after Postmodernism*. New York: T & T Clark International, 2004.

Yi, Won Gyu. *Hanguk gyohoeui wigiwa huimang* [*The Crisis and Hope of Korean Christianity: The Perspective of Sociology of Religion*]. Seoul: Doseochulpan, 2010.

———. *Hanguk gidoggyoui wigiwa huimang* [*The Crisis and Hope of Korean Protestantism: The Perspective of Sociology of Religion*]. Seoul: Christian Literature Society, 2015.

Contributors

Don Baker is Professor of Korean Civilization in the department of Asian Studies at the University of British Columbia in Vancouver, Canada. He first became interested in Korea as a Peace Corps volunteer from 1971 to 1974, earned his PhD in Korean history at the University of Washington in 1983, and has been teaching at UBC since 1987. He is the author of *Chosŏn Hugi Yugyo wa Chŏnjugyo ŭi Taerip* [*The Confrontation between Confucianism and Catholicism in the Latter Half of the Chosŏn Dynasty*] and *Korean Spirituality*. His teaching and research focus on Korean history, religion, philosophy, and traditional science, especially the writings of Tasan Chŏng Yagyong (1762–1836).

Young-Ho Chun is Professor of Systematic Theology at Saint Paul School of Theology, in Overland Park, Kansas. His research interests include Paul Tillich, the relation between philosophy and theology in nineteenth-century German thinkers in dialogue with the Patristic period, and the comparative culture of East and West. He is the author of, among others, *Tillich and Religion: Toward a Theology of World Religions* (1998), and many articles in *The Global Dictionary of Theology*, *Tillich-Studien* (volumes 2, 3, and 10), and *The Cambridge Companion to the Trinity* (2011). He is currently working on a comparative study of Tillich and Otto and a translation of the works of Wolfhart Pannenberg into Korean.

Namsoon Kang is Professor of Theology and Religion at Brite Divinity School, Texas Christian University. Her most recent books include *Cosmopolitanism and Religion* (2015 in Korean), *Diasporic Feminist Theology* (2014), *Cosmopolitan Theology* (2013), and *Handbook of Theological Education in World Christianity* (2010) (co-edited). Teaching, researching, and writing from interdisciplinary spaces, her particular theoretical interests are in discourses of deconstruction, postmodernism, postcolonialism, gender studies, and diaspora.

Jongmyung Kim earned his Ph.D. in Korean Buddhism from the University of California at Los Angeles in 1994 and is Professor of Korean and Buddhist Studies at the Academy of Korean Studies and is former Founding Director of International Korean Studies. In addition to numerous journal articles, he published in Korean *Korean Kings' Buddhist Views and Statecraft* (2013), which was awarded a book of the year prize by the National Academy of Sciences, the Republic of Korea, in 2014, *Buddhist World Heritage Properties* (2008), and *Buddhist Rituals in Medieval Korea* (2001). He contributed to *Zen Buddhist Rhetoric in China, Korea, and Japan* (Brill, 2012), *Makers of Modern Korean Buddhism* (SUNY Press, 2010), *Traditions and Traditional Theories* (LIT Verlag, 2006), *Korea and Globalization* (RoutledgeCurzon, 2002), and the forthcoming volumes, *East Asian Esoteric Buddhist Art* and *Koryŏ—The Dynamics of Inner and Outer*. He is authoring *The Nature of Koryŏ Buddhist Rituals: A Reillumination* in Korean, and is editing *Buddhist Rituals in Pre-modern Korea and China*.

Un-sunn Lee is Professor of Asian Studies and Philosophy of Education at Sejong University, Seoul, Korea. She received the Dr. Theol. from Basel University, Switzerland, and the PhD from Sungkyungkwan University, Seoul, Korea. Her major works are in feminist transversal studies in Confucianism and Christianity. In addition to numerous articles and books, she has authored *In Search for the Lost Transcendent: The Religiosity of Korean Confucianism and Feminism* (2009), *Korean Feminist Theology of Life-giving Spirituality* (2011), *Politics and Education in the Era of Biosphere Politics: Dialogue between H. Arendt and Confucianism* (2013), and *The Other Confucianism, the Other Christianity* (2016).

Anselm K. Min is Professor of Religion at Claremont Graduate University with a specialization in Philosophy of Religion and Theology. He is the author of, among others, *Dialectic of Salvation: Issues in Theology of Liberation* (1989), *The Solidarity of Others: A Postmodern Theology after Postmodernism* (2004), *Paths to the Triune God: An Encounter between Aquinas and Recent Thought* (2005), *Korean Catholicism in the 1970s* (1974), and numerous essays on Aquinas, Hegel, postmodern theology, liberation theology, religious pluralism, various areas of systematic theology, and Asian and Korean theologies. His current project is the construction of a theology of globalization that retrieves the depth of the classical Christian tradition and broadens it by appropriating the insights and challenges of the contemporary world.

A. Charles Muller is Professor in the Graduate School of Humanities and Sociology, University of Tokyo. His main work lies in the fields of Korean Buddhism, East Asian Yogâcāra, East Asian classical lexicography, and online scholarly resource development. Among his major works are *The Sūtra of Perfect Enlightenment: Korean Buddhism's Guide to Meditation* (SUNY Press, 1999) and *Wŏnhyo's Philosophy of Mind* (University of Hawai'i Press, 2012). He has also published over two dozen articles on Korean and East Asian Buddhism. He is the editor and primary translator of three volumes in the *Collected Works of Korean Buddhism*, and is the publication chairman for the Numata BDK sutra translation project. Among his online digital projects are the *Digital Dictionary of Buddhism* (http://www.buddhism-dict.net/ddb), the *CJKV-E Dictionary* (http://www.buddhism-dict.net/ddb), the *H-Buddhism Buddhist Scholars Information Network* (http://www.h-net.org/~buddhism), and most recently, the *H-Buddhism Bibliography Project* (https://www.zotero.org/groups/h-buddhism_bibliography_project).

Sung-Deuk Oak is Dongsoon Im and Mija Im Endowed Chair Associate Professor of Korean Christianity at the University of California–Los Angeles. His monograph, *The Making of Korean Christianity: Protestant Encounters with Korean Religions, 1876–1915*, was awarded the book of the year prize by *Books and Culture* in 2013. His major field is the history of Korean Protestantism and its ways of appropriating Anglo-American, Chinese, Japanese, and Korean elements, and its global connections. His current projects include writing *The History of the Korean Bible Society, Vol. III. 1945–2000* and editing the ten-volume series of *Samuel Austin Moffett Papers, 1868–1939*.

Young-chan Ro is Professor of Religious Studies and Director of the Korean Studies Center, George Mason University. He authored *The Korean Neo-Confucianism of Yi Yulgok* (SUNY Press, 1987) and co-authored *The Four-Seven Debate: The Most Famous Controversy in Korean Neo-Confucianism* (SUNY Press, 1995). He also contributed several book chapters on Neo-Confucianism including "Ecological Implications of Yi

Yulgok's Cosmology" in Mary Evelyn Tucker and John Berthrong (ed.), *Confucianism and Ecology* (Harvard UP, 1998) and "Morality, Spirituality, and Spontaneity in Korean Neo-Confucianism" in Tu Weiming and Mary Evelyn Tucker (ed.), *Confucian Spirituality, II* (Crossroad, 2004). His publications also include many articles in Korean studies, Confucian studies, and comparative religion.

Young-bae Song is Professor of Philosophy emeritus at Seoul National University, where he also served as chair of the department. His doctoral dissertation at the University of Frankfurt, Germany, "Konfuzianismus, Konfuzische Gesellschaft und die Sinisierung des Marxismus" [Confucianism, Confucian Society and the Sinicization of Marxism] was translated into Korean in 1986. In 1994 he published *Thoughts of Zezabaigga* [諸子百家의 思想, *Hundred Schools of Thought*] dealing with representative thinkers of the Spring and Autumn period and the Warring States period in Chinese history (770 BCE–221 BCE). Also a well-known scholar of Matteo Ricci, Song published an annotated translation of Ricci's *Tianzhu Shiyi* [天主實義, *The True Meaning of the Heavenly Lord*] [originally published in 1603) in 1999, and another volume of annotated translation containing Ricci's *Jiaoyoulun* [交友論, *Treatise on Friendship*] (1595), *Ershiwuyan* [二十五言, *Twenty-Five Proverbs*] (1599), and *Jiren shipian* [琦人十篇, *Ten Essays of an Eccentric Man*] (1608) in 2000, both volumes by Seoul National University Press.

Index

A Handbook of Comparative Religion, 161-62
afterlife, 25-26, 28, 32, 37, 67, 91, 102, 107-111, 116, 146
ahimsā, 71
An Chong-bok, 102
An-Naim, Abdullahi A., 215
Analects, 57, 72, 77, 256
ancestor worship, veneration, 23, 30, 92, 101, 159, 163, 166, 169-173, 177, 222. See also filial piety
animism, 158, 162-163, 172
Appenzeller, Henry G., 157-160, 184
Aquinas, Thomas, 120, 123, 128
Arendt, Hannah, 248-49, 250-252
Aristotle, 120-121, 128, 221
atheism, 90
Augustine, 120

Baker, Don, 6, 89-118, 311
Bible, Christian, 160, 165, 167, 177, 190, 192-194, 196, 202, 298
Book of History, 23
Book of Rites, 23, 243, 247
bodhisattva, 26-27, 33, 68
Buddhism
  Buddha(s), 22, 26, 28-39, 45n32, 46n42, 55, 73, 79, 162, 177, 180-181, 198, 204, 289
  canons, 22, 29-32, 37-38, 44n17, 46n44, 70, 182, 190, 211

Chinese, 21-22, 26, 33-34, 36
critique of Confucianism, 61-63, 70-75
good fortune, 31-32
hagiography, 64
Mahāyāna, 46n43, 61, 67
monks, monasticism, 28-31, 33, 35-36, 55, 61, 211
political impact of, 22, 25-29, 33-36, 38, 54, 59
religion, 21, 24-25, 31-33
temple, 27-30, 35-36, 59, 91, 182-183
Zen, 29-30, 47n49, 54-58, 61, 68, 78n7, 194
Bulseong, 198, 204
Bulssi japbyeon, 60-61, 64-65, 70, 74, 77, 78n4, 80n22-n23

Caputo, John D., 249
Catholicism
  clerical authoritarianism, 289, 300-301, 304
  conversion to, 89, 95, 100-101, 105, 108-109
  doctrine, 103-112
  humanism, 168
  persecution of, 109-111, 287 [martyrdom]
cessationism, 156, 167, 175-176
Ch'ae Chegong, 97-98

315

Ch'ae Ch'ungsun, 24–25, 28, 32
Chan. *See* Buddhism, Zen
Cheng brothers, 57, 58, 60, 71–73, 80n25
Cheng Hao. *See* Cheng brothers
chi. *See qi*
Ch'oe Pyŏnghŏn, 162, 168, 178–179, 181–184
Ch'oe Sŭngno, 23–25
Chŏnju, 106
Chŏng Chisang, 32
Chŏng Yagyong, (John), 89, 94, 96, 99–101, 105–107, 109, 119–120, 130–131, 149
Chŏng Yakchong, (Augustine), 90, 101–102, 108–109, 112
Chosŏn Dynasty, 21, 34, 39, 45n24, 45n29, 45n34, 46n44, 91–94, 103, 116n49, 165, 221, 231, 263, 265, 277–278, 305
Chu Hsi, 250–251
Chun Koh, Hesung, 247
Chun Young-ho, 11, 189–212, 311
Clarke, James F., 157–159, 184
Communism, 242, 265, 269–270
Confucianism
  Chinese, 22–23, 36, 38, 54–58, 71, 75, 169, 172, 181–182, 263, 267–268
  critique of Buddhism, 5, 57–60, 64, 67, 73–74, 92
  modernization, 266
  namin, 93, 98–100, 102–103
  Neo-Confucianism, 2, 4–5, 56–57, 71, 90, 98, 110, 125–126, 128, 133, 136, 145
  political, 1–5, 20–25, 103
  virtues, 21, 31, 62, 79n19, 93, 103–104, 106, 108–109, 122, 140, 145, 200–201, 216, 219, 241, 247, 252, 257, 276
Confucius, 62, 65, 71–72, 134, 146, 162, 170, 177, 180, 204, 217, 222, 243, 252, 256, 272–273

continuationism, 156, 167, 174, 176
Corea, the Hermit Nation, 159–160
cosmology, 36–37, 56–57, 67, 189, 220

Dao, Tao, Way, 70, 77, 126, 131–132, 135–136 141–142, 274, 287
Daoism, 4–5, 21, 25, 30, 34, 53–55, 62, 65, 71, 75–76, 78, 78n1, 81n30, 116n49, 141, 171–172, 181–182, 189, 195, 305n3
Daode jing, 77
Dasan. *See* Chŏng Yagyong
Daseok. *See* Ryu Yongmo
degradation theory, 160, 163–165, 177–178, 184. *See also* fulfillment theory
democracy, 14–15, 220, 229, 235, 264–279, 304
demons, 167, 174–176
Demon Possession, 166
desire, 34, 98–99, 107, 122–123, 135, 197
Dharma, 33, 38
Doctrine of the Mean, 77, 142, 245, 250, 255, 280n3
Donghak, 302

Ellinwood, Frank Field, 160, 184
Engel, George O., 173
Eol, 11–12, 190, 195–204, 209–210
Errors of Ancestor Worship, 166
essence-function, 56, 68, 70, 76–77
Evidences of Christianity, 167
exclusivism, 59, 79n14, 160, 195, 288–289

feminism, 215–216, 218–220, 223–226, 229–230, 233–239, 243, 246–250, 256–261
  theology, 233–234, 303
filial piety, 4, 8, 21–23, 25, 28–29, 31, 36, 38, 43n10, 92, 101, 103–105,

108–109, 112, 169, 200–202, 222, 227, 265, 291, 304. *See also* ancestor worship
Fingarette, Herbert, 81n31
Four Noble Truths, 4, 30, 34, 36, 46n37
free will, 121–124, 134–137, 145
fulfillment theory, 161–164, 178, 180, 183–184. *See also* degradation theory

Gihwa, 4–5, 62–65, 70–74, 77, 80n22, 81n30
globalization, 216, 285–287, 292–299, 304
Goryeo Dynasty, 1–6, 19–39, 58–59, 63
God
  Buddhist, 28, 32
  Christian, 102–112, 126, 128–130, 146, 166, 177–178, 201–202, 204–205, 207, 226
  Confucian, 90–91, 112, 145, 161, 170, 197
  shamanist, 176
Grant, George M., 161–162, 181–182
Griffis, William E., 159

Haet'a-ron, 180–181
Hallyu, 241–242, 245
Ham Suk-hun, 250
Han Dynasty, 22
Han Yu, 4, 55, 62–63, 78n2
Hanui, 94
hsiao. See filial piety
Huayan, 54–56, 61–62, 65, 77
human nature, 98–99, 121–126, 130–140, 163, 197–201, 250, 269–280
humaneness, 68, 71–73, 77, 122, 235
humanism, 14, 167, 227–228, 264, 268, 271, 274, 280n3
Hwang Sayŏng, 90, 100, 102

Hyeonjeong non, 69–70, 75, 80n22–n23
hyo. See filial piety
Hyŏnjong, King, 20, 23–25, 29, 31–32, 34–35, 44n13, 45n29

iconoclasm, 56, 165–166, 176
idolatry, 103, 158, 160, 163, 165–166, 169–171, 179, 200
inclusivism, 5, 156
India, 35, 37, 76, 164, 292, 297
individualism, 12–13, 16, 217–219, 226, 229–230, 235–236, 238, 249, 297, 298–299
interreligious dialogue, 75–76, 203
Islam, 21, 92

Japan, 38, 90, 155–157, 159, 164–165, 168, 177, 193–194, 208n12, 216, 294
  Japanese colonial period, 46n35, 159
Jen, 21, 235–236, 248, 250–252, 257
Jeong Yagyong. *See* Chŏng Yagyong
Jeong Dojeon, 4–5, 60, 62–63, 67–68, 74, 77
Jesus, 174–177, 180, 190, 192–196, 199–204, 206, 224–226, 228, 288, 299
  Death, 103, 105–106, 110, 166–167
  Divinity, 102, 104, 112, 166, 200
  Incarnation, 8, 103, 105, 112, 190, 200, 204
Jesuit, 94, 110, 184
Jones, G. Herber, 172–173, 181–184
Joseon Dynasty, 4, 59–60, 63, 77, 79n14, 145–146, 192, 244–245, 247
Judaism, 158
Judeo-Christian, 92, 225–226

Kang, Namsoon, 12, 215–239, 311
Kang, Wansuk Kollumba, 111

Kang, Wi Jo, ix–x
karma, 32, 36–37, 39, 55, 60, 62, 67, 71
Kellog, Samuel H., 161–163
Kil Sŏnju, 174, 178, 180–181, 184
Kim, Jongmyung, 3, 19–52, 312
Koryŏ Dynasty. *See* Goryeo Dynasty

Laozi, 62, 65, 162
Lee, Ki-Dong, 250
Lee, Kuan Yew, 216–217, 266–267
Lee, Un-sunn, xiii, 13, 241–262, 312
Legge, James, 157, 163, 170–171, 177, 179, 184
li, 55–57, 77, 81, 85, 81n33, 98–99, 106, 125–128, 133–134, 140–141, 145, 222, 237n17, 276–277, 277, 279, 302
liberation theology, 204, 303
Lincoln, Abraham, President, 275–276

Madison, James, President, 275
Mao Zedong, 217
Martin, William A.P., 167–168, 171
Medieval Korea. See *Goryeo Dynasty*
Mencius, or Menzius, 56, 71–73, 131, 137, 139, 146, 170, 192, 221, 243, 246, 248, 253–255, 257, 266, 268, 276, 282n18
Min, Anselm Kyongsuk 1–16, 207n1, 285–308, 312
monotheism, 90–91, 109, 158, 160–161, 163–164, 166–167, 176–178
Muller, A. Charles, 4, 53–85, 313
multi-religious society, 4, 21, 204

Neville, Robert C., 257, 277
Nevius, John L., 165–167, 171, 176, 184
No-self, 37
nothingness. *See* void

Oak, Sung-Deuk, 9, 155–187, 313

Oriental Religions and Christianity, 160
Orientalism, 159, 206, 217–218

Pan Ku, 127
pantheism, 163
Park Chung Hee, President, 264–267, 280n4
pluralism, 21, 38, 195
polytheism, 91, 158, 160–161, 163, 177
Pope Francis, 103, 110
prayer, 35, 91, 97–98, 167, 174–176
Protestantism, 156
  fragmentation, 298–299, 304
  Methodist, 157, 162, 165
  Missionaries, 155–156, 164, 172, 175–176, 183
  Presbyterian, 157, 162, 165
  Unitarian, 158

qi, 56–57, 77, 122, 130–134, 137–138, 140–141, 302
Qin Dynasty, 277

Rhee Syngman, President, 264
Ricci, Matteo, 101, 120–128, 130, 135, 138, 141, 143–146, 168, 181
ritual, 91–93, 106, 176, 253, 277
  Buddhist, 3, 21–22, 30–31, 37, 39, 44n15, 44n16, 45n34, 47n49, 47n51, 93, 183
  Confucian, 23, 30, 72, 91, 101, 105, 108, 112n1–3, 220, 245, 279
Ro, Young-chan, 14, 263–283, 313
Ryu Yongmo, 189–212
  Christology, 195–203

Said, Edward, 206
Samgha, 32–33, 35, 64, 71
samsara, 133
Sangje, 105–107, 141, 143
Scripture, Christian. *See* Bible

Second Vatican Council, 288, 301
seong, 11, 67, 197, 209
shamanism, 3, 30, 91, 172, 175–177
Shanghai Mission Conferences, 170–171
Shao Gong, 79n21
Silk Letter, 90, 100, 102, 111
Silla, 20, 24, 27–29, 31, 33, 43n1, 44n19
Sin Sa-im-dang, 247–248
Song Dynasty, 26, 55, 57, 59, 61, 71, 78n11, 137
Song Young-bae, 8, 119–151, 314
Songho Yi Ik, 98–99
soul, 67, 76, 91, 120–122, 128–129, 131, 161, 196
Spivak, Gayatri Chakravorty, 219
Student Volunteer Movement for Foreign Missions, 157, 161, 163–164
SVM. *See* Student Volunteer Movement for Foreign Missions
Syŏngsan Myŏnggyŏng, 181

T'aejo, King, 20–23, 26–30, 32, 35, 44n12, 44n13, 44n21, 46n38
taiji, 126, 128, 141, 148n38, 149n38
Tang Dynasty, 4, 26, 53–55, 61, 179
Taoism. See *Daoism*
Tasan. *See* Chŏng Yagyong
Tatsuo, Inoue, 215
Ten Commandments, 104, 109, 227
Ten Great Religions, 158
The Religions of Eastern Asia, 176
The Religions of the World in Relation to Christianity, 161
"The Spirit Worship in Korea," 172
Theory of Heavenly Warning, 22, 36–37, 44n22, 47n49

Three Kingdom period, 19, 43n1, 44n19, 46n39
Tianzhu shiyi, 120, 130–131, 134–145, 168
T'oegye Yi Hwang, 98

Underwood, Horace G., 157, 176–179, 184

Vedantists, 76
void, 74, 127, 142, 190, 203–204, 211

Wei Dynasty, 33, 79n19
Wu Dynasty, 21, 33

Xunzi, 15, 276–278, 282

Yates, Matthew T., 170
Yi Dynasty. *See* Chosŏn Dynasty
Yi Ki-baik, 93
Yi Pyok, 90, 94, 100–102
Yi Sunghun, 100–101, 103
Yi Suni, Luthgarde, 111, 117n60
Yi Toegye, 119, 250–251
Yi Yulgok, 247–248, 252
yin and yang, 22, 36, 56, 67, 79n19, 130, 148n38, 169, 219, 243–244
Yun Chich'ung, (Paul), 102
Yun, Sung Bum, 225–226

zhou, 104, 110
Zhou Dunyi, 71, 78n10
Zhou Dynasty, 79n21, 179
Zhou Gongdan, 79n21
Zhu Xi, 56–58, 60, 68, 73, 78n8, 80n24–n25, 131–133, 278
Zongmi, 4, 61–63, 65, 70, 80n22, 80n30

Made in the USA
Monee, IL
24 October 2020